Contents

X-Men Misfits

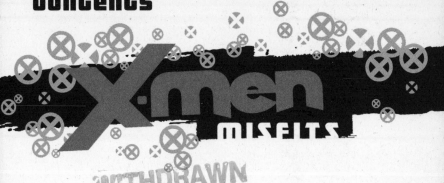

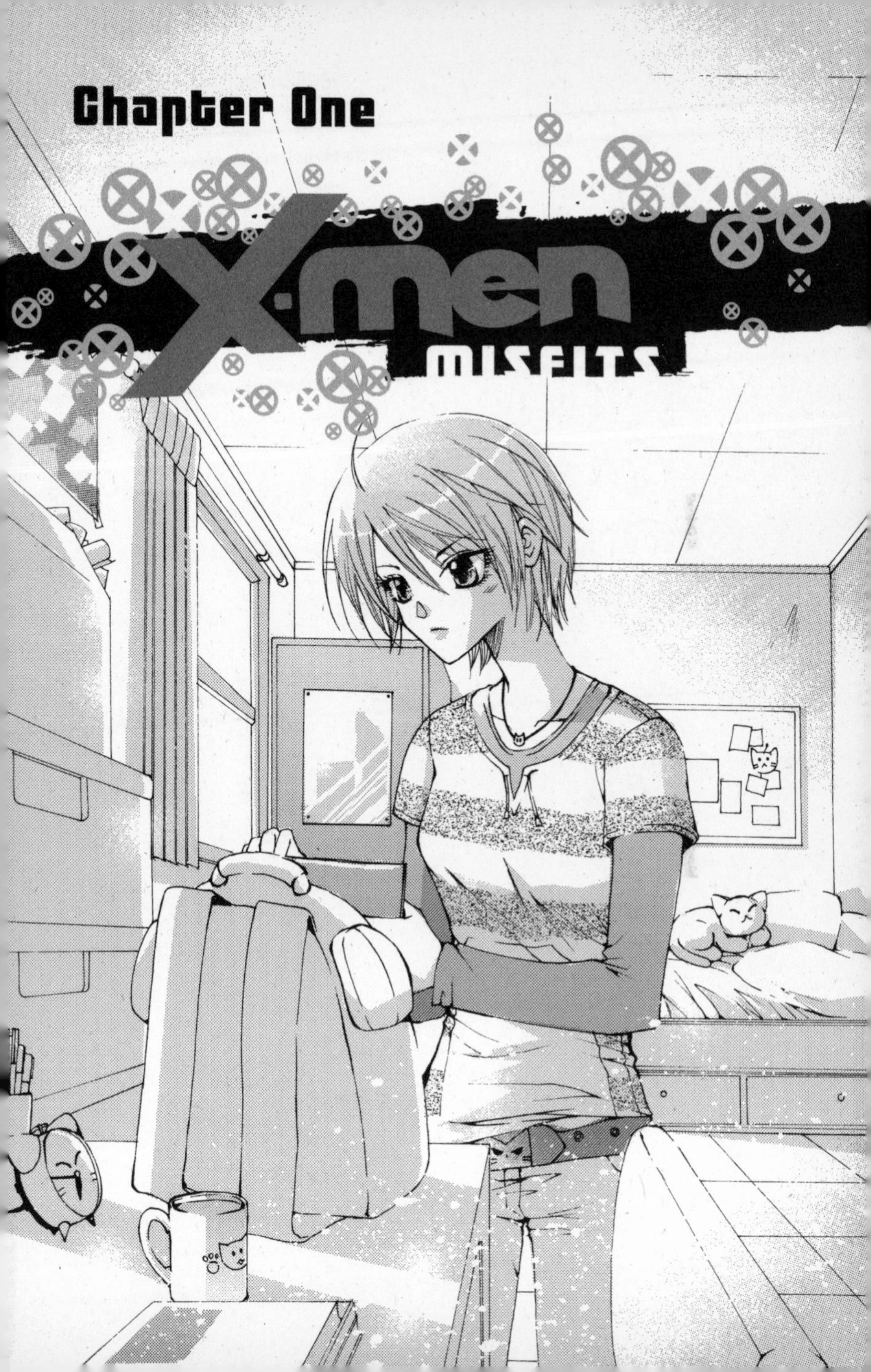
Chapter One
X-men
MISFITS

XAVIER'S SCHOOL • FOR GIFTED YOUNGSTERS

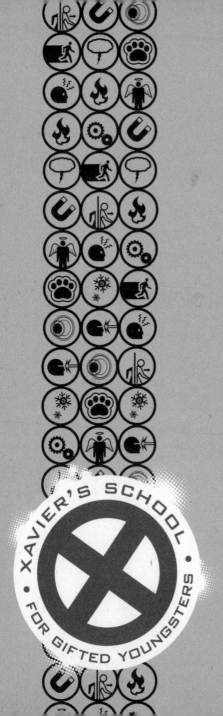

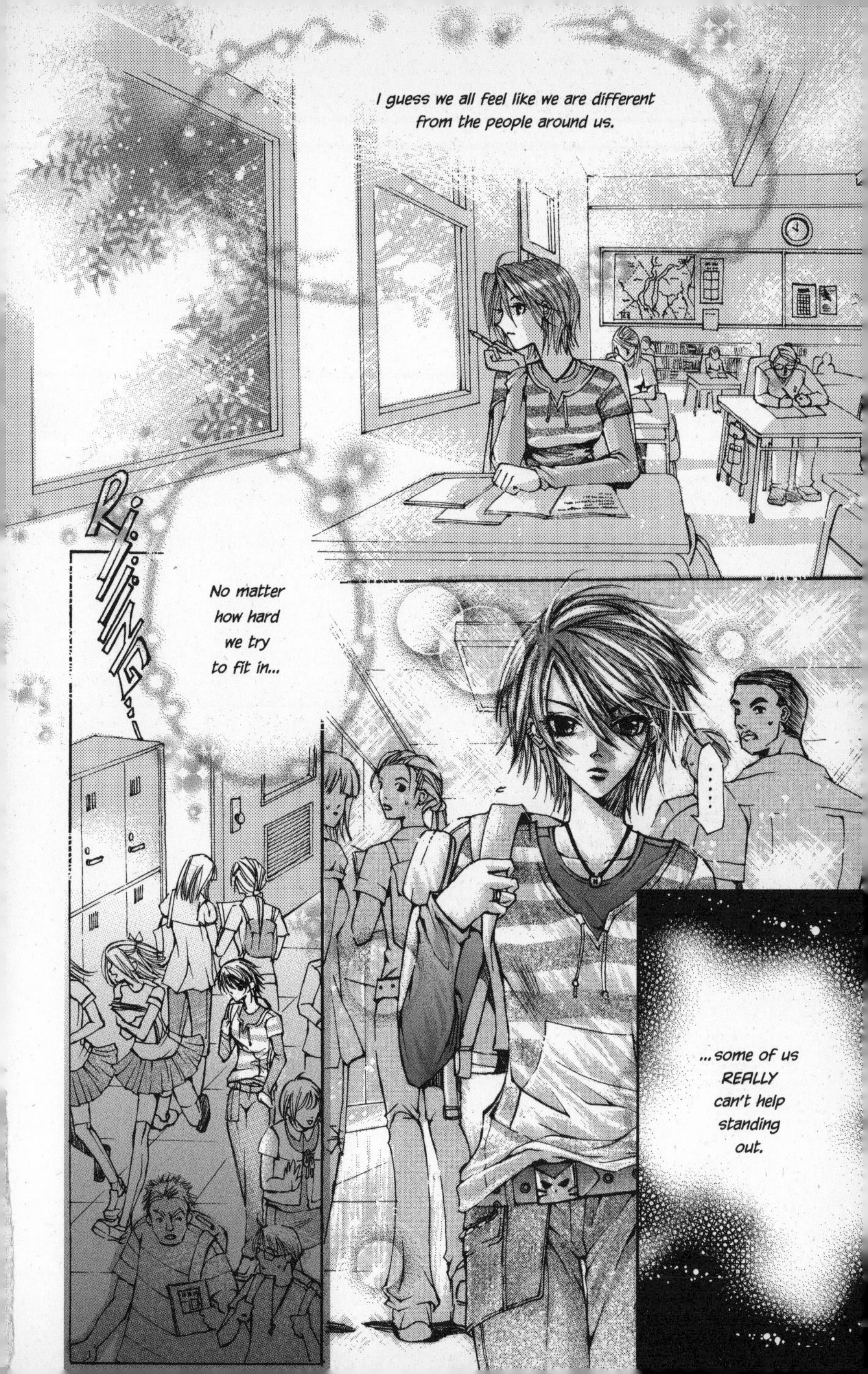
I guess we all feel like we are different from the people around us.
Riiiing...
No matter how hard we try to fit in...
......
...some of us REALLY can't help standing out.

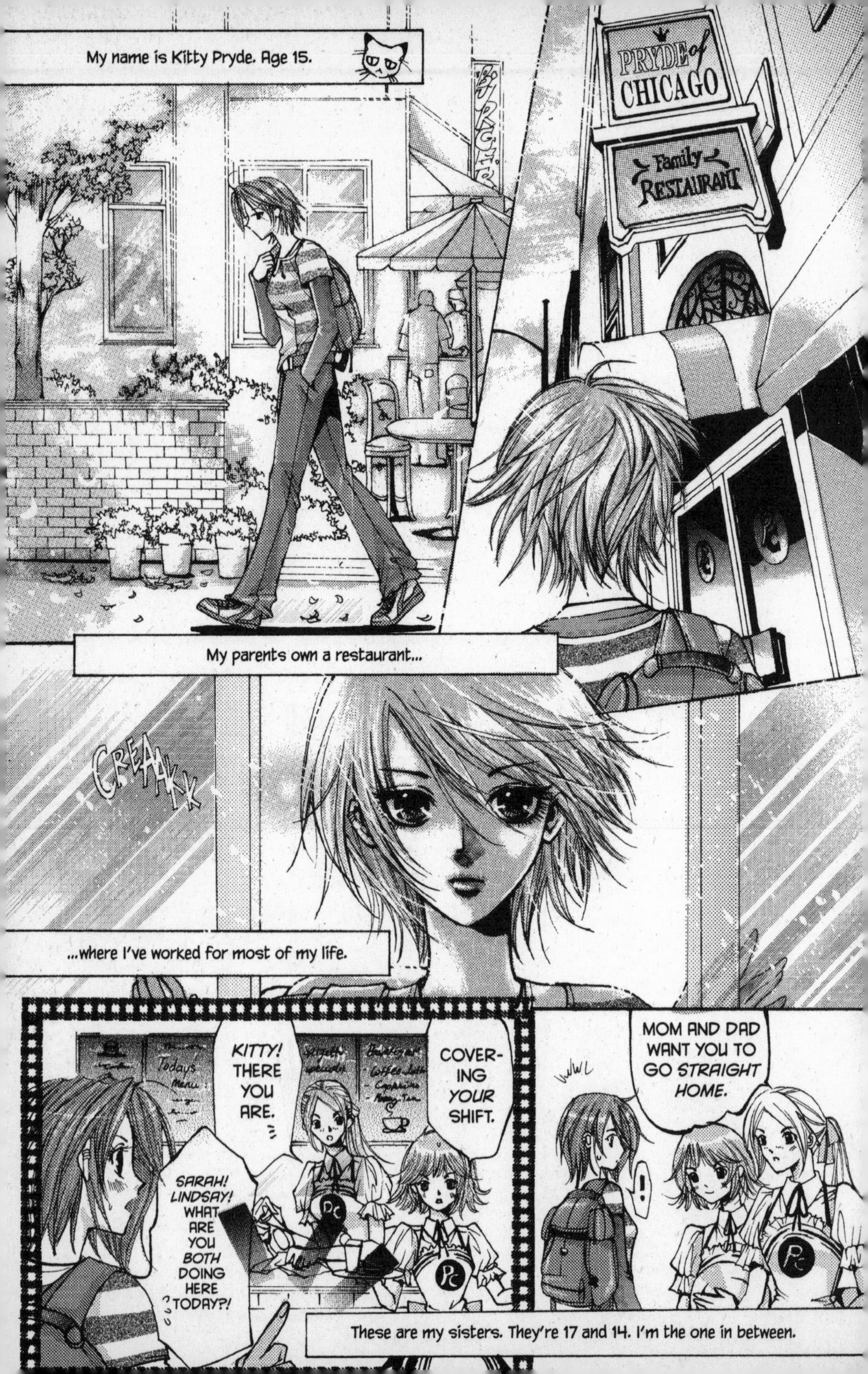

My name is Kitty Pryde. Age 15.
PRYDE of CHICAGO
Family RESTAURANT
My parents own a restaurant...
CREAAKK
...where I've worked for most of my life.
Todays menu
KITTY! THERE YOU ARE.
SARAH! LINDSAY! WHAT ARE YOU BOTH DOING HERE TODAY?!
COVER-ING YOUR SHIFT.
MOM AND DAD WANT YOU TO GO STRAIGHT HOME.
!
These are my sisters. They're 17 and 14. I'm the one in between.

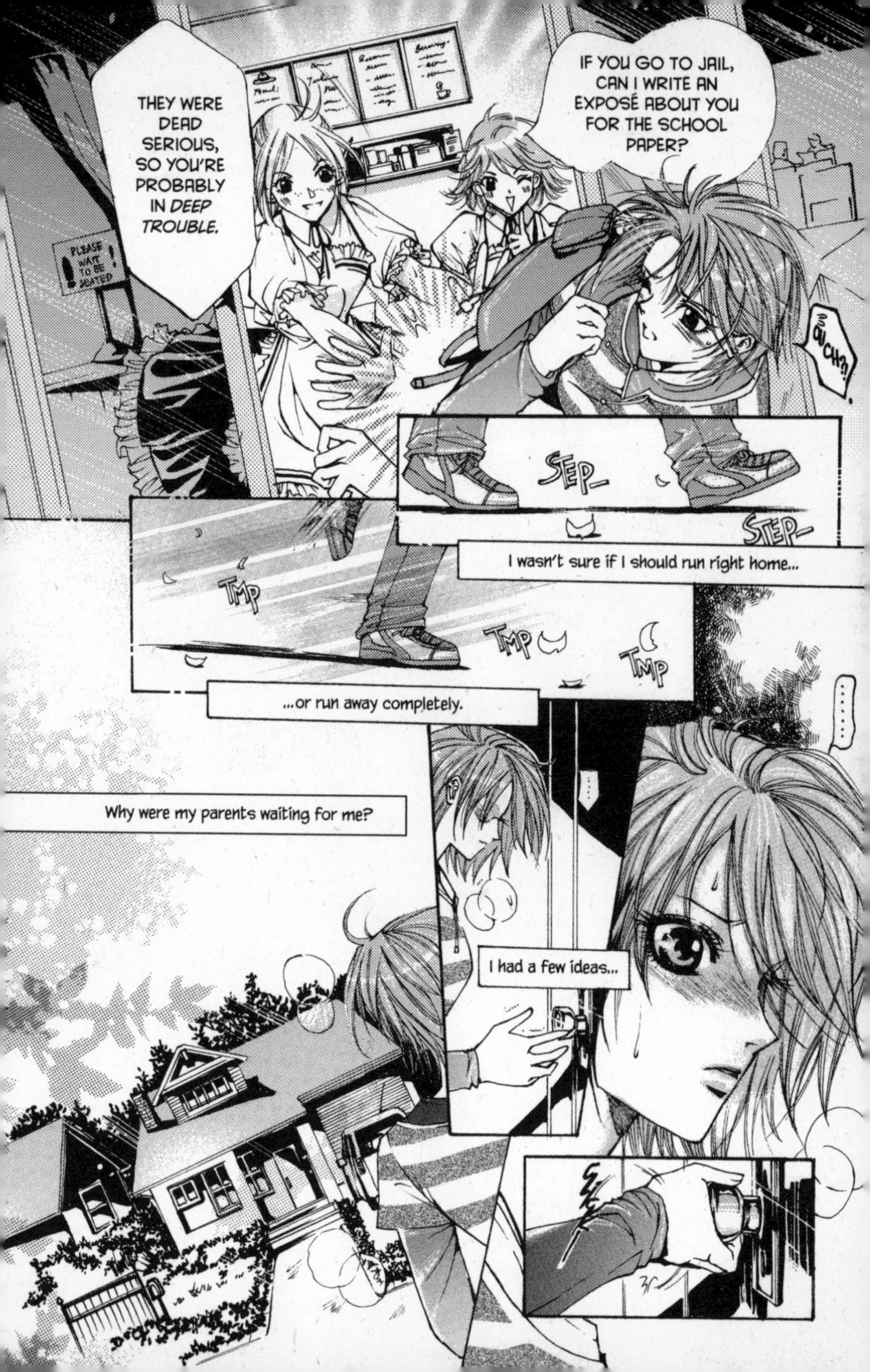
THEY WERE DEAD SERIOUS, SO YOU'RE PROBABLY IN *DEEP TROUBLE.*
PLEASE WAIT TO BE SEATED
IF YOU GO TO JAIL, CAN I WRITE AN EXPOSÉ ABOUT YOU FOR THE SCHOOL PAPER?
OUCH?!
STEP_
STEP-
I wasn't sure if I should run right home...
TMP
TMP
TMP
...or run away completely.
Why were my parents waiting for me?
....
......
I had a few ideas...

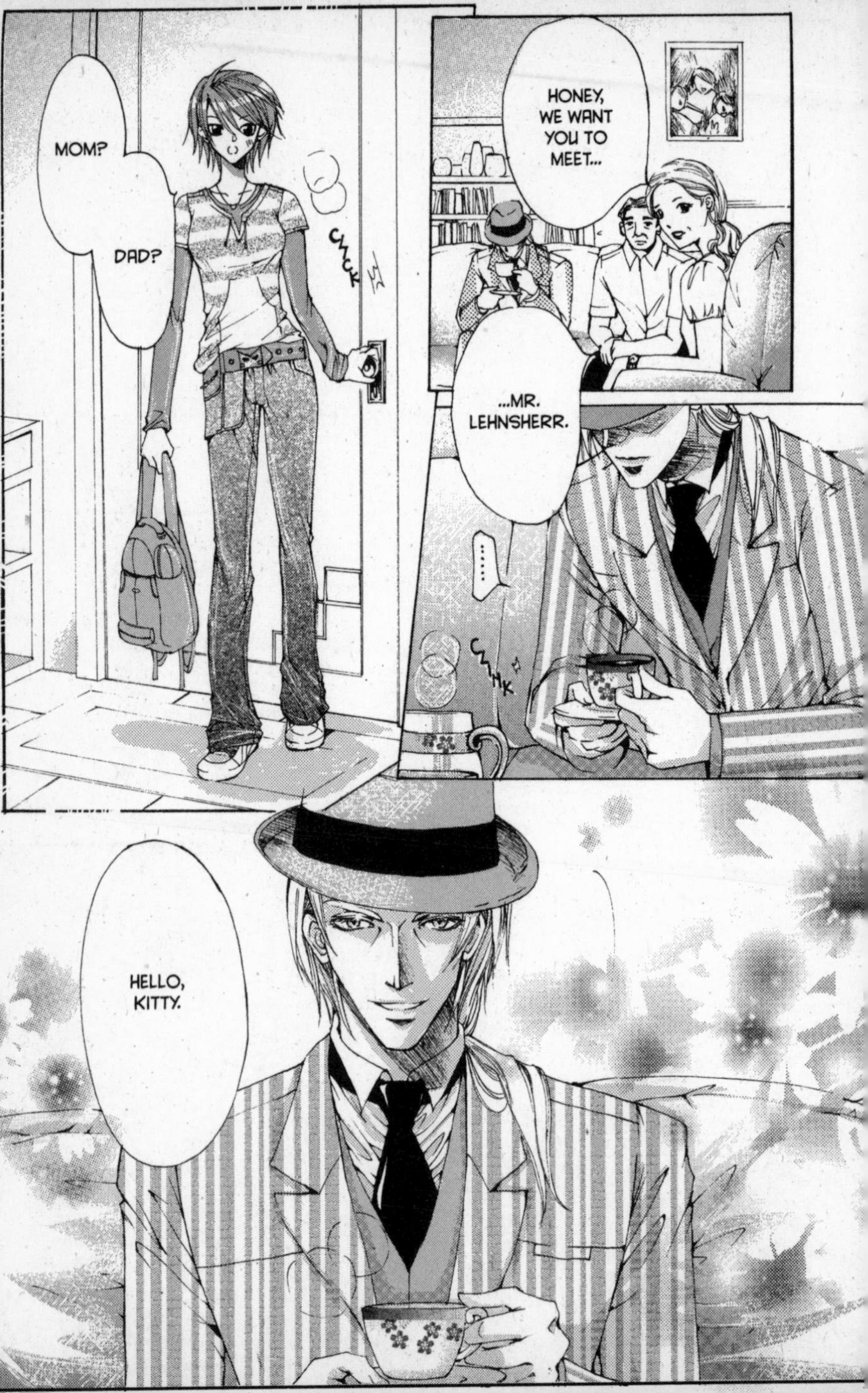
MOM?
DAD?
CLICK
HONEY, WE WANT YOU TO MEET...
...MR. LEHNSHERR.
......
CLINK
HELLO, KITTY.

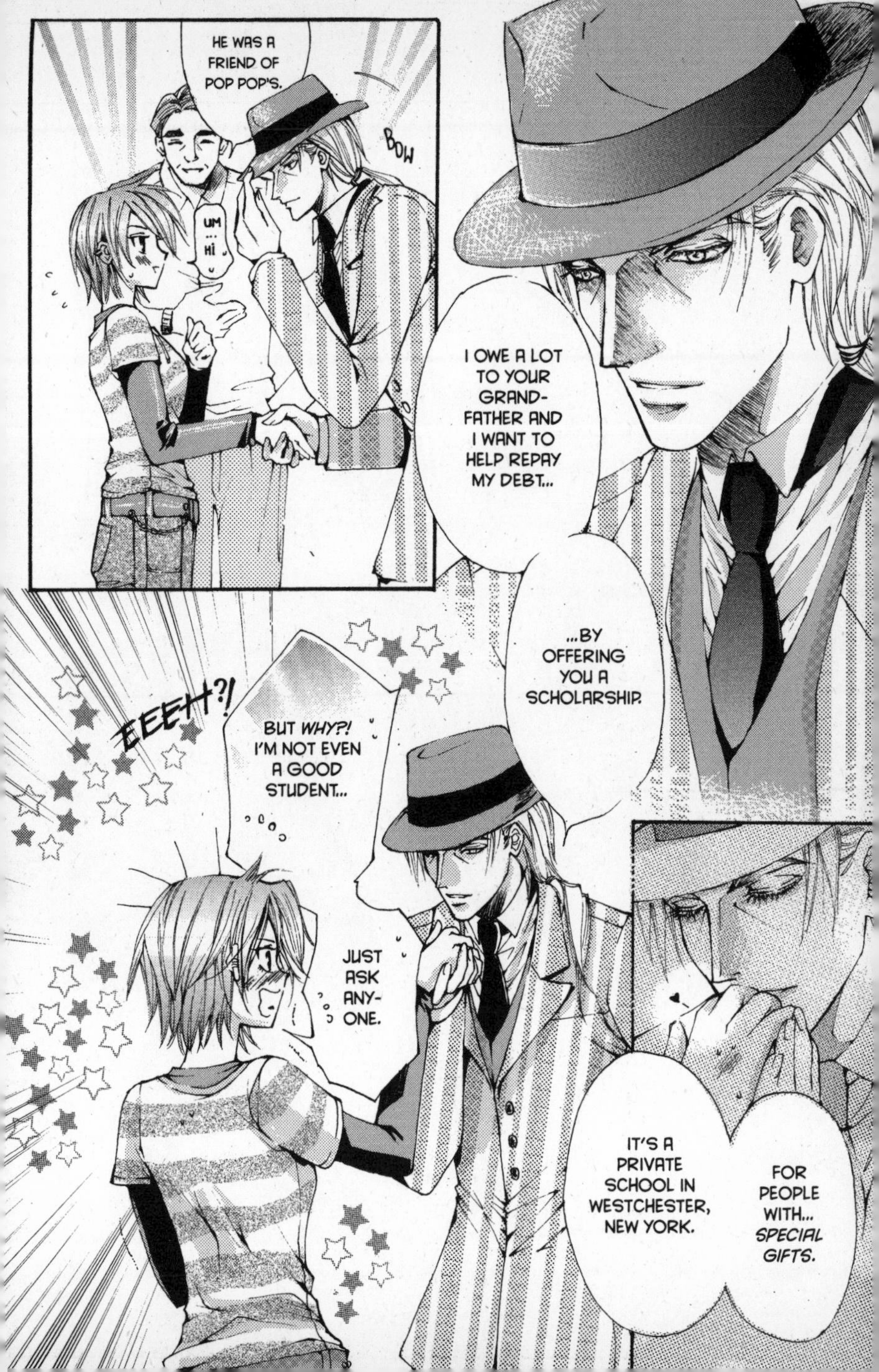
HE WAS A FRIEND OF POP POP'S.
BOW
UM ... HI
I OWE A LOT TO YOUR GRAND-FATHER AND I WANT TO HELP REPAY MY DEBT...
...BY OFFERING YOU A SCHOLARSHIP.
EEEH?!
BUT *WHY?!* I'M NOT EVEN A GOOD STUDENT...
JUST ASK ANY-ONE.
IT'S A PRIVATE SCHOOL IN WESTCHESTER, NEW YORK.
FOR PEOPLE WITH... *SPECIAL GIFTS.*

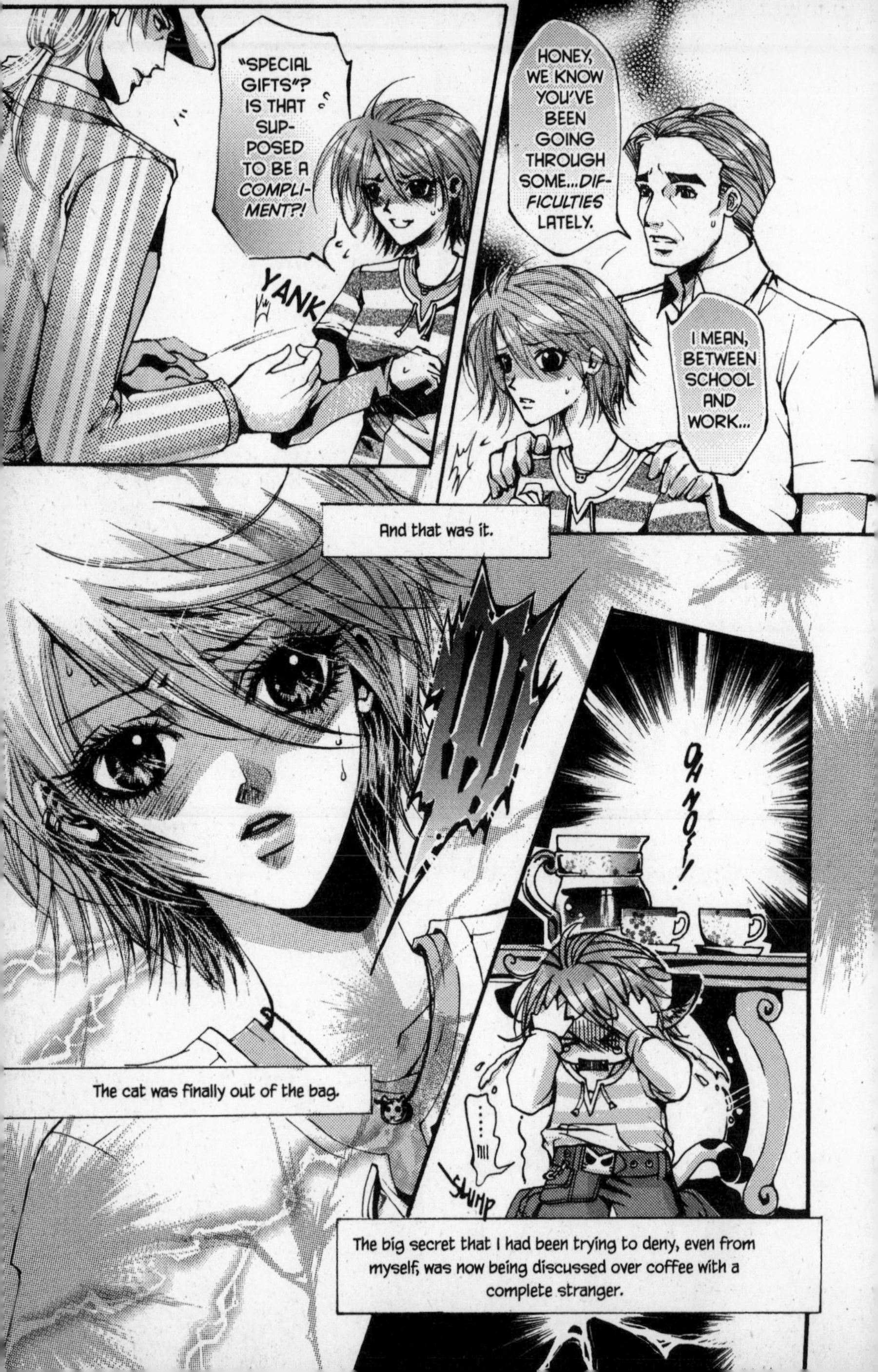
"SPECIAL GIFTS"? IS THAT SUP-POSED TO BE A COMPLI-MENT?!
YANK
HONEY, WE KNOW YOU'VE BEEN GOING THROUGH SOME...DIF-FICULTIES LATELY.
I MEAN, BETWEEN SCHOOL AND WORK...
And that was it.
The cat was finally out of the bag.
The big secret that I had been trying to deny, even from myself, was now being discussed over coffee with a complete stranger.

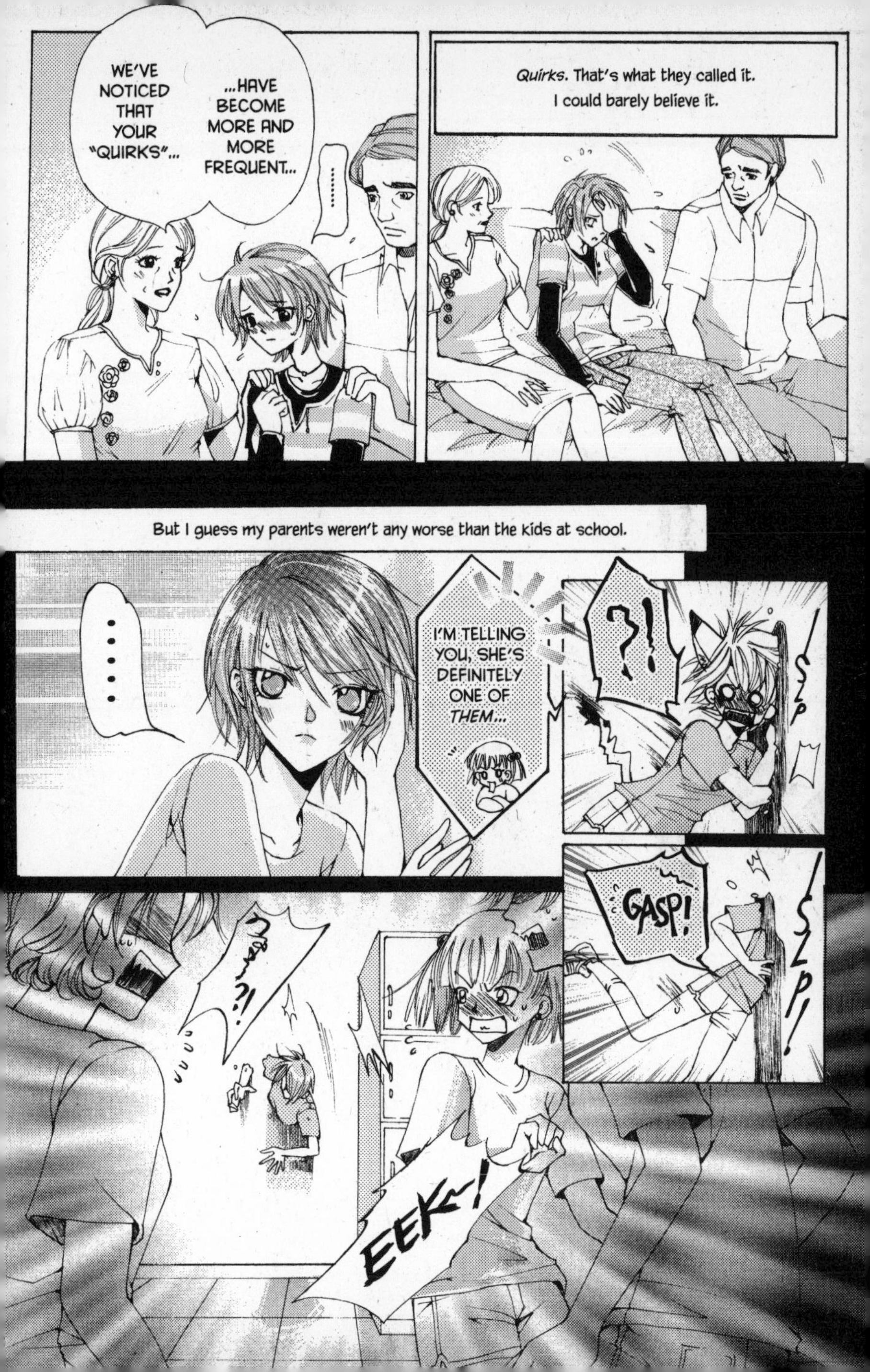
WE'VE NOTICED THAT YOUR "QUIRKS"...
...HAVE BECOME MORE AND MORE FREQUENT...
......
Quirks. That's what they called it. I could barely believe it.
But I guess my parents weren't any worse than the kids at school.
.....
I'M TELLING YOU, SHE'S DEFINITELY ONE OF *THEM*...
?!
SLP
GASP!
SLP!
EEK~!

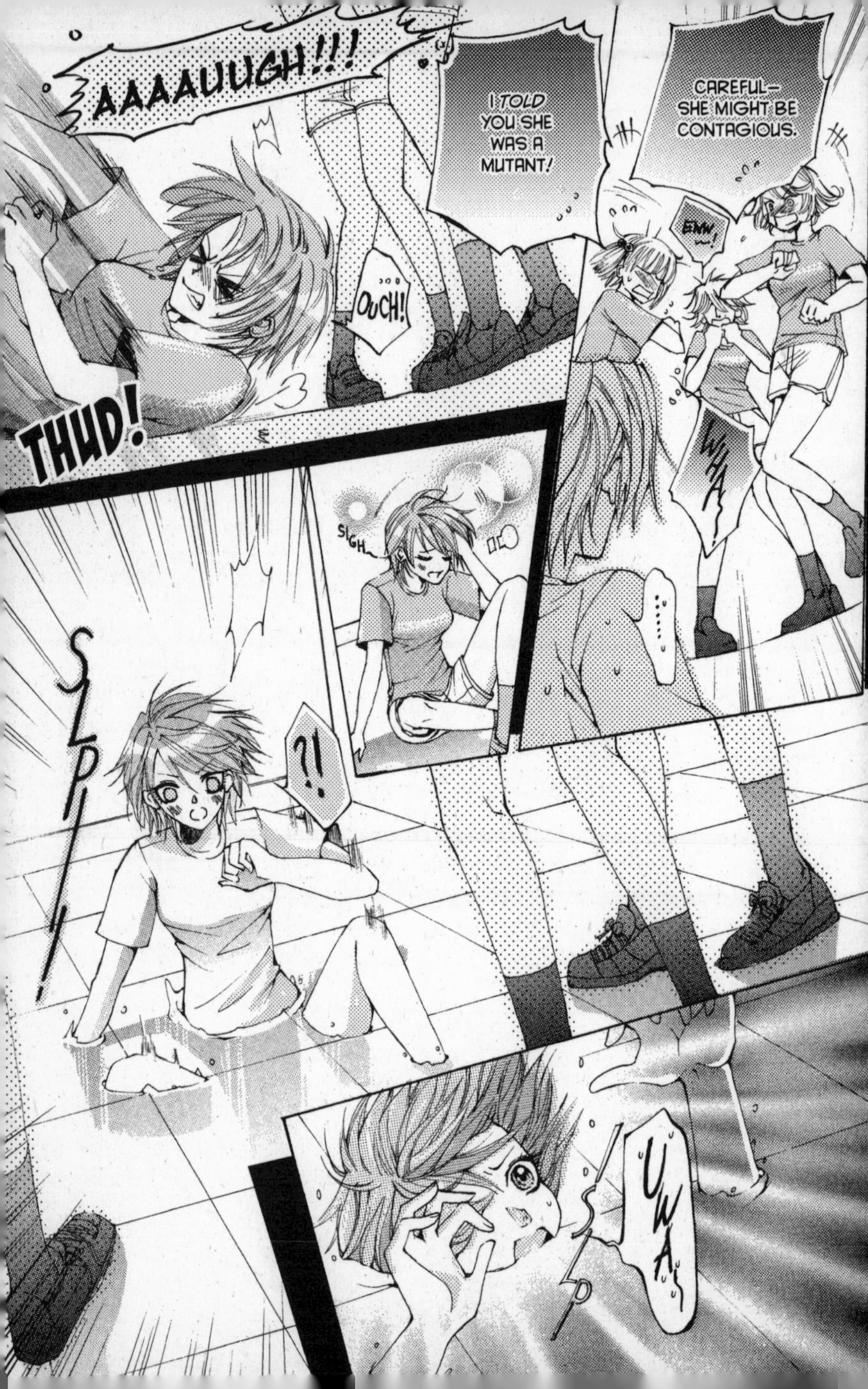
AAAAUUGH!!!
OUCH!
THUD!
I TOLD YOU SHE WAS A MUTANT!
CAREFUL—SHE MIGHT BE CONTAGIOUS.
EWW!
WHA
SIGH~
......
SLIP
?!
UWA

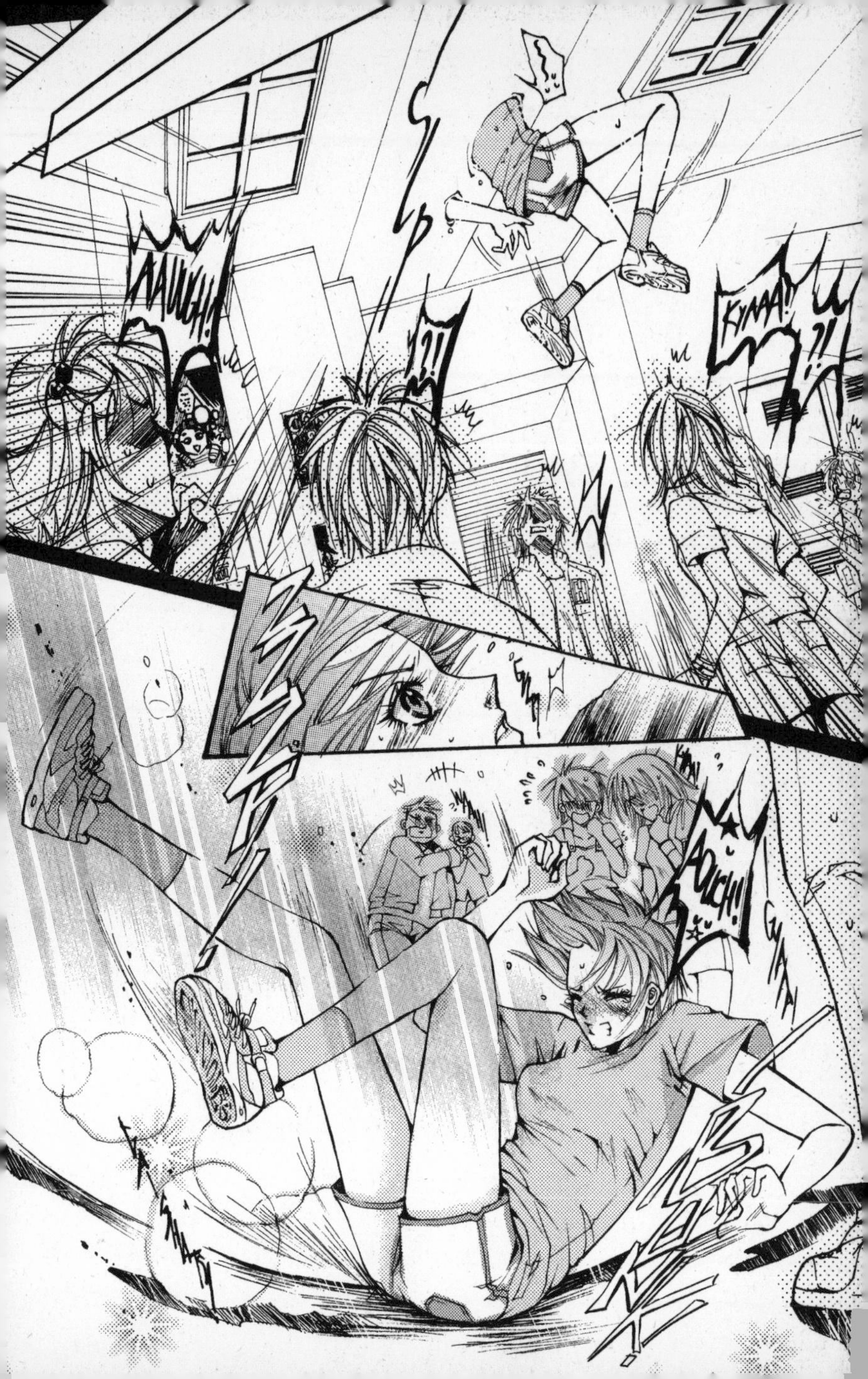
AAUUGH!
KYAAA!
AOUCH!

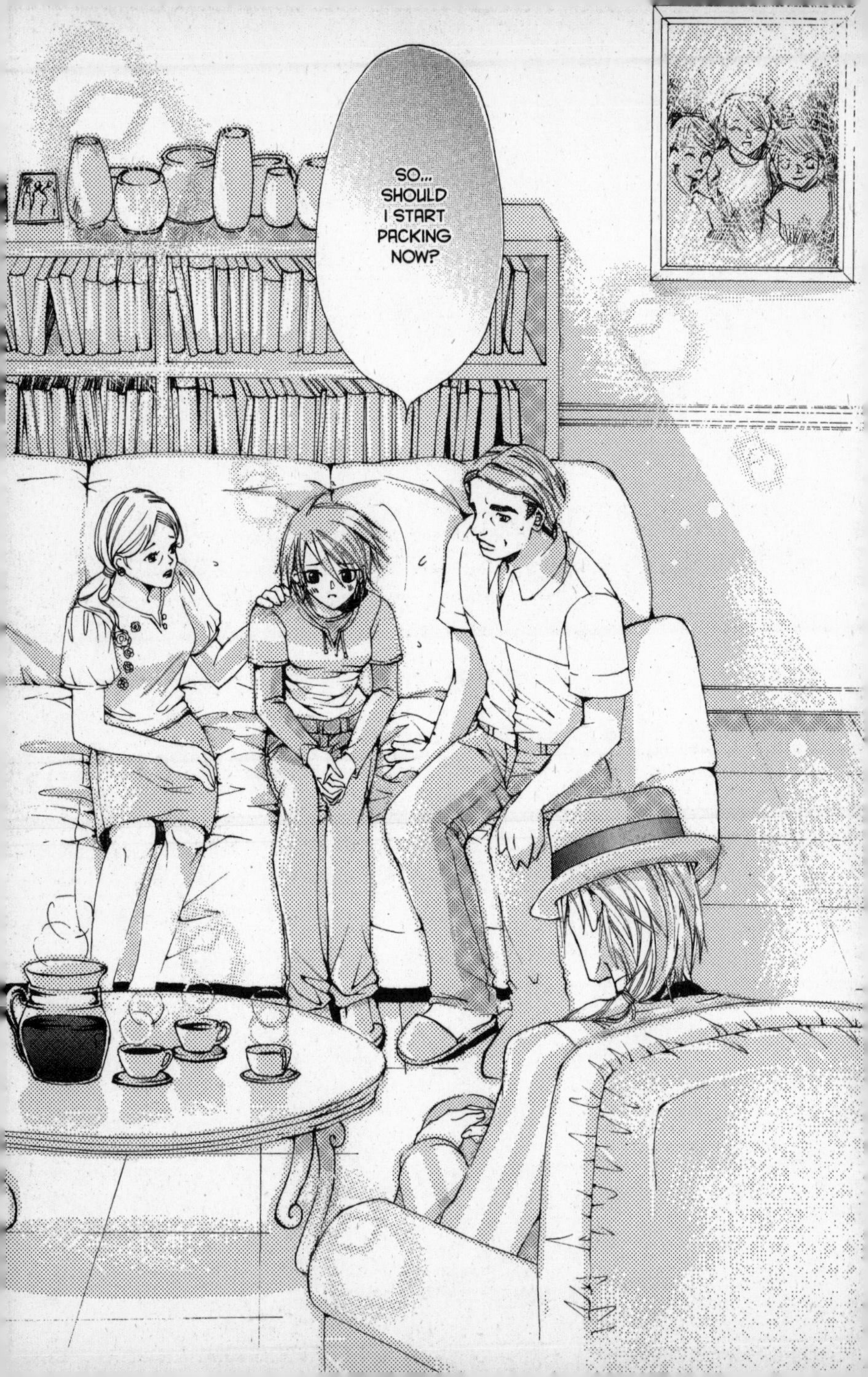
SO... SHOULD I START PACKING NOW?

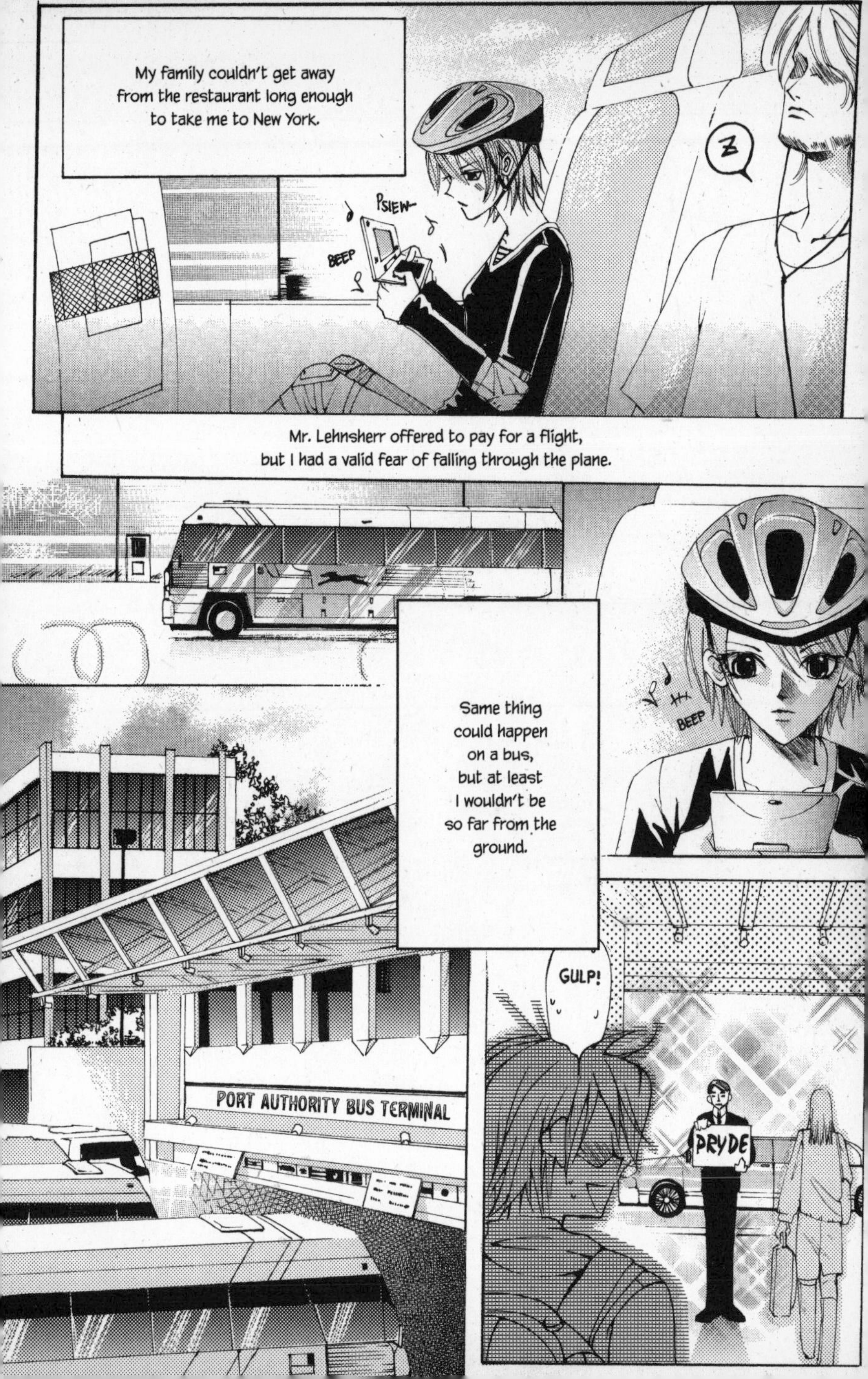
My family couldn't get away from the restaurant long enough to take me to New York.
PSIEW-
BEEP
Z
Mr. Lehnsherr offered to pay for a flight, but I had a valid fear of falling through the plane.
Same thing could happen on a bus, but at least I wouldn't be so far from the ground.
BEEP
PORT AUTHORITY BUS TERMINAL
GULP!
PRYDE

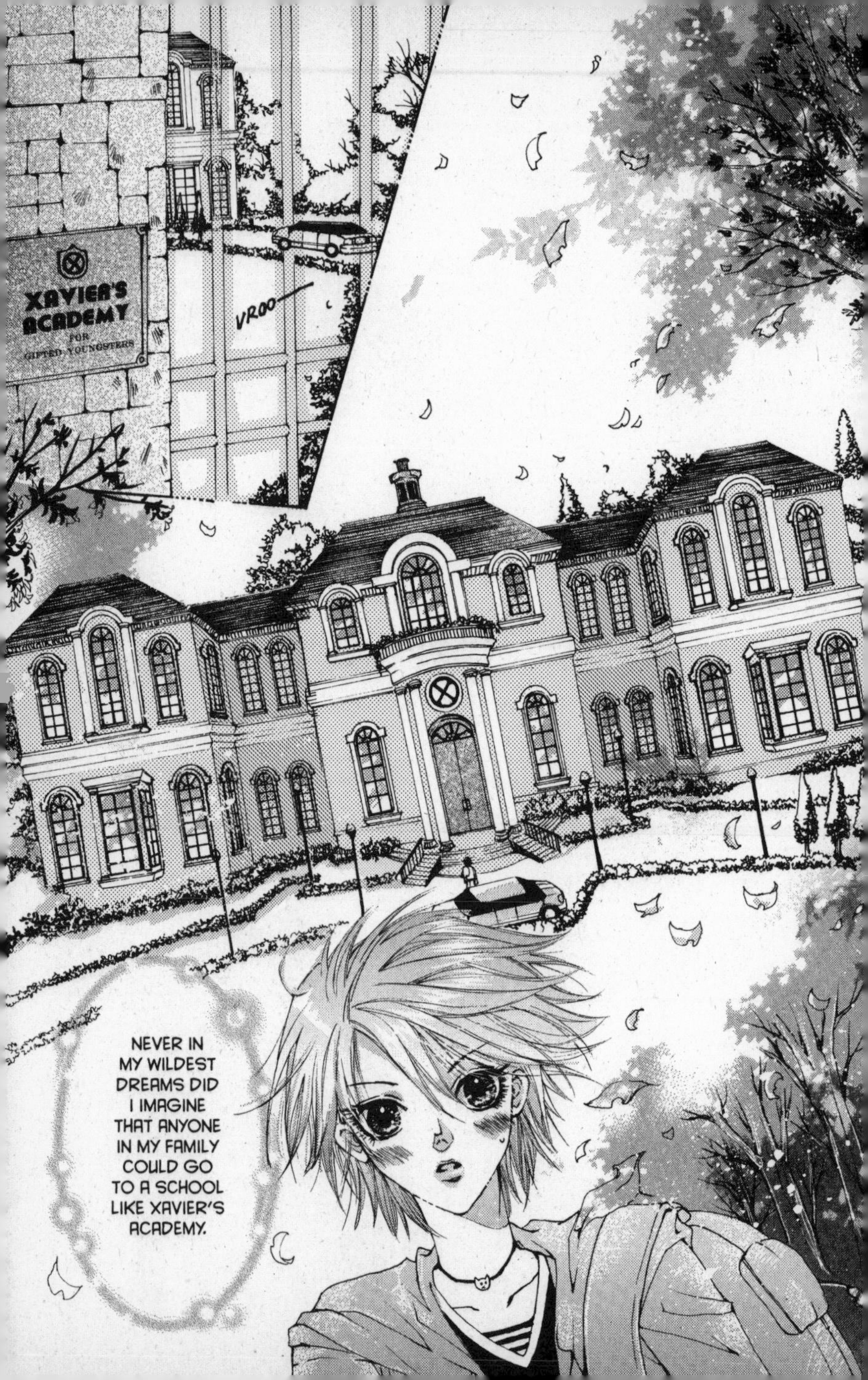
XAVIER'S ACADEMY
FOR GIFTED YOUNGSTERS
VROO—
NEVER IN MY WILDEST DREAMS DID I IMAGINE THAT ANYONE IN MY FAMILY COULD GO TO A SCHOOL LIKE XAVIER'S ACADEMY.

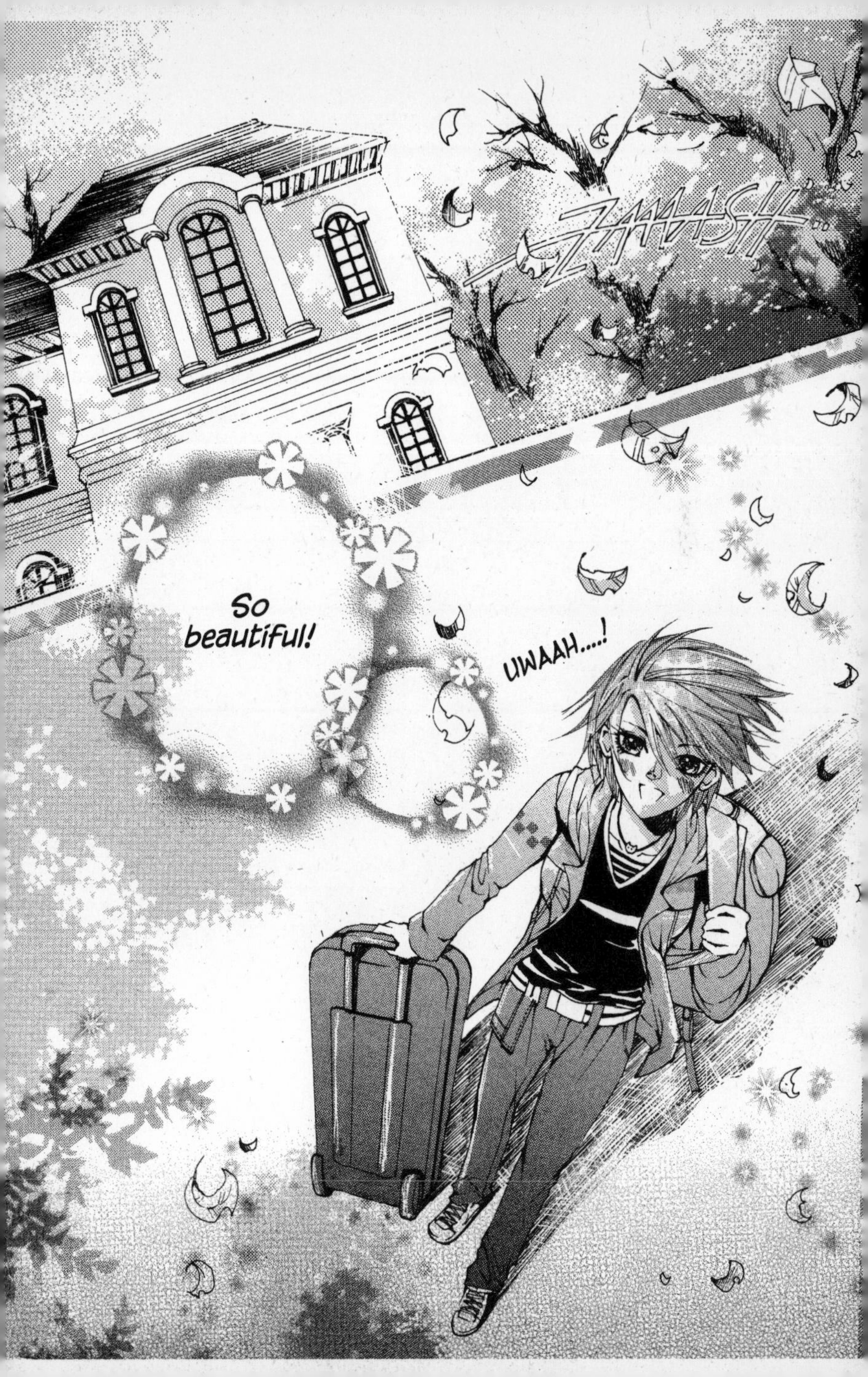
ZAAAASH
So beautiful!
UWAAH...!

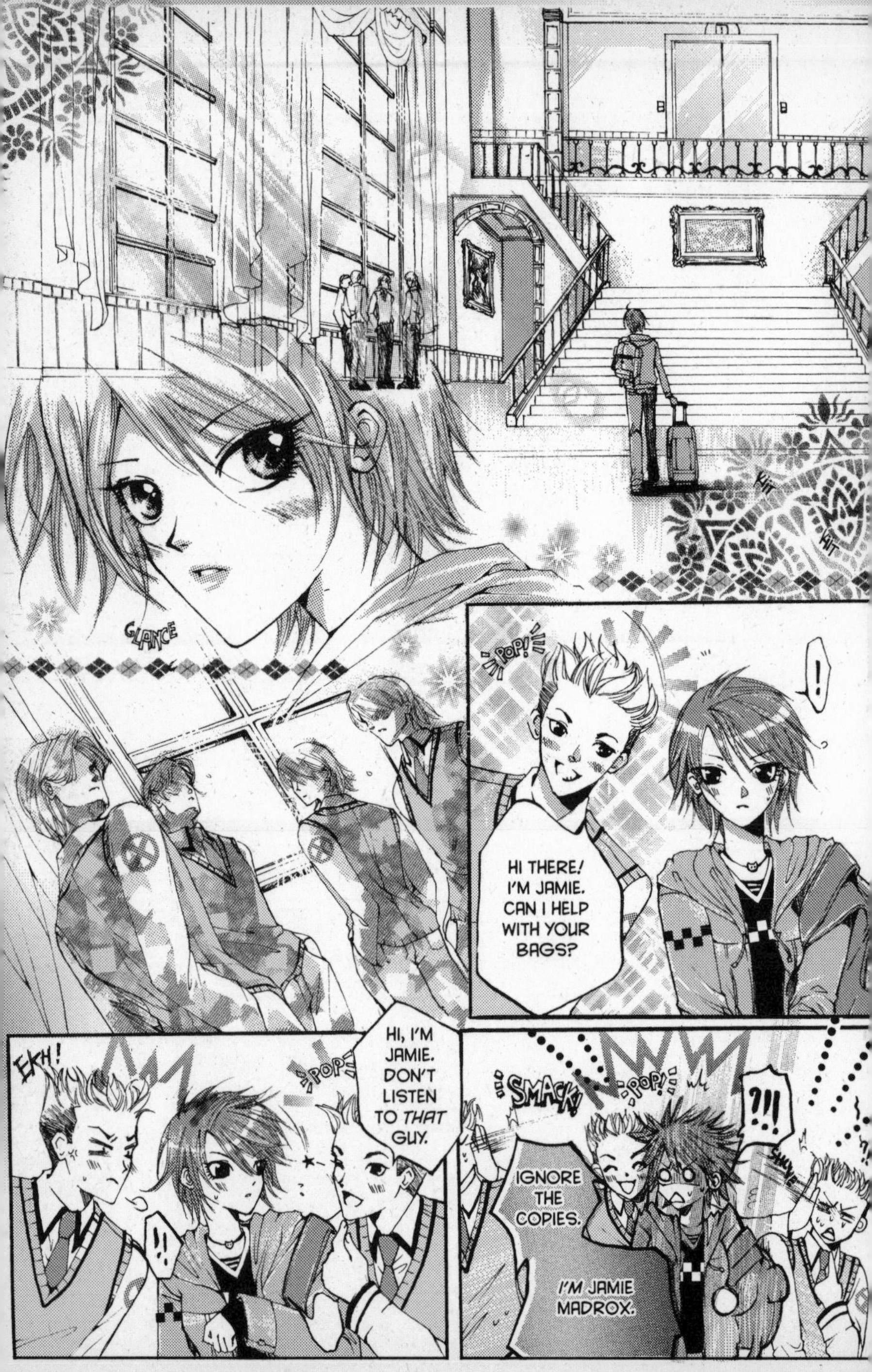
KLIT
KLIT
GLANCE
POP!
!
HI THERE! I'M JAMIE. CAN I HELP WITH YOUR BAGS?
EKH!
!!
POP
HI, I'M JAMIE. DON'T LISTEN TO *THAT* GUY.
SMACK!
POP!
IGNORE THE COPIES.
I'M JAMIE MADROX.
?!!
SHOVE
?!

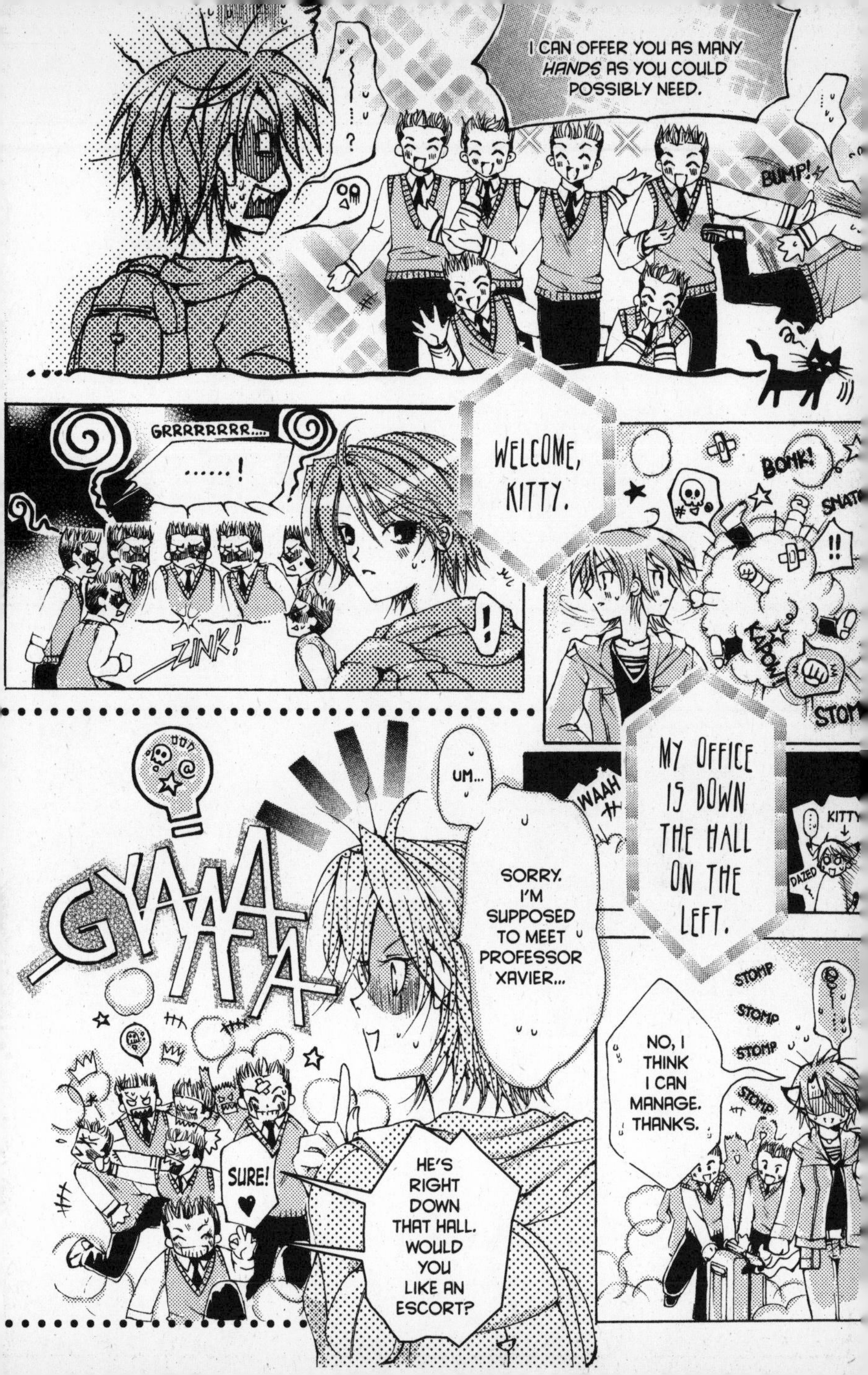
...?
I CAN OFFER YOU AS MANY *HANDS* AS YOU COULD POSSIBLY NEED.
BUMP!
GRRRRRRRR...
......!
ZINK!
!
WELCOME, KITTY.
BONK!
!!
KAPOW!
GYAAAAA
UM...
SORRY. I'M SUPPOSED TO MEET PROFESSOR XAVIER...
SURE!
HE'S RIGHT DOWN THAT HALL. WOULD YOU LIKE AN ESCORT?
MY OFFICE IS DOWN THE HALL ON THE LEFT.
WAAH
KITTY
DAZED
NO, I THINK I CAN MANAGE. THANKS.
STOMP
STOMP
STOMP
STOMP

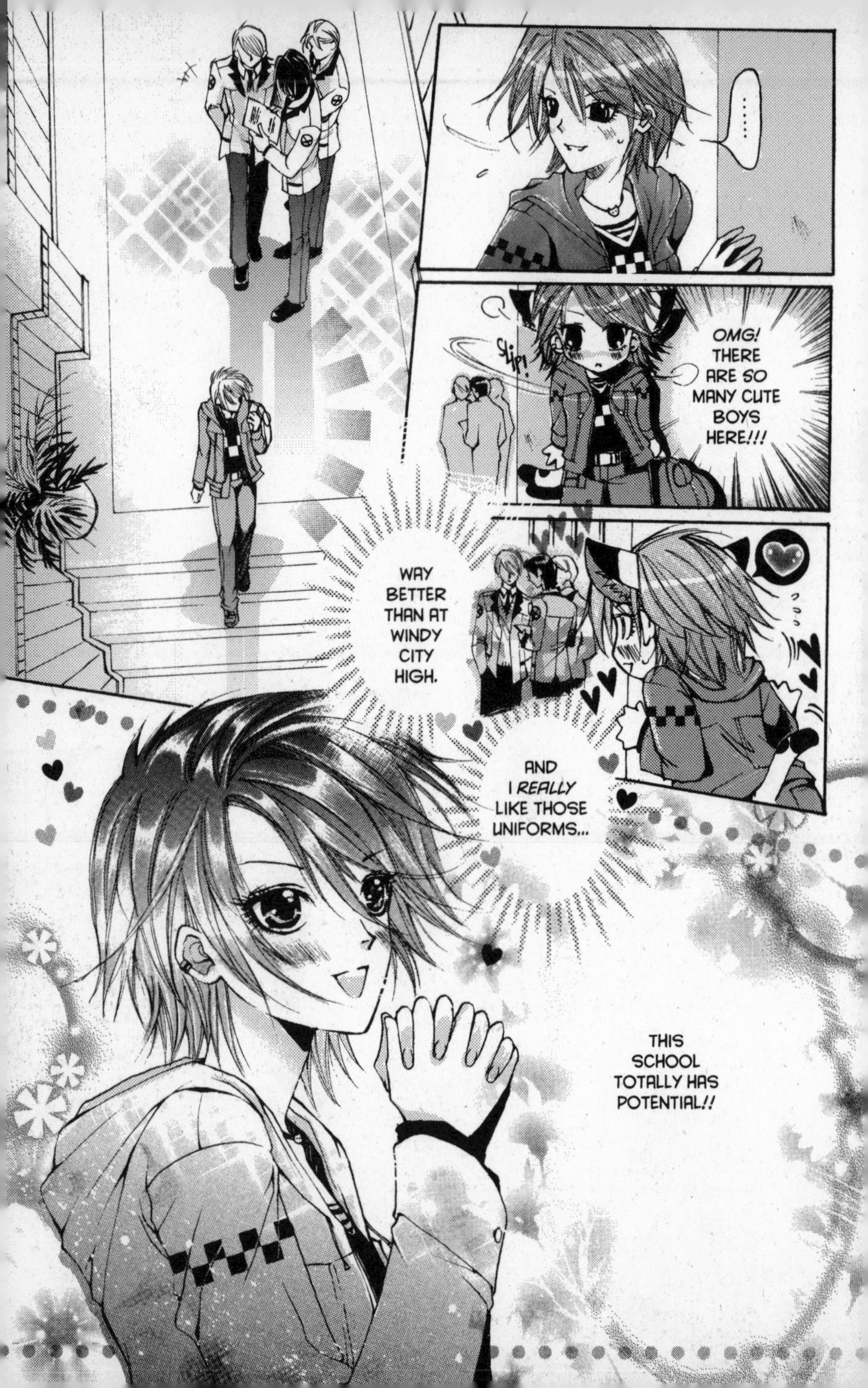
......
OMG! THERE ARE SO MANY CUTE BOYS HERE!!!
WAY BETTER THAN AT WINDY CITY HIGH.
AND I *REALLY* LIKE THOSE UNIFORMS...
THIS SCHOOL TOTALLY HAS POTENTIAL!!

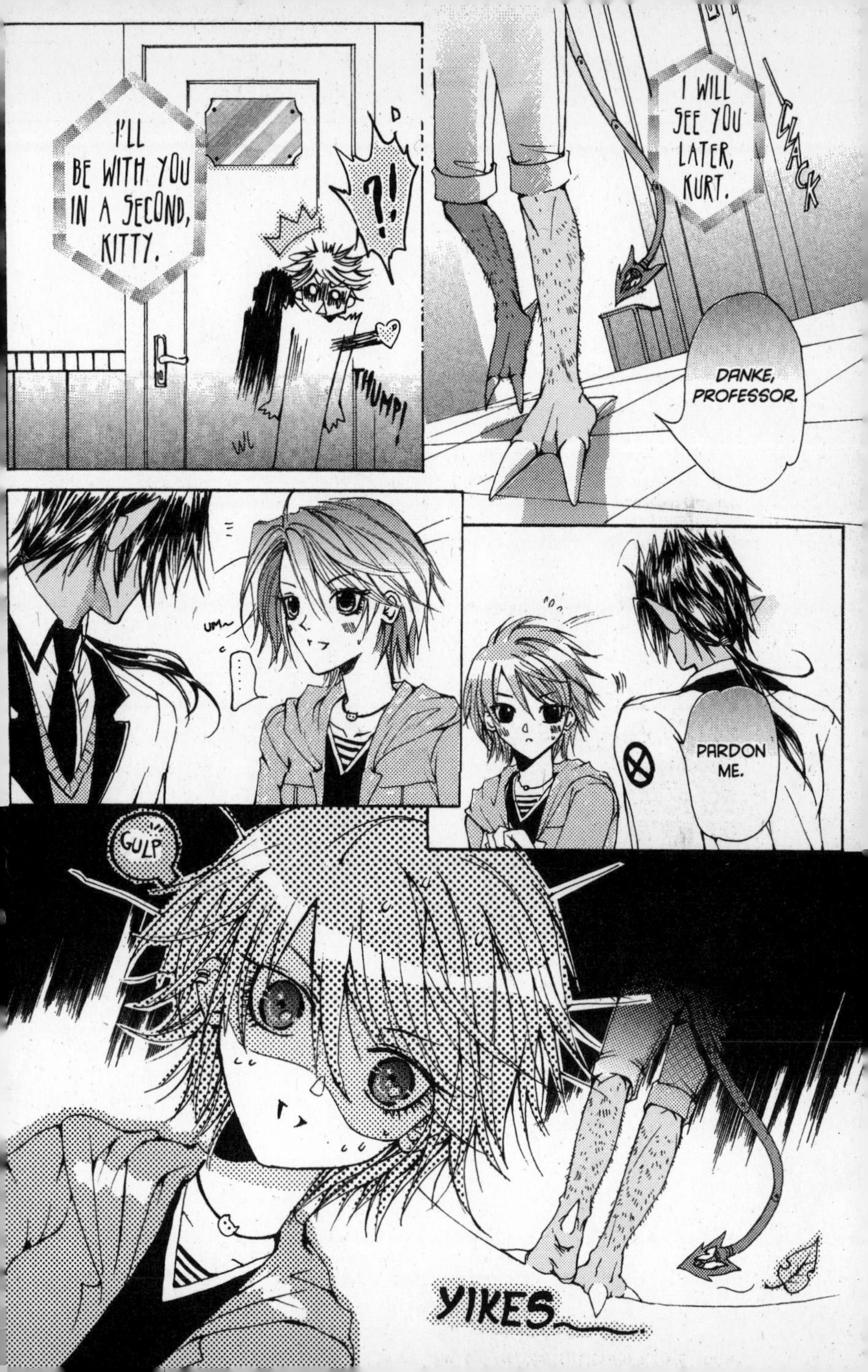
I'LL BE WITH YOU IN A SECOND, KITTY.
?!
THUMP!
I WILL SEE YOU LATER, KURT.
CLACK
DANKE, PROFESSOR.
UM~
......
PARDON ME.
GULP
YIKES

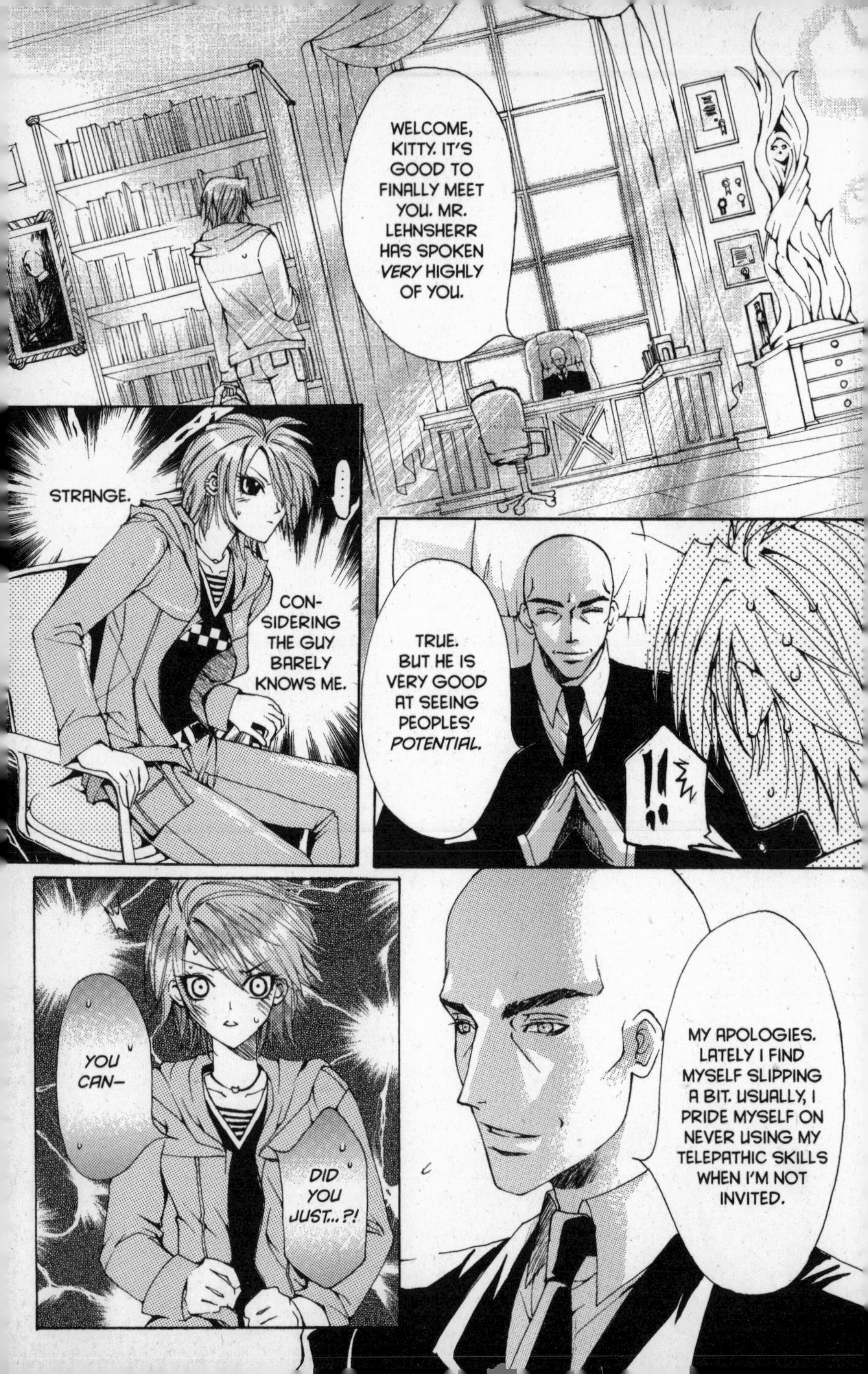
WELCOME, KITTY. IT'S GOOD TO FINALLY MEET YOU. MR. LEHNSHERR HAS SPOKEN *VERY* HIGHLY OF YOU.
STRANGE.
...
CON-SIDERING THE GUY BARELY KNOWS ME.
TRUE. BUT HE IS VERY GOOD AT SEEING PEOPLES' *POTENTIAL*.
!!
YOU CAN–
DID YOU JUST...?!
MY APOLOGIES. LATELY I FIND MYSELF SLIPPING A BIT. USUALLY, I PRIDE MYSELF ON NEVER USING MY TELEPATHIC SKILLS WHEN I'M NOT INVITED.

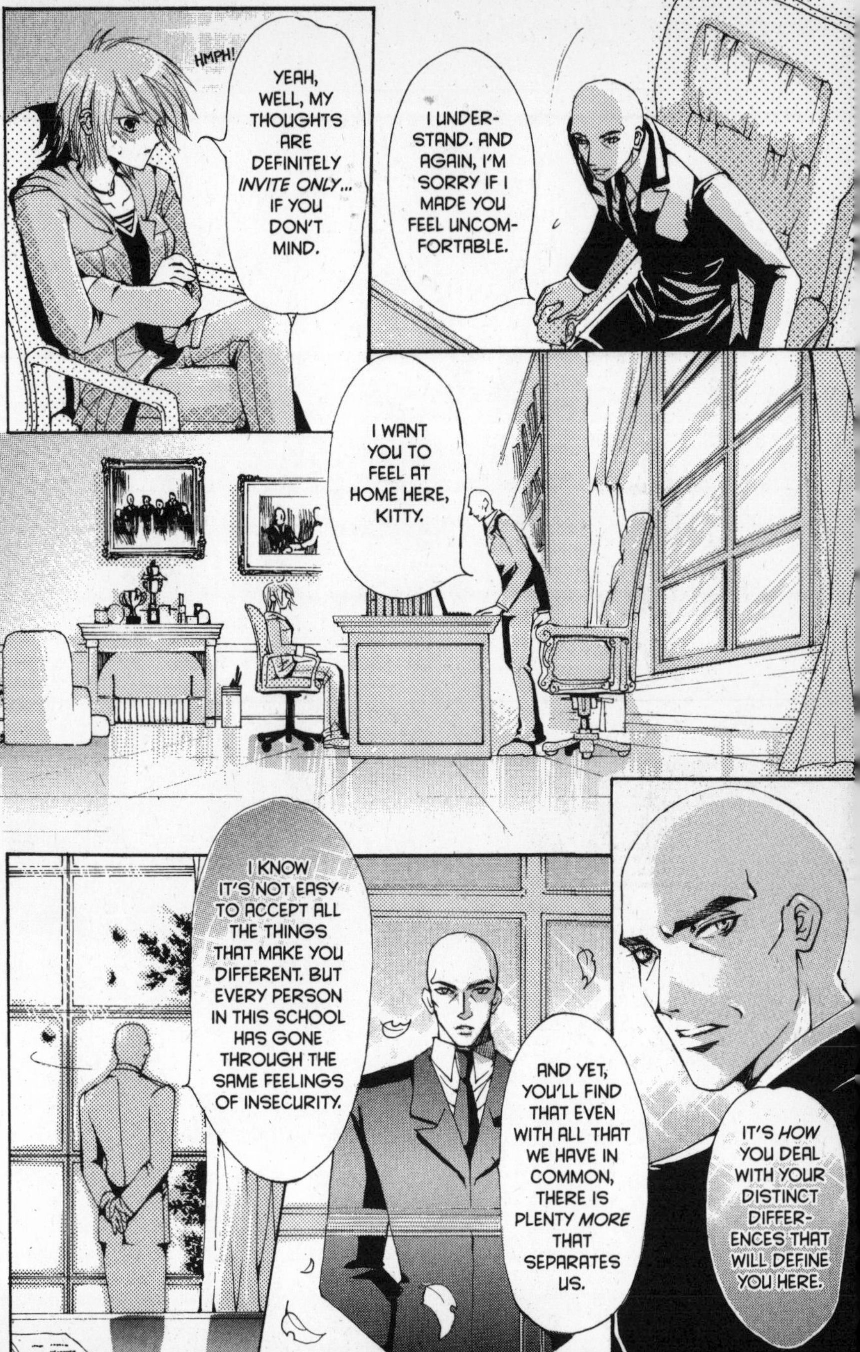
HMPH!
YEAH, WELL, MY THOUGHTS ARE DEFINITELY *INVITE ONLY*... IF YOU DON'T MIND.
I UNDERSTAND. AND AGAIN, I'M SORRY IF I MADE YOU FEEL UNCOMFORTABLE.
I WANT YOU TO FEEL AT HOME HERE, KITTY.
I KNOW IT'S NOT EASY TO ACCEPT ALL THE THINGS THAT MAKE YOU DIFFERENT. BUT EVERY PERSON IN THIS SCHOOL HAS GONE THROUGH THE SAME FEELINGS OF INSECURITY.
AND YET, YOU'LL FIND THAT EVEN WITH ALL THAT WE HAVE IN COMMON, THERE IS PLENTY *MORE* THAT SEPARATES US.
IT'S *HOW* YOU DEAL WITH YOUR DISTINCT DIFFERENCES THAT WILL DEFINE YOU HERE.

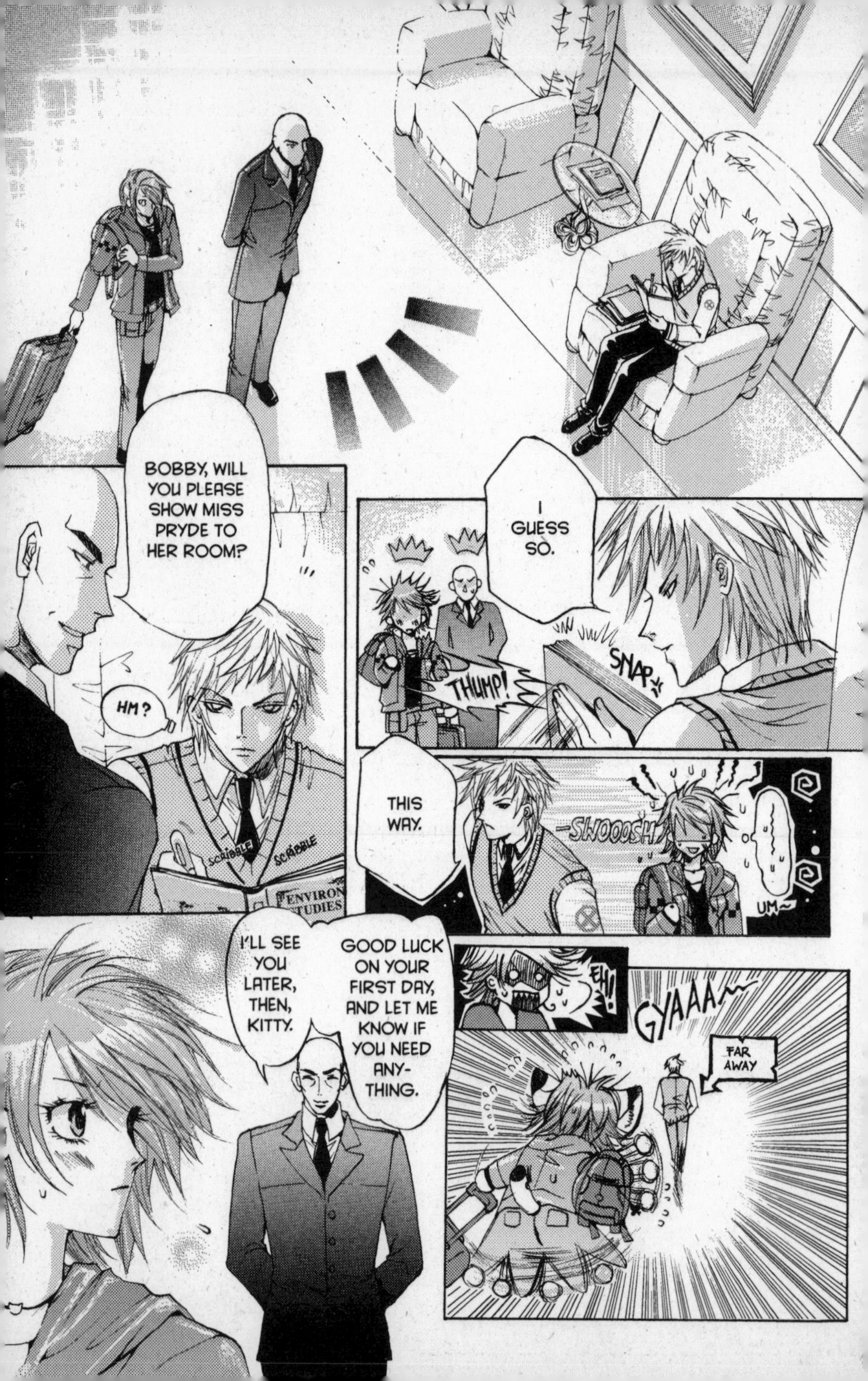
BOBBY, WILL YOU PLEASE SHOW MISS PRYDE TO HER ROOM?
HM?
SCRIBBLE
SCRIBBLE
ENVIRON STUDIES
I GUESS SO.
THUMP!
SNAP
THIS WAY.
SWOOOSH
UM~
I'LL SEE YOU LATER, THEN, KITTY.
GOOD LUCK ON YOUR FIRST DAY, AND LET ME KNOW IF YOU NEED ANY-THING.
EH!!
GYAAA~
FAR AWAY

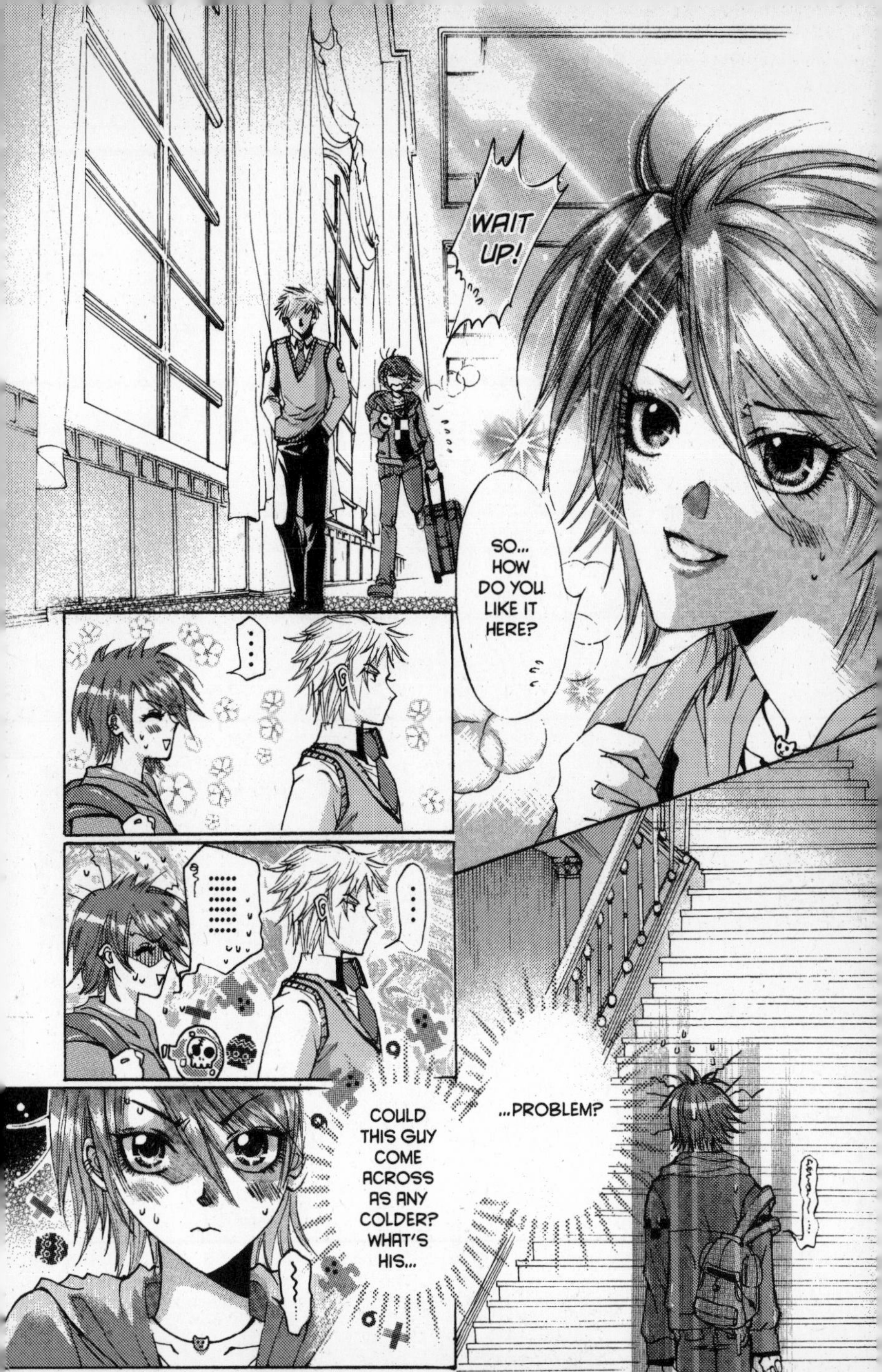
WAIT UP!
SO... HOW DO YOU LIKE IT HERE?
....
....
COULD THIS GUY COME ACROSS AS ANY COLDER? WHAT'S HIS...
...PROBLEM?

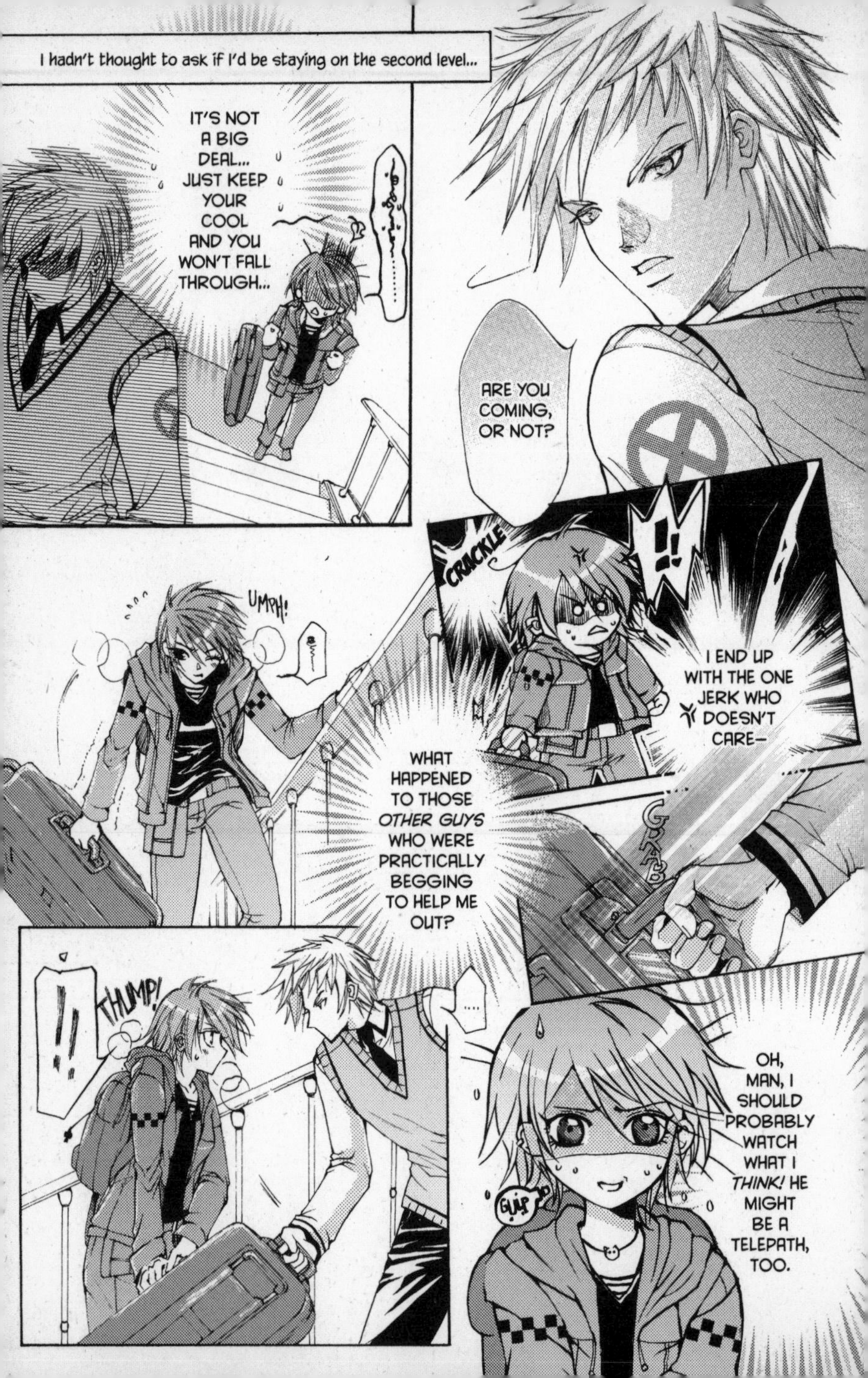
I hadn't thought to ask if I'd be staying on the second level...
IT'S NOT A BIG DEAL... JUST KEEP YOUR COOL AND YOU WON'T FALL THROUGH...
ARE YOU COMING, OR NOT?
UMPH!
CRACKLE
!!
I END UP WITH THE ONE JERK WHO DOESN'T CARE—
WHAT HAPPENED TO THOSE *OTHER GUYS* WHO WERE PRACTICALLY BEGGING TO HELP ME OUT?
GRAB
!!
THUMP!
....
GULP
OH, MAN, I SHOULD PROBABLY WATCH WHAT I *THINK!* HE MIGHT BE A TELEPATH, TOO.

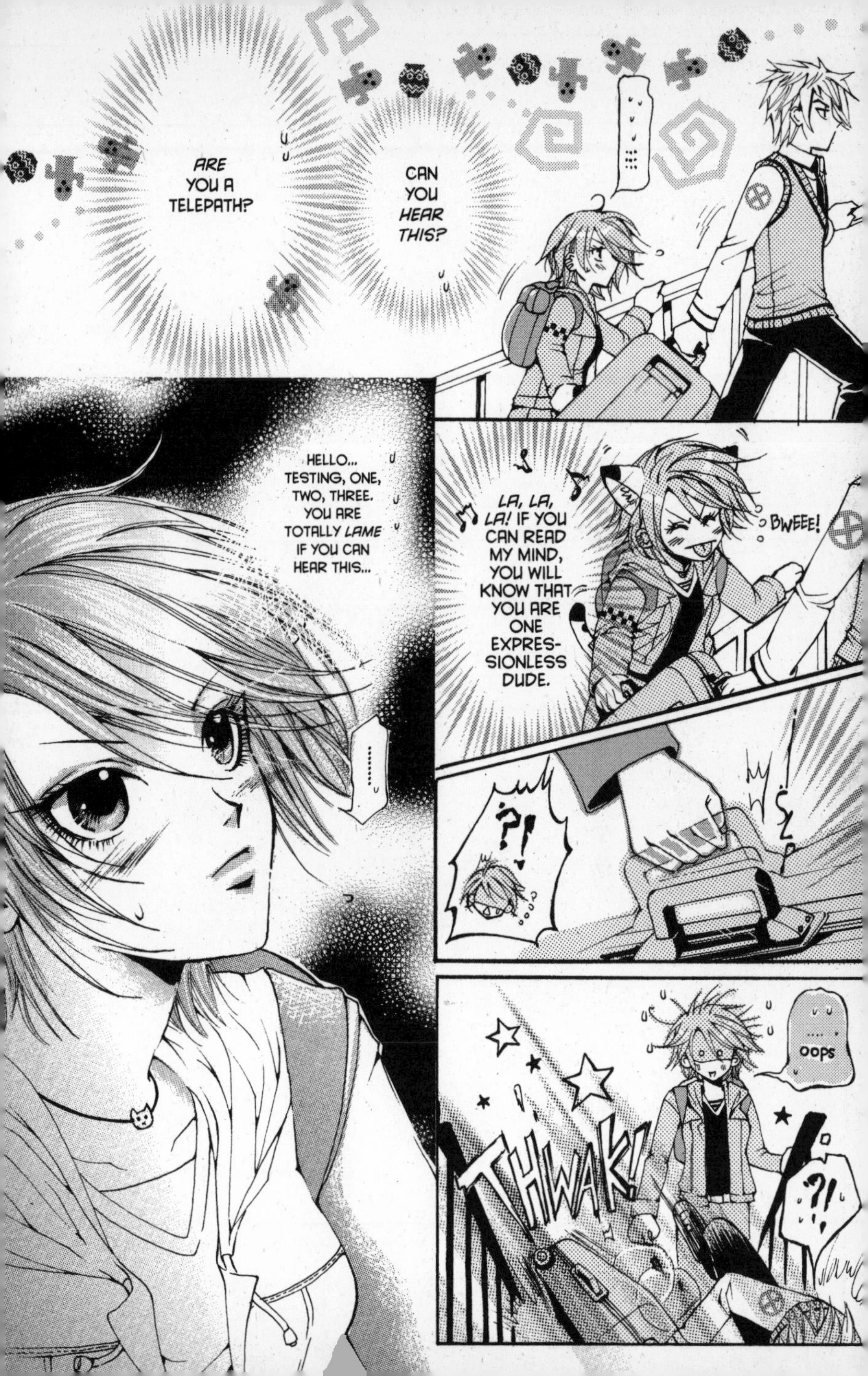

ARE YOU A TELEPATH?
CAN YOU HEAR THIS?
HELLO... TESTING, ONE, TWO, THREE. YOU ARE TOTALLY LAME IF YOU CAN HEAR THIS...
LA, LA, LA! IF YOU CAN READ MY MIND, YOU WILL KNOW THAT YOU ARE ONE EXPRES-SIONLESS DUDE.
BWEEE!
?!
THWAK!
OOPS
?!

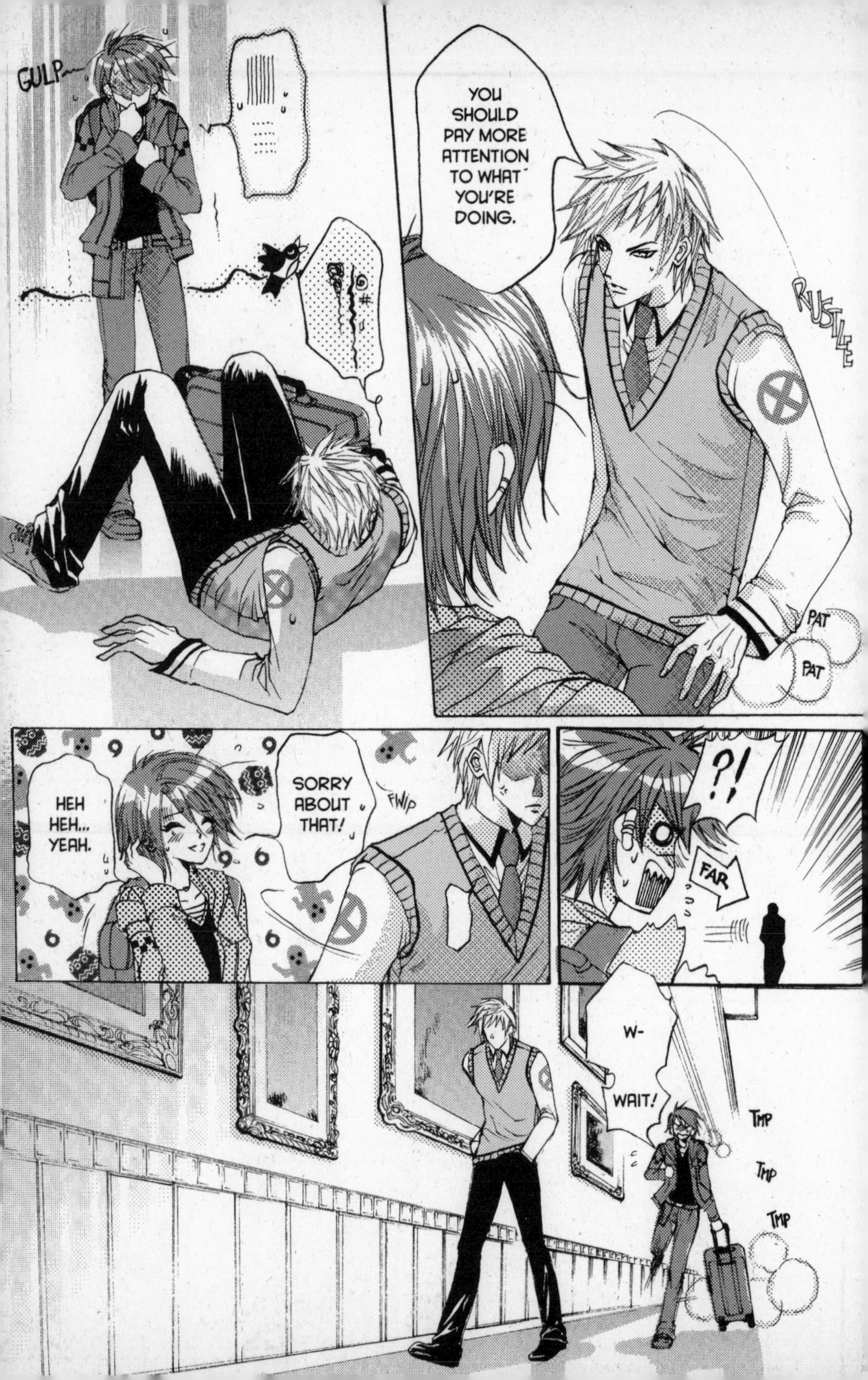
GULP
YOU SHOULD PAY MORE ATTENTION TO WHAT YOU'RE DOING.
RUSTLE
PAT
PAT
HEH HEH... YEAH.
SORRY ABOUT THAT!
FWIP
?!
FAR
W-
WAIT!
TMP
TMP
TMP

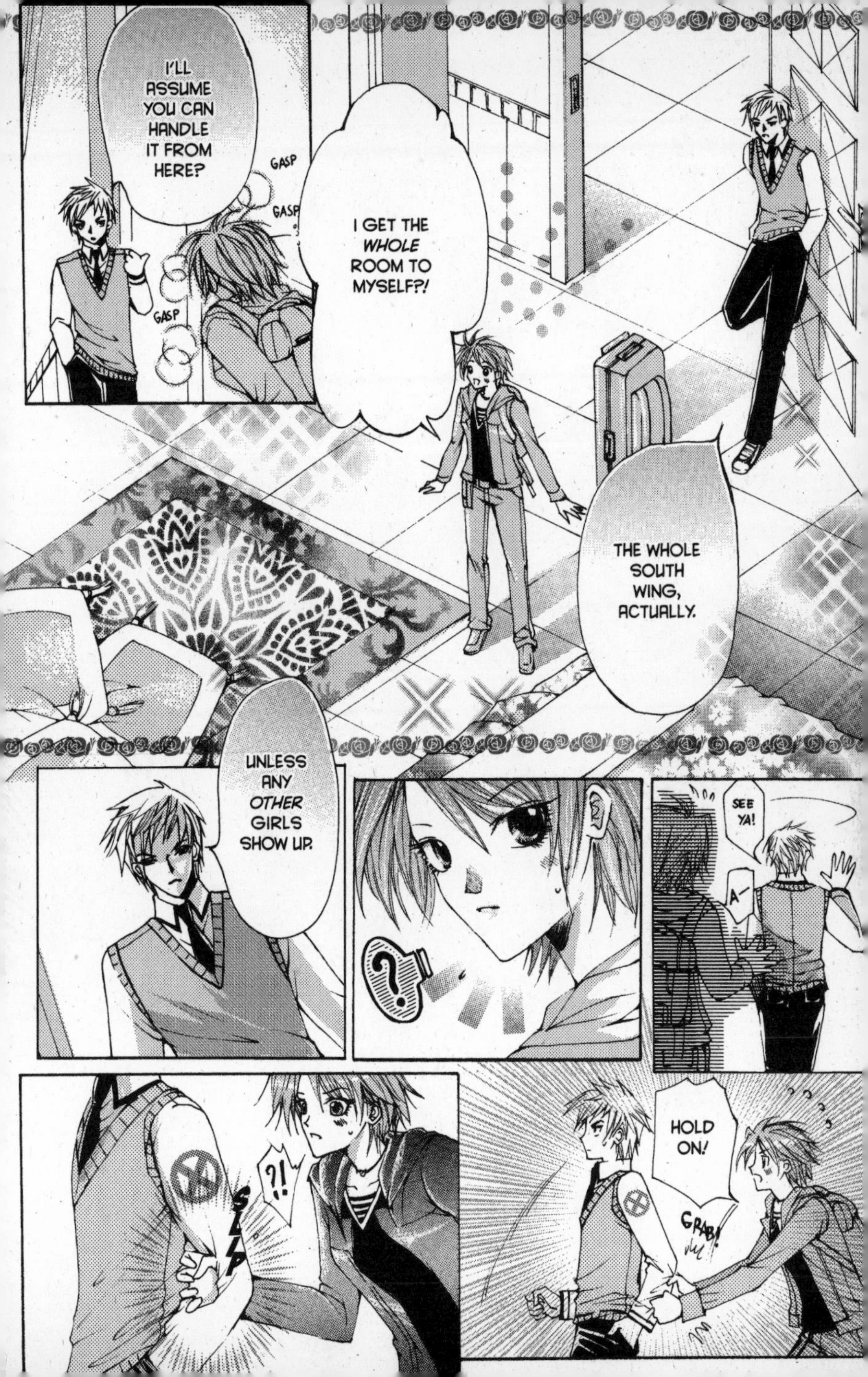
I'LL ASSUME YOU CAN HANDLE IT FROM HERE?
GASP
GASP
GASP
I GET THE *WHOLE* ROOM TO MYSELF?!
THE WHOLE SOUTH WING, ACTUALLY.
UNLESS ANY *OTHER* GIRLS SHOW UP.
?
SEE YA!
A—
?!
HOLD ON!
GRAB!

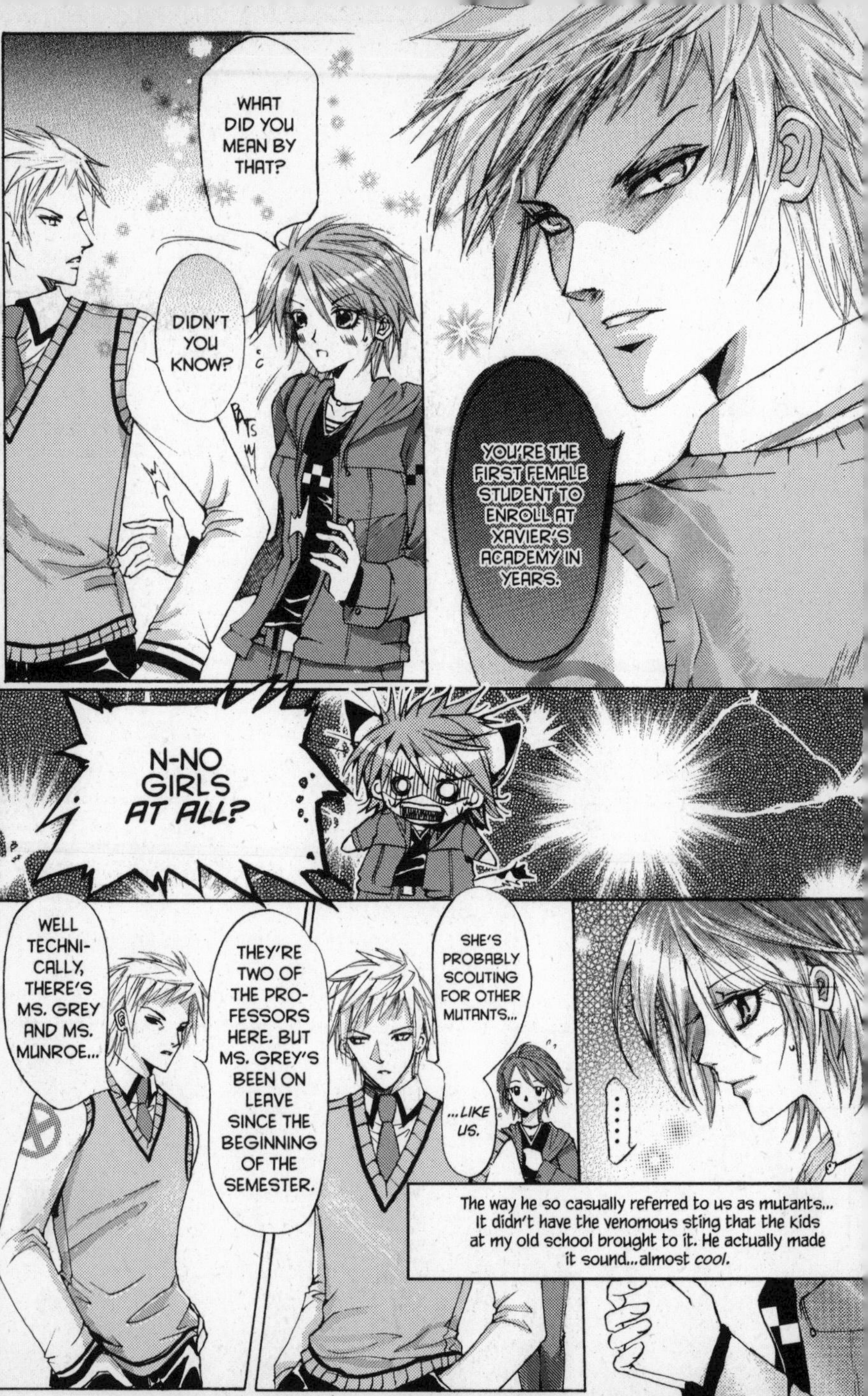
WHAT DID YOU MEAN BY THAT?
DIDN'T YOU KNOW?
YOU'RE THE FIRST FEMALE STUDENT TO ENROLL AT XAVIER'S ACADEMY IN YEARS.
N-NO GIRLS *AT ALL?*
WELL TECHNICALLY, THERE'S MS. GREY AND MS. MUNROE...
THEY'RE TWO OF THE PROFESSORS HERE. BUT MS. GREY'S BEEN ON LEAVE SINCE THE BEGINNING OF THE SEMESTER.
SHE'S PROBABLY SCOUTING FOR OTHER MUTANTS...
...LIKE US.
......
The way he so casually referred to us as mutants... It didn't have the venomous sting that the kids at my old school brought to it. He actually made it sound...almost *cool.*

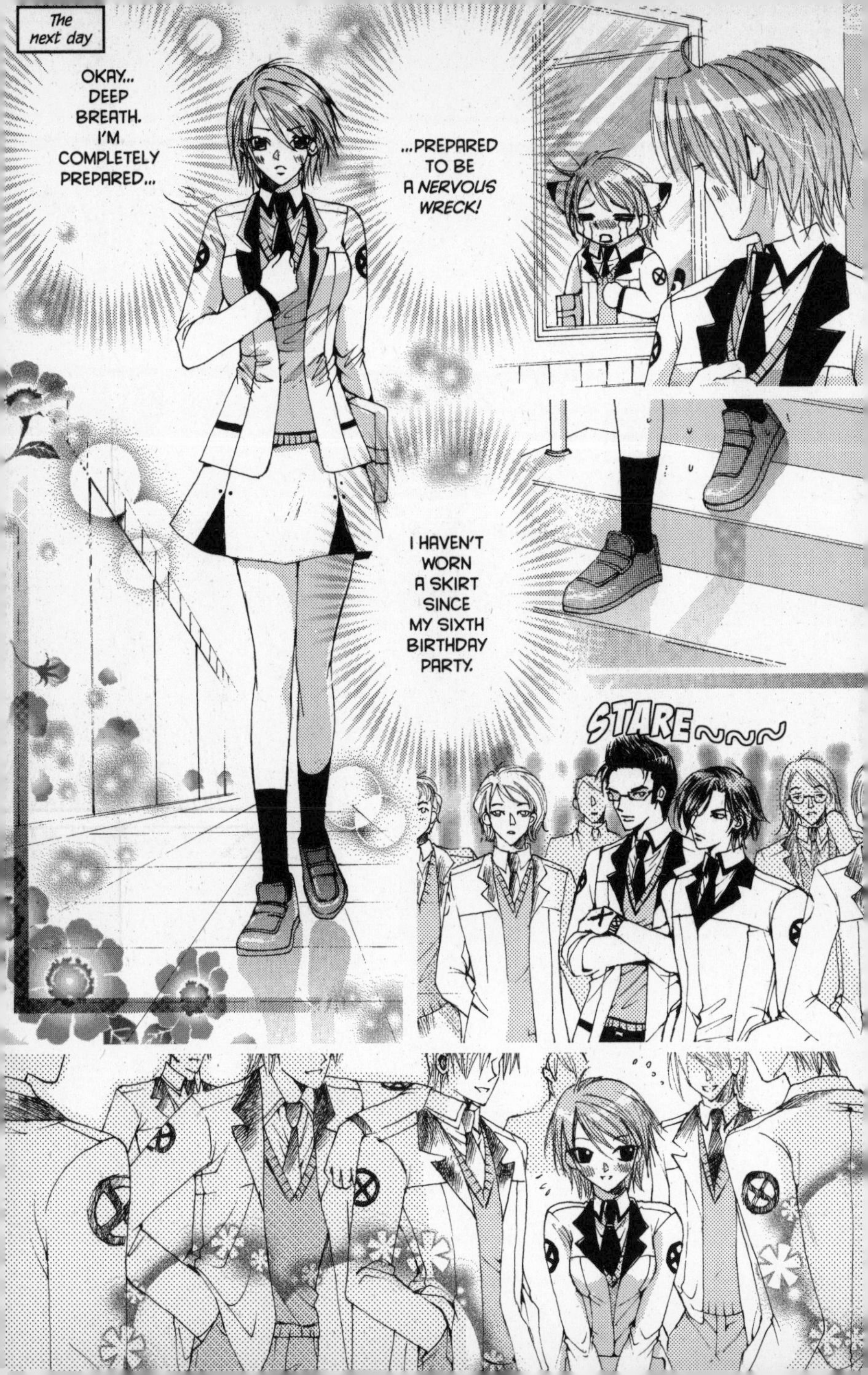
The next day
OKAY... DEEP BREATH. I'M COMPLETELY PREPARED...
...PREPARED TO BE A NERVOUS WRECK!
I HAVEN'T WORN A SKIRT SINCE MY SIXTH BIRTHDAY PARTY.
STARE~~~

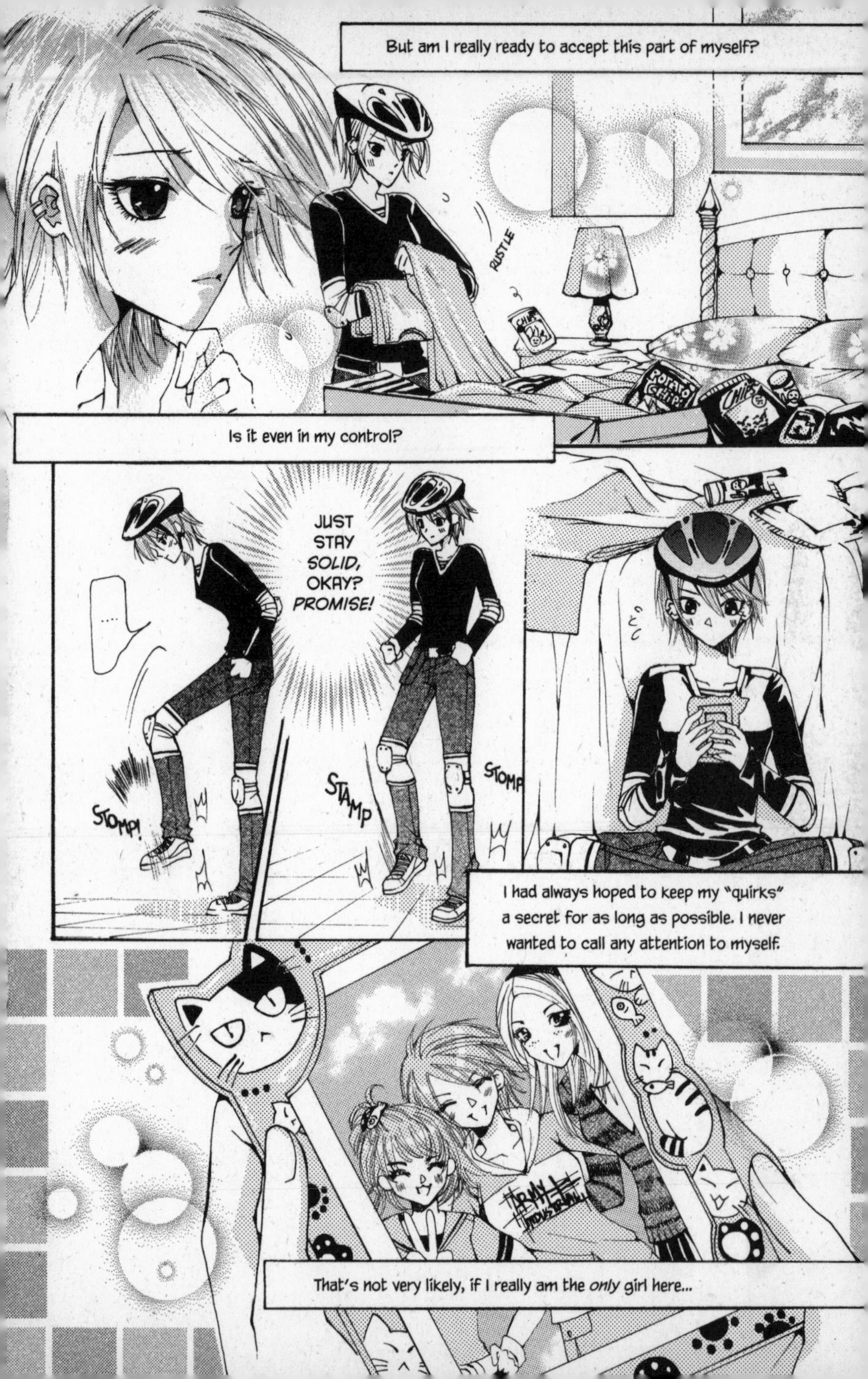
But am I really ready to accept this part of myself?
RUSTLE
Is it even in my control?
...
JUST STAY SOLID, OKAY? PROMISE!
STOMP!
STAMP
STOMP
I had always hoped to keep my "quirks" a secret for as long as possible. I never wanted to call any attention to myself.
That's not very likely, if I really am the *only* girl here...

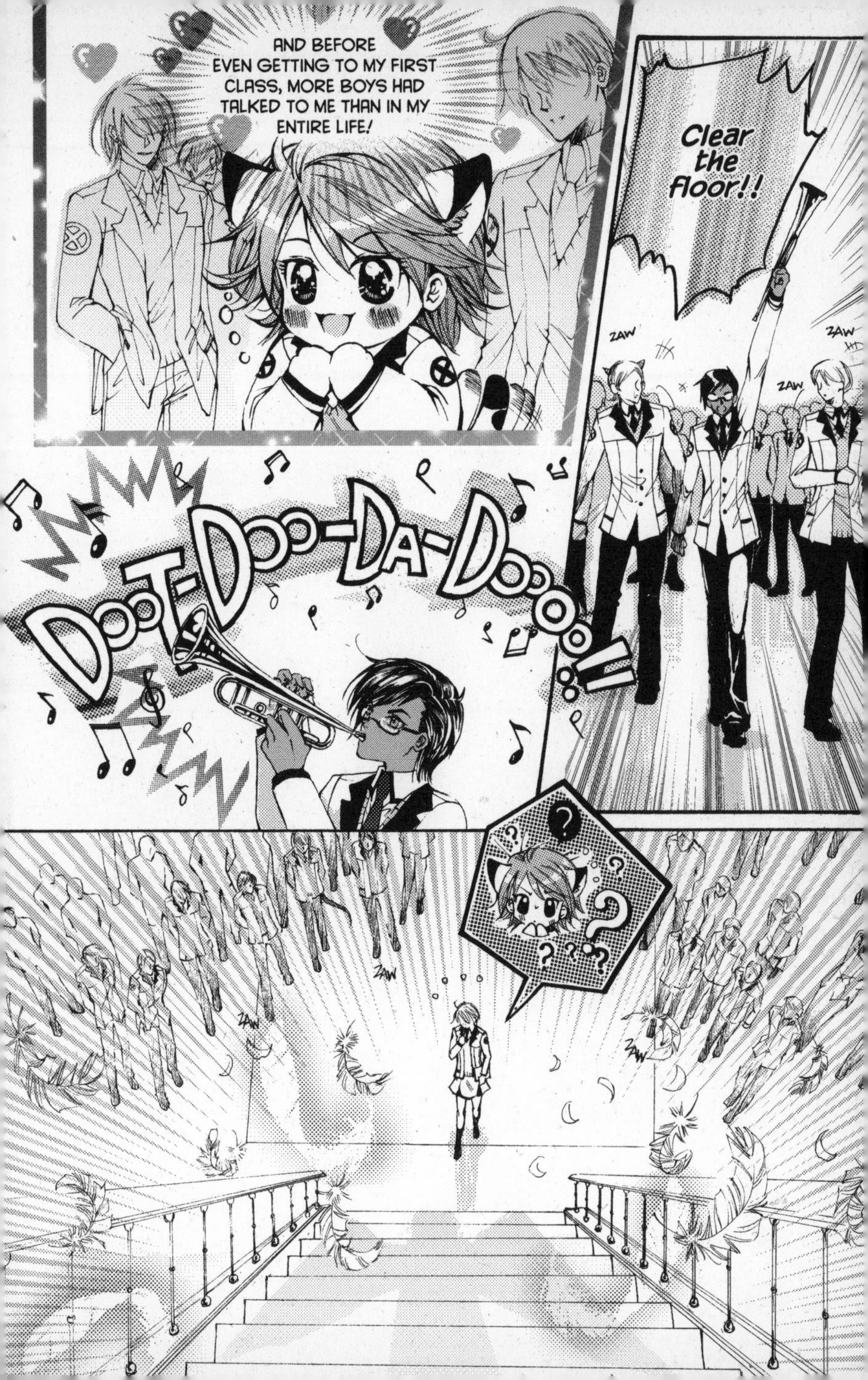
AND BEFORE EVEN GETTING TO MY FIRST CLASS, MORE BOYS HAD TALKED TO ME THAN IN MY ENTIRE LIFE!
DOOT-DOOO-DA-DOOOOO!!
Clear the floor!!
ZAW
ZAW
ZAW
ZAW
ZAW
ZAW
ZAW

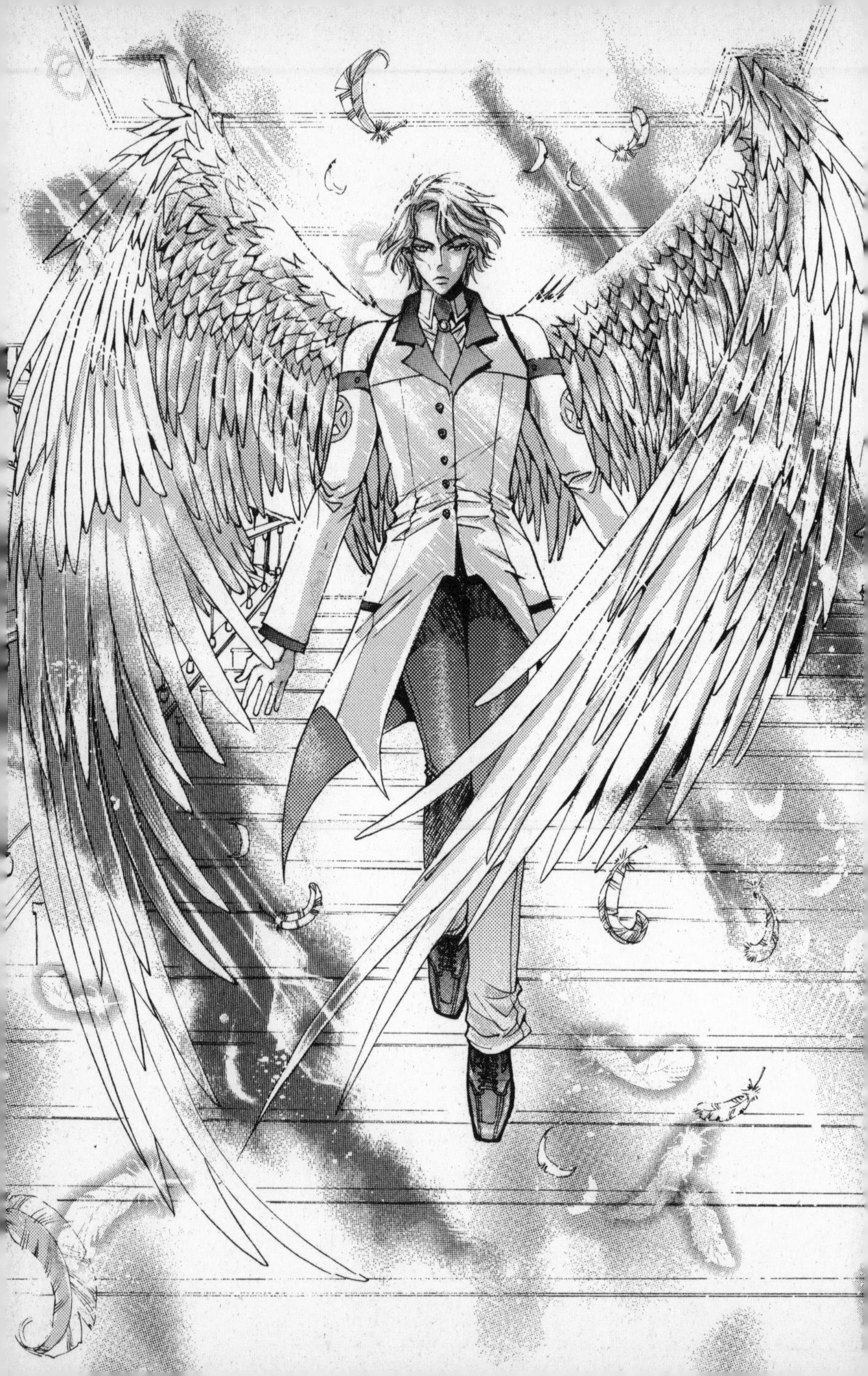

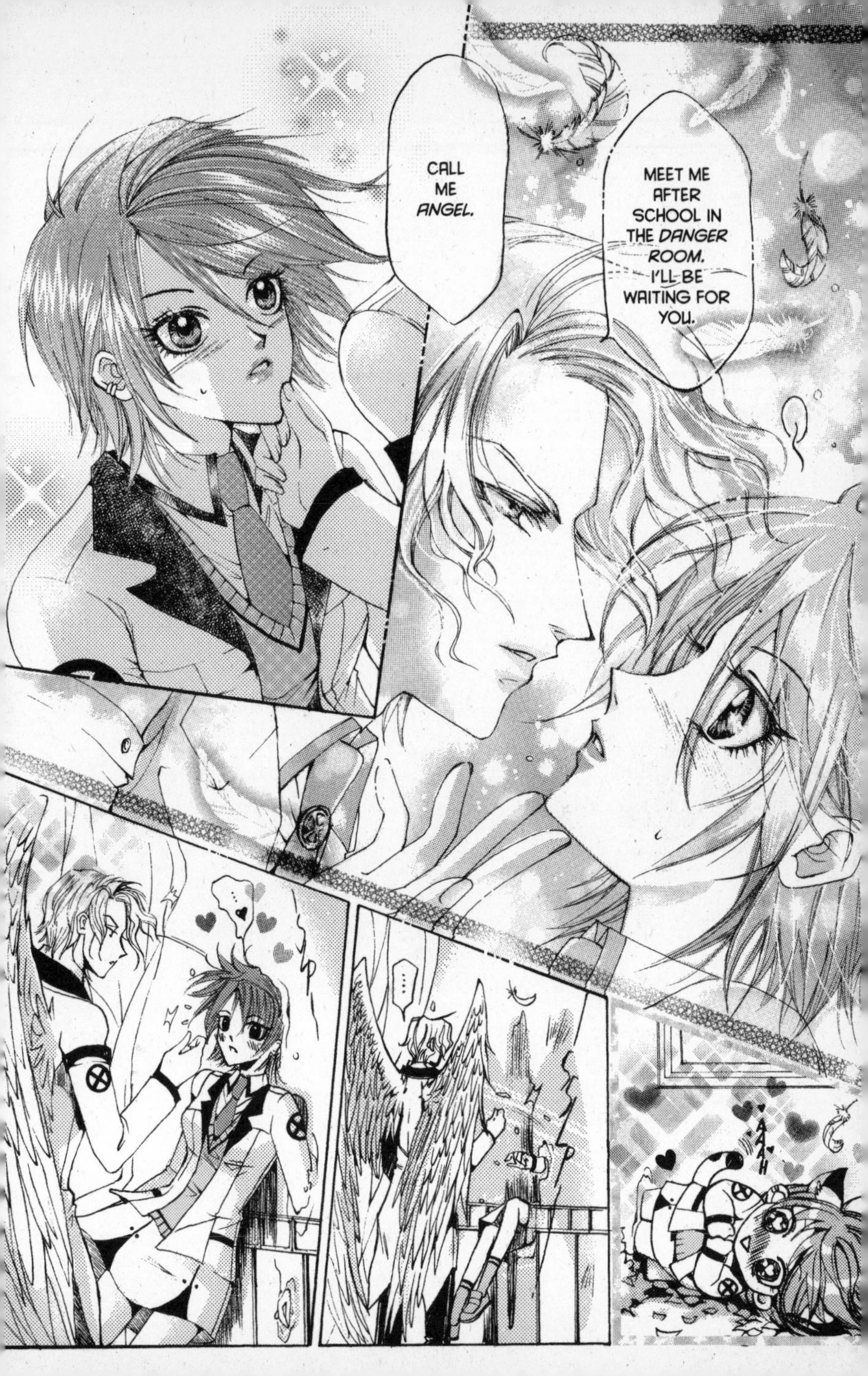
CALL ME *ANGEL.*
MEET ME AFTER SCHOOL IN THE *DANGER ROOM.* I'LL BE WAITING FOR YOU.

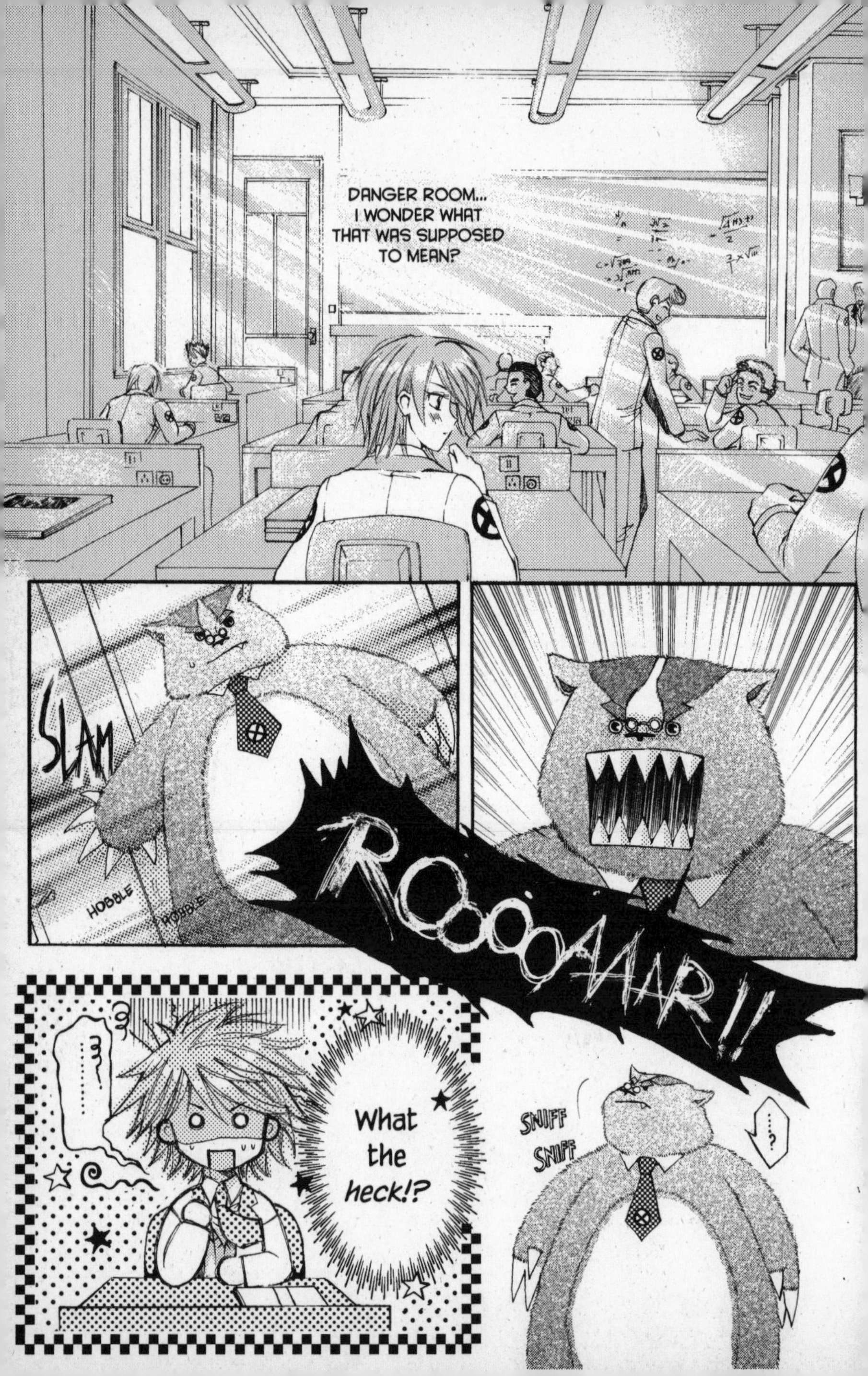
DANGER ROOM... I WONDER WHAT THAT WAS SUPPOSED TO MEAN?
SLAM
HOBBLE
HOBBLE
ROOOOAAAR!!
...!!
What the heck!?
SNIFF
SNIFF
...?

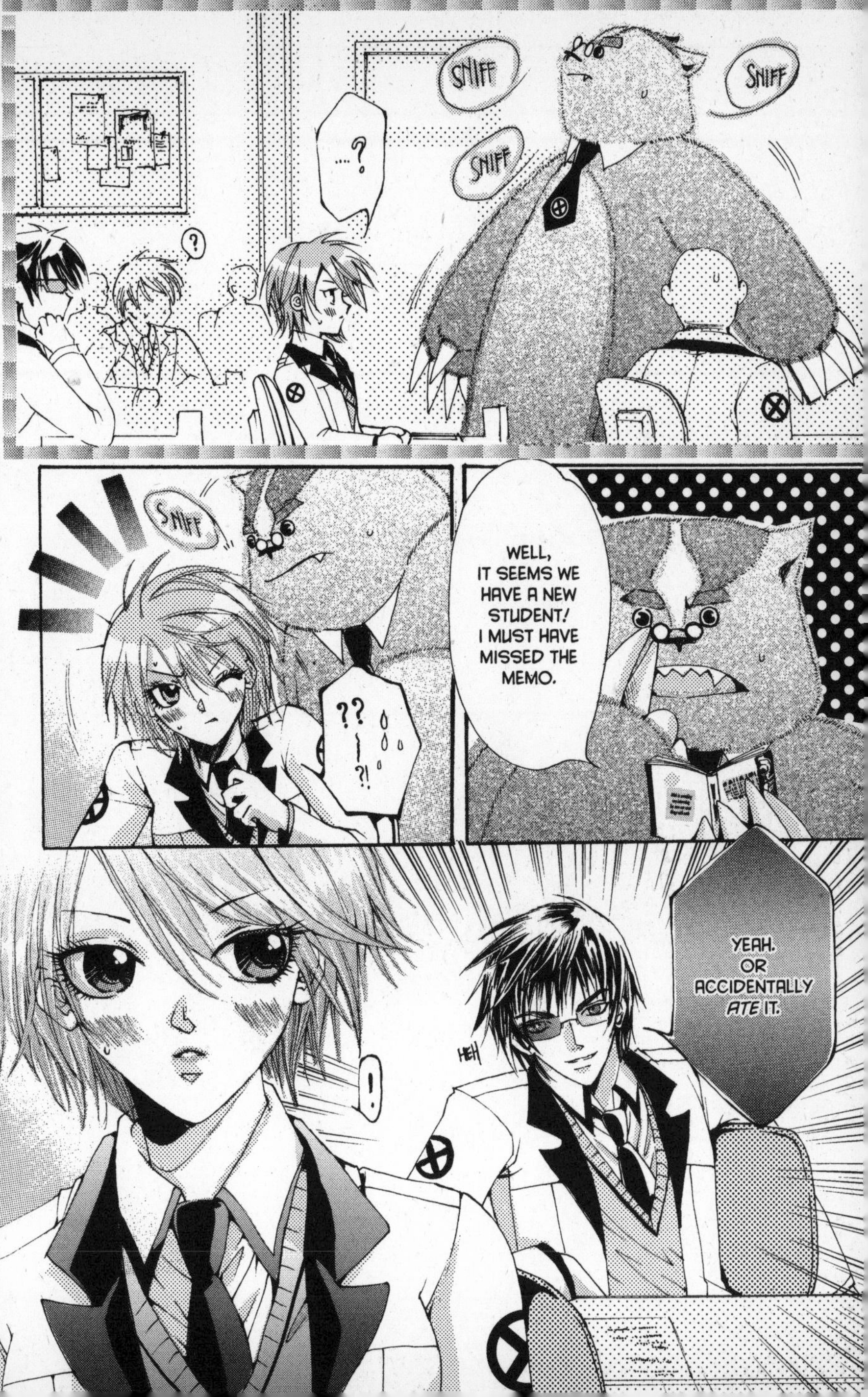
....?
SNIFF
SNIFF
SNIFF
?
SNIFF
??—?!
WELL, IT SEEMS WE HAVE A NEW STUDENT! I MUST HAVE MISSED THE MEMO.
!
HEH
YEAH. OR ACCIDENTALLY *ATE* IT.

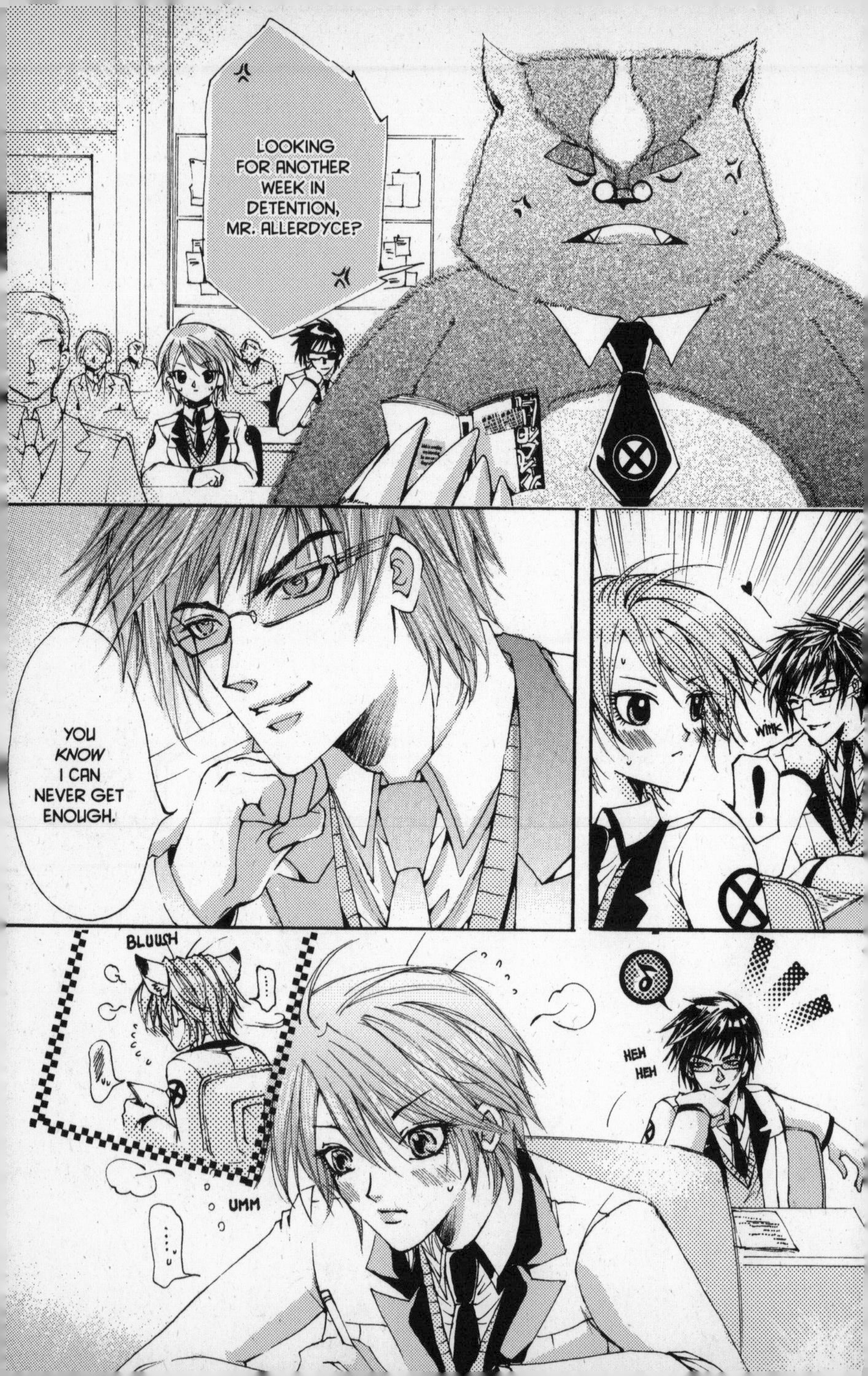
LOOKING FOR ANOTHER WEEK IN DETENTION, MR. ALLERDYCE?
YOU *KNOW* I CAN NEVER GET ENOUGH.
WINK
!
BLUUSH
...
HEH HEH
UMM
...

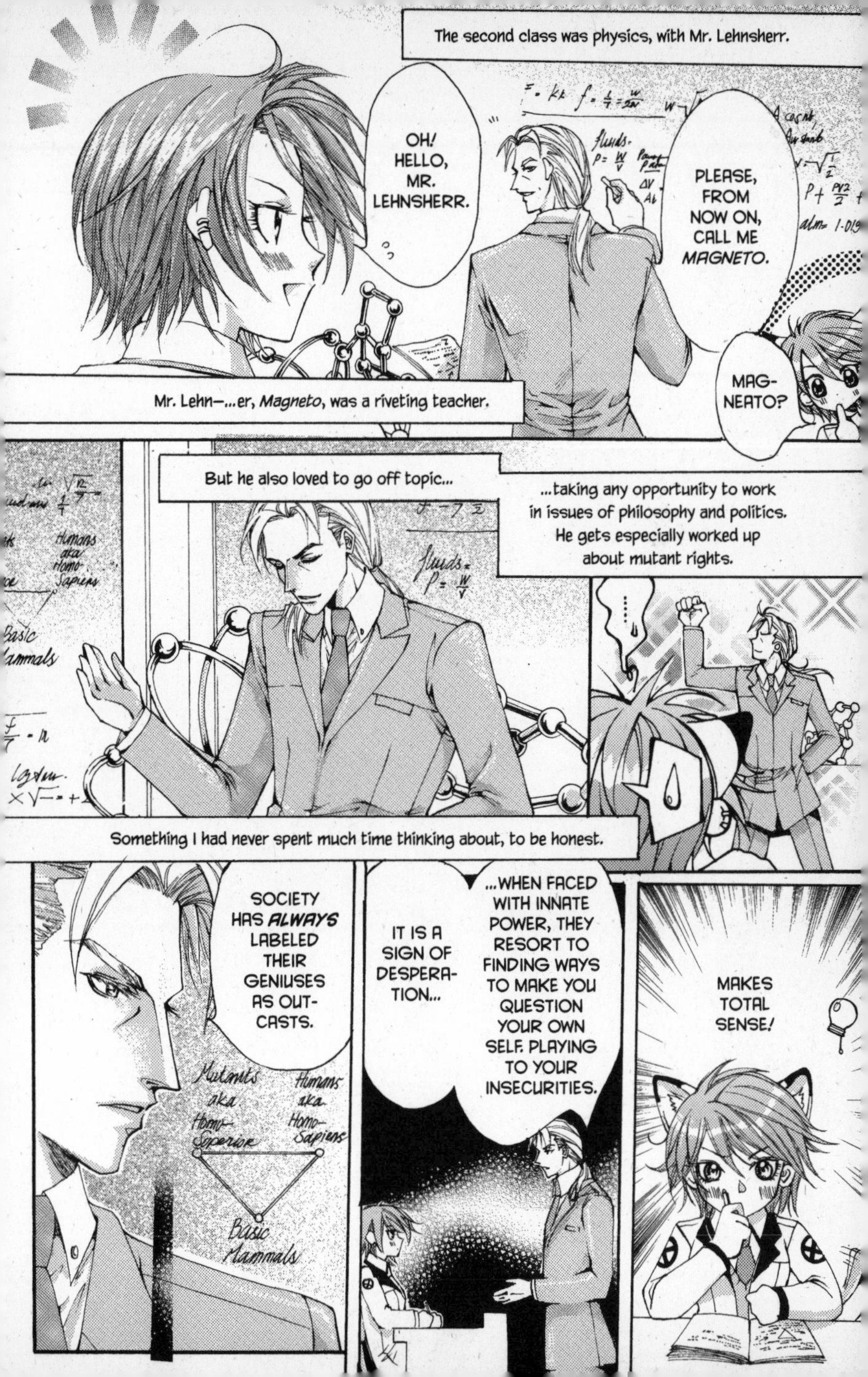
The second class was physics, with Mr. Lehnsherr.
OH! HELLO, MR. LEHNSHERR.
PLEASE, FROM NOW ON, CALL ME *MAGNETO*.
Mr. Lehn—...er, *Magneto*, was a riveting teacher.
MAG-NEATO?
But he also loved to go off topic...
...taking any opportunity to work in issues of philosophy and politics. He gets especially worked up about mutant rights.
Humans aka Homo-Sapiens
Basic Mammals
Something I had never spent much time thinking about, to be honest.
SOCIETY HAS ***ALWAYS*** LABELED THEIR GENIUSES AS OUT-CASTS.
Mutants aka Homo-Superior
Humans aka Homo-Sapiens
Basic Mammals
IT IS A SIGN OF DESPERA-TION...
...WHEN FACED WITH INNATE POWER, THEY RESORT TO FINDING WAYS TO MAKE YOU QUESTION YOUR OWN SELF. PLAYING TO YOUR INSECURITIES.
MAKES TOTAL SENSE!

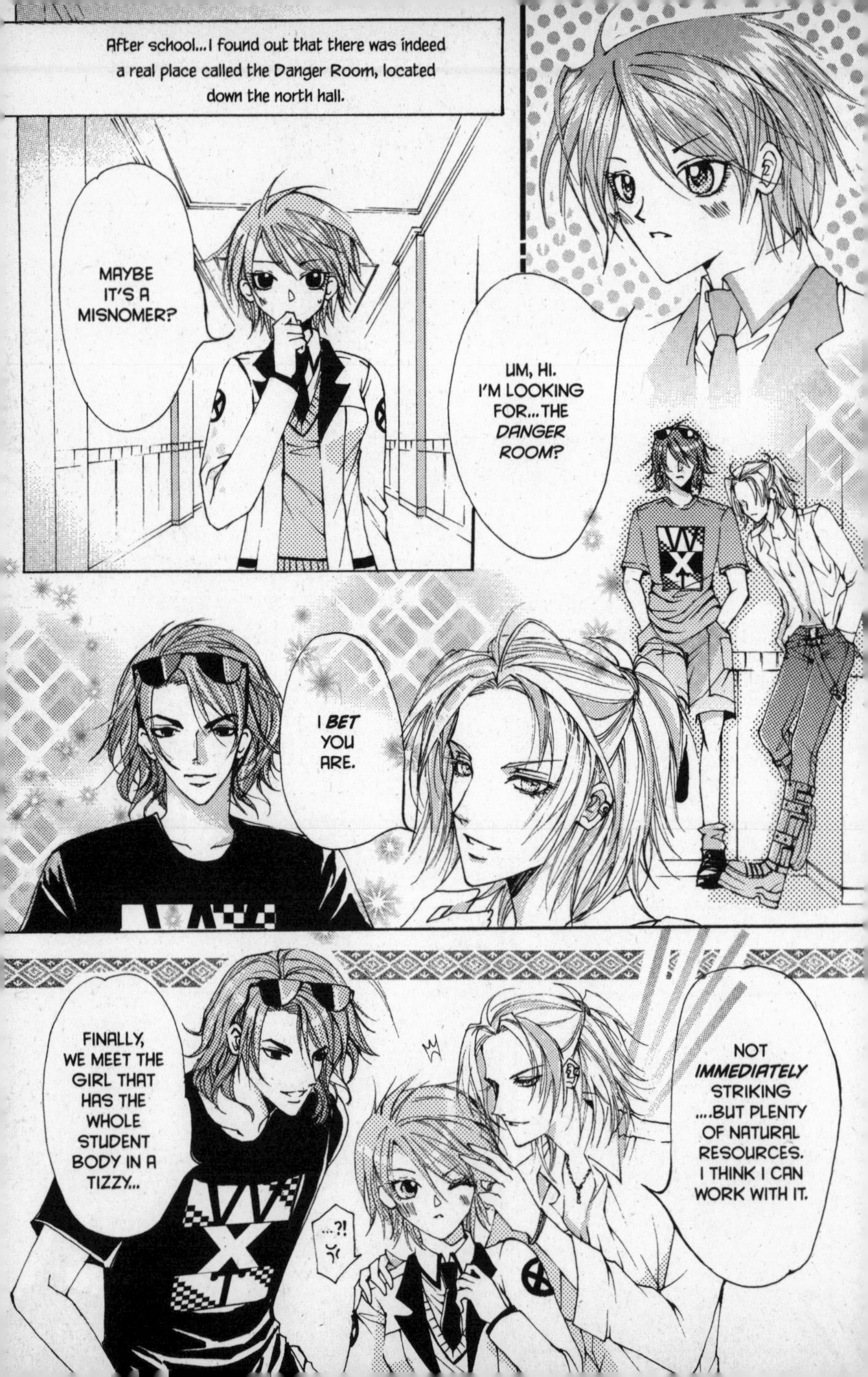
After school...I found out that there was indeed a real place called the Danger Room, located down the north hall.
MAYBE IT'S A MISNOMER?
UM, HI. I'M LOOKING FOR...THE *DANGER ROOM?*
I *BET* YOU ARE.
FINALLY, WE MEET THE GIRL THAT HAS THE WHOLE STUDENT BODY IN A TIZZY...
...?!
NOT *IMMEDIATELY* STRIKING ....BUT PLENTY OF NATURAL RESOURCES. I THINK I CAN WORK WITH IT.

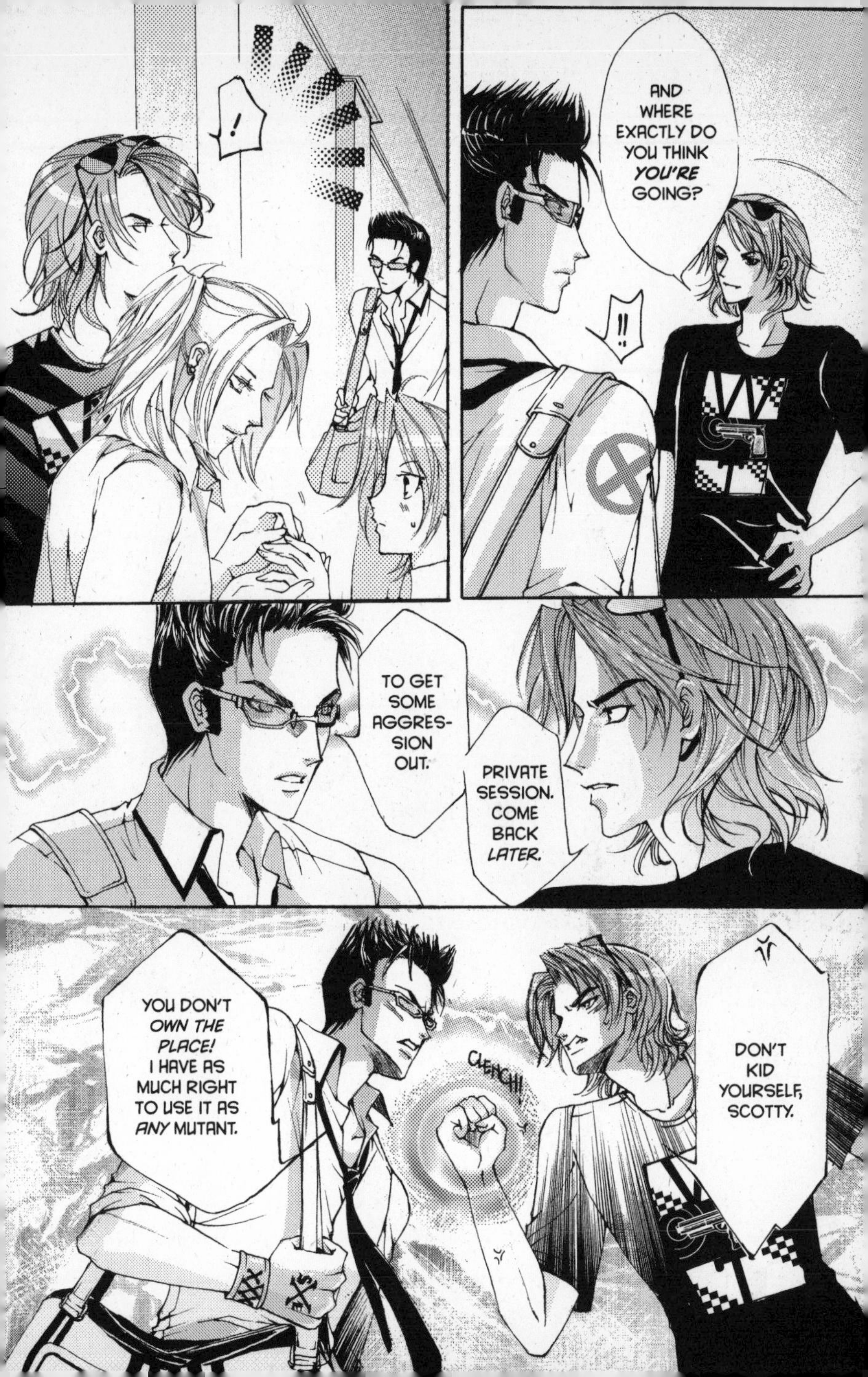
!
AND WHERE EXACTLY DO YOU THINK YOU'RE GOING?
!!
TO GET SOME AGGRES-SION OUT.
PRIVATE SESSION. COME BACK LATER.
YOU DON'T OWN THE PLACE! I HAVE AS MUCH RIGHT TO USE IT AS ANY MUTANT.
CLENCH!!
DON'T KID YOURSELF, SCOTTY.

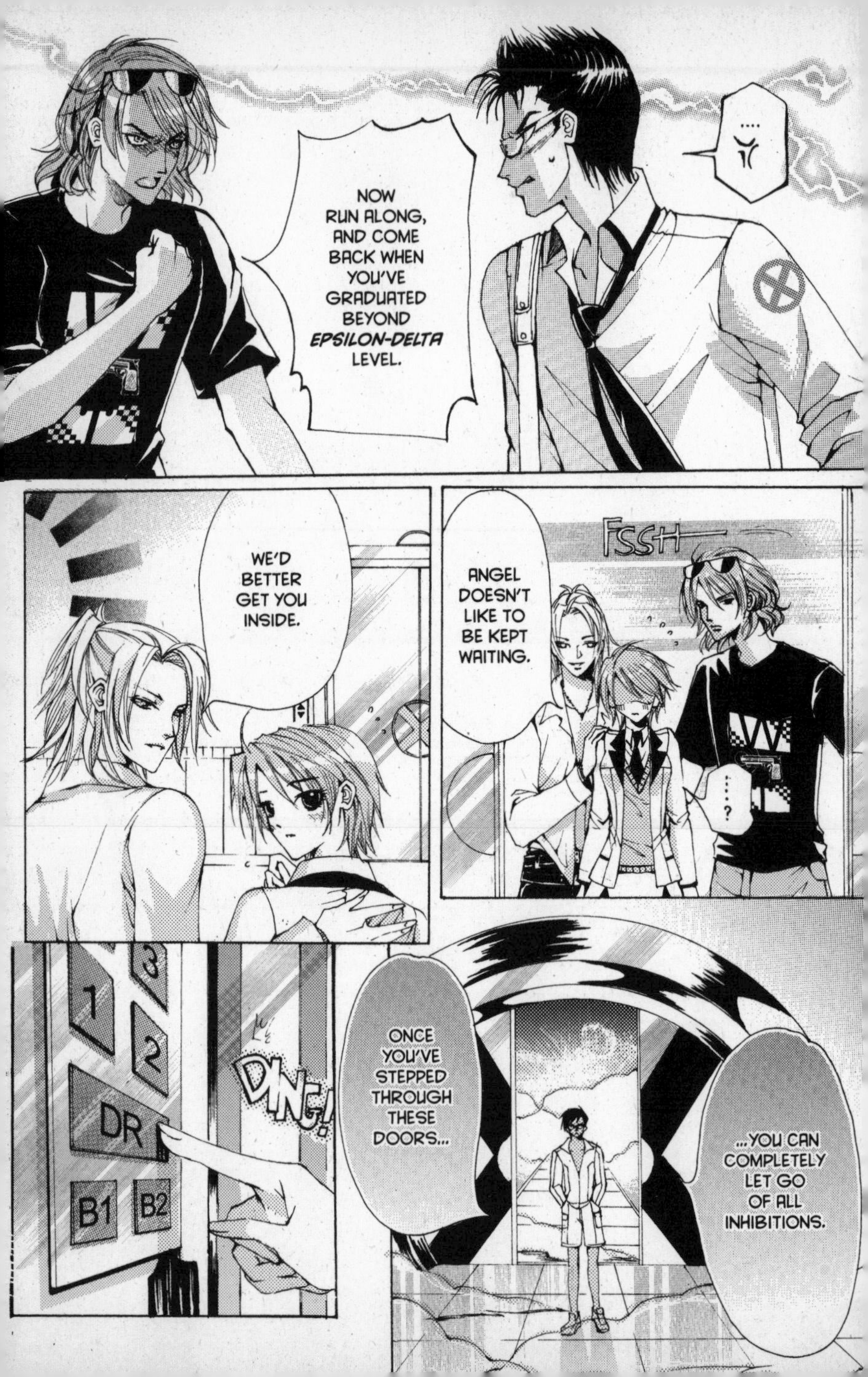
NOW RUN ALONG, AND COME BACK WHEN YOU'VE GRADUATED BEYOND EPSILON-DELTA LEVEL.
....
WE'D BETTER GET YOU INSIDE.
FSSH
ANGEL DOESN'T LIKE TO BE KEPT WAITING.
....?
3
1
2
DR
B1
B2
DING!
ONCE YOU'VE STEPPED THROUGH THESE DOORS...
...YOU CAN COMPLETELY LET GO OF ALL INHIBITIONS.

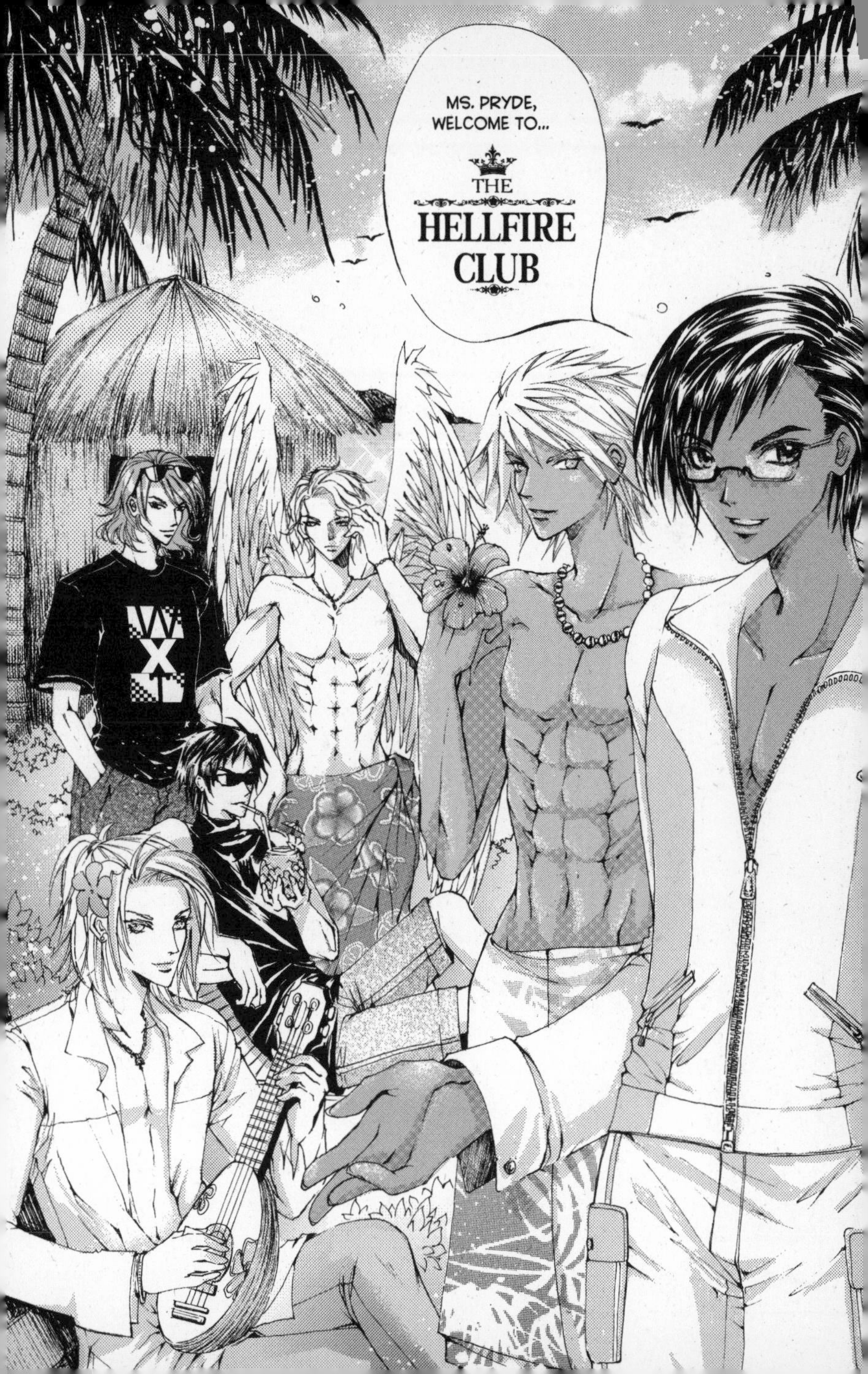
MS. PRYDE, WELCOME TO...
THE HELLFIRE CLUB
WX

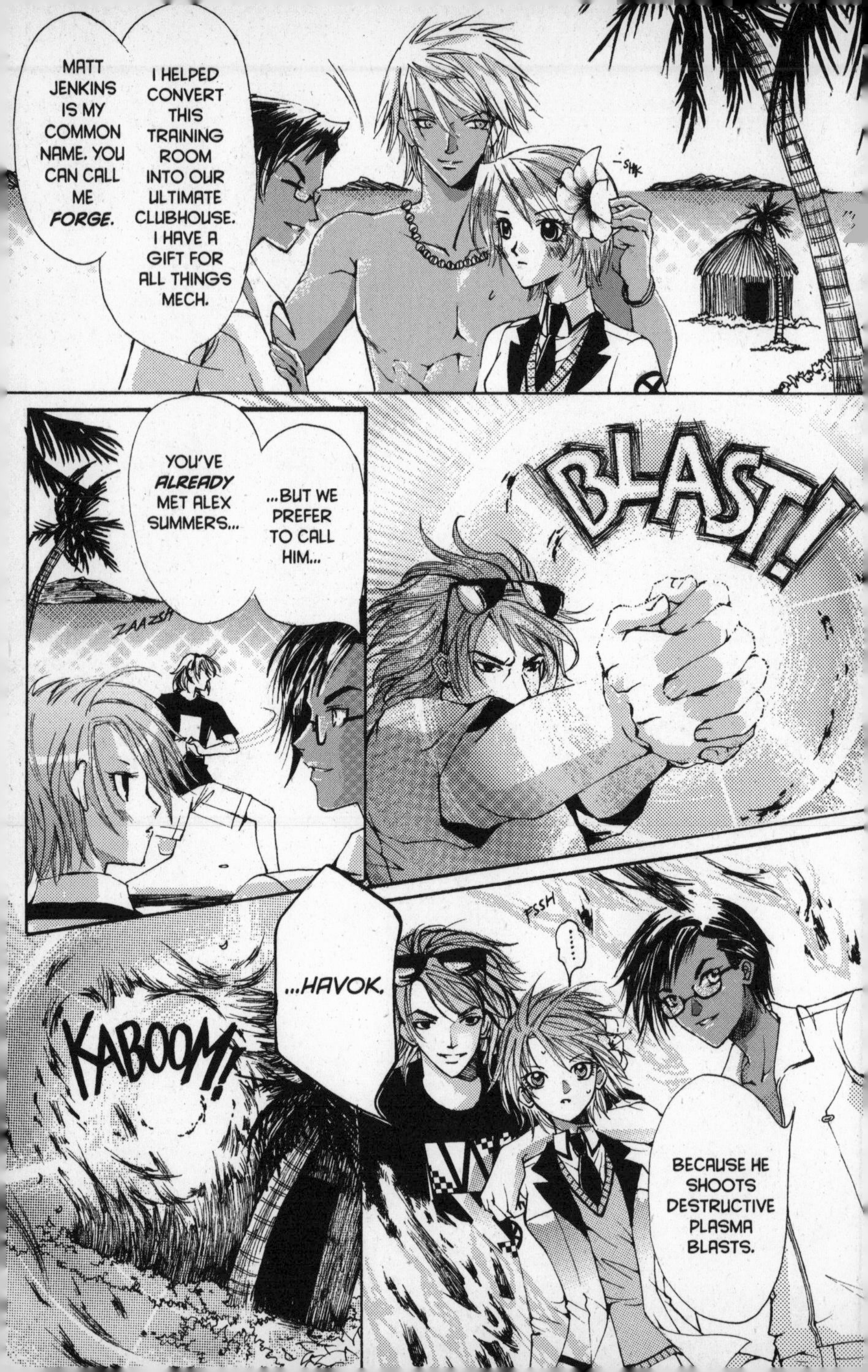
MATT JENKINS IS MY COMMON NAME. YOU CAN CALL ME *FORGE*.
I HELPED CONVERT THIS TRAINING ROOM INTO OUR ULTIMATE CLUBHOUSE. I HAVE A GIFT FOR ALL THINGS MECH.
SHIK
YOU'VE *ALREADY* MET ALEX SUMMERS...
...BUT WE PREFER TO CALL HIM...
ZAASH
BLAST!
KABOOM!
...HAVOK.
FSSH
......
BECAUSE HE SHOOTS DESTRUCTIVE PLASMA BLASTS.

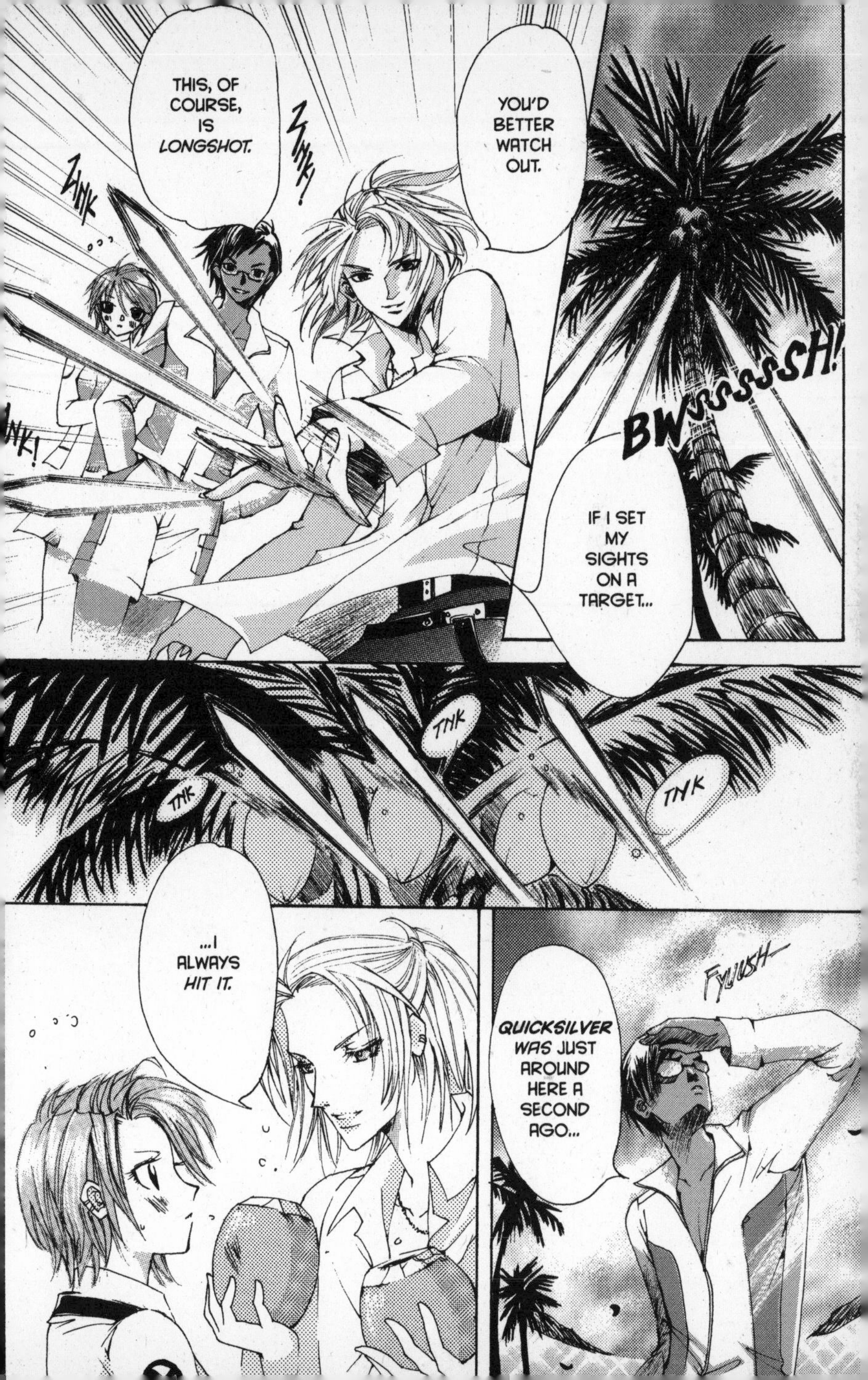
THIS, OF COURSE, IS *LONGSHOT.*
YOU'D BETTER WATCH OUT.
BWSSSSSH!
IF I SET MY SIGHTS ON A TARGET...
TNK
TNK
TNK
...I ALWAYS *HIT IT.*
FYUUSH
QUICKSILVER WAS JUST AROUND HERE A SECOND AGO...

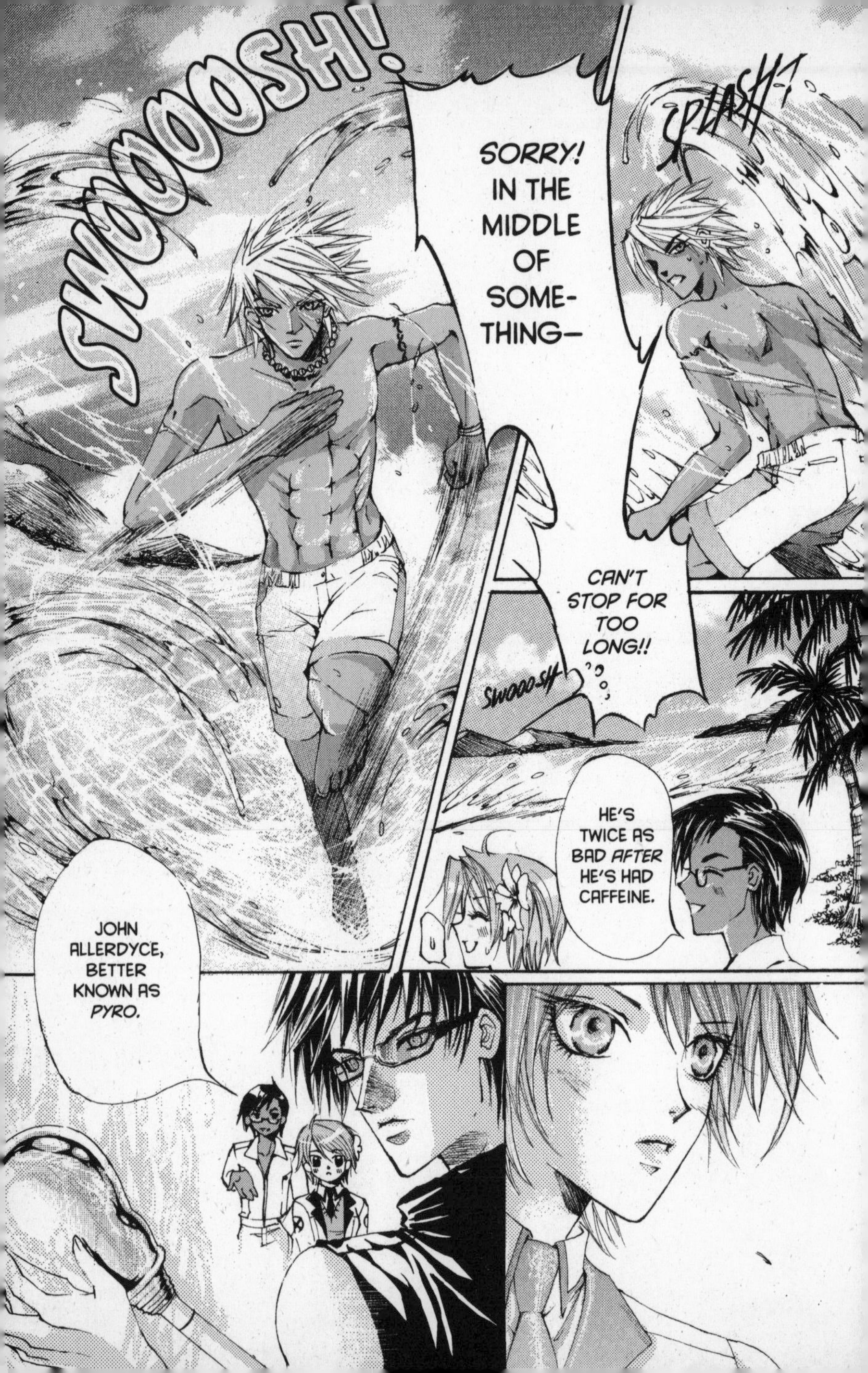
SWOOOOSH!
SORRY! IN THE MIDDLE OF SOME-THING—
SPLASH!?
CAN'T STOP FOR TOO LONG!!
SWOOOSH
HE'S TWICE AS BAD AFTER HE'S HAD CAFFEINE.
JOHN ALLERDYCE, BETTER KNOWN AS PYRO.

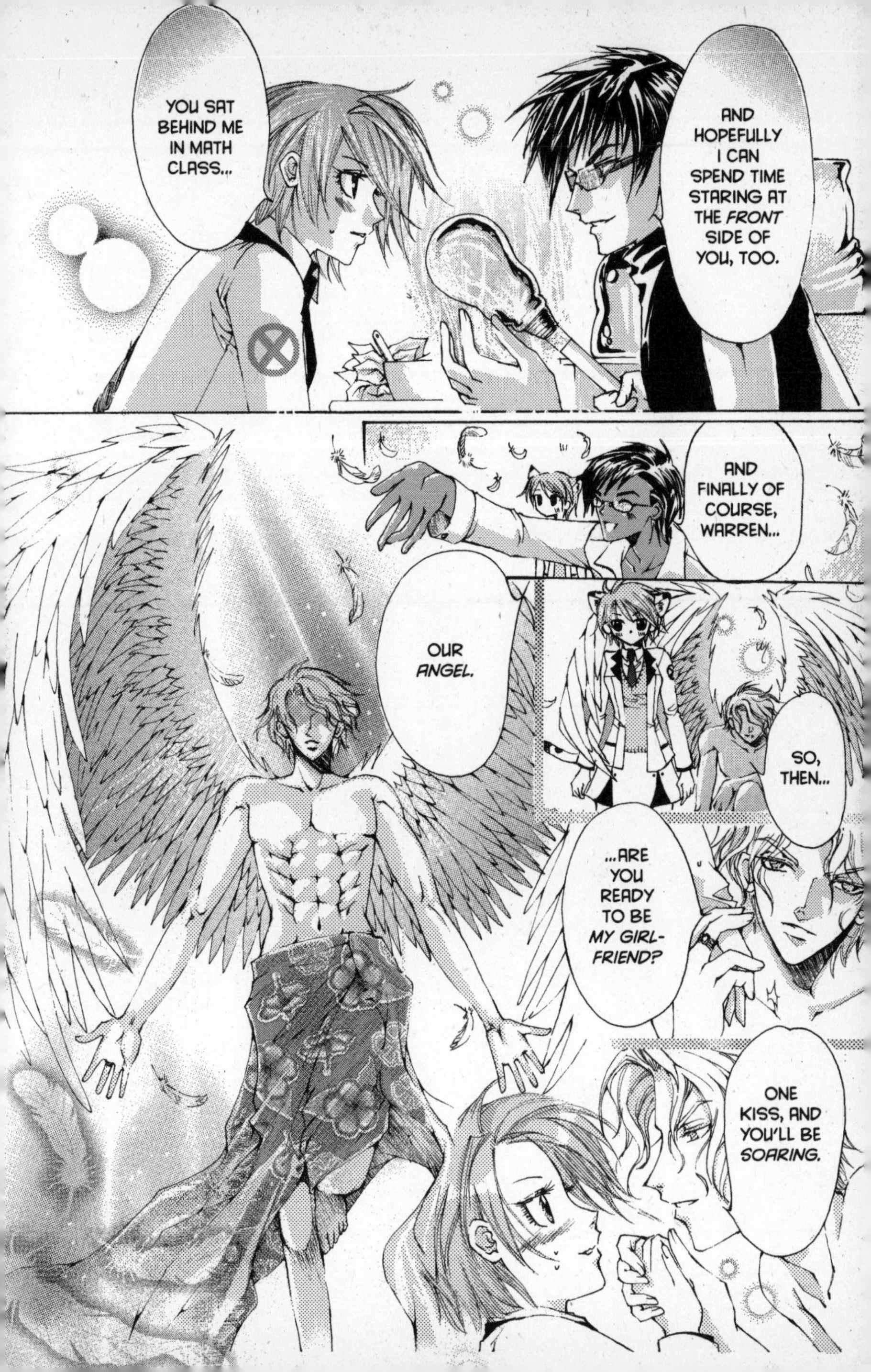
YOU SAT BEHIND ME IN MATH CLASS...
AND HOPEFULLY I CAN SPEND TIME STARING AT THE *FRONT* SIDE OF YOU, TOO.
OUR *ANGEL.*
AND FINALLY OF COURSE, WARREN...
SO, THEN...
...ARE YOU READY TO BE *MY GIRL-FRIEND?*
ONE KISS, AND YOU'LL BE *SOARING.*

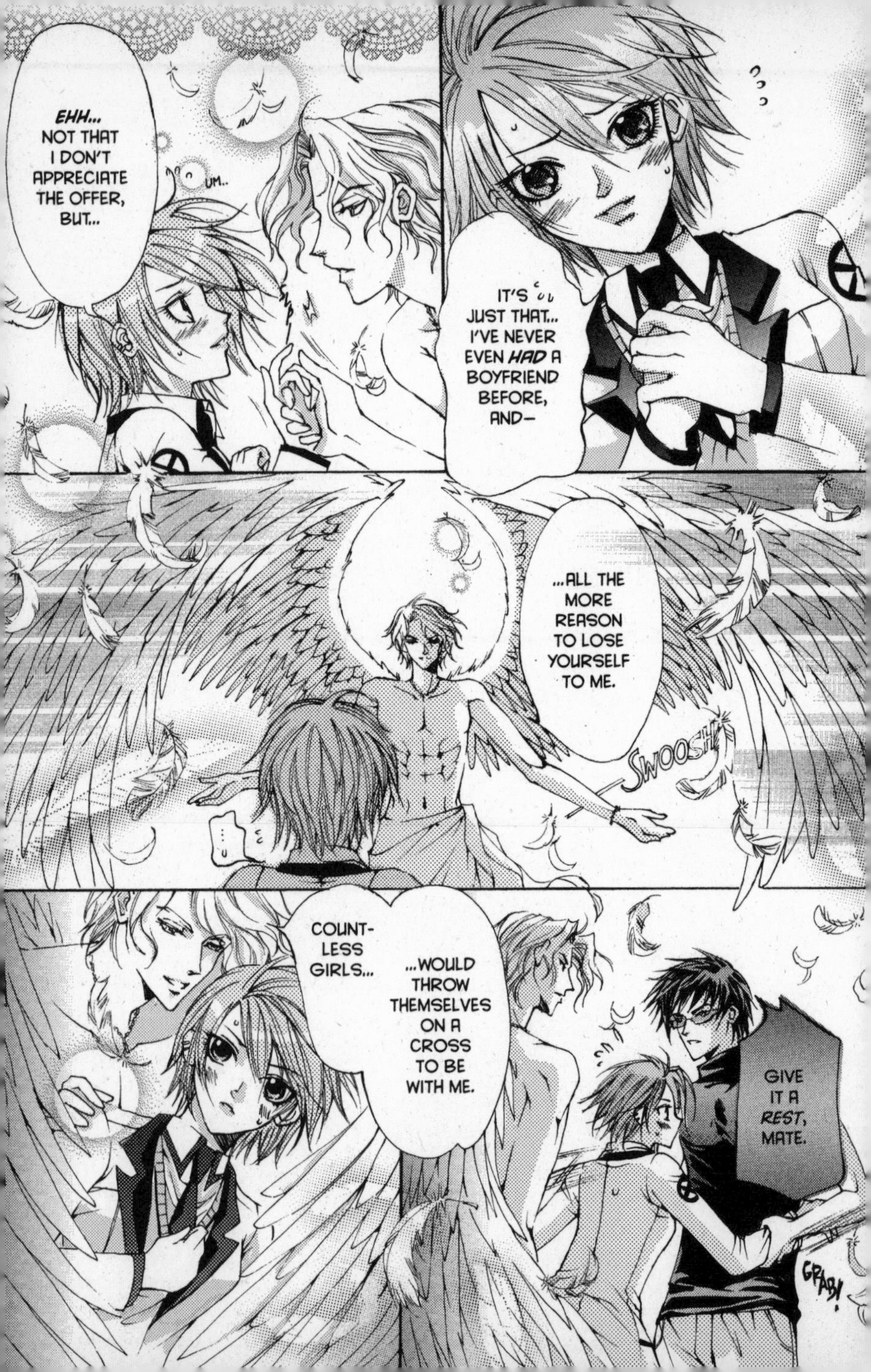

EHH... NOT THAT I DON'T APPRECIATE THE OFFER, BUT...
UM..
IT'S JUST THAT... I'VE NEVER EVEN HAD A BOYFRIEND BEFORE, AND—
...ALL THE MORE REASON TO LOSE YOURSELF TO ME.
SWOOSH
...
COUNT-LESS GIRLS...
...WOULD THROW THEMSELVES ON A CROSS TO BE WITH ME.
GIVE IT A REST, MATE.
GRAB!

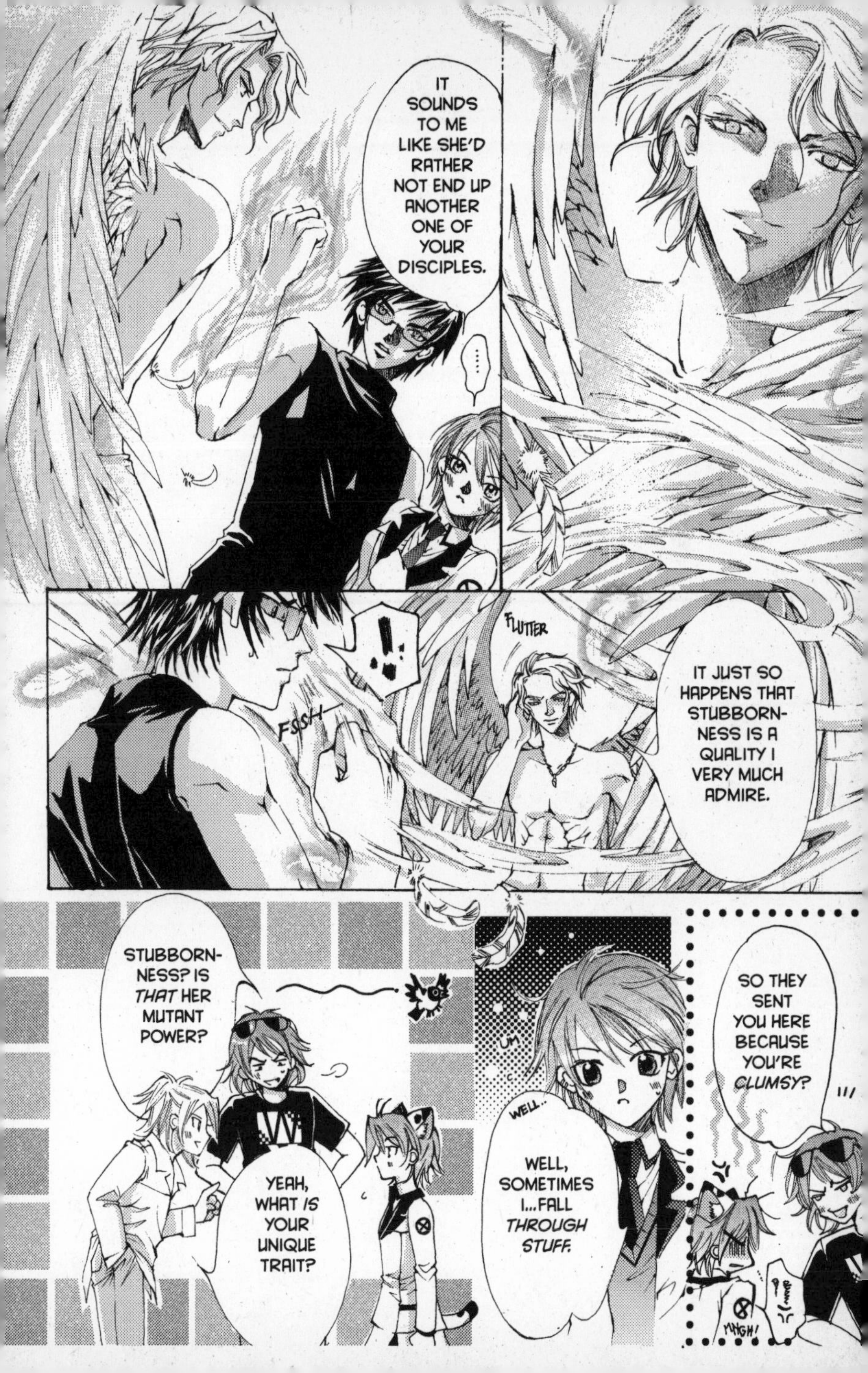
IT SOUNDS TO ME LIKE SHE'D RATHER NOT END UP ANOTHER ONE OF YOUR DISCIPLES.
...
!
FSSH
FLUTTER
IT JUST SO HAPPENS THAT STUBBORN-NESS IS A QUALITY I VERY MUCH ADMIRE.
STUBBORN-NESS? IS *THAT* HER MUTANT POWER?
YEAH, WHAT *IS* YOUR UNIQUE TRAIT?
UM
WELL...
WELL, SOMETIMES I...FALL *THROUGH* *STUFF.*
SO THEY SENT YOU HERE BECAUSE YOU'RE *CLUMSY?*
MNGH!

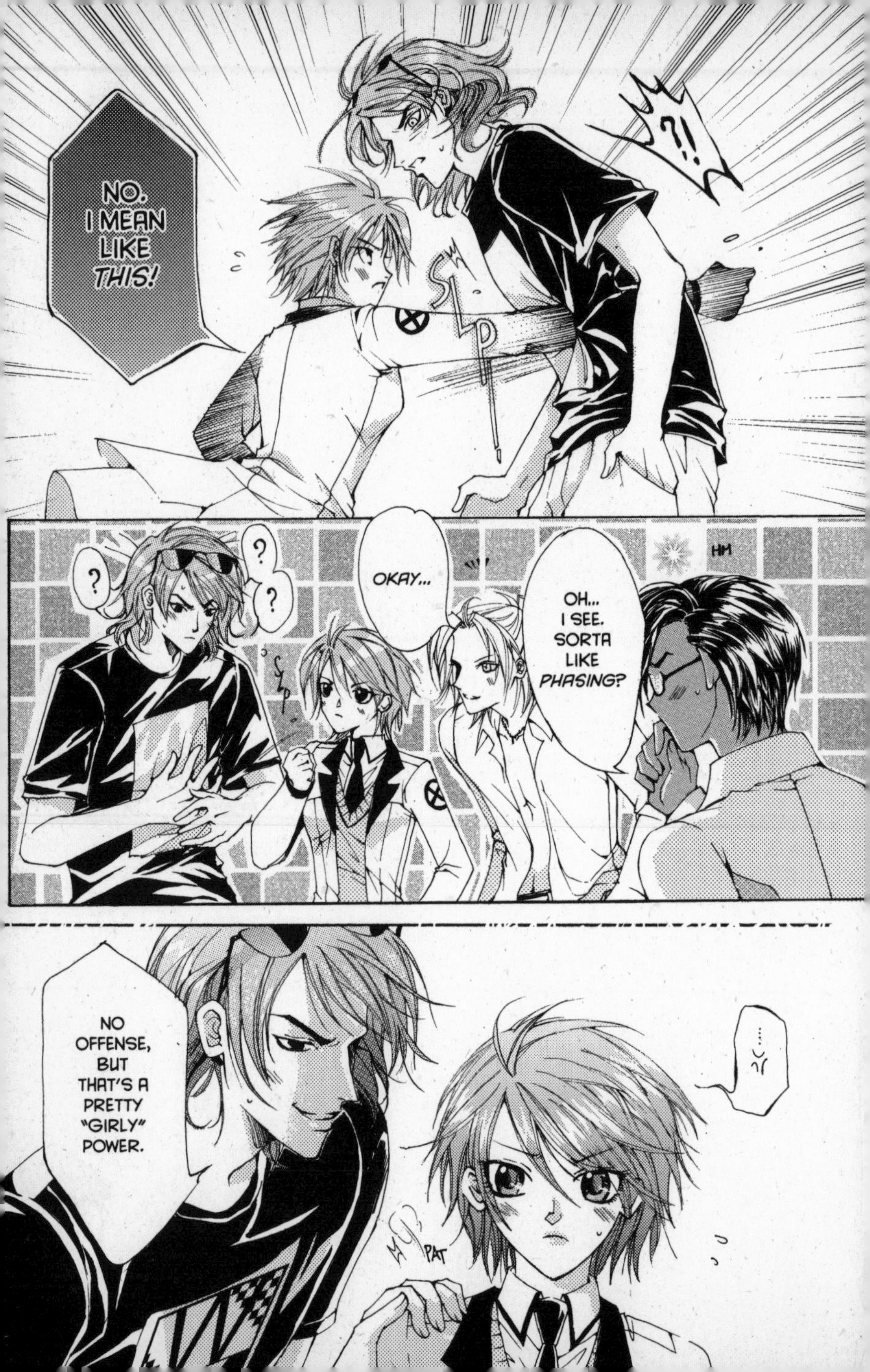
NO. I MEAN LIKE *THIS!*
?!!
SLP
?
?
?
SLP
OKAY...
OH... I SEE. SORTA LIKE *PHASING?*
HM
NO OFFENSE, BUT THAT'S A PRETTY "GIRLY" POWER.
...!
PAT

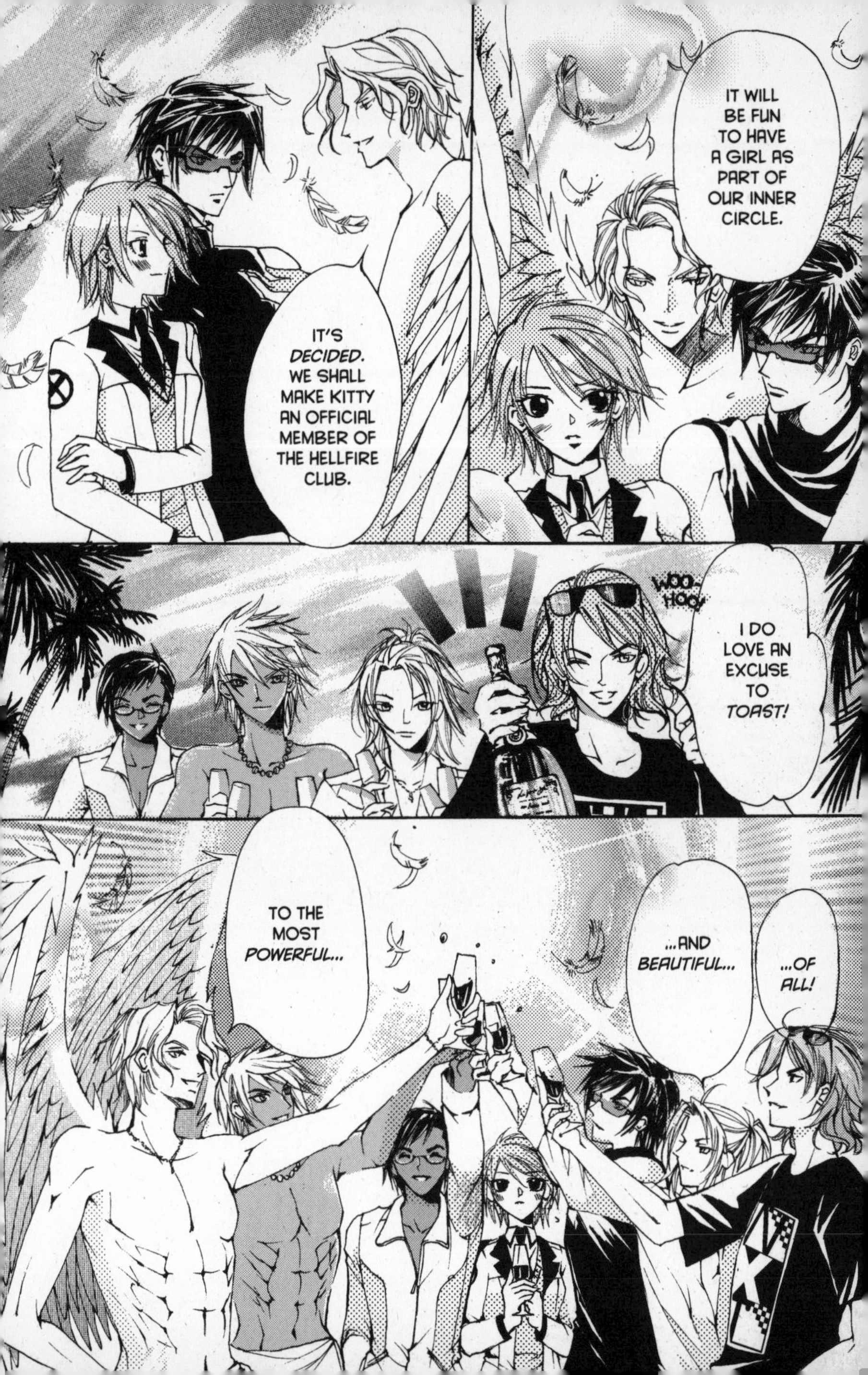
IT'S *DECIDED*. WE SHALL MAKE KITTY AN OFFICIAL MEMBER OF THE HELLFIRE CLUB.
IT WILL BE FUN TO HAVE A GIRL AS PART OF OUR INNER CIRCLE.
WOO-HOO!
I DO LOVE AN EXCUSE TO *TOAST!*
TO THE MOST *POWERFUL...*
...AND *BEAUTIFUL...*
...OF *ALL!*

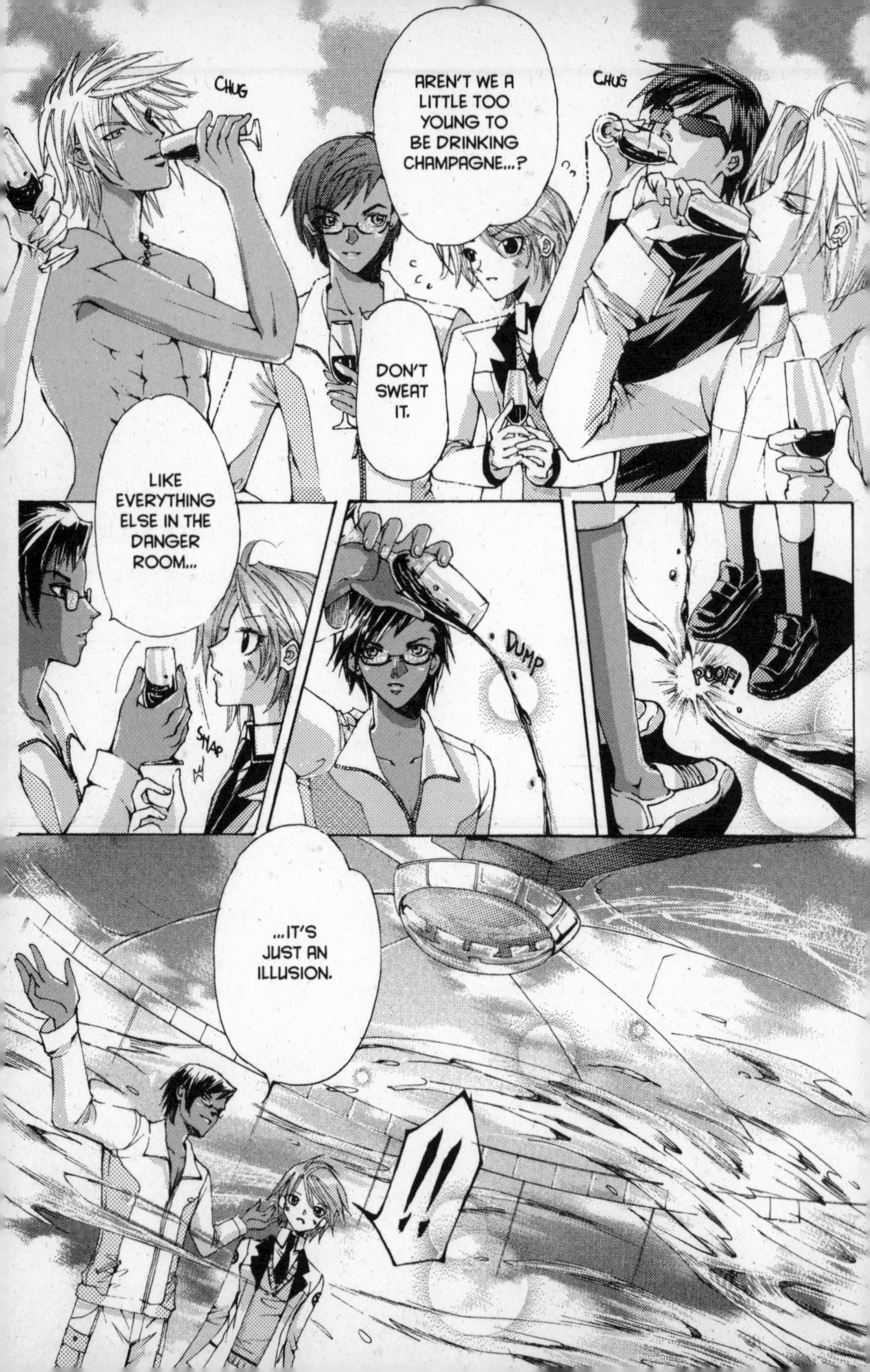

CHUG
AREN'T WE A LITTLE TOO YOUNG TO BE DRINKING CHAMPAGNE...?
CHUG
DON'T SWEAT IT.
LIKE EVERYTHING ELSE IN THE DANGER ROOM...
SNAP
DUMP
POOF!
...IT'S JUST AN ILLUSION.
!!

Chapter Two

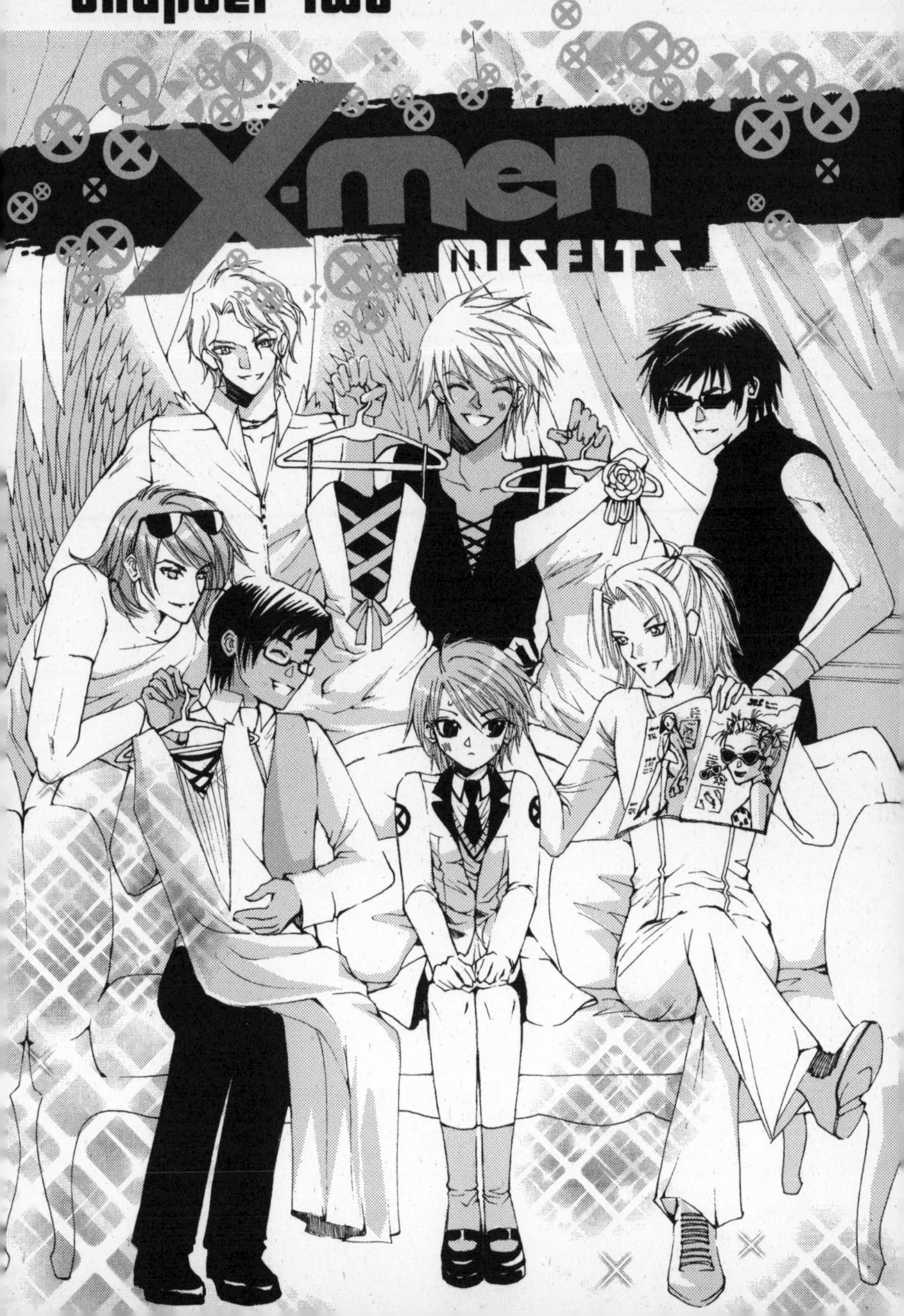
X-men
MISFITS

XAVIER'S SCHOOL • FOR GIFTED YOUNGSTERS •

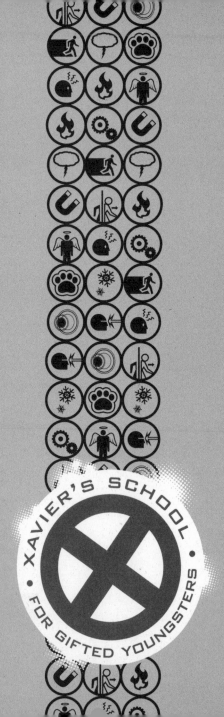

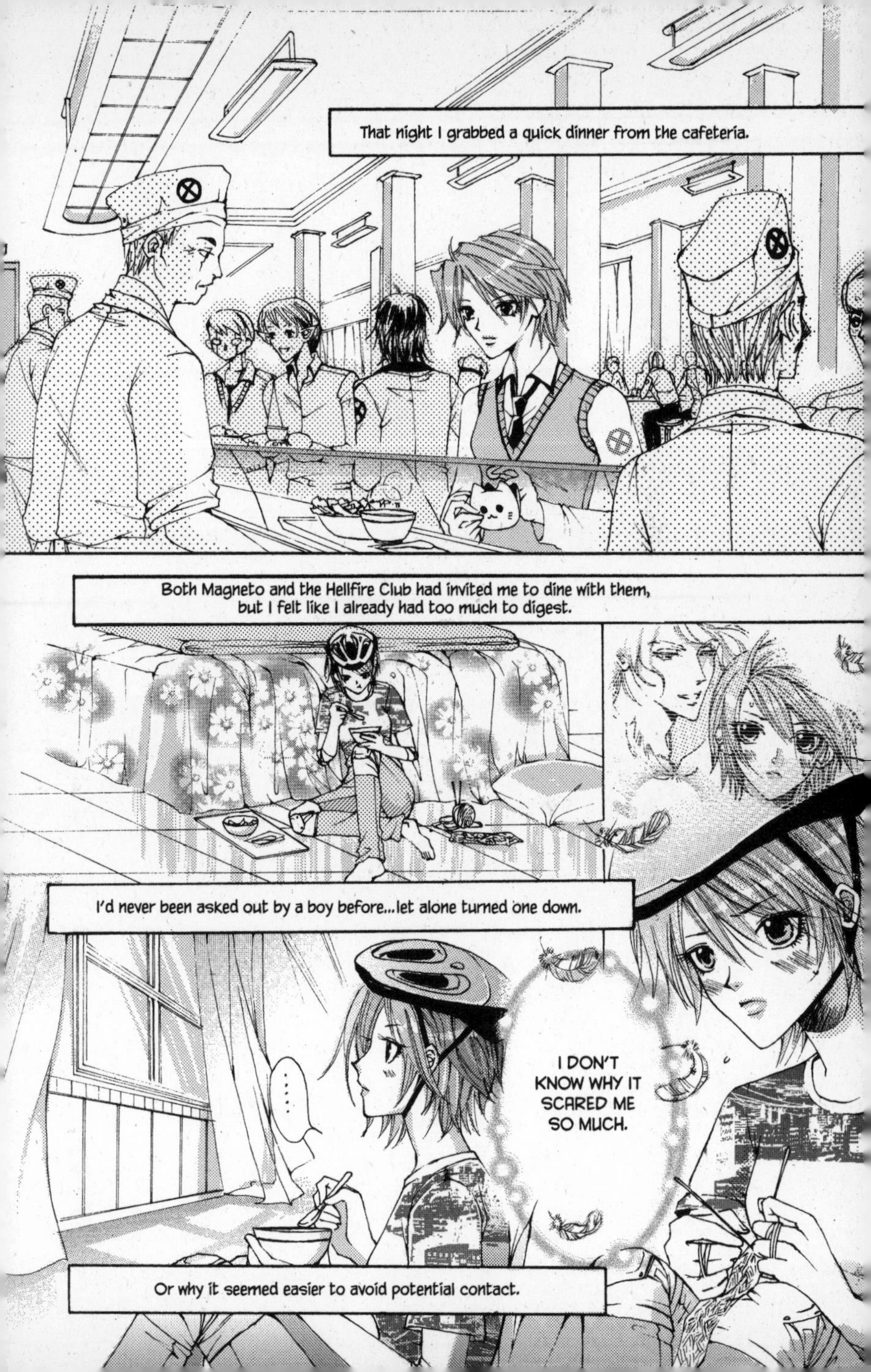
That night I grabbed a quick dinner from the cafeteria.
Both Magneto and the Hellfire Club had invited me to dine with them, but I felt like I already had too much to digest.
I'd never been asked out by a boy before...let alone turned one down.
....
I DON'T KNOW WHY IT SCARED ME SO MUCH.
Or why it seemed easier to avoid potential contact.

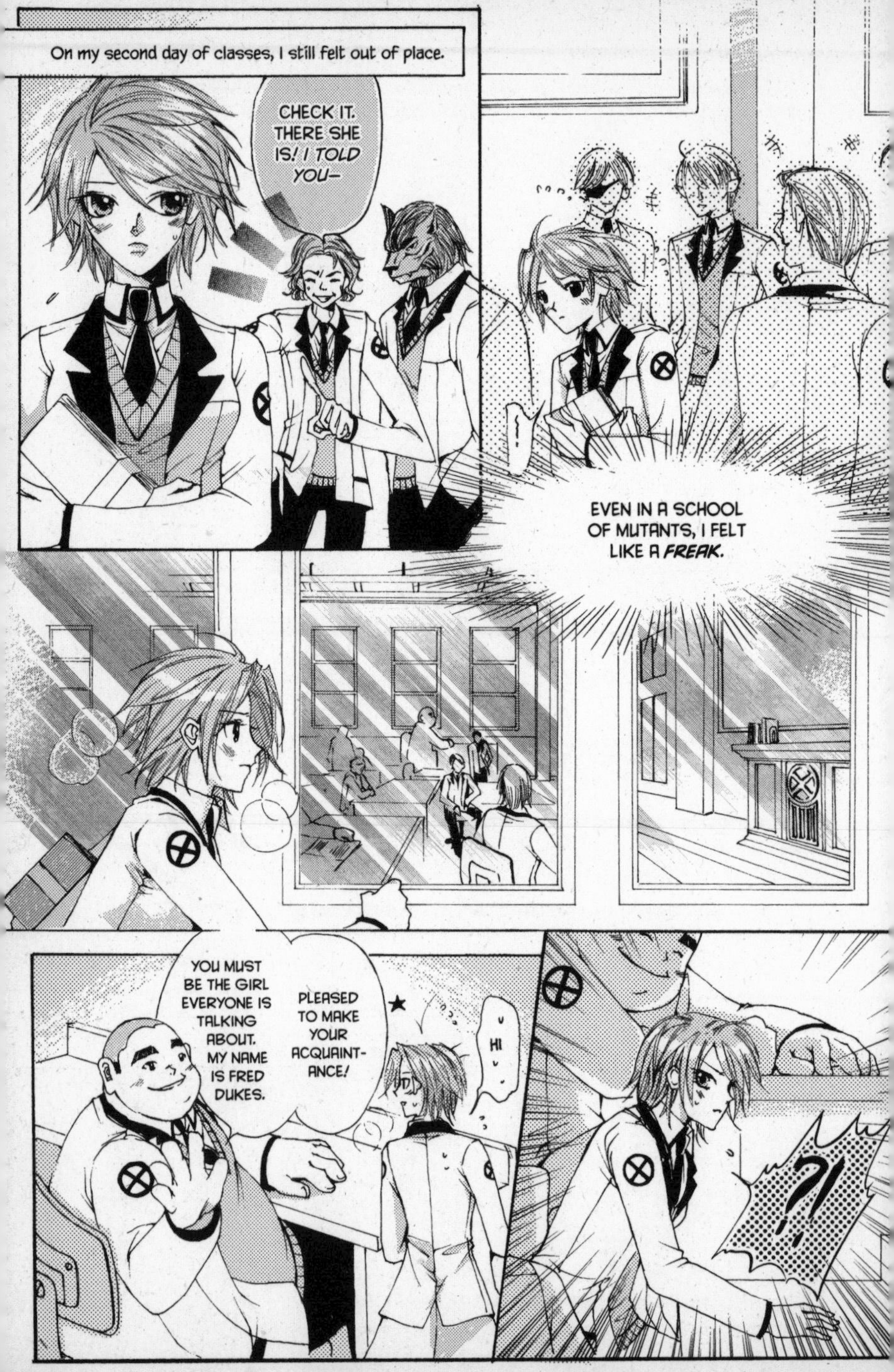
On my second day of classes, I still felt out of place.
CHECK IT. THERE SHE IS! I TOLD YOU—
EVEN IN A SCHOOL OF MUTANTS, I FELT LIKE A *FREAK*.
YOU MUST BE THE GIRL EVERYONE IS TALKING ABOUT. MY NAME IS FRED DUKES.
PLEASED TO MAKE YOUR ACQUAINT-ANCE!
HI
?!

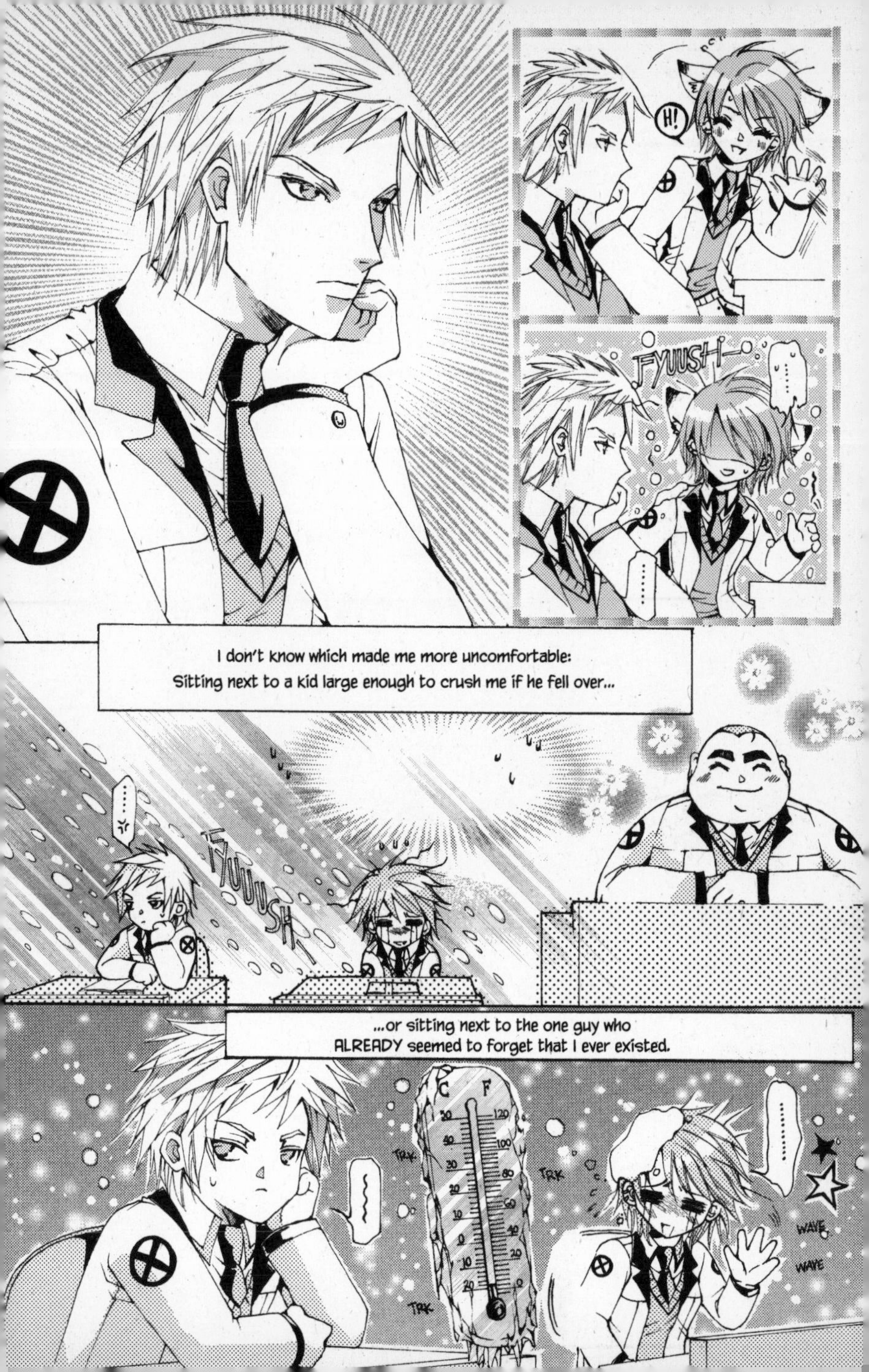
H!
FYUUSH—
......
......
I don't know which made me more uncomfortable:
Sitting next to a kid large enough to crush me if he fell over...
......
FYUUUSH
...or sitting next to the one guy who
ALREADY seemed to forget that I ever existed.
TRK
TRK
TRK
....
WAVE
WAVE

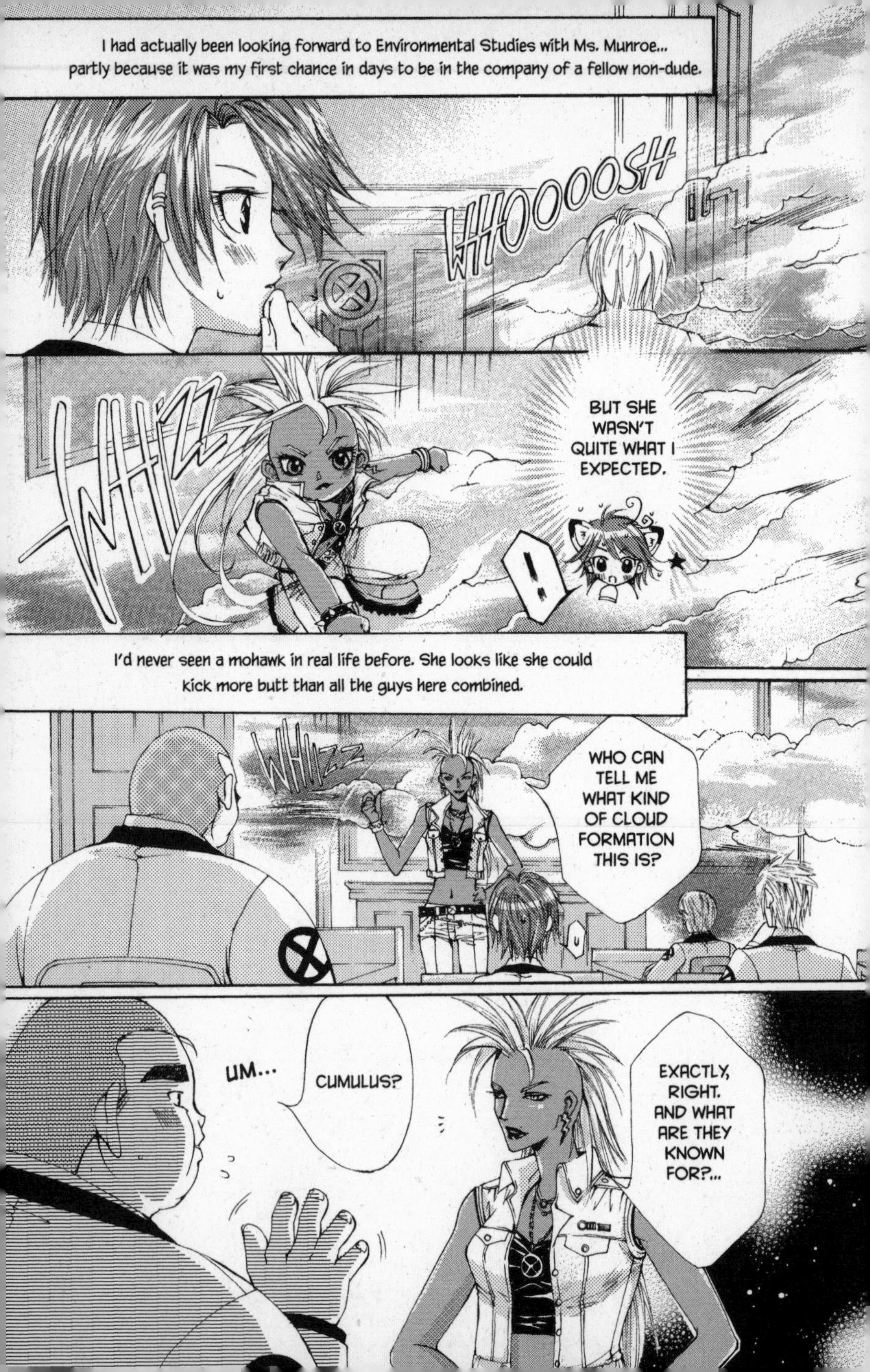
I had actually been looking forward to Environmental Studies with Ms. Munroe... partly because it was my first chance in days to be in the company of a fellow non-dude.
WHOOOOSH
WHIZZ
BUT SHE WASN'T QUITE WHAT I EXPECTED.
!
I'd never seen a mohawk in real life before. She looks like she could kick more butt than all the guys here combined.
WHIZZ
WHO CAN TELL ME WHAT KIND OF CLOUD FORMATION THIS IS?
UM...
CUMULUS?
EXACTLY, RIGHT. AND WHAT ARE THEY KNOWN FOR?...

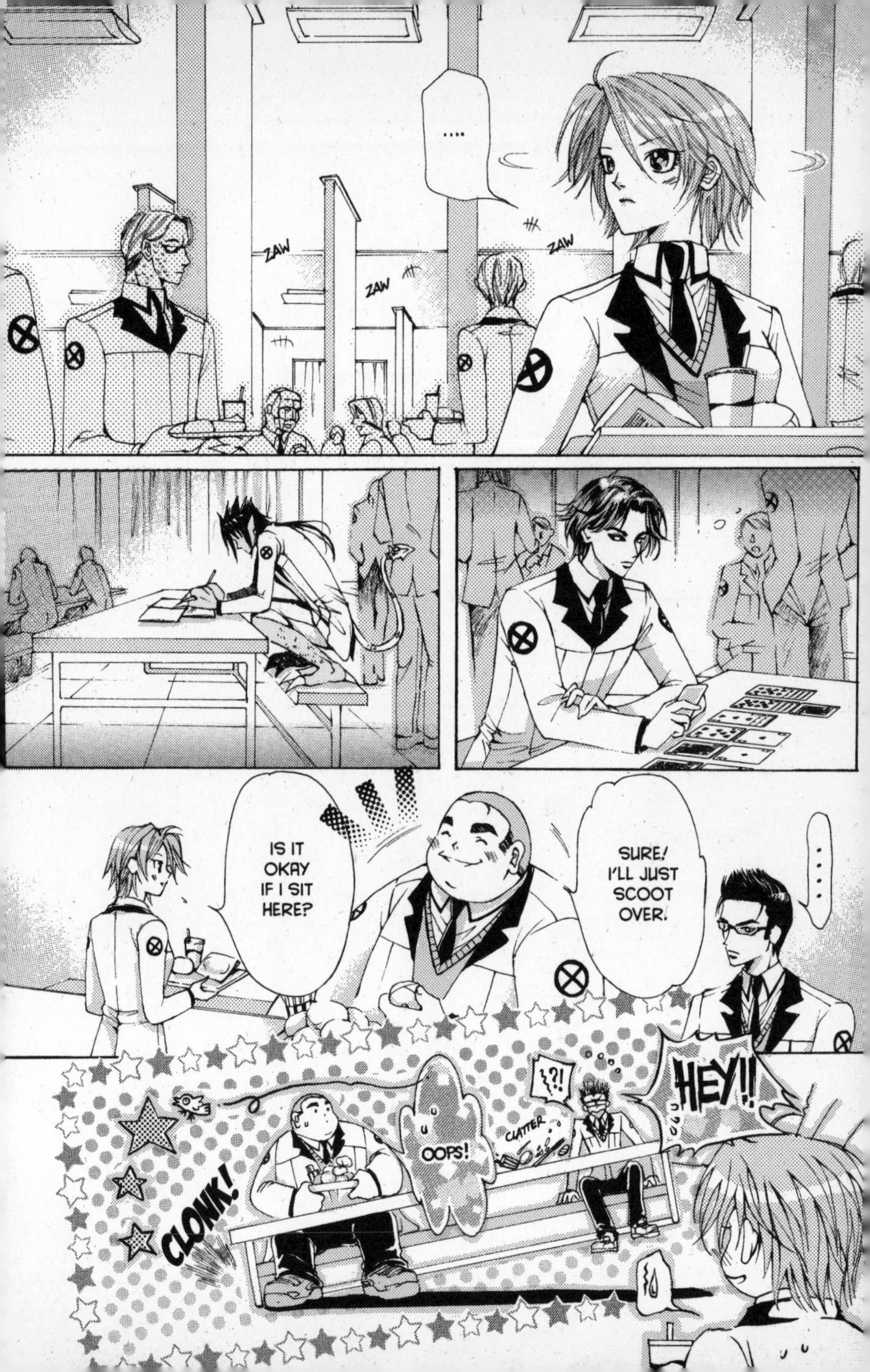
....
ZAW
ZAW
ZAW
IS IT OKAY IF I SIT HERE?
SURE! I'LL JUST SCOOT OVER.
....
CLONK!
OOPS!
CLATTER
?!
HEY!!

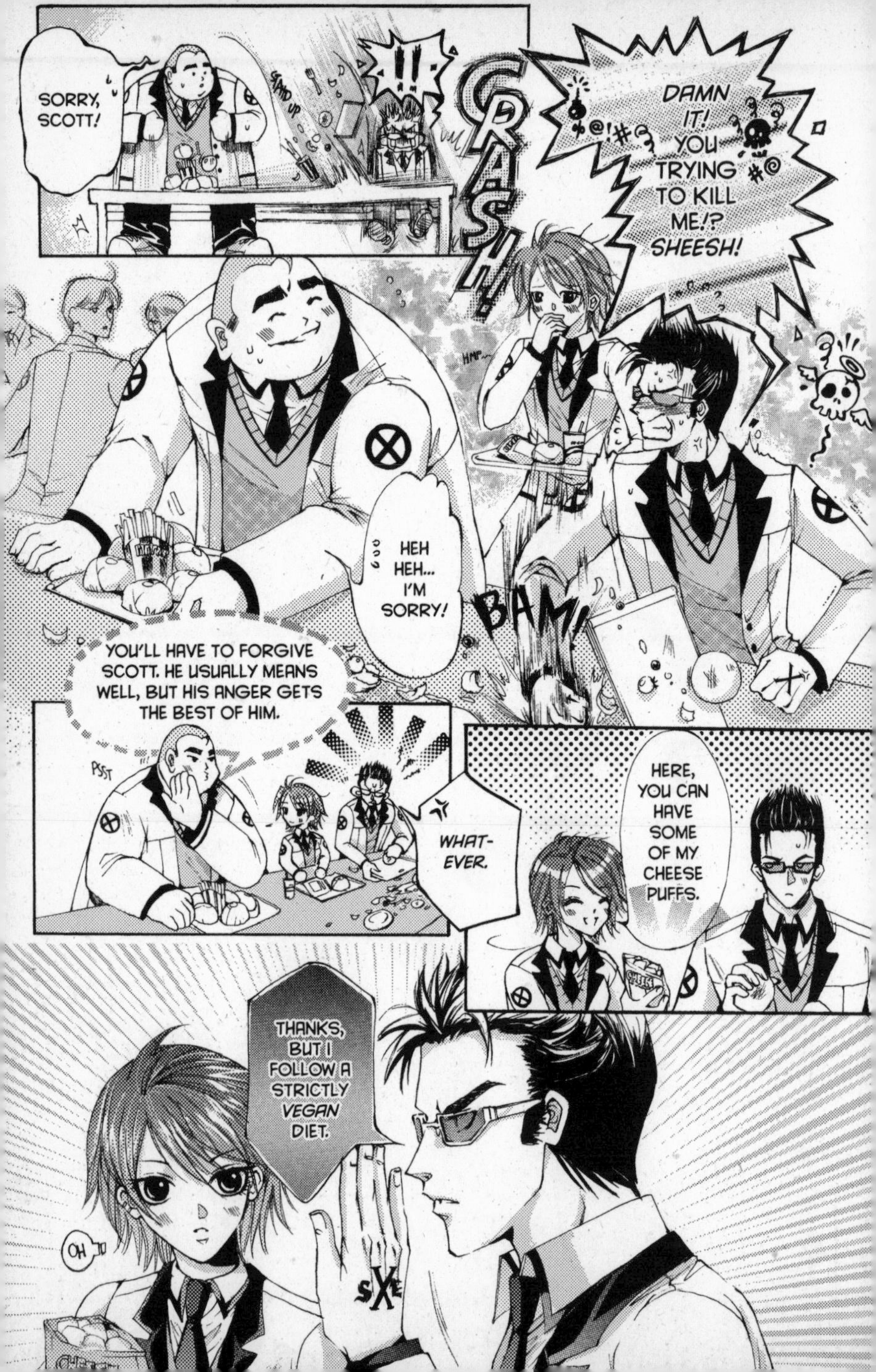
SORRY, SCOTT!
!!
CRASH!
DAMN IT! YOU TRYING TO KILL ME!? SHEESH!
HEH HEH... I'M SORRY!
BAM!
YOU'LL HAVE TO FORGIVE SCOTT. HE USUALLY MEANS WELL, BUT HIS ANGER GETS THE BEST OF HIM.
PSST
WHAT-EVER.
HERE, YOU CAN HAVE SOME OF MY CHEESE PUFFS.
THANKS, BUT I FOLLOW A STRICTLY VEGAN DIET.
OH
sXe

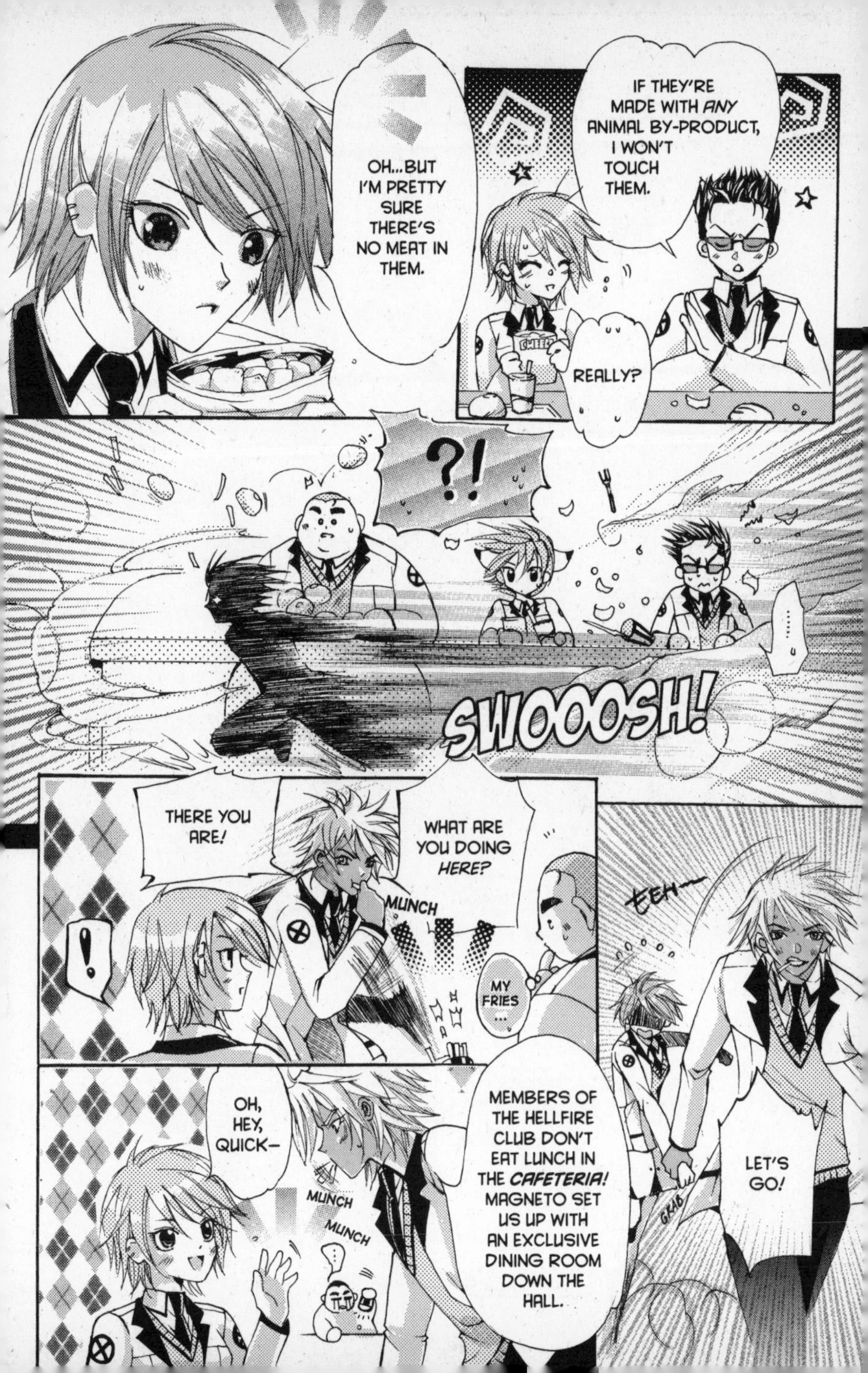
OH...BUT I'M PRETTY SURE THERE'S NO MEAT IN THEM.
IF THEY'RE MADE WITH *ANY* ANIMAL BY-PRODUCT, I WON'T TOUCH THEM.
REALLY?
?!
SWOOOSH!
.....
THERE YOU ARE!
!
WHAT ARE YOU DOING *HERE?*
MUNCH
MY FRIES...
OH, HEY, QUICK—
MUNCH
MUNCH
MEMBERS OF THE HELLFIRE CLUB DON'T EAT LUNCH IN THE *CAFETERIA!* MAGNETO SET US UP WITH AN EXCLUSIVE DINING ROOM DOWN THE HALL.
EEH—
GRAB
LET'S GO!

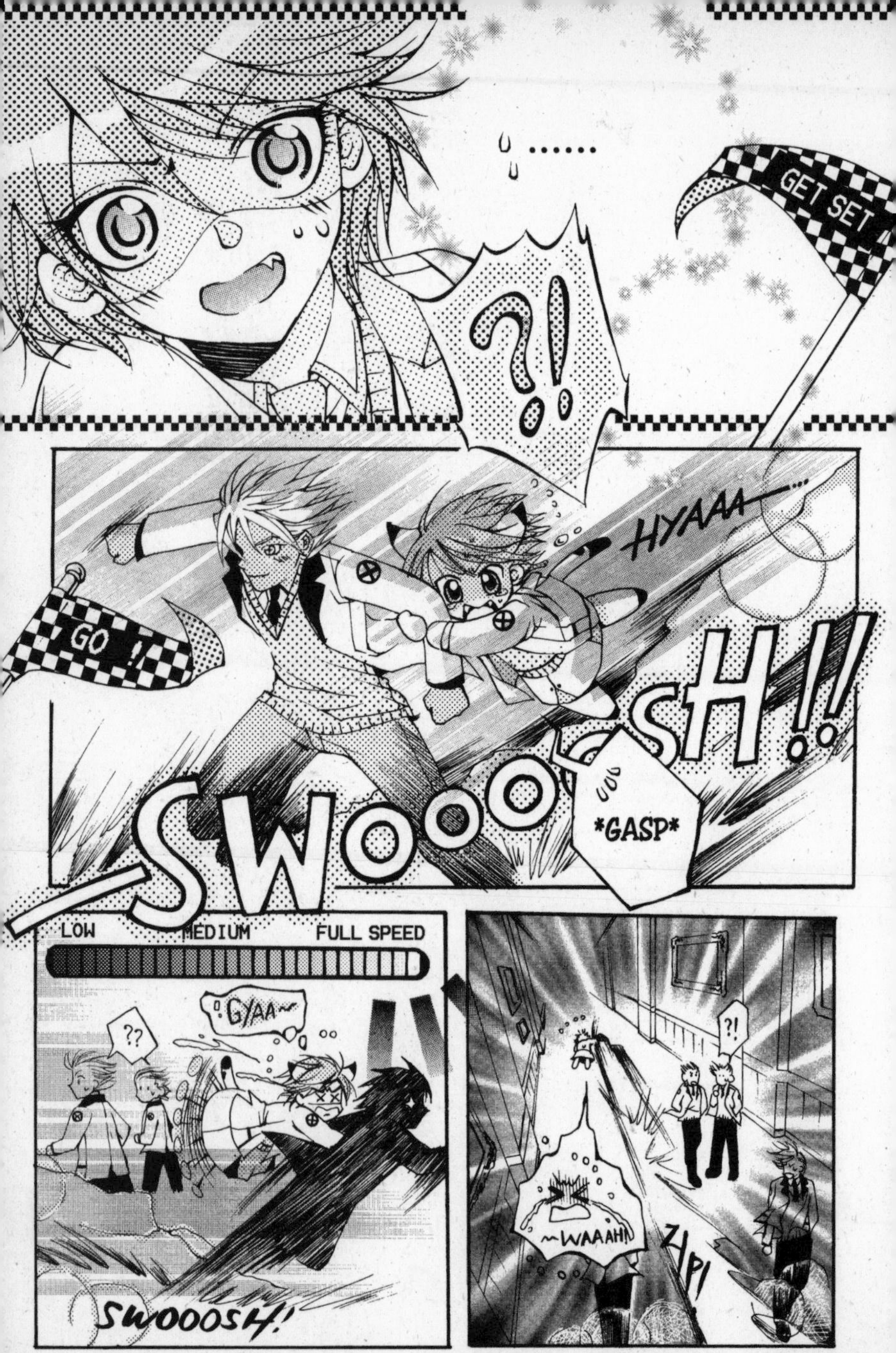

......
GET SET
?!
GO!!
HYAAA—
SWOOOOSH!!
GASP
LOW
MEDIUM
FULL SPEED
GYAA~
??
SWOOOSH!
?!
~WAAAH!
ZIP!

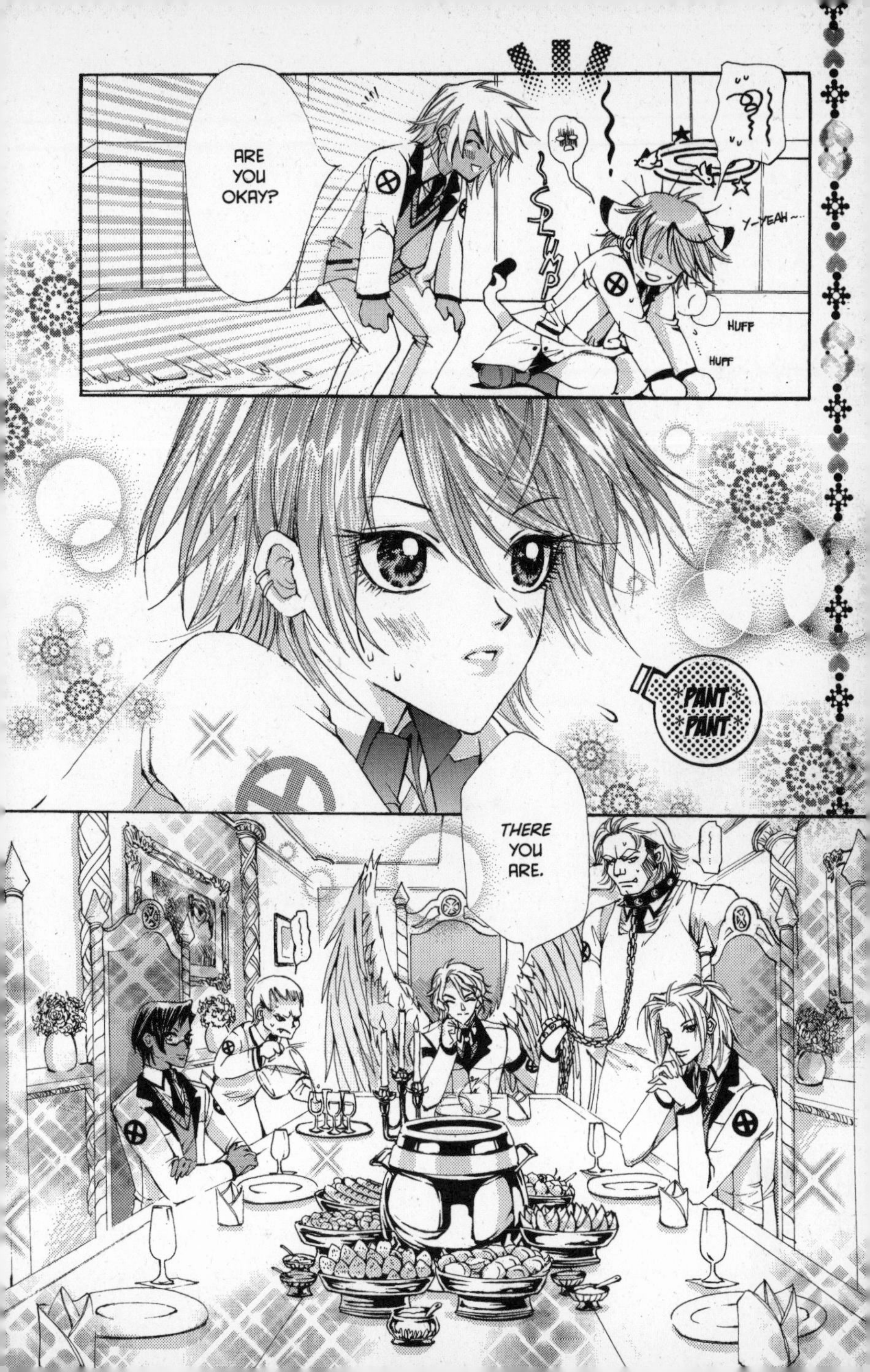
ARE YOU OKAY?
SLUMP
Y-YEAH...
HUFF
HUFF
PANT *PANT*
THERE YOU ARE.

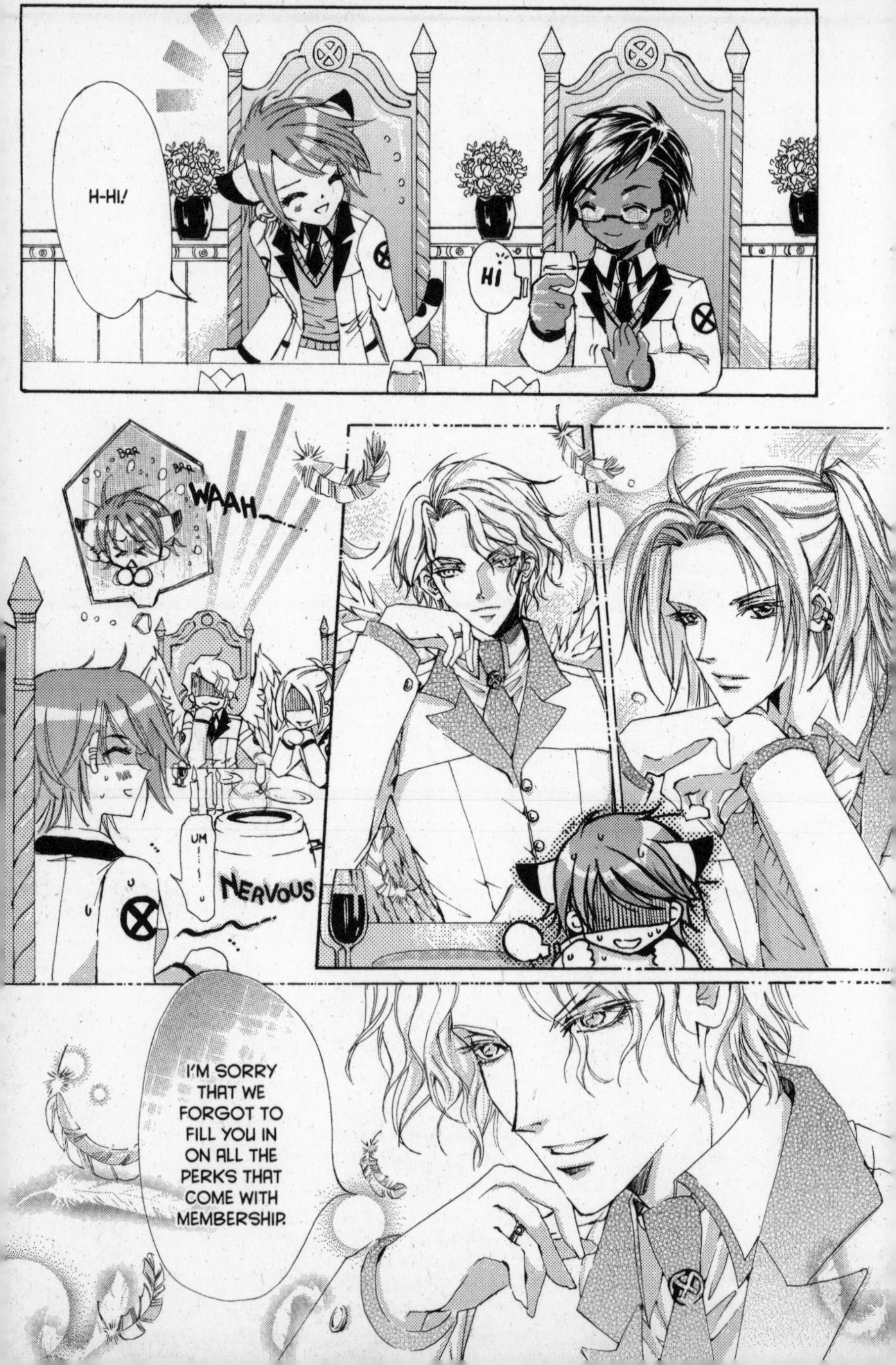
H-HI!
HI
BRR
BRR
WAAH
UM
NERVOUS
I'M SORRY THAT WE FORGOT TO FILL YOU IN ON ALL THE PERKS THAT COME WITH MEMBERSHIP.

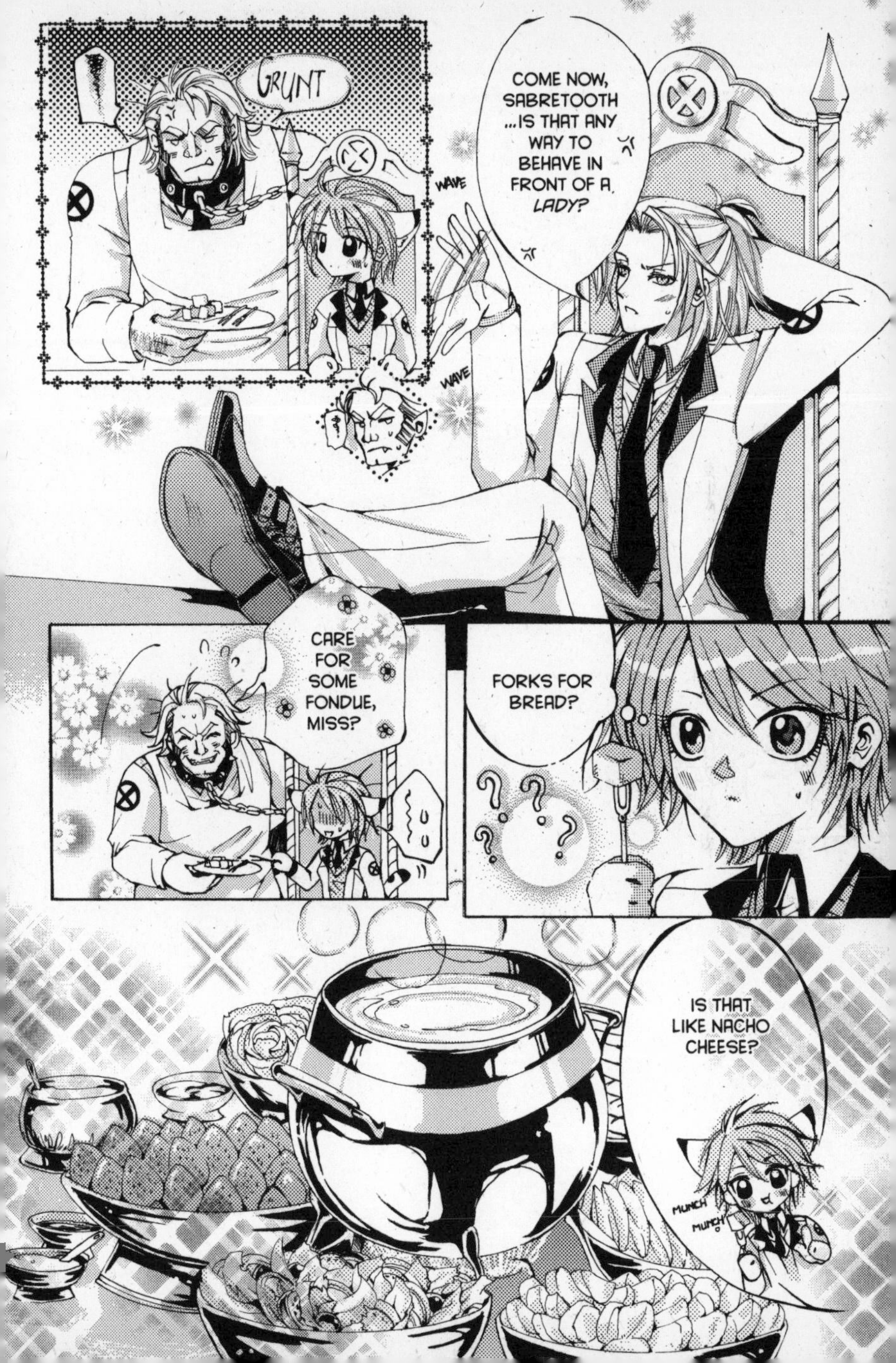
GRUNT
WAVE
WAVE
COME NOW, SABRETOOTH ...IS THAT ANY WAY TO BEHAVE IN FRONT OF A *LADY?*
CARE FOR SOME FONDUE, MISS?
FORKS FOR BREAD?
IS THAT LIKE NACHO CHEESE?
MUNCH
MUNCH

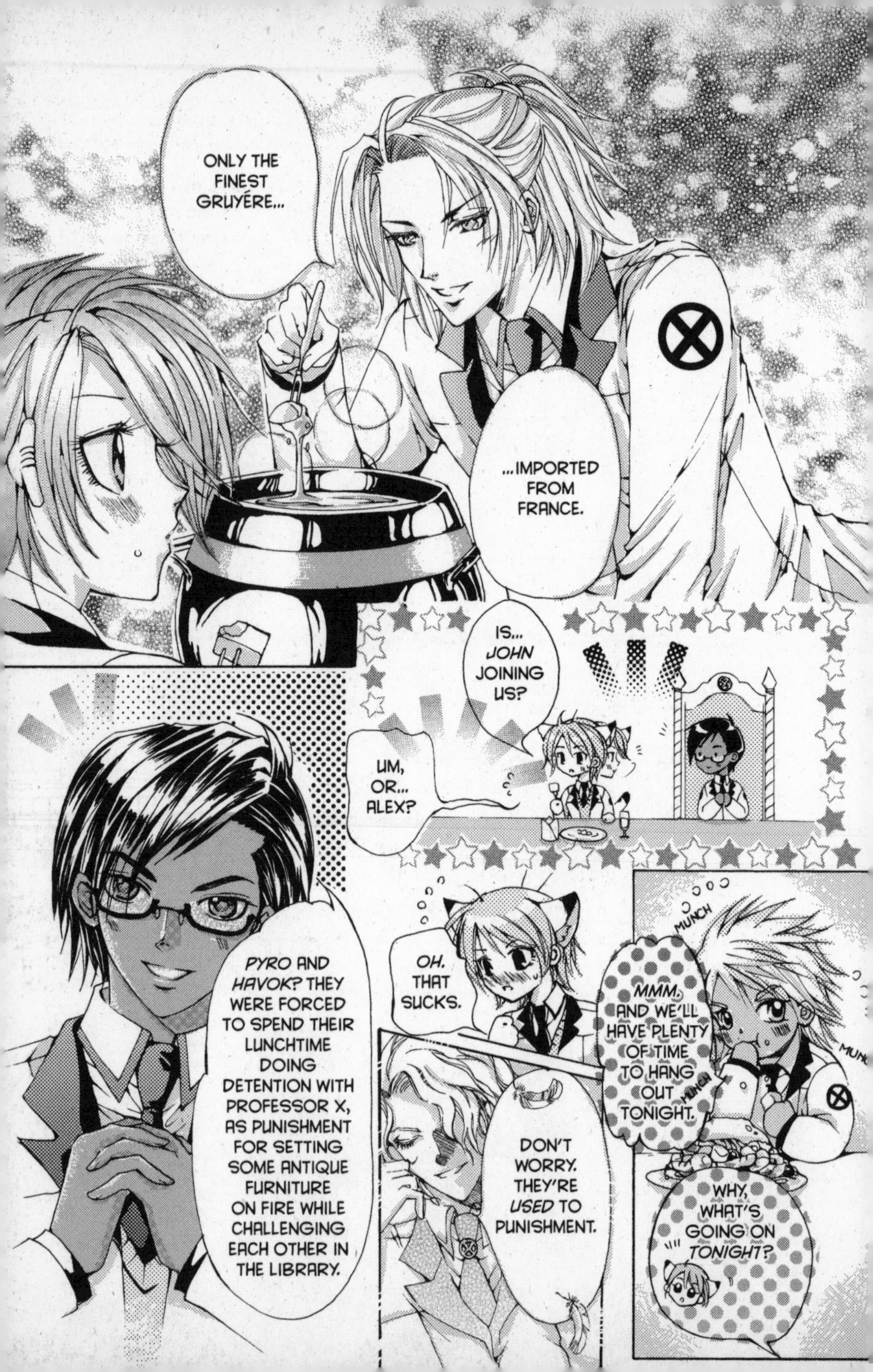
ONLY THE FINEST GRUYÉRE...
...IMPORTED FROM FRANCE.
IS... *JOHN* JOINING US?
UM, OR... ALEX?
PYRO AND *HAVOK*? THEY WERE FORCED TO SPEND THEIR LUNCHTIME DOING DETENTION WITH PROFESSOR X, AS PUNISHMENT FOR SETTING SOME ANTIQUE FURNITURE ON FIRE WHILE CHALLENGING EACH OTHER IN THE LIBRARY.
OH. THAT SUCKS.
DON'T WORRY. THEY'RE *USED* TO PUNISHMENT.
MUNCH
MMM, AND WE'LL HAVE PLENTY OF TIME TO HANG OUT TONIGHT.
WHY, WHAT'S GOING ON *TONIGHT*?

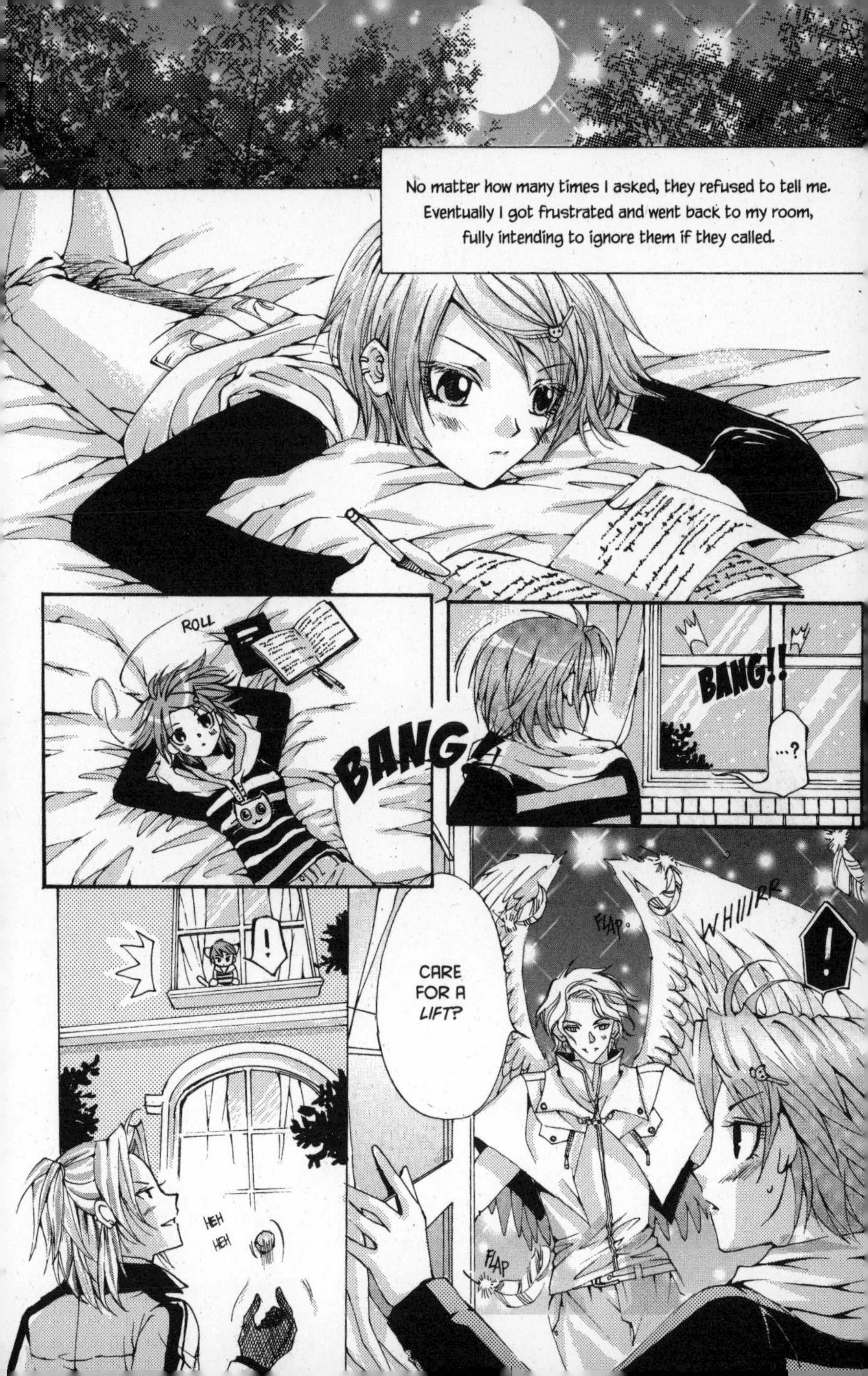
No matter how many times I asked, they refused to tell me.
Eventually I got frustrated and went back to my room,
fully intending to ignore them if they called.
ROLL
BANG!
BANG!!
...?
!
HEH
HEH
CARE FOR A LIFT?
FLAP
WHIIIRR
!
FLAP

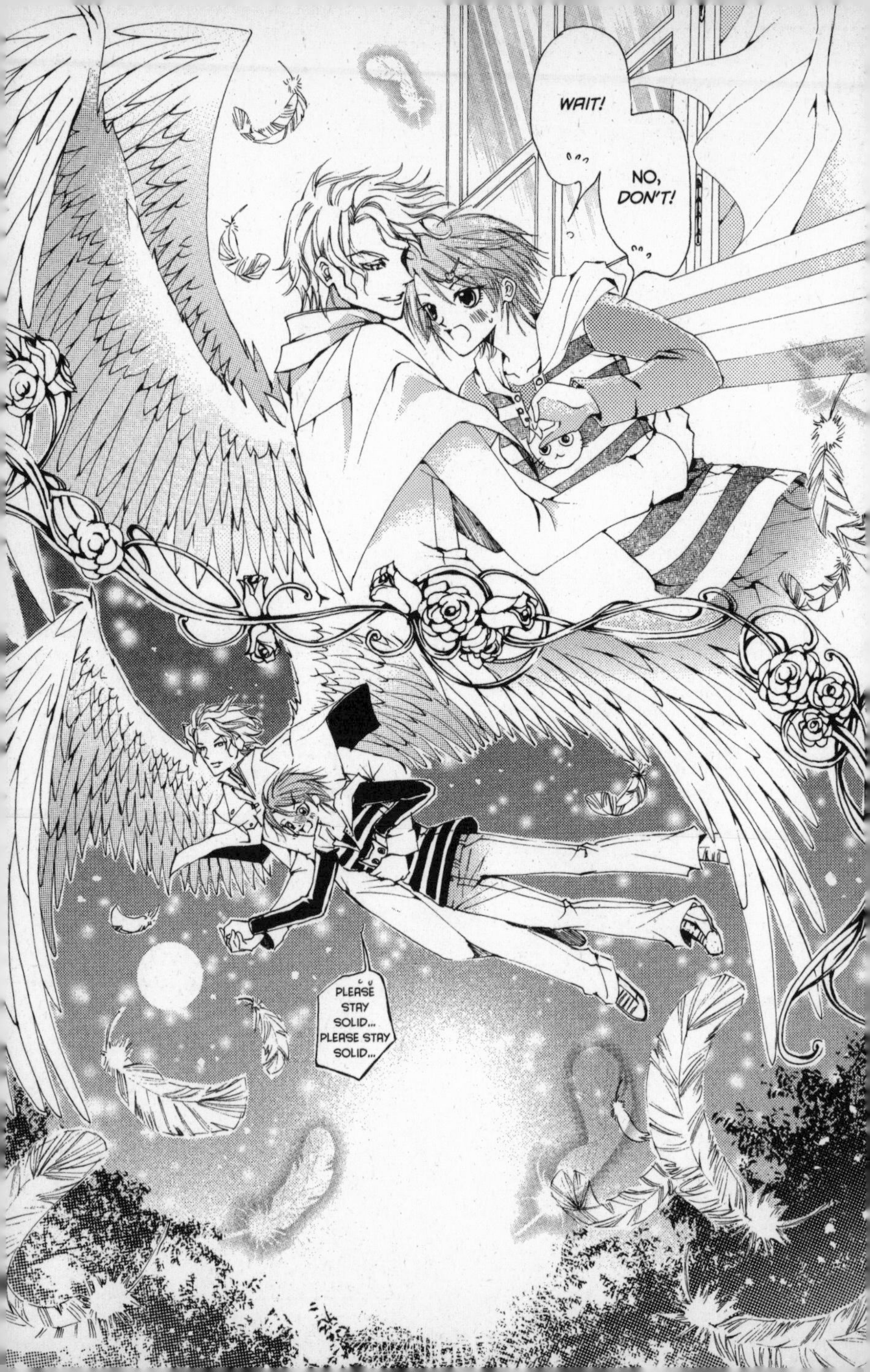
WAIT!
NO, DON'T!
PLEASE STAY SOLID... PLEASE STAY SOLID...

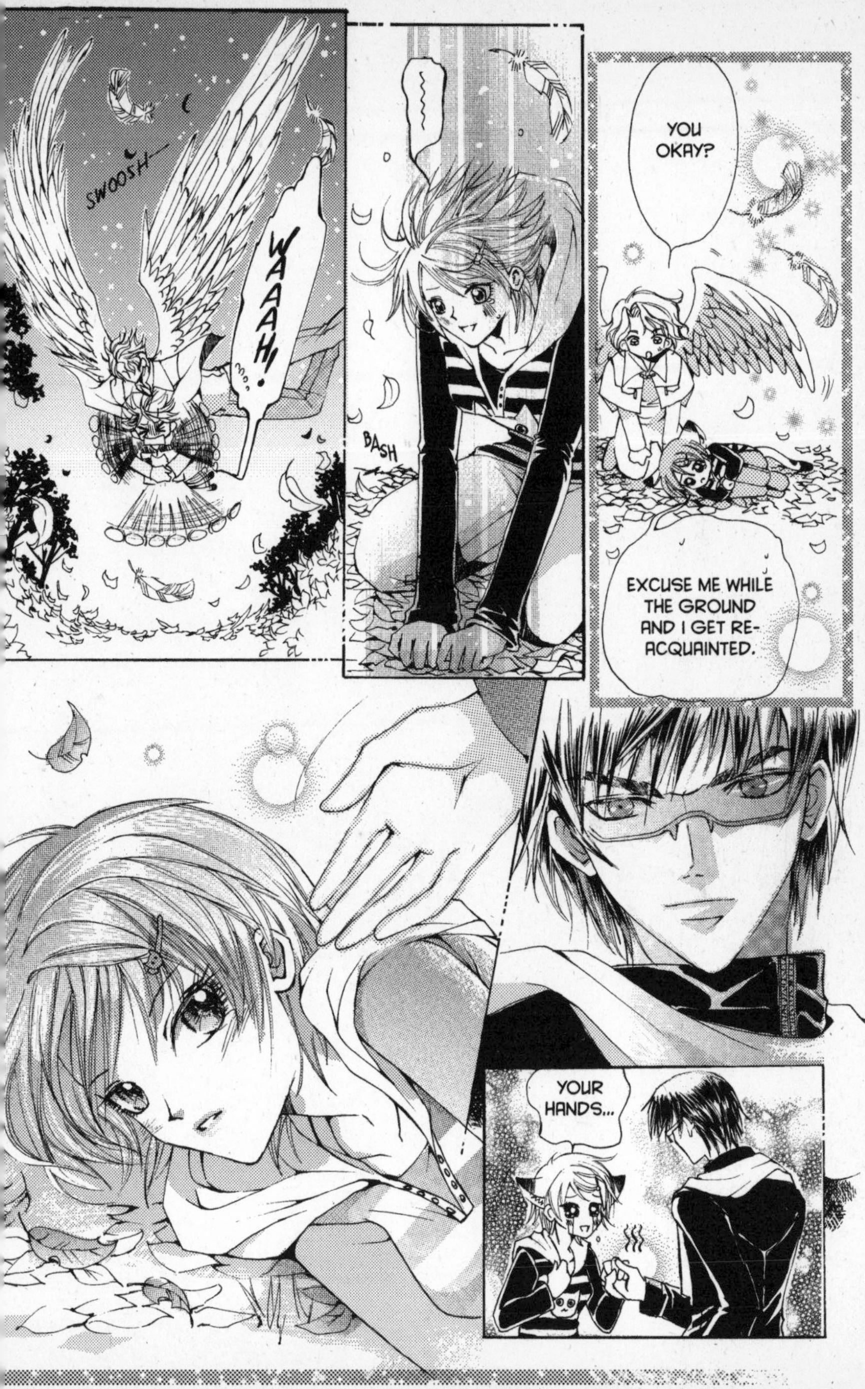
SWOOSH
WAAAAH!
BASH
YOU OKAY?
EXCUSE ME WHILE THE GROUND AND I GET RE-ACQUAINTED.
YOUR HANDS...

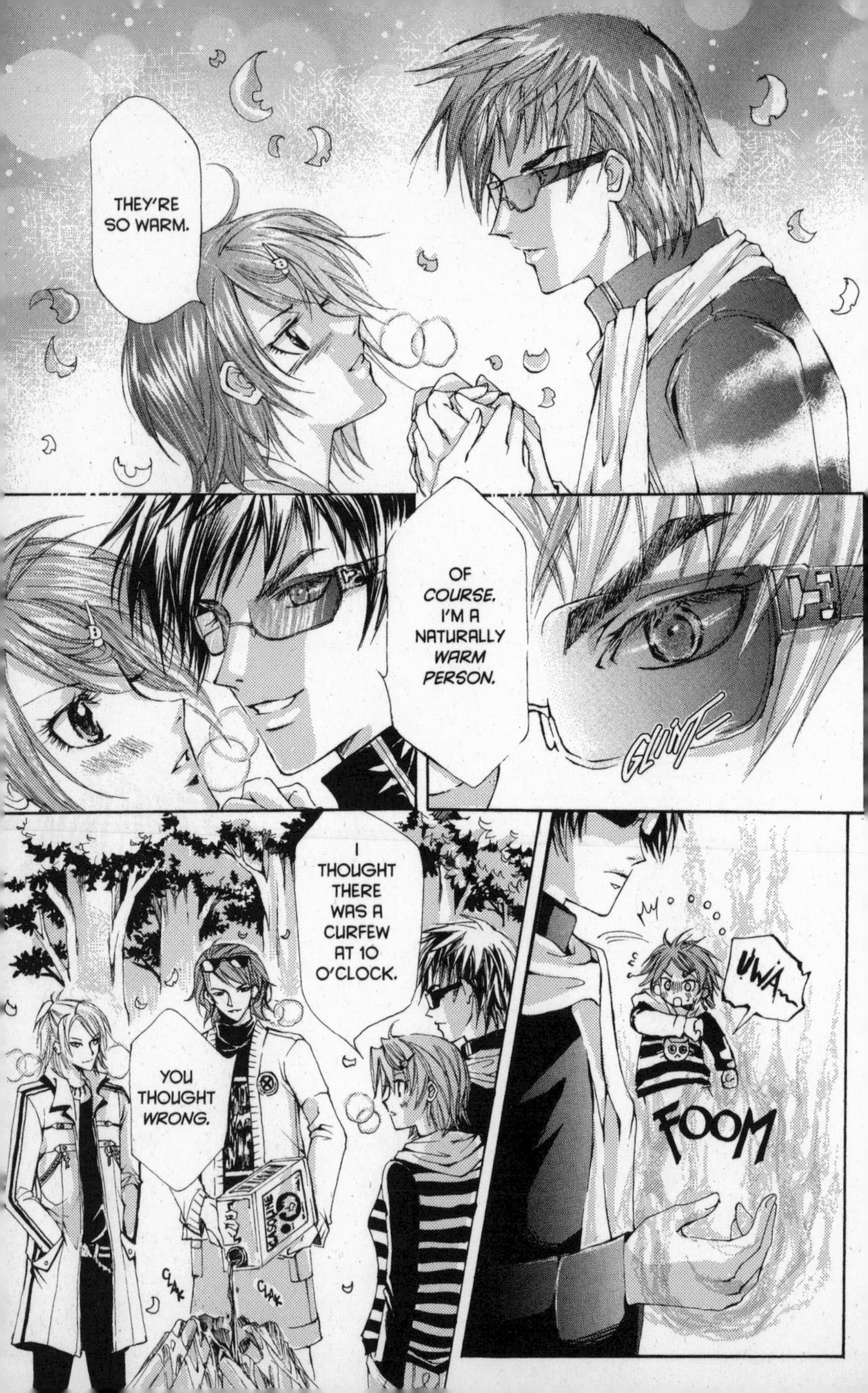
THEY'RE SO WARM.
OF COURSE. I'M A NATURALLY WARM PERSON.
GLINT
I THOUGHT THERE WAS A CURFEW AT 10 O'CLOCK.
YOU THOUGHT WRONG.
GASOLINE
CLAK
CLAK
UWA
FOOM

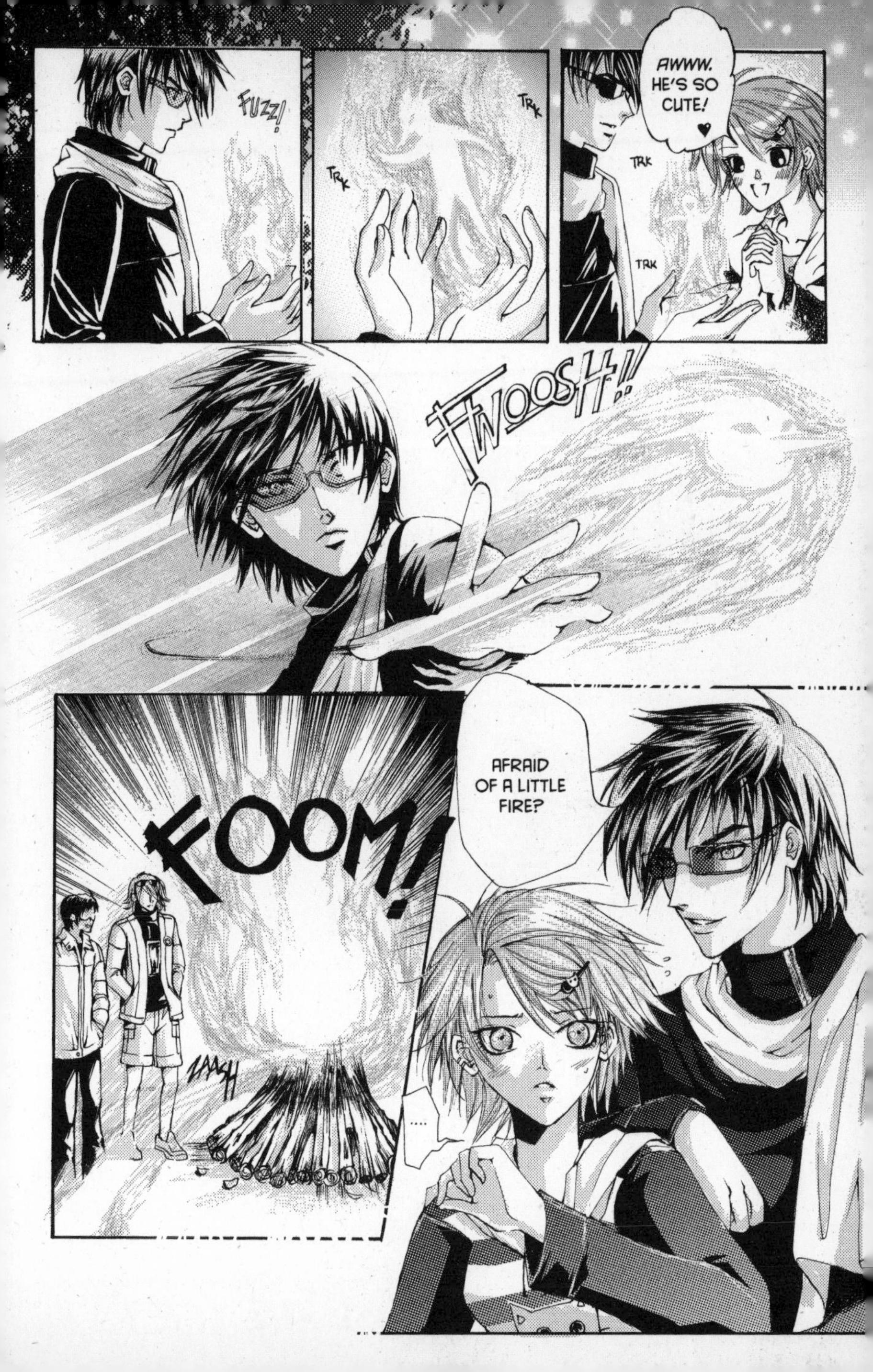
FUZZ!
TRK
TRK
TRK
AWWW. HE'S SO CUTE! ♥
TRK
FWOOSH!!
FOOM!
ZAASH
AFRAID OF A LITTLE FIRE?
....

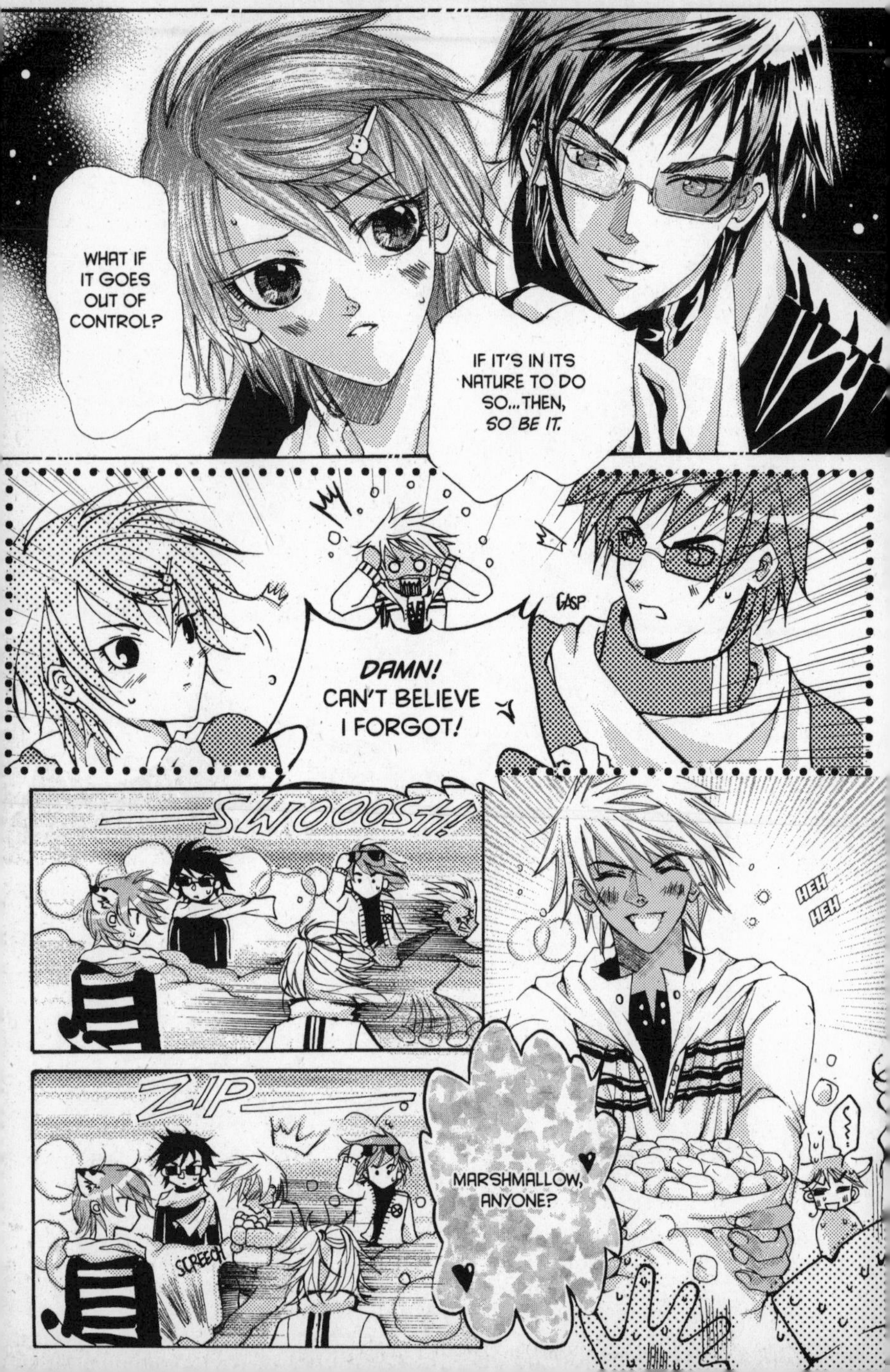
WHAT IF IT GOES OUT OF CONTROL?
IF IT'S IN ITS NATURE TO DO SO...THEN, *SO BE IT.*
GASP
DAMN! CAN'T BELIEVE I FORGOT!
SWOOOSH!
ZIP
SCREECH
HEH HEH
MARSHMALLOW, ANYONE?

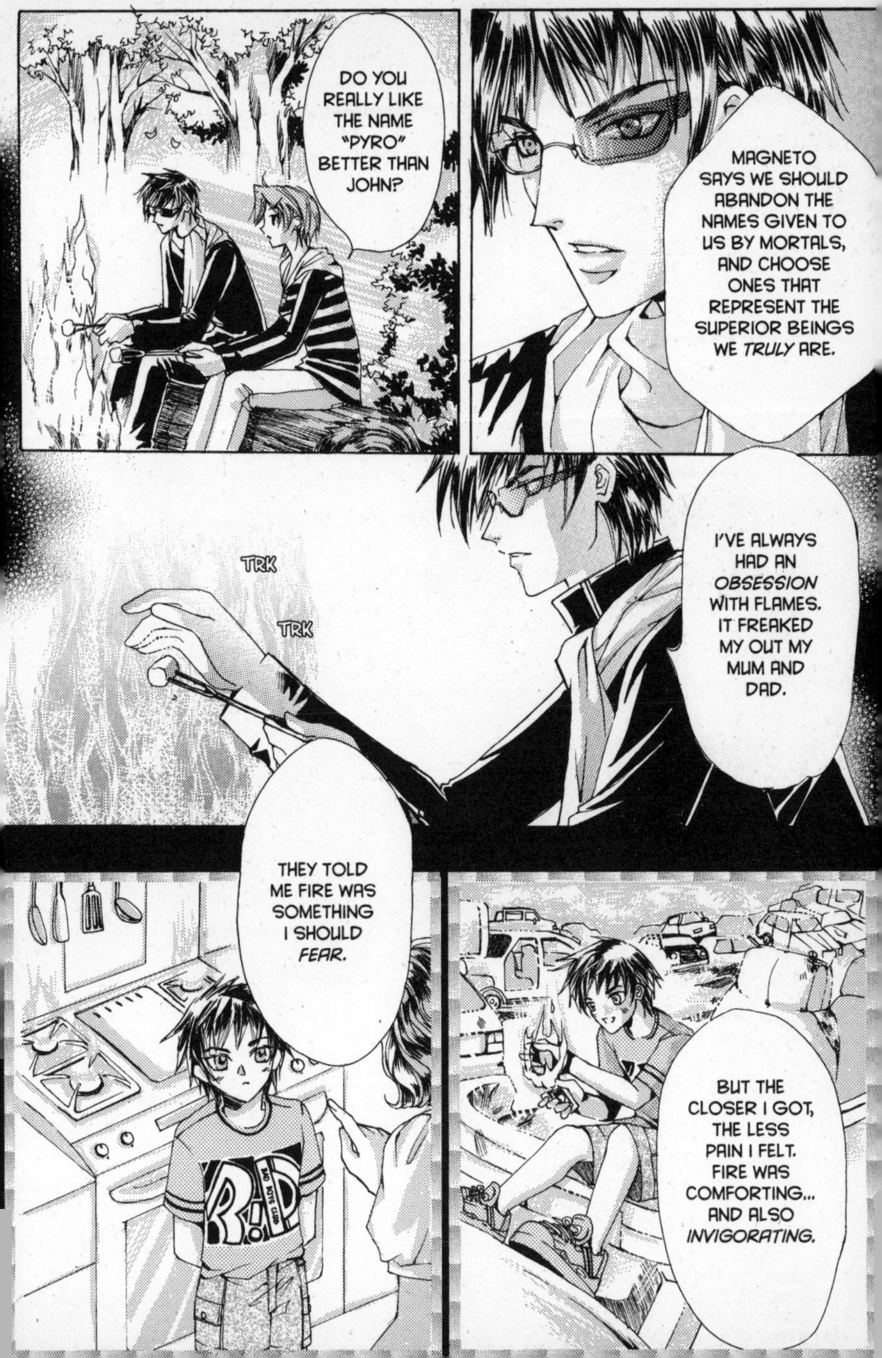
DO YOU REALLY LIKE THE NAME "PYRO" BETTER THAN JOHN?
MAGNETO SAYS WE SHOULD ABANDON THE NAMES GIVEN TO US BY MORTALS, AND CHOOSE ONES THAT REPRESENT THE SUPERIOR BEINGS WE TRULY ARE.
TRK
TRK
I'VE ALWAYS HAD AN OBSESSION WITH FLAMES. IT FREAKED MY OUT MY MUM AND DAD.
THEY TOLD ME FIRE WAS SOMETHING I SHOULD FEAR.
BUT THE CLOSER I GOT, THE LESS PAIN I FELT. FIRE WAS COMFORTING... AND ALSO INVIGORATING.

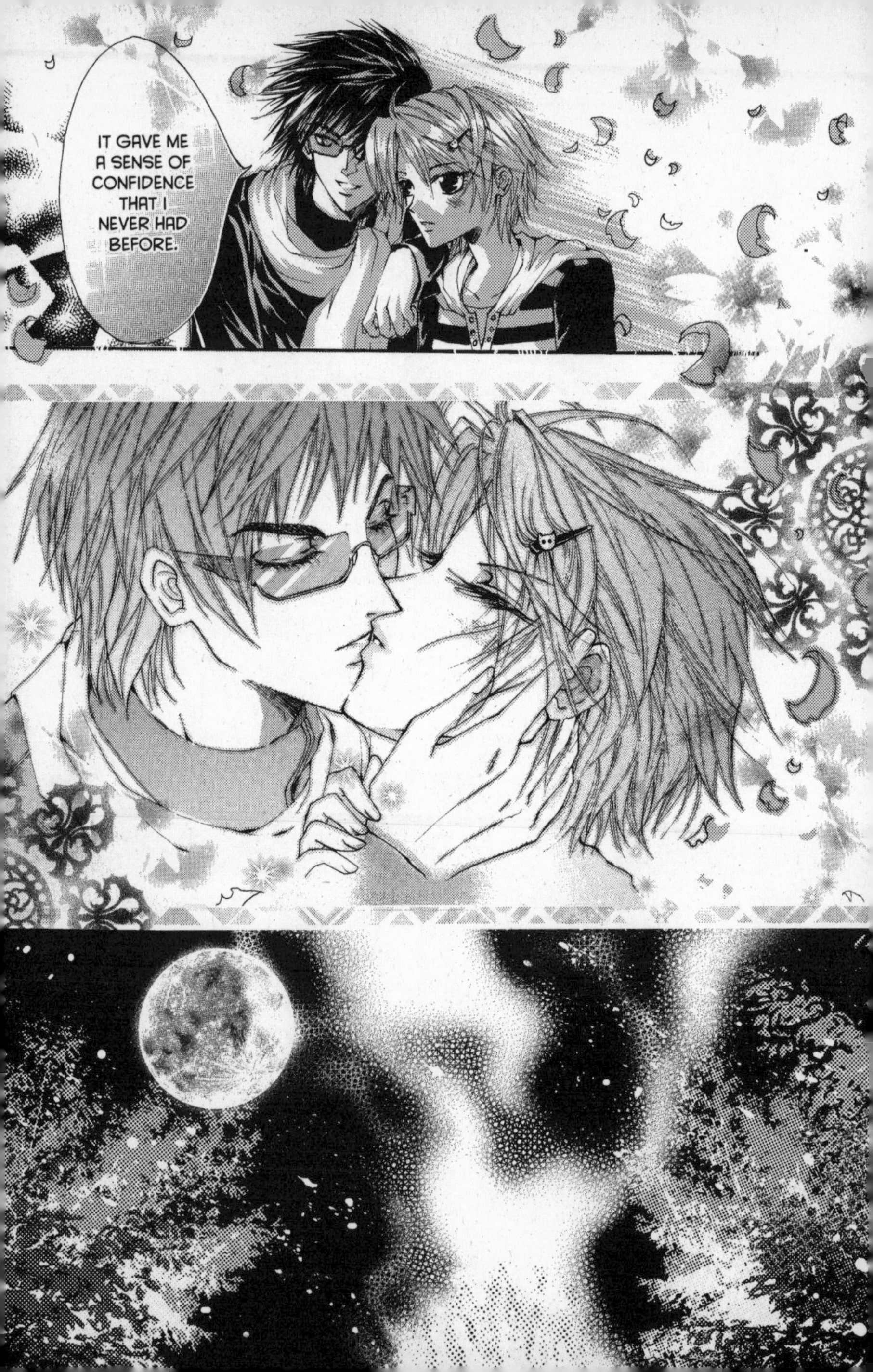
IT GAVE ME A SENSE OF CONFIDENCE THAT I NEVER HAD BEFORE.

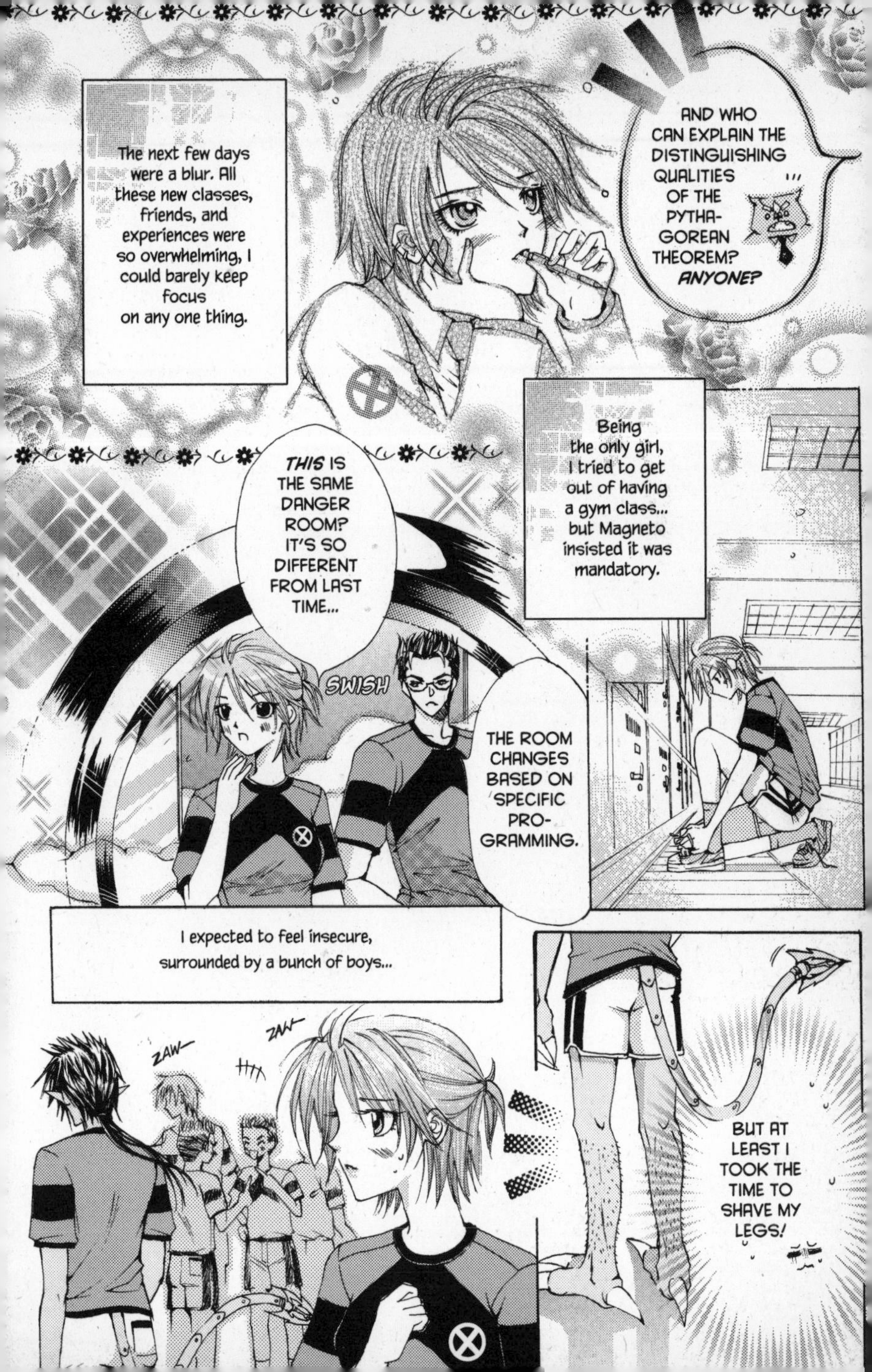
The next few days were a blur. All these new classes, friends, and experiences were so overwhelming, I could barely keep focus on any one thing.
AND WHO CAN EXPLAIN THE DISTINGUISHING QUALITIES OF THE PYTHA-GOREAN THEOREM? ANYONE?
THIS IS THE SAME DANGER ROOM? IT'S SO DIFFERENT FROM LAST TIME...
SWISH
THE ROOM CHANGES BASED ON SPECIFIC PRO-GRAMMING.
Being the only girl, I tried to get out of having a gym class... but Magneto insisted it was mandatory.
I expected to feel insecure, surrounded by a bunch of boys...
ZAW
ZAW
BUT AT LEAST I TOOK THE TIME TO SHAVE MY LEGS!

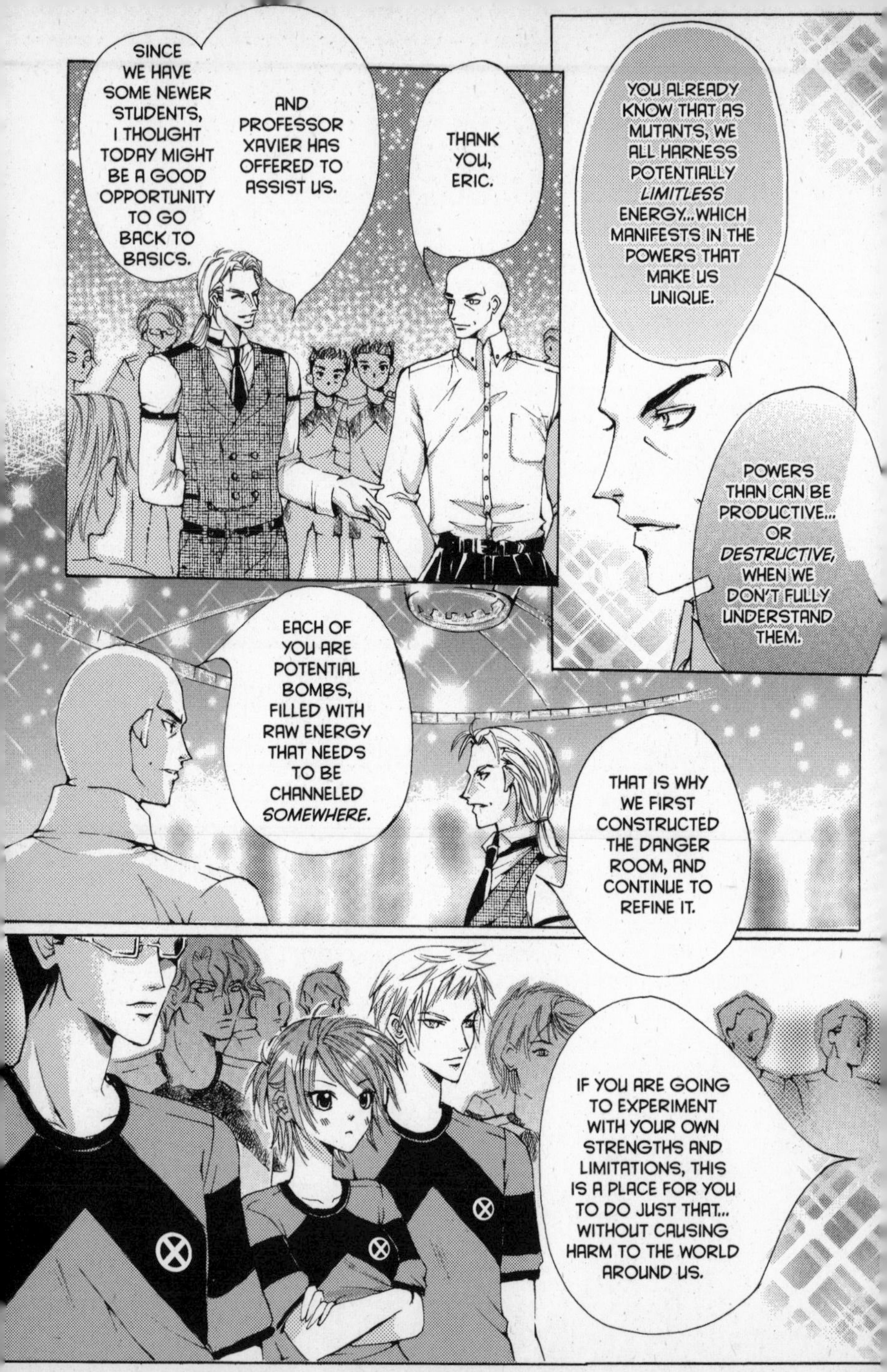
SINCE WE HAVE SOME NEWER STUDENTS, I THOUGHT TODAY MIGHT BE A GOOD OPPORTUNITY TO GO BACK TO BASICS.
AND PROFESSOR XAVIER HAS OFFERED TO ASSIST US.
THANK YOU, ERIC.
YOU ALREADY KNOW THAT AS MUTANTS, WE ALL HARNESS POTENTIALLY *LIMITLESS* ENERGY...WHICH MANIFESTS IN THE POWERS THAT MAKE US UNIQUE.
POWERS THAN CAN BE PRODUCTIVE... OR *DESTRUCTIVE,* WHEN WE DON'T FULLY UNDERSTAND THEM.
EACH OF YOU ARE POTENTIAL BOMBS, FILLED WITH RAW ENERGY THAT NEEDS TO BE CHANNELED *SOMEWHERE.*
THAT IS WHY WE FIRST CONSTRUCTED THE DANGER ROOM, AND CONTINUE TO REFINE IT.
IF YOU ARE GOING TO EXPERIMENT WITH YOUR OWN STRENGTHS AND LIMITATIONS, THIS IS A PLACE FOR YOU TO DO JUST THAT... WITHOUT CAUSING HARM TO THE WORLD AROUND US.

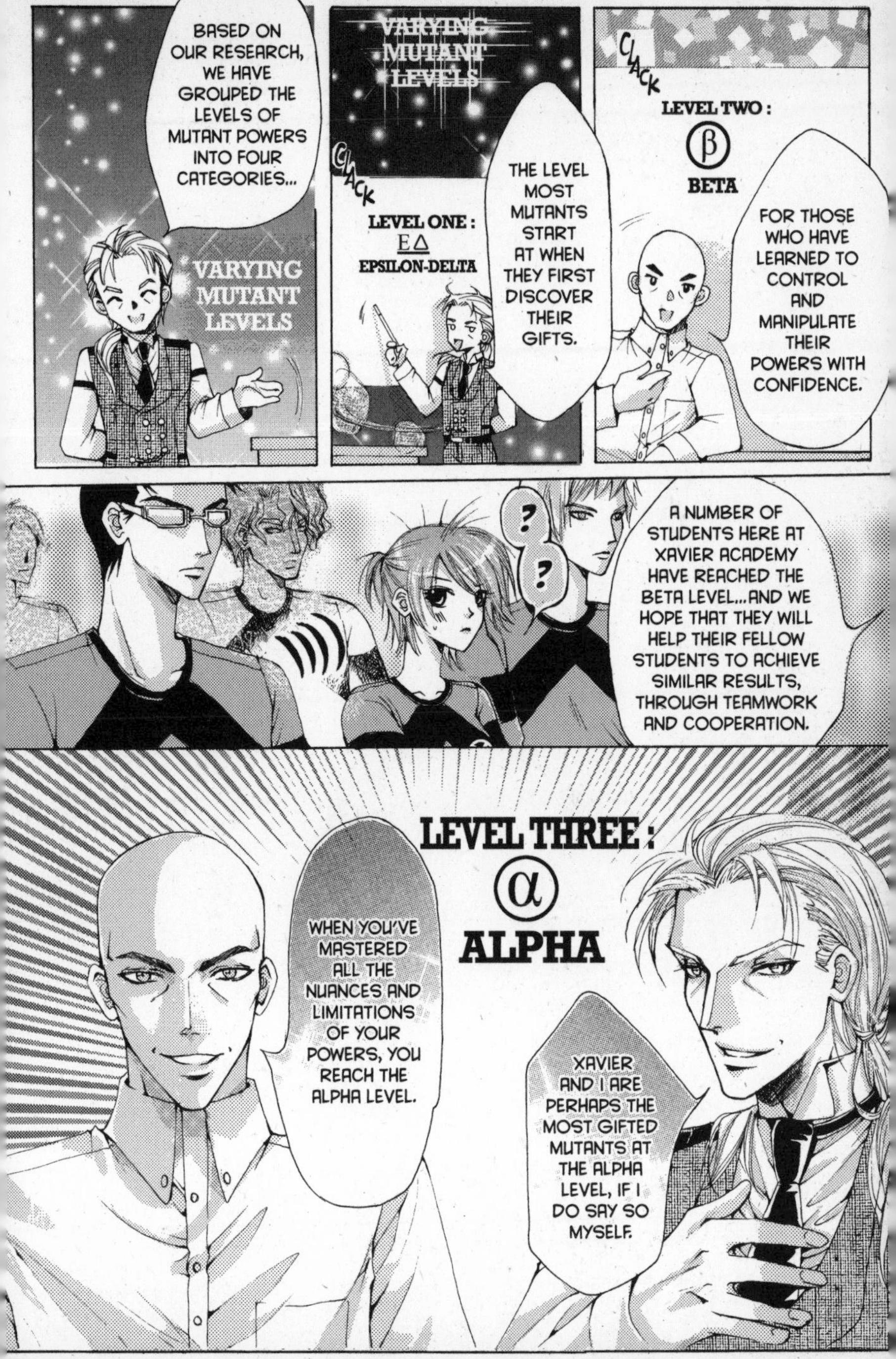

BASED ON OUR RESEARCH, WE HAVE GROUPED THE LEVELS OF MUTANT POWERS INTO FOUR CATEGORIES...
VARYING MUTANT LEVELS
VARYING MUTANT LEVELS
CLACK
LEVEL ONE : EΔ EPSILON-DELTA
THE LEVEL MOST MUTANTS START AT WHEN THEY FIRST DISCOVER THEIR GIFTS.
CLACK
LEVEL TWO : β BETA
FOR THOSE WHO HAVE LEARNED TO CONTROL AND MANIPULATE THEIR POWERS WITH CONFIDENCE.
?
?
A NUMBER OF STUDENTS HERE AT XAVIER ACADEMY HAVE REACHED THE BETA LEVEL...AND WE HOPE THAT THEY WILL HELP THEIR FELLOW STUDENTS TO ACHIEVE SIMILAR RESULTS, THROUGH TEAMWORK AND COOPERATION.
LEVEL THREE : α ALPHA
WHEN YOU'VE MASTERED ALL THE NUANCES AND LIMITATIONS OF YOUR POWERS, YOU REACH THE ALPHA LEVEL.
XAVIER AND I ARE PERHAPS THE MOST GIFTED MUTANTS AT THE ALPHA LEVEL, IF I DO SAY SO MYSELF.

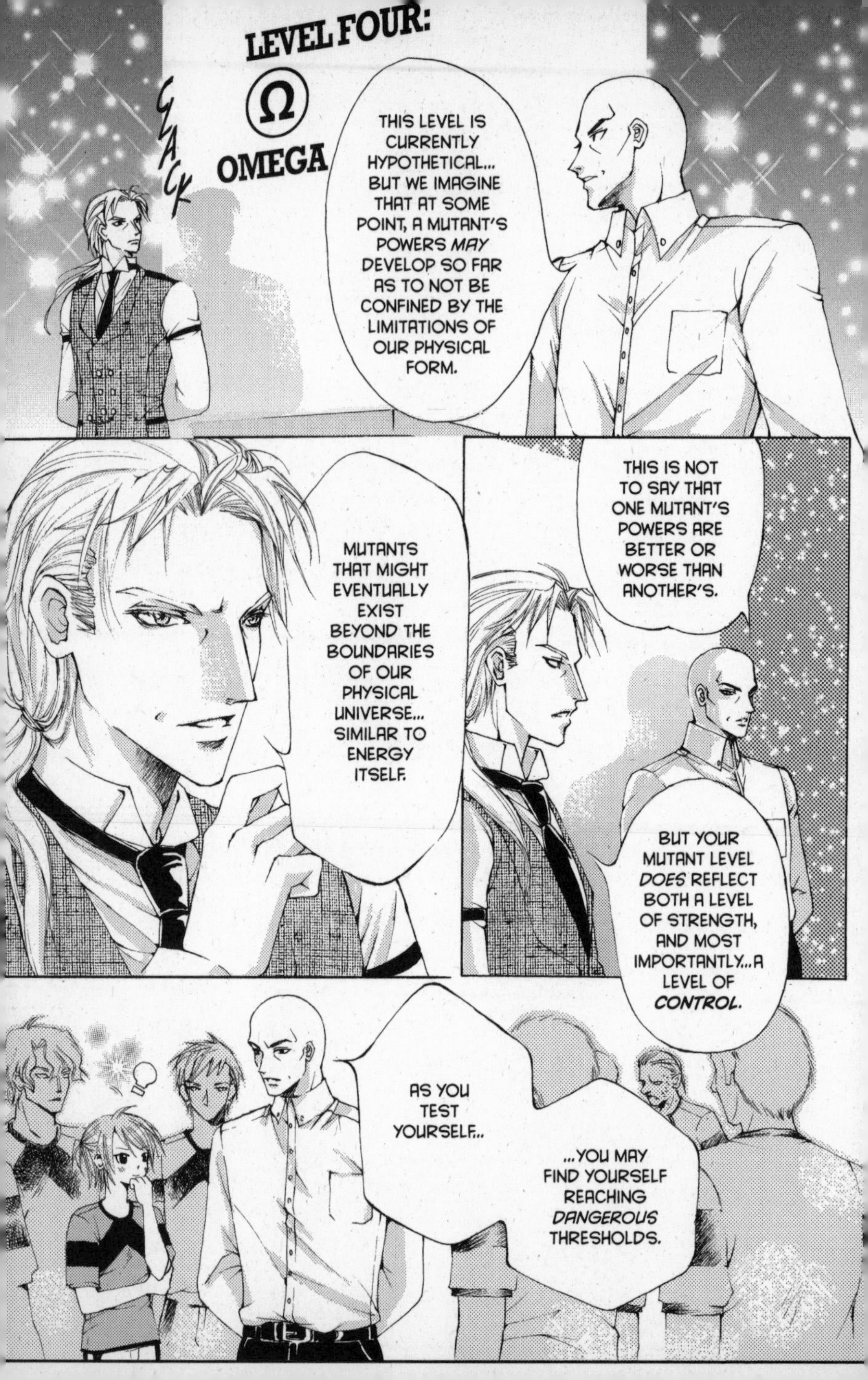
LEVEL FOUR:
Ω
OMEGA
CLACK
THIS LEVEL IS CURRENTLY HYPOTHETICAL... BUT WE IMAGINE THAT AT SOME POINT, A MUTANT'S POWERS *MAY* DEVELOP SO FAR AS TO NOT BE CONFINED BY THE LIMITATIONS OF OUR PHYSICAL FORM.
MUTANTS THAT MIGHT EVENTUALLY EXIST BEYOND THE BOUNDARIES OF OUR PHYSICAL UNIVERSE... SIMILAR TO ENERGY ITSELF.
THIS IS NOT TO SAY THAT ONE MUTANT'S POWERS ARE BETTER OR WORSE THAN ANOTHER'S.
BUT YOUR MUTANT LEVEL *DOES* REFLECT BOTH A LEVEL OF STRENGTH, AND MOST IMPORTANTLY...A LEVEL OF ***CONTROL.***
AS YOU TEST YOURSELF...
...YOU MAY FIND YOURSELF REACHING *DANGEROUS* THRESHOLDS.

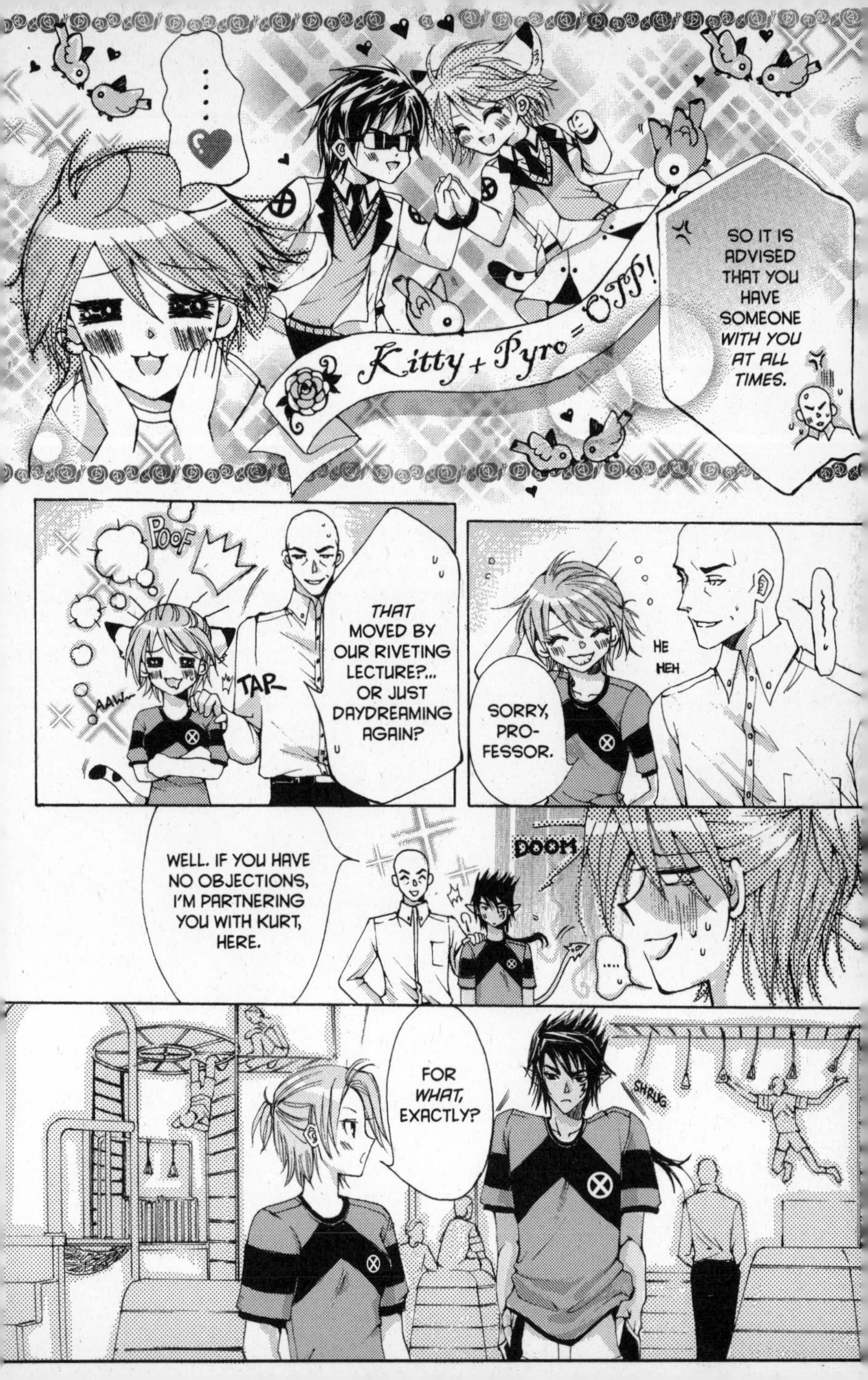
...
Kitty + Pyro = OTP!
SO IT IS ADVISED THAT YOU HAVE SOMEONE WITH YOU AT ALL TIMES.
POOF
AAW~
TAP
THAT MOVED BY OUR RIVETING LECTURE?... OR JUST DAYDREAMING AGAIN?
HE HEH
SORRY, PRO-FESSOR.
WELL. IF YOU HAVE NO OBJECTIONS, I'M PARTNERING YOU WITH KURT, HERE.
DOOM
....
FOR WHAT, EXACTLY?
SHRUG

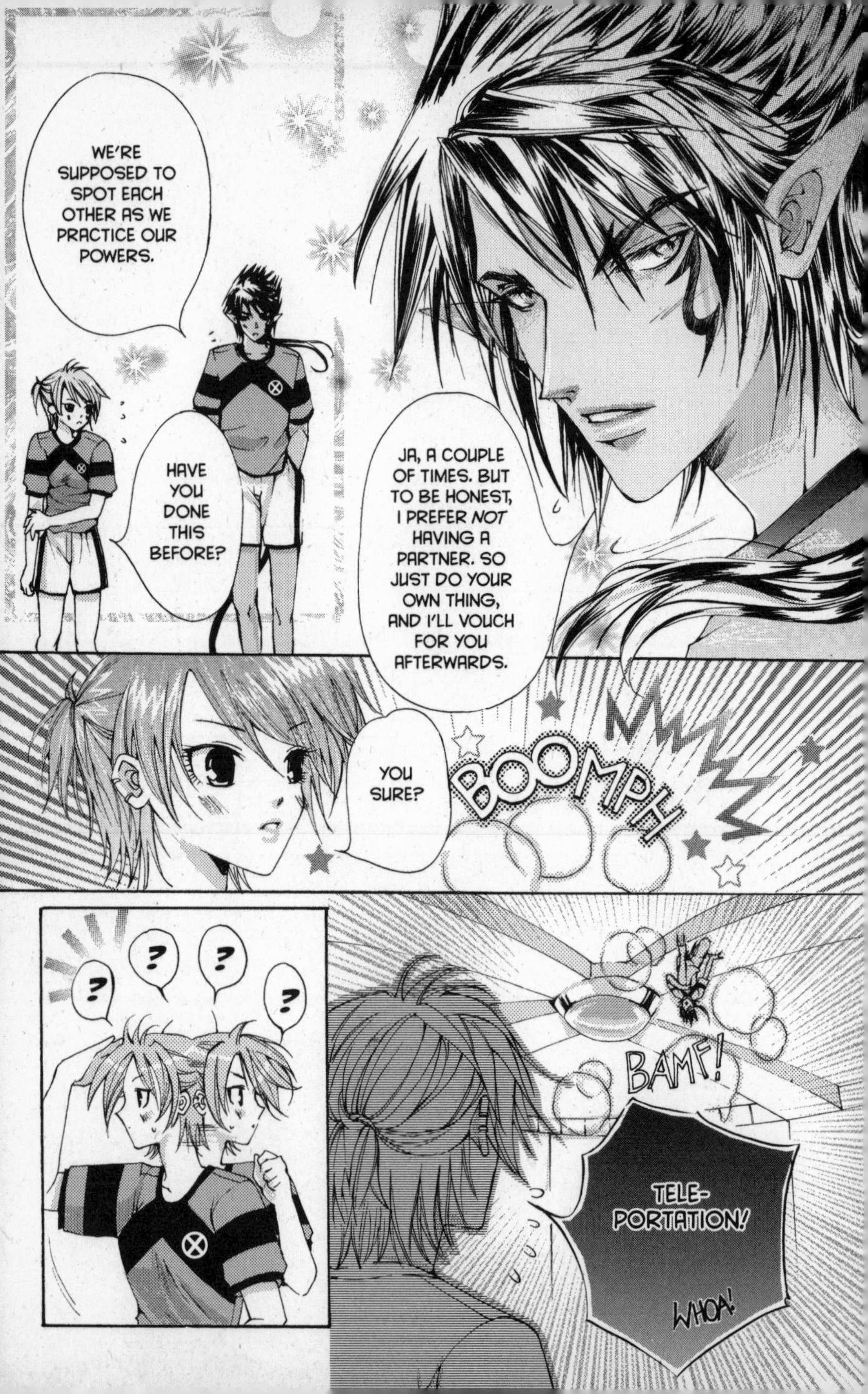
WE'RE SUPPOSED TO SPOT EACH OTHER AS WE PRACTICE OUR POWERS.
HAVE YOU DONE THIS BEFORE?
JA, A COUPLE OF TIMES. BUT TO BE HONEST, I PREFER *NOT* HAVING A PARTNER. SO JUST DO YOUR OWN THING, AND I'LL VOUCH FOR YOU AFTERWARDS.
YOU SURE?
BOOMPH
?
?
?
?
BAMF!
TELE-PORTATION!
WHOA!

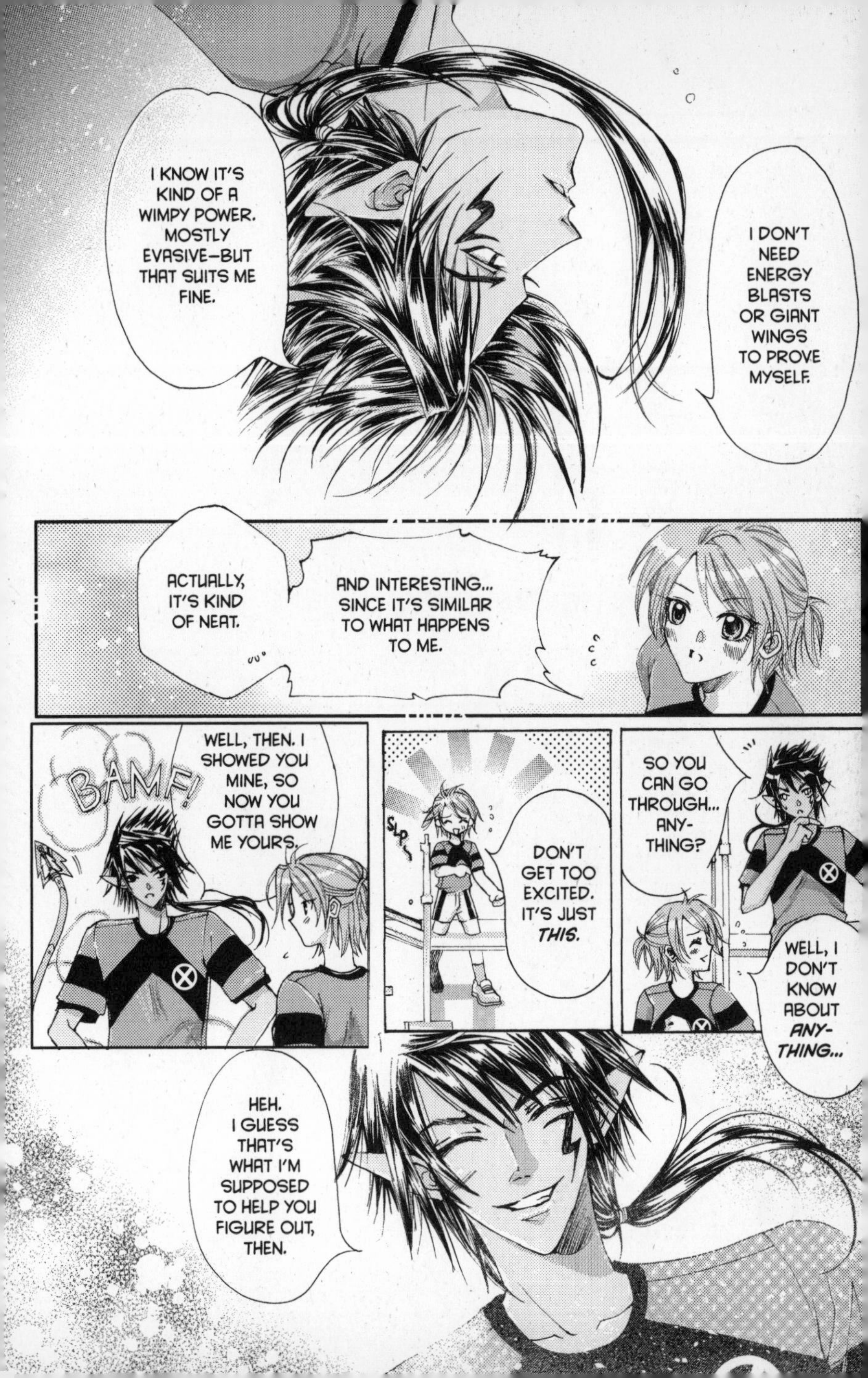
I KNOW IT'S KIND OF A WIMPY POWER. MOSTLY EVASIVE—BUT THAT SUITS ME FINE.
I DON'T NEED ENERGY BLASTS OR GIANT WINGS TO PROVE MYSELF.
ACTUALLY, IT'S KIND OF NEAT.
AND INTERESTING... SINCE IT'S SIMILAR TO WHAT HAPPENS TO ME.
BAMF!
WELL, THEN. I SHOWED YOU MINE, SO NOW YOU GOTTA SHOW ME YOURS.
SLP
DON'T GET TOO EXCITED. IT'S JUST *THIS.*
SO YOU CAN GO THROUGH... ANY-THING?
WELL, I DON'T KNOW ABOUT *ANY-THING...*
HEH. I GUESS THAT'S WHAT I'M SUPPOSED TO HELP YOU FIGURE OUT, THEN.

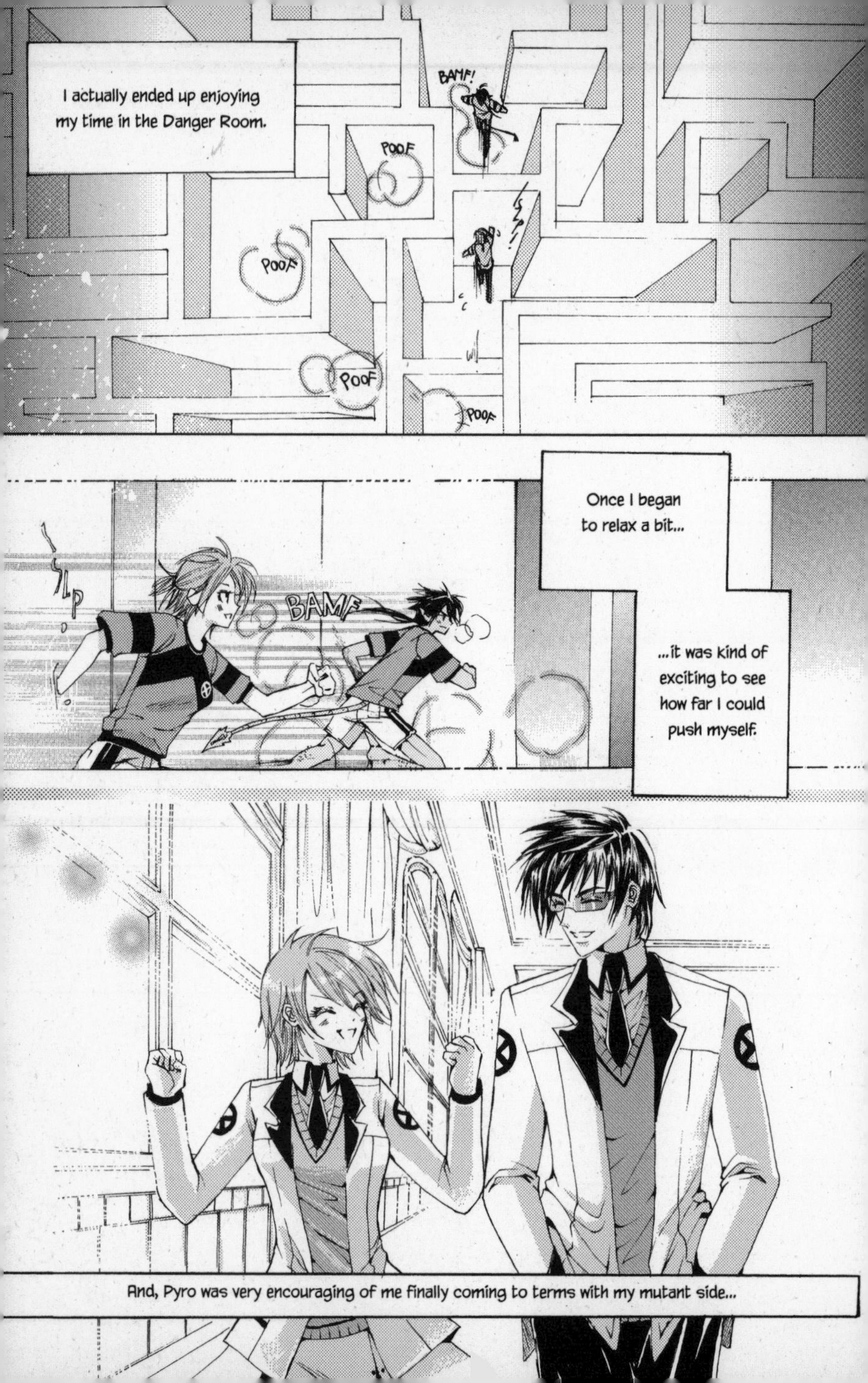
I actually ended up enjoying my time in the Danger Room.
BAMF!
POOF
POOF
POOF
POOF
BAMF
Once I began to relax a bit...
...it was kind of exciting to see how far I could push myself.
And, Pyro was very encouraging of me finally coming to terms with my mutant side...

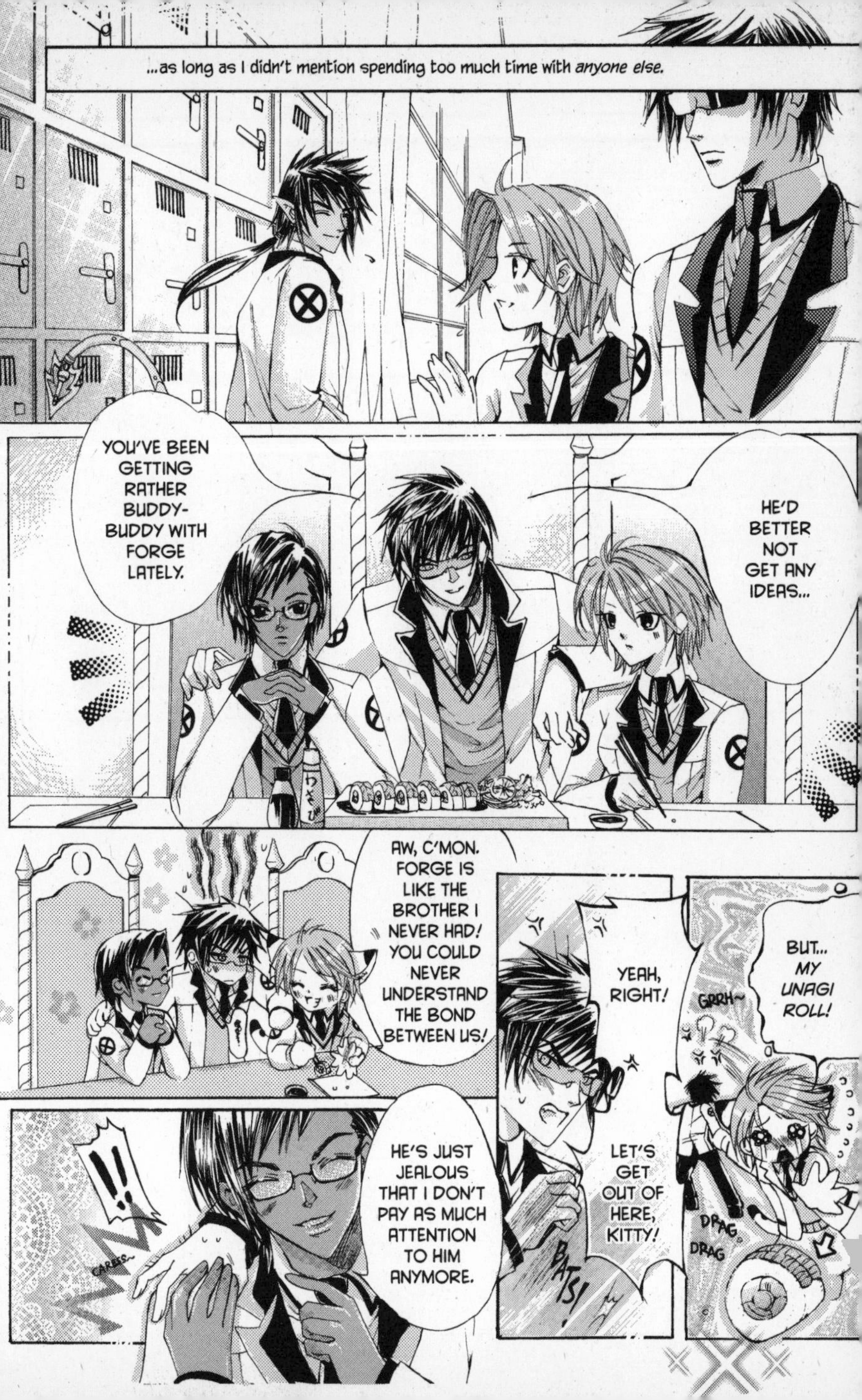
...as long as I didn't mention spending too much time with *anyone else.*
YOU'VE BEEN GETTING RATHER BUDDY-BUDDY WITH FORGE LATELY.
HE'D BETTER NOT GET ANY IDEAS...
AW, C'MON. FORGE IS LIKE THE BROTHER I NEVER HAD! YOU COULD NEVER UNDERSTAND THE BOND BETWEEN US!
!!
CARESS..
HE'S JUST JEALOUS THAT I DON'T PAY AS MUCH ATTENTION TO HIM ANYMORE.
YEAH, RIGHT!
LET'S GET OUT OF HERE, KITTY!
BATS!
BUT... MY UNAGI ROLL!
GRRH~
DRAG DRAG

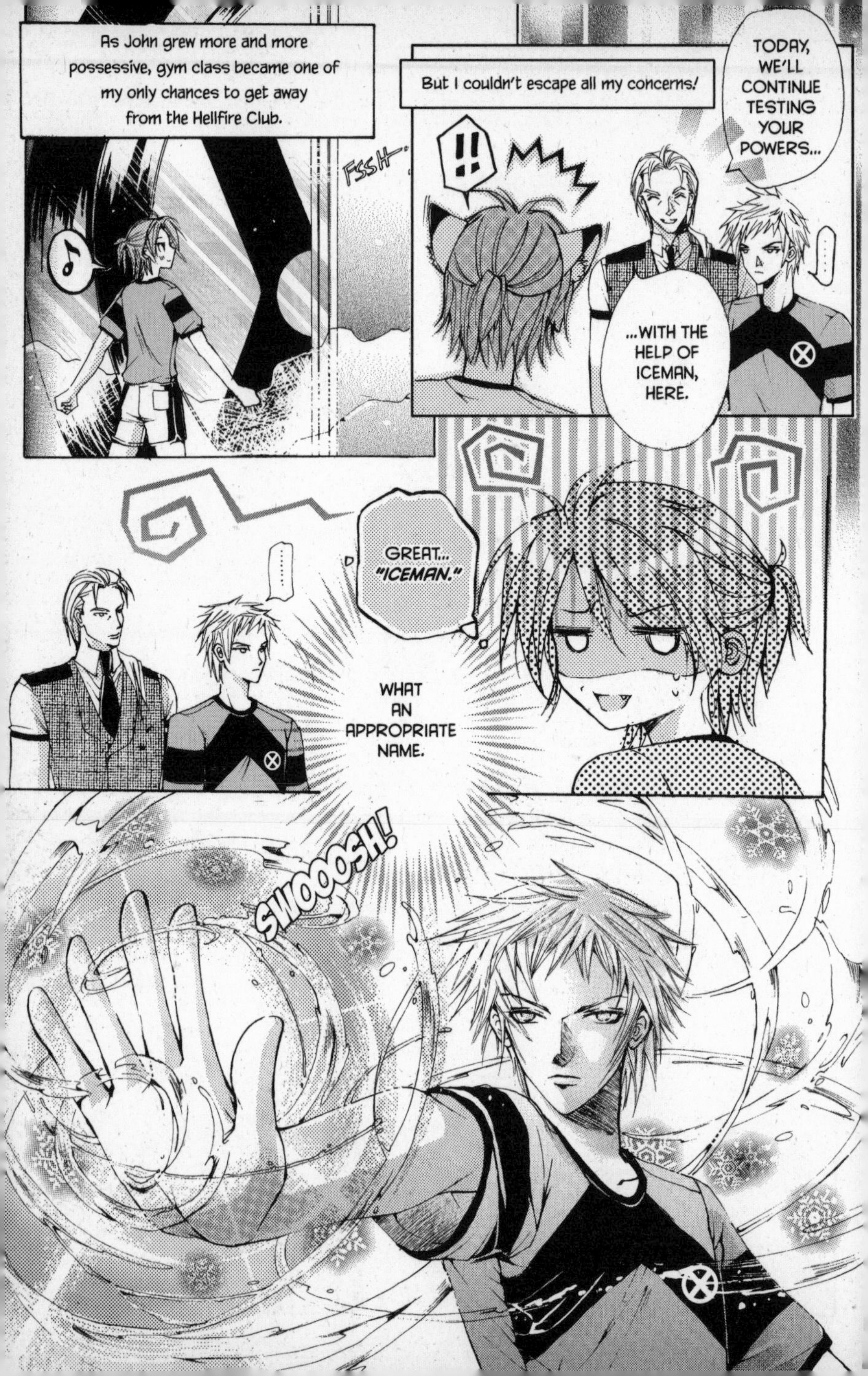
As John grew more and more possessive, gym class became one of my only chances to get away from the Hellfire Club.
FSSH
But I couldn't escape all my concerns!
!!
TODAY, WE'LL CONTINUE TESTING YOUR POWERS...
...
...WITH THE HELP OF ICEMAN, HERE.
...
GREAT... "ICEMAN."
WHAT AN APPROPRIATE NAME.
SWOOOSH!

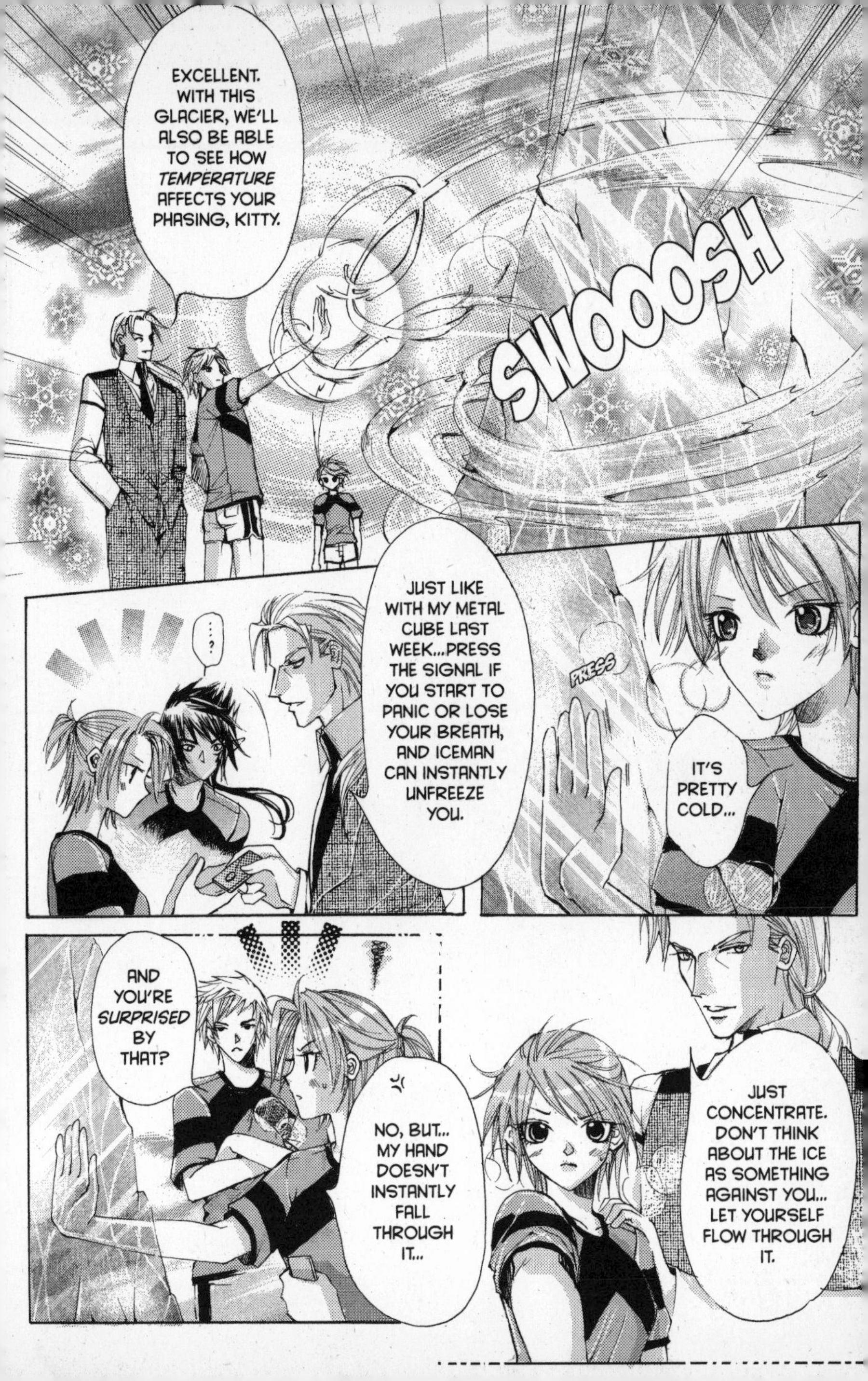
EXCELLENT. WITH THIS GLACIER, WE'LL ALSO BE ABLE TO SEE HOW *TEMPERATURE* AFFECTS YOUR PHASING, KITTY.
SWOOOSH
...?
JUST LIKE WITH MY METAL CUBE LAST WEEK...PRESS THE SIGNAL IF YOU START TO PANIC OR LOSE YOUR BREATH, AND ICEMAN CAN INSTANTLY UNFREEZE YOU.
PRESS
IT'S PRETTY COLD...
AND YOU'RE *SURPRISED* BY THAT?
NO, BUT... MY HAND DOESN'T INSTANTLY FALL THROUGH IT...
JUST CONCENTRATE. DON'T THINK ABOUT THE ICE AS SOMETHING AGAINST YOU... LET YOURSELF FLOW THROUGH IT.

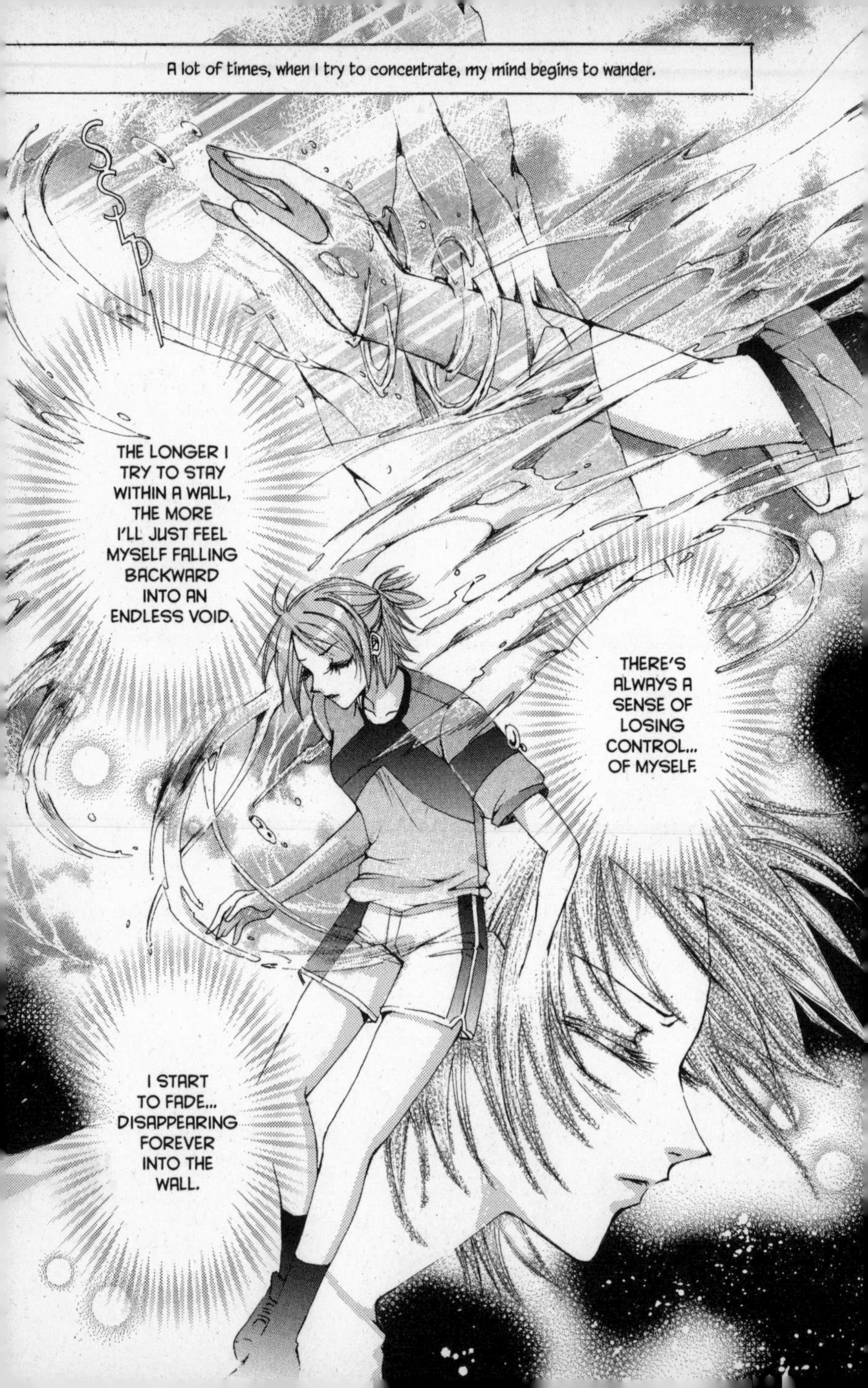
A lot of times, when I try to concentrate, my mind begins to wander.
THE LONGER I TRY TO STAY WITHIN A WALL, THE MORE I'LL JUST FEEL MYSELF FALLING BACKWARD INTO AN ENDLESS VOID.
THERE'S ALWAYS A SENSE OF LOSING CONTROL... OF MYSELF.
I START TO FADE... DISAPPEARING FOREVER INTO THE WALL.

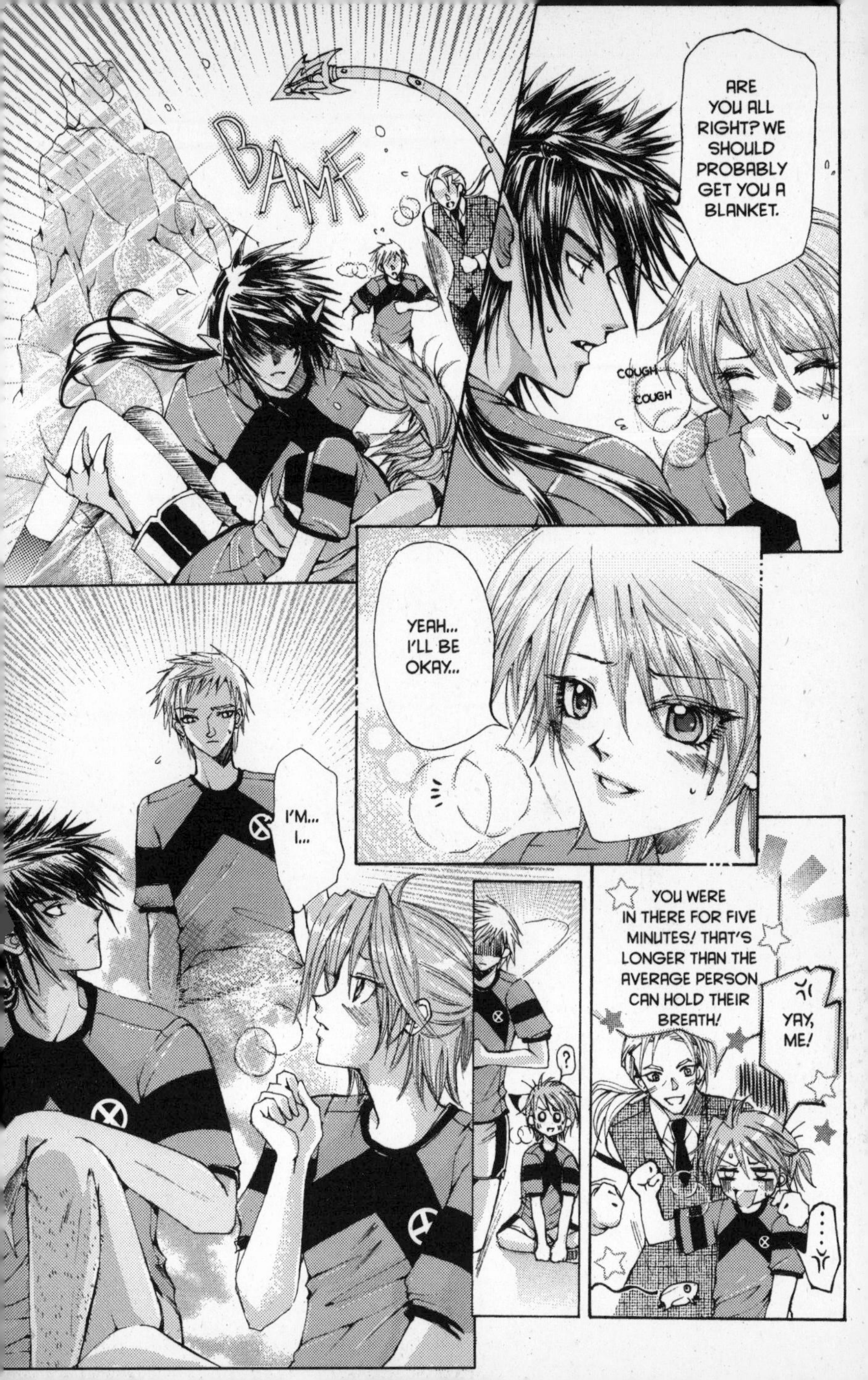
BAMF
ARE YOU ALL RIGHT? WE SHOULD PROBABLY GET YOU A BLANKET.
COUGH
COUGH
I'M... I...
YEAH... I'LL BE OKAY...
?
YOU WERE IN THERE FOR FIVE MINUTES! THAT'S LONGER THAN THE AVERAGE PERSON CAN HOLD THEIR BREATH!
YAY, ME!
.....

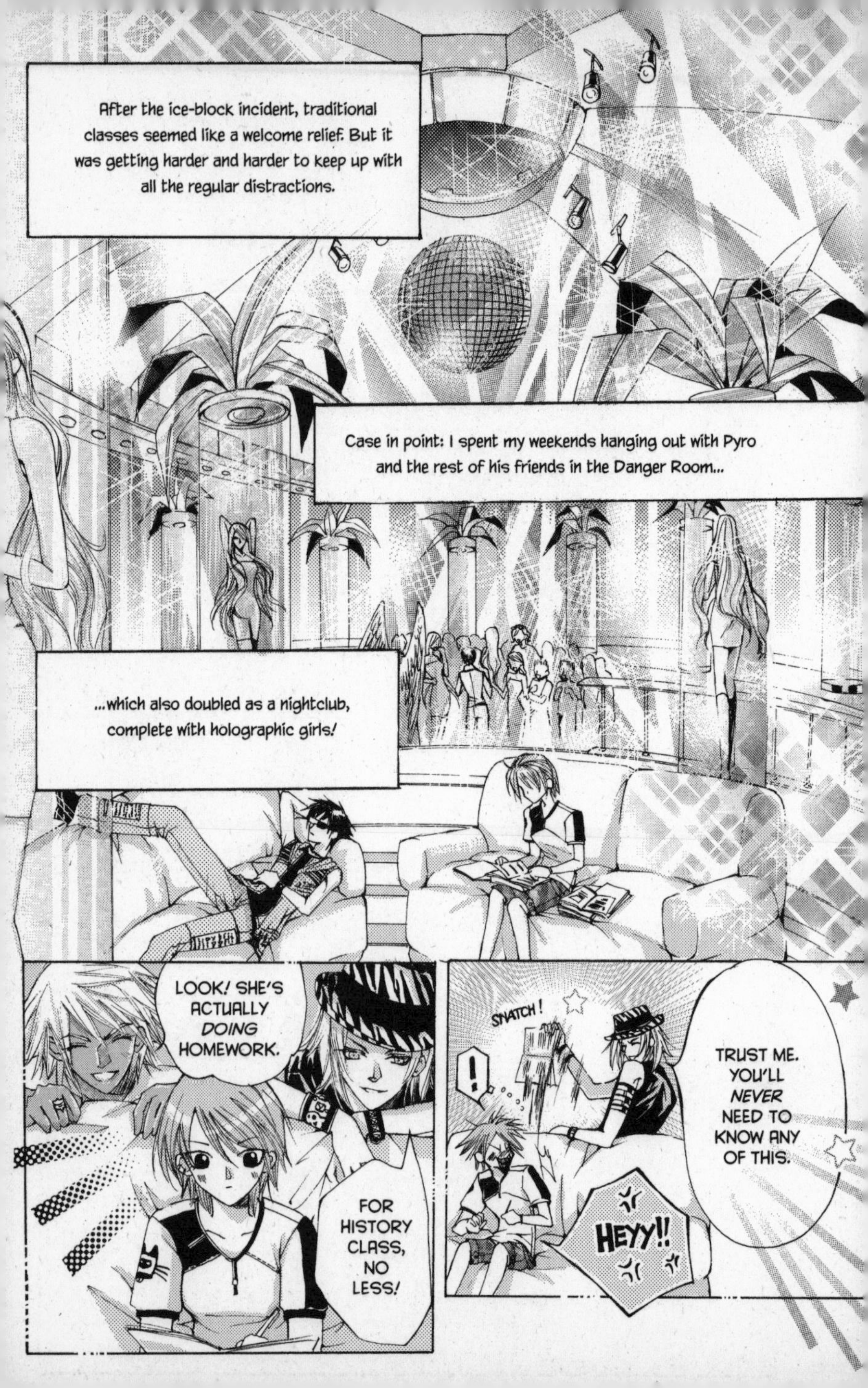
After the ice-block incident, traditional classes seemed like a welcome relief. But it was getting harder and harder to keep up with all the regular distractions.
Case in point: I spent my weekends hanging out with Pyro and the rest of his friends in the Danger Room...
...which also doubled as a nightclub, complete with holographic girls!
LOOK! SHE'S ACTUALLY *DOING* HOMEWORK.
FOR HISTORY CLASS, NO LESS!
SNATCH!
!
TRUST ME. YOU'LL *NEVER* NEED TO KNOW ANY OF THIS.
HEYY!!

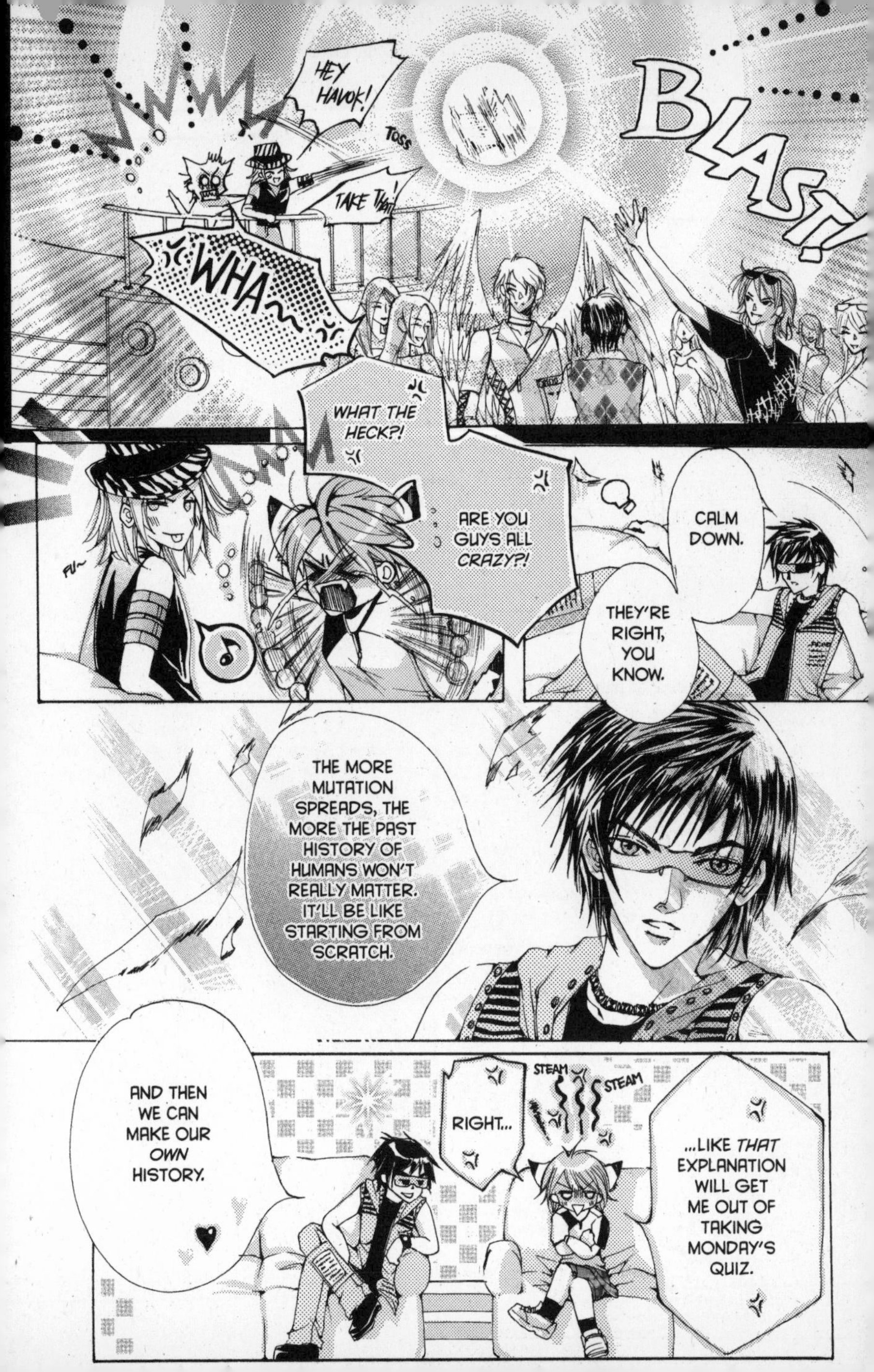
HEY HAVOK!
TOSS
BLAST!!
TAKE THAT!
WHA~
WHAT THE HECK?!
FU~
ARE YOU GUYS ALL CRAZY?!
CALM DOWN.
THEY'RE RIGHT, YOU KNOW.
THE MORE MUTATION SPREADS, THE MORE THE PAST HISTORY OF HUMANS WON'T REALLY MATTER. IT'LL BE LIKE STARTING FROM SCRATCH.
AND THEN WE CAN MAKE OUR OWN HISTORY.
RIGHT...
STEAM
STEAM
...LIKE THAT EXPLANATION WILL GET ME OUT OF TAKING MONDAY'S QUIZ.

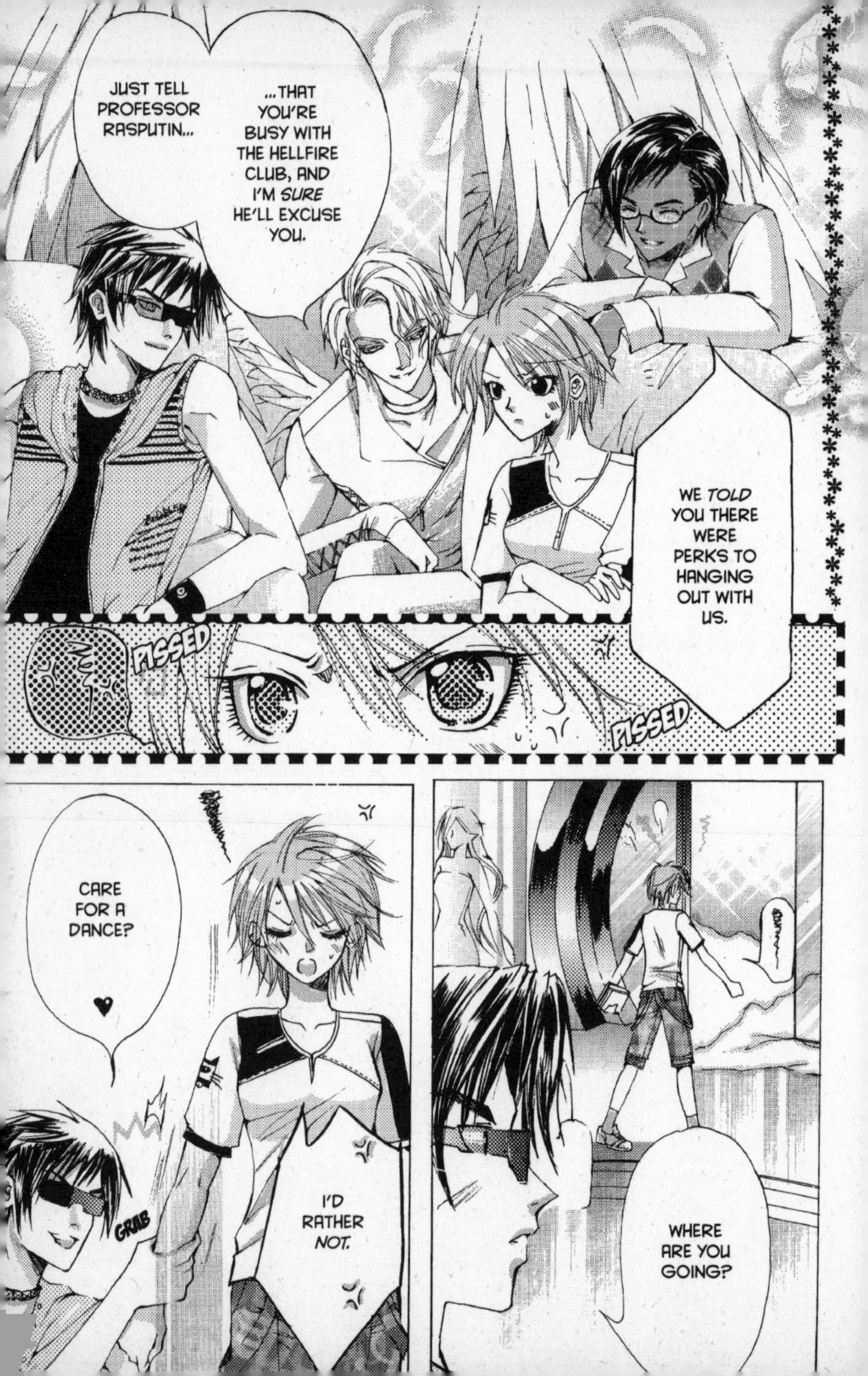
JUST TELL PROFESSOR RASPUTIN...
...THAT YOU'RE BUSY WITH THE HELLFIRE CLUB, AND I'M *SURE* HE'LL EXCUSE YOU.
WE *TOLD* YOU THERE WERE PERKS TO HANGING OUT WITH US.
PISSED
PISSED
CARE FOR A DANCE? ♥
GRAB
I'D RATHER *NOT.*
WHERE ARE YOU GOING?

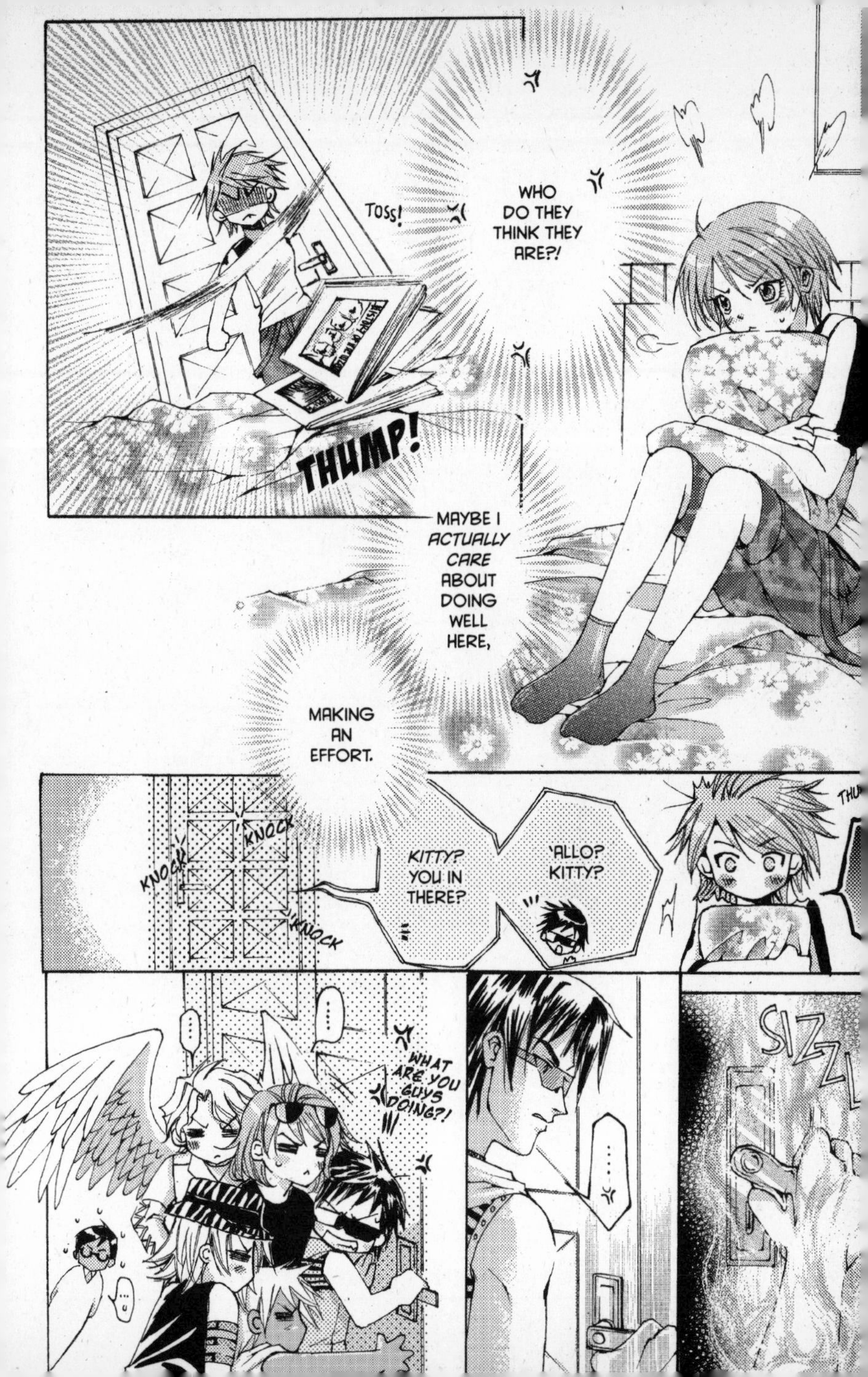
TOSS!
THUMP!
WHO DO THEY THINK THEY ARE?!
MAYBE I ACTUALLY CARE ABOUT DOING WELL HERE,
MAKING AN EFFORT.
KNOCK
KNOCK
KNOCK
KITTY? YOU IN THERE?
'ALLO? KITTY?
...
...
WHAT ARE YOU GUYS DOING?!
...
...

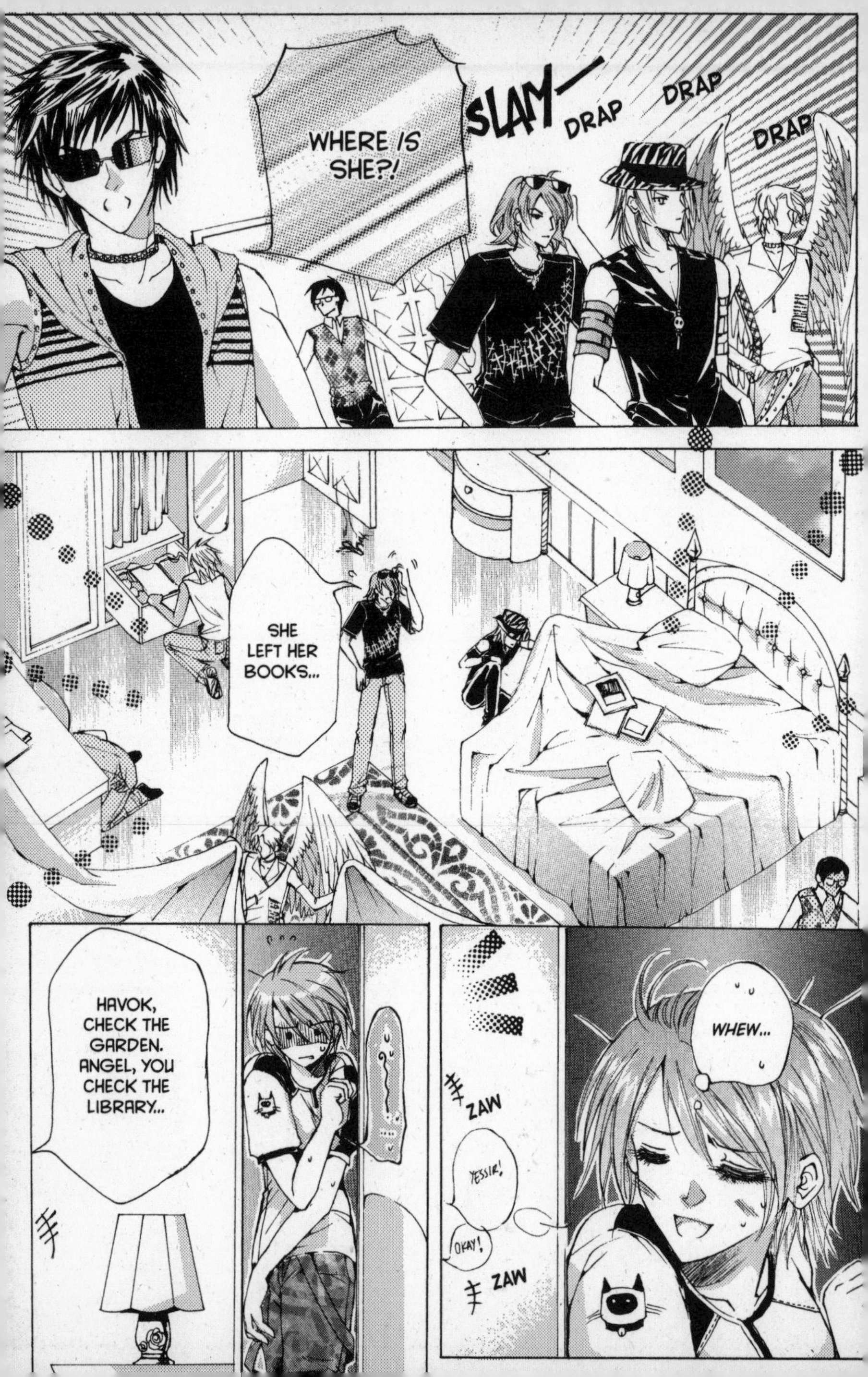
WHERE IS SHE?!
SLAM—
DRAP
DRAP
DRAP
SHE LEFT HER BOOKS...
HAVOK, CHECK THE GARDEN. ANGEL, YOU CHECK THE LIBRARY...
ZAW
YESSIR!
OKAY!
ZAW
WHEW...

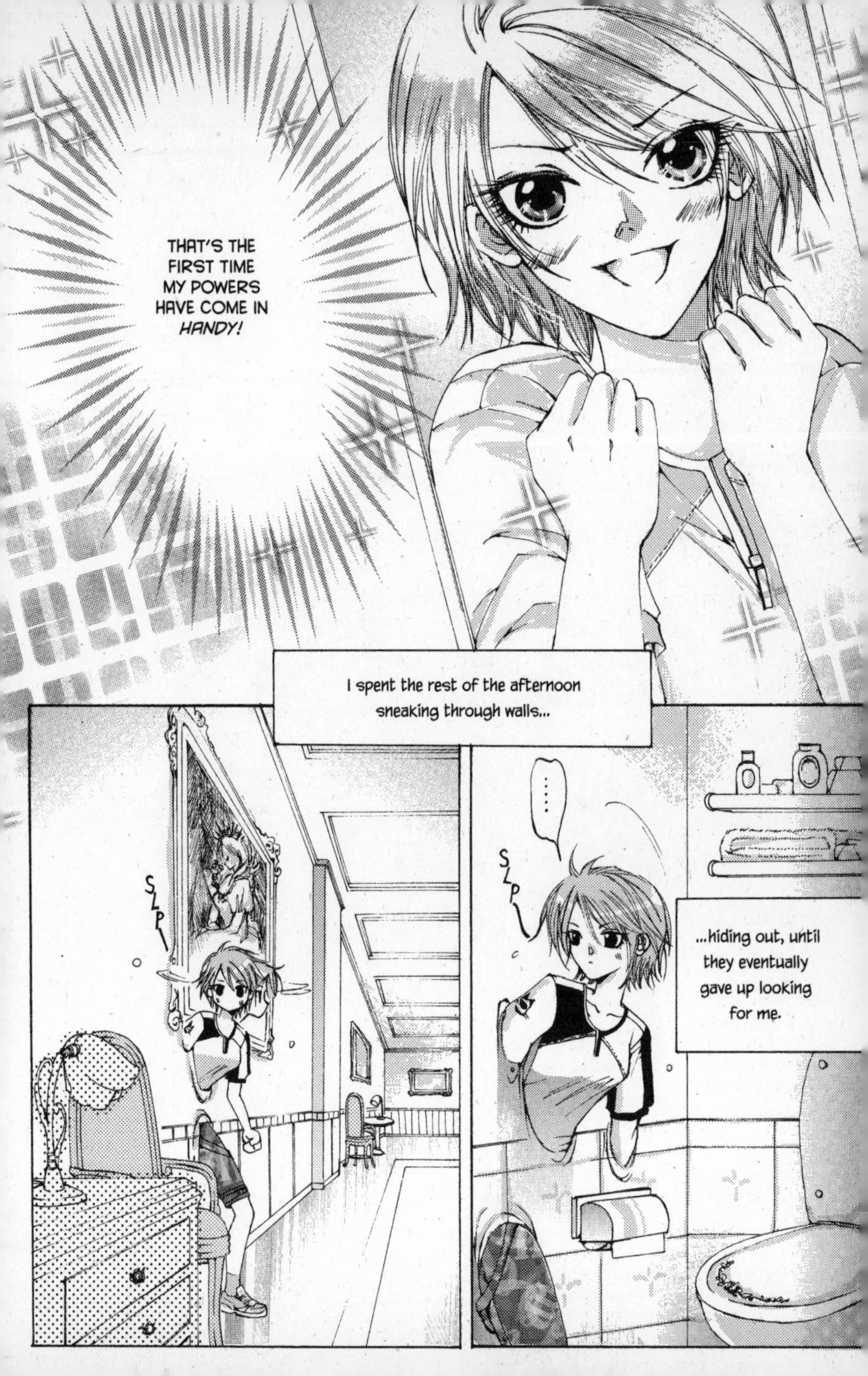
THAT'S THE FIRST TIME MY POWERS HAVE COME IN HANDY!
I spent the rest of the afternoon sneaking through walls...
SLP
SLP
......
...hiding out, until they eventually gave up looking for me.

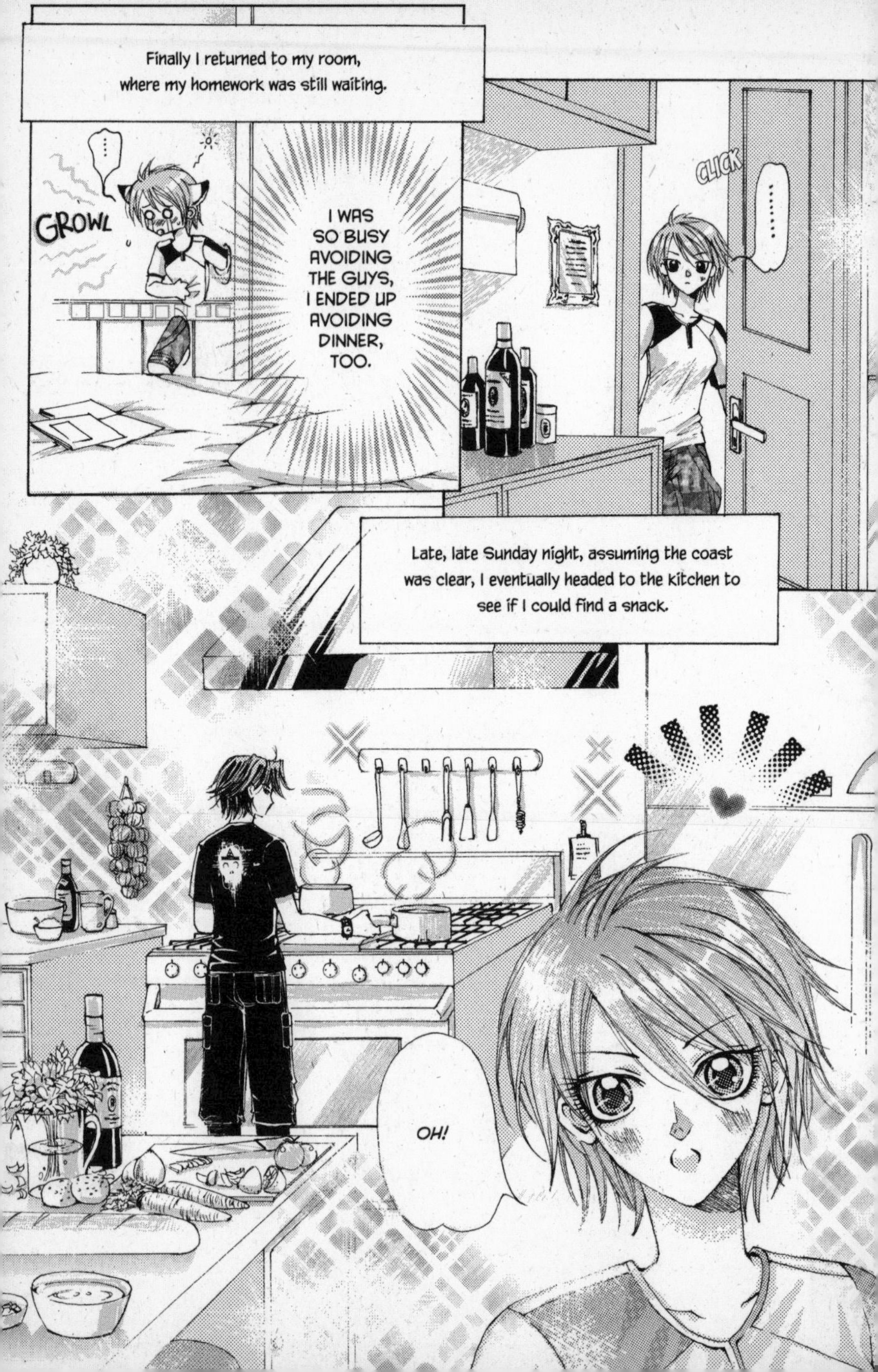
Finally I returned to my room, where my homework was still waiting.
...
GROWL
I WAS SO BUSY AVOIDING THE GUYS, I ENDED UP AVOIDING DINNER, TOO.
CLICK
......
Late, late Sunday night, assuming the coast was clear, I eventually headed to the kitchen to see if I could find a snack.
OH!

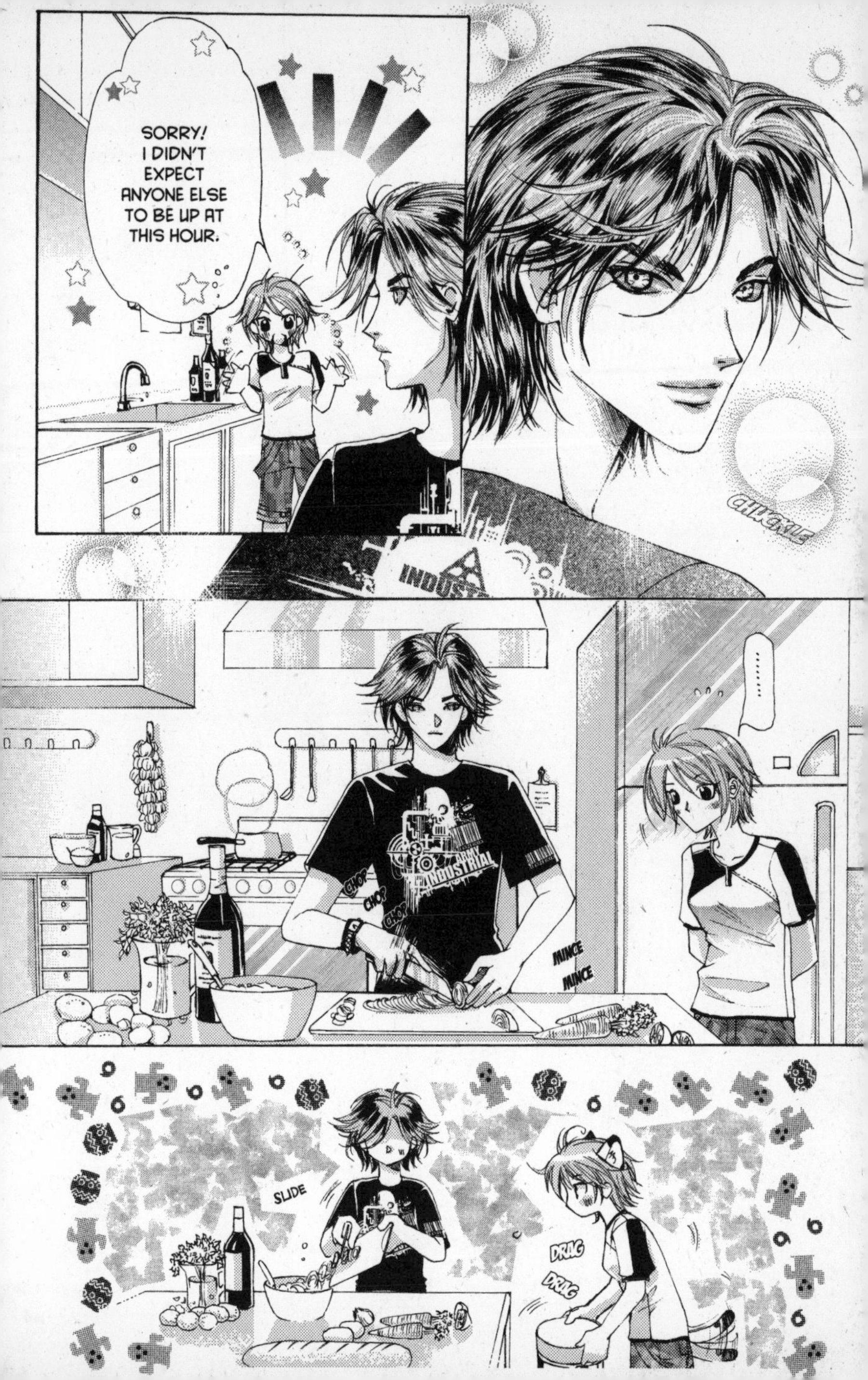
SORRY! I DIDN'T EXPECT ANYONE ELSE TO BE UP AT THIS HOUR.
CHUCKLE
INDUSTRIAL
......
CHOP
CHOP
CHOP
INDUSTRIAL
MINCE
MINCE
SLIDE
DRAG
DRAG

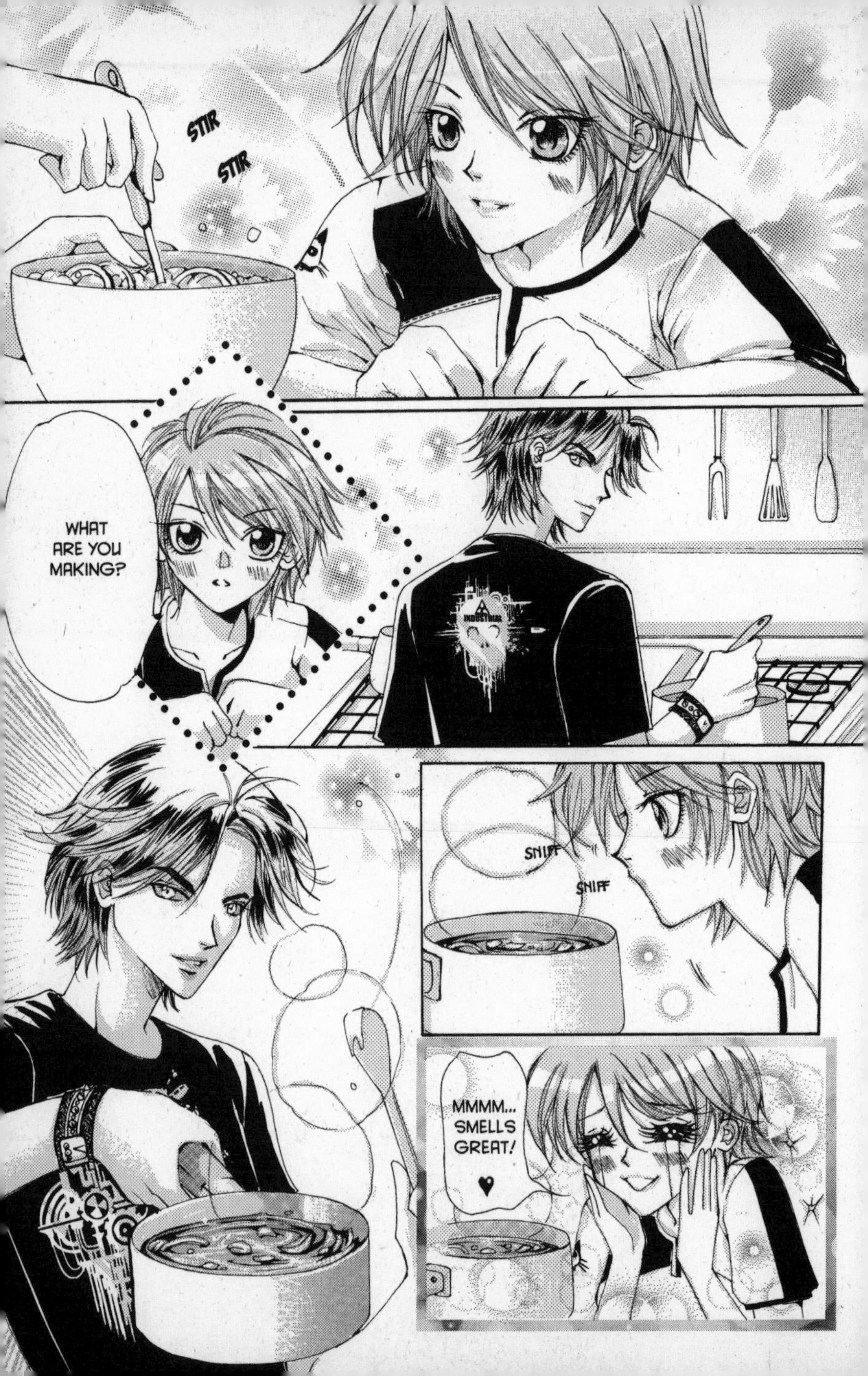
STIR
STIR
WHAT ARE YOU MAKING?
SNIFF
SNIFF
MMMM... SMELLS GREAT! ♥

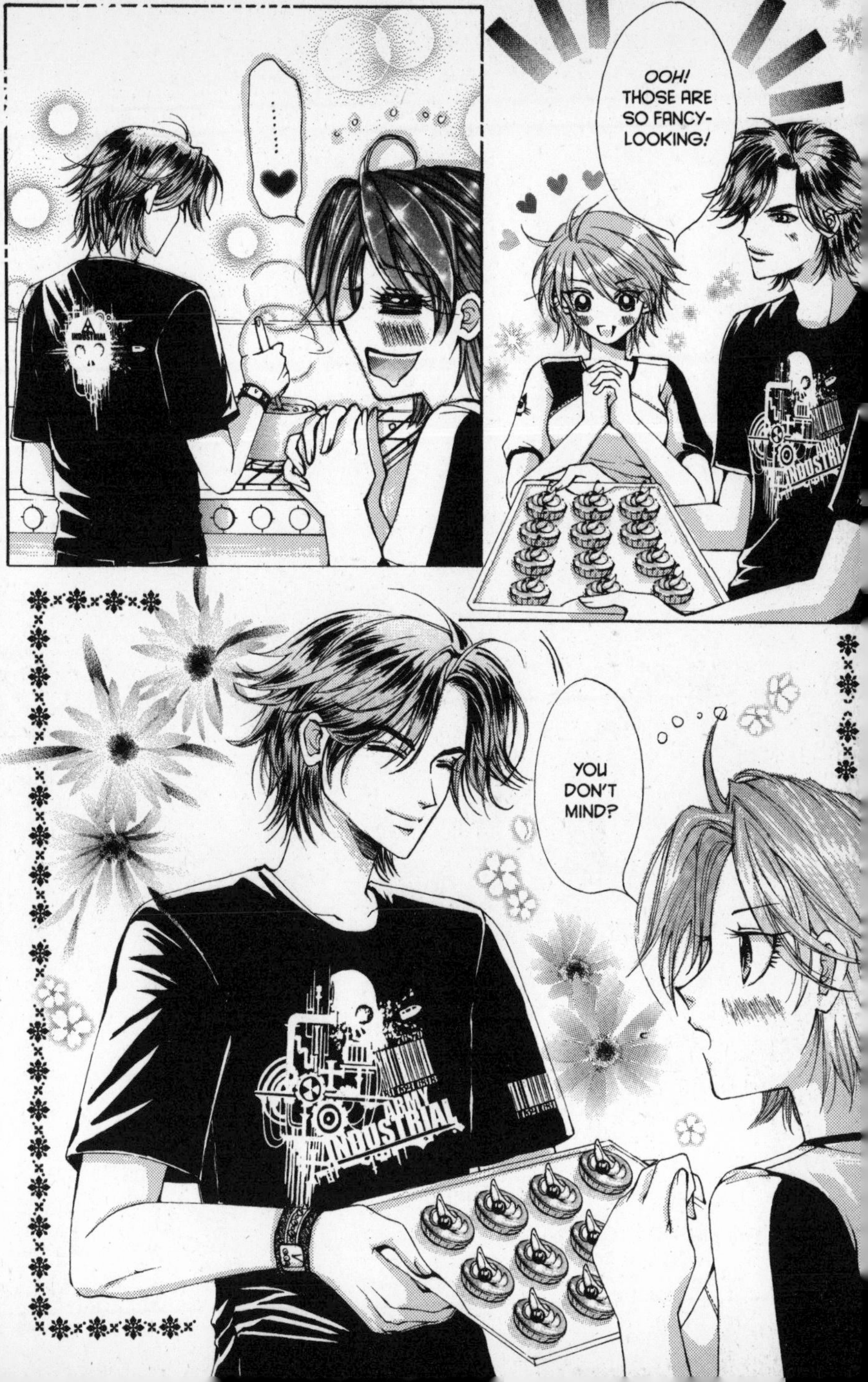
......
OOH! THOSE ARE SO FANCY-LOOKING!
YOU DON'T MIND?

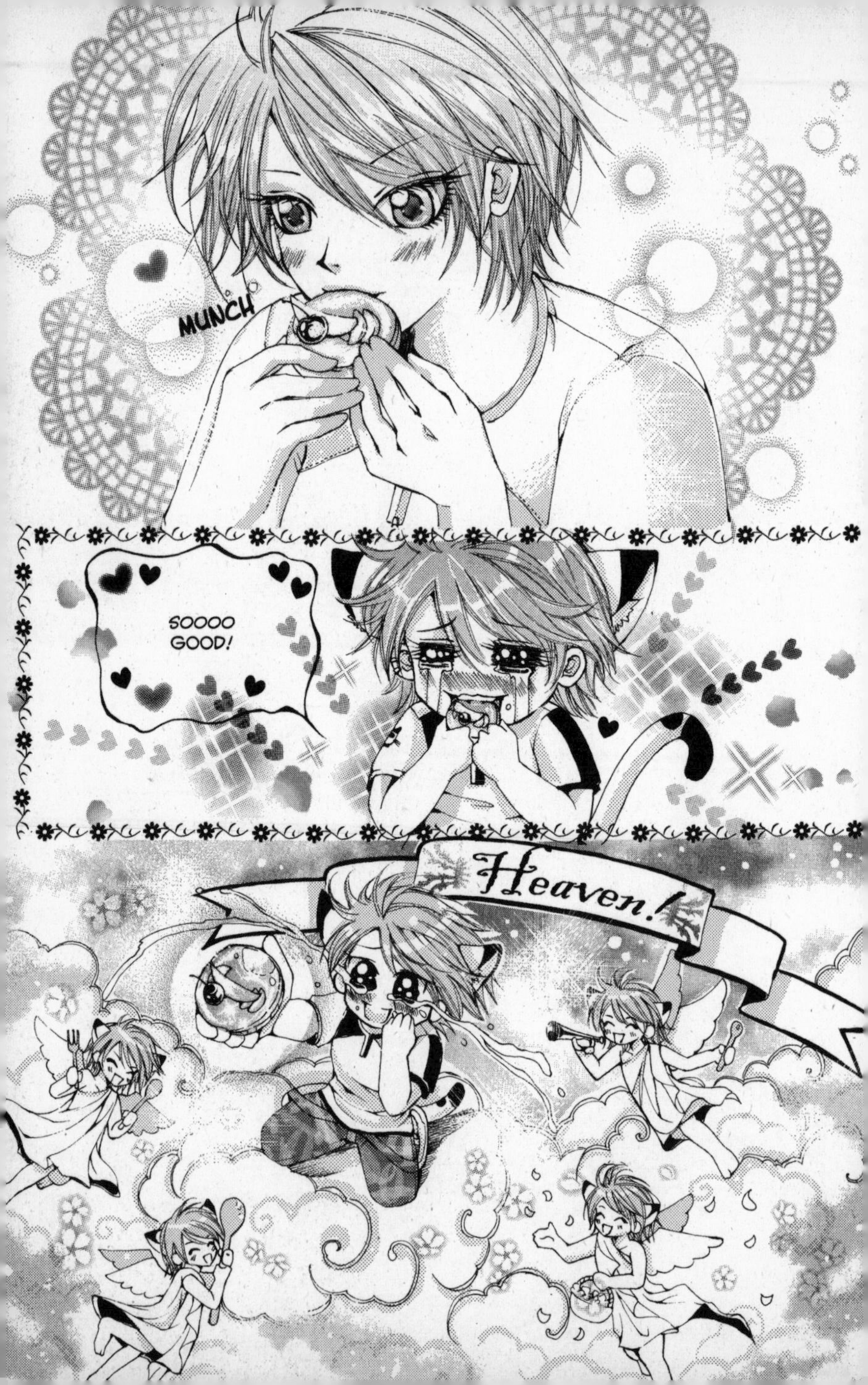
MUNCH
SOOOO GOOD!
Heaven!

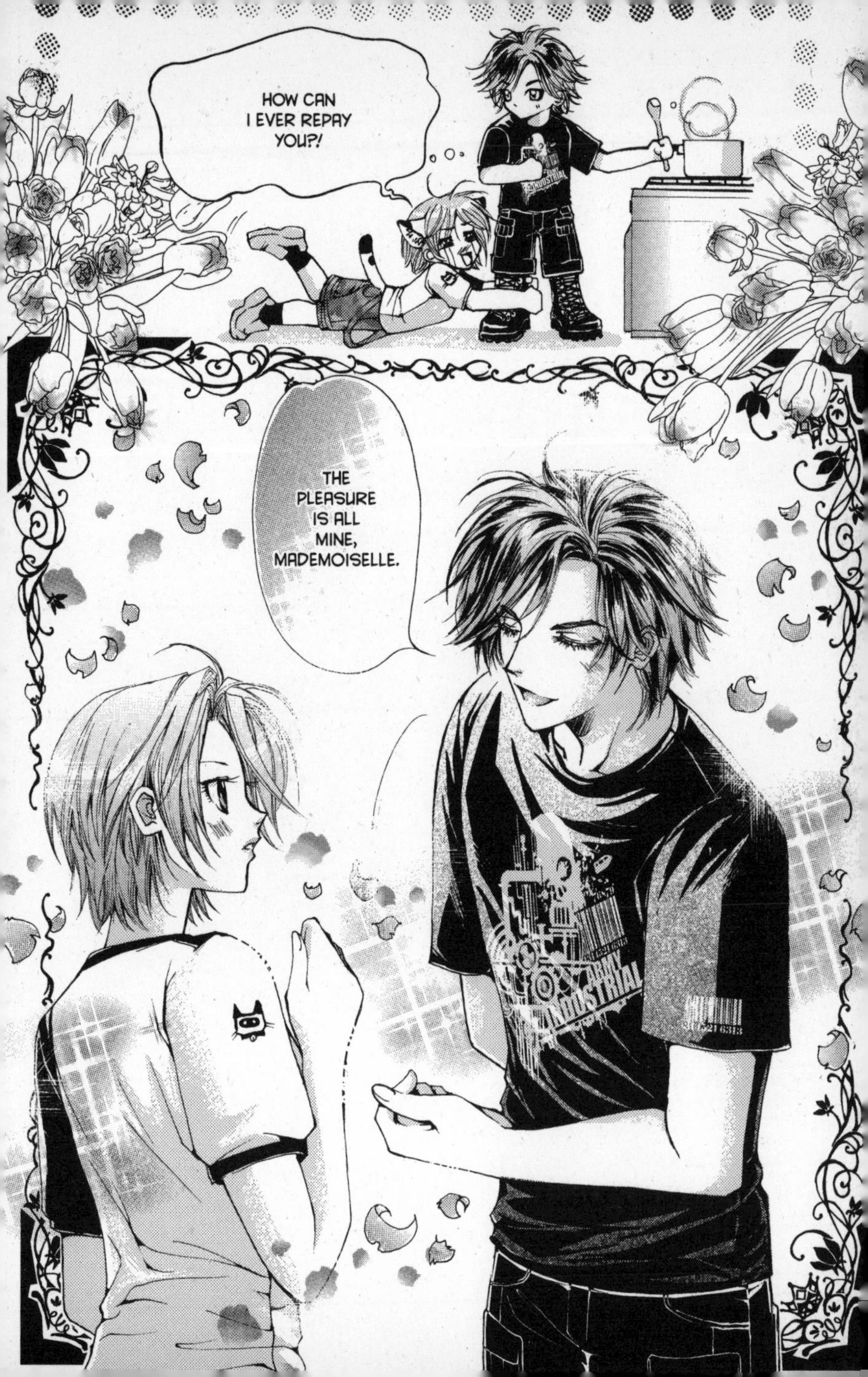
HOW CAN I EVER REPAY YOU?!
THE PLEASURE IS ALL MINE, MADEMOISELLE.

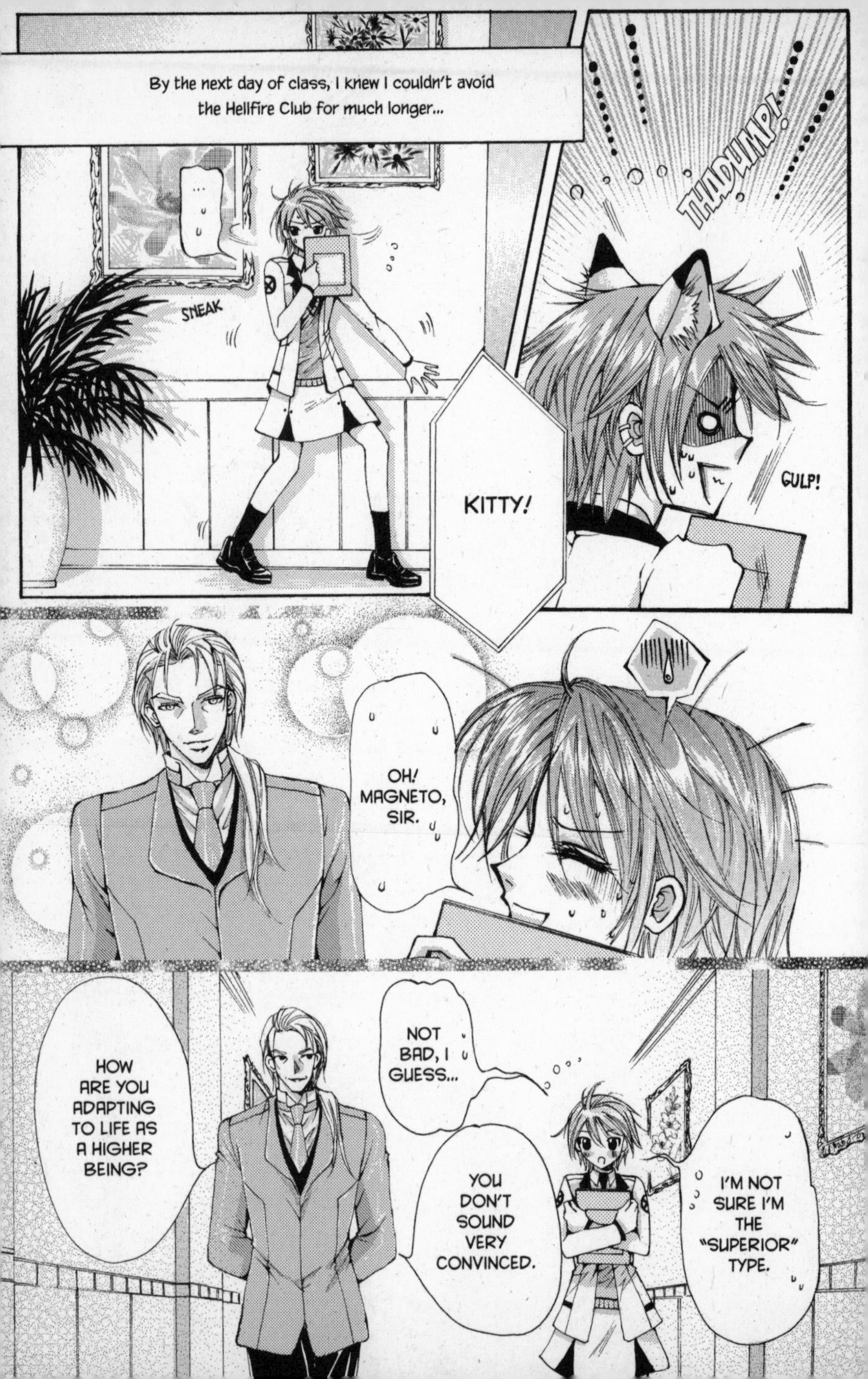
By the next day of class, I knew I couldn't avoid the Hellfire Club for much longer...
...
SNEAK
THADUMP!
KITTY!
GULP!
OH! MAGNETO, SIR.
HOW ARE YOU ADAPTING TO LIFE AS A HIGHER BEING?
NOT BAD, I GUESS...
YOU DON'T SOUND VERY CONVINCED.
I'M NOT SURE I'M THE "SUPERIOR" TYPE.

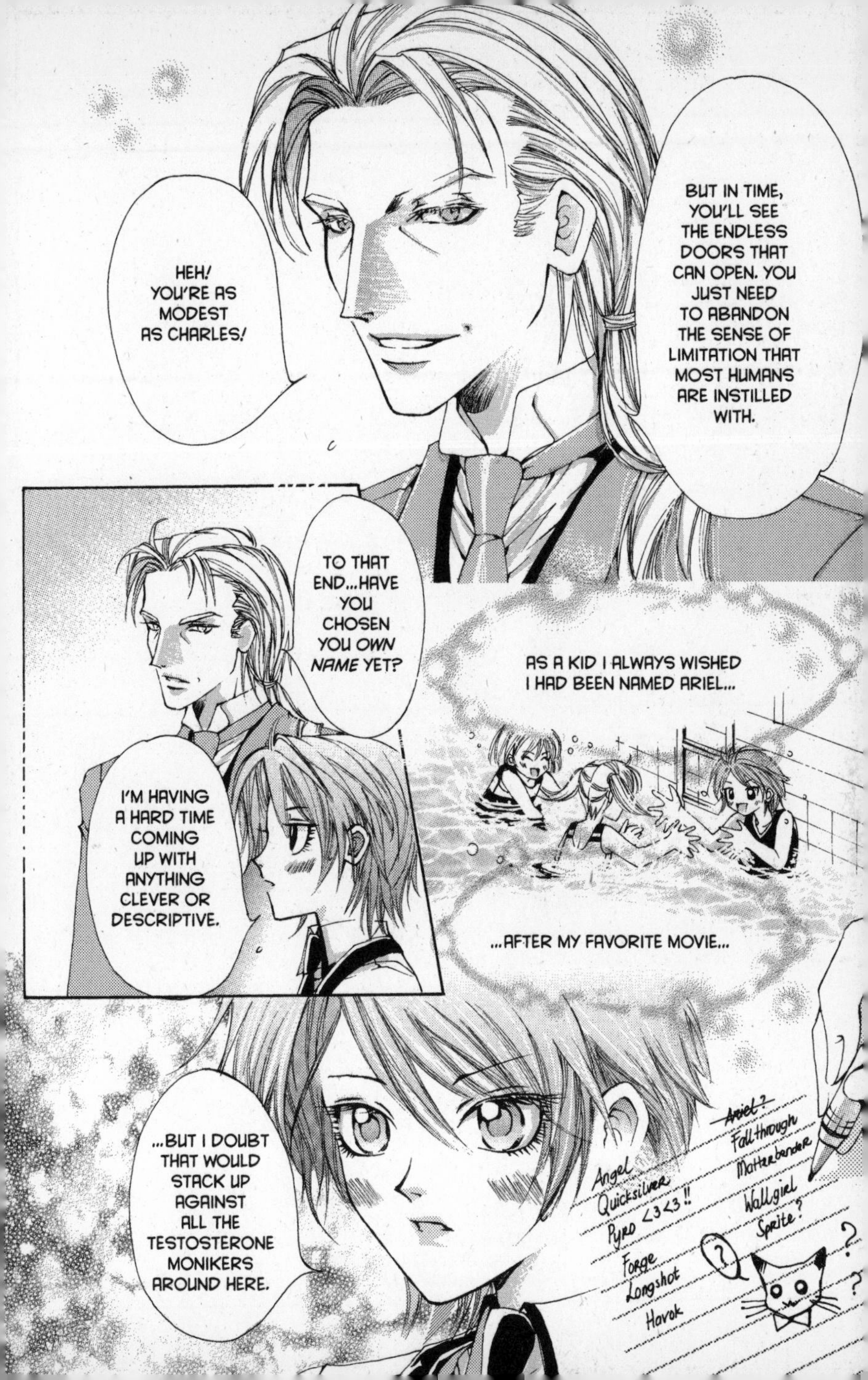
HEH! YOU'RE AS MODEST AS CHARLES!
BUT IN TIME, YOU'LL SEE THE ENDLESS DOORS THAT CAN OPEN. YOU JUST NEED TO ABANDON THE SENSE OF LIMITATION THAT MOST HUMANS ARE INSTILLED WITH.
TO THAT END...HAVE YOU CHOSEN YOU *OWN NAME* YET?
I'M HAVING A HARD TIME COMING UP WITH ANYTHING CLEVER OR DESCRIPTIVE.
AS A KID I ALWAYS WISHED I HAD BEEN NAMED ARIEL...
...AFTER MY FAVORITE MOVIE...
...BUT I DOUBT THAT WOULD STACK UP AGAINST ALL THE TESTOSTERONE MONIKERS AROUND HERE.
Angel
Quicksilver
Pyro <3<3!!
Forge
Longshot
Havok
Ariel?
Fallthrough
Matterbender
Wallgirl
Sprite?
?

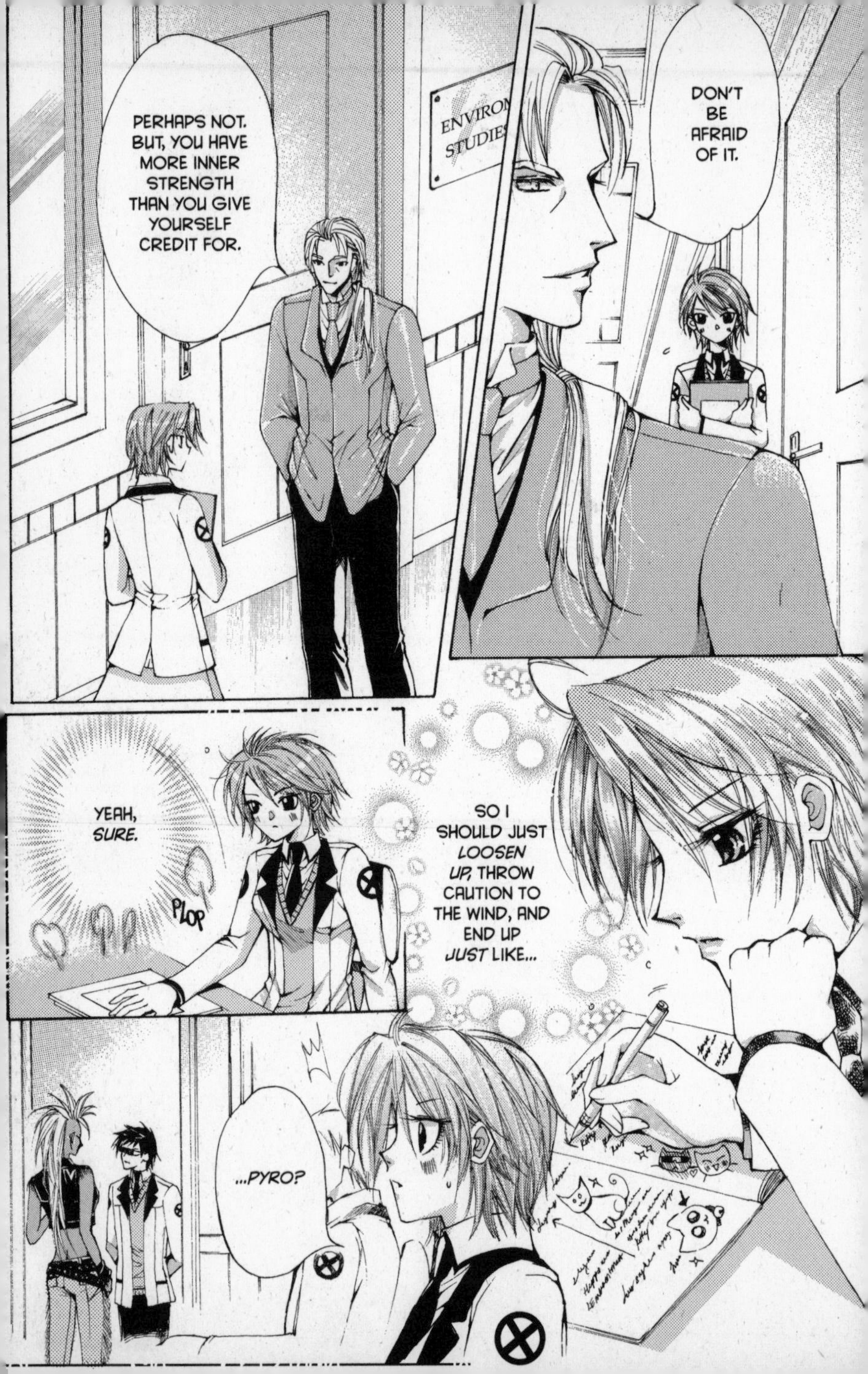
PERHAPS NOT. BUT, YOU HAVE MORE INNER STRENGTH THAN YOU GIVE YOURSELF CREDIT FOR.
ENVIRON
STUDIES
DON'T BE AFRAID OF IT.
YEAH, *SURE.*
PLOP
SO I SHOULD JUST *LOOSEN UP,* THROW CAUTION TO THE WIND, AND END UP *JUST* LIKE...
...PYRO?

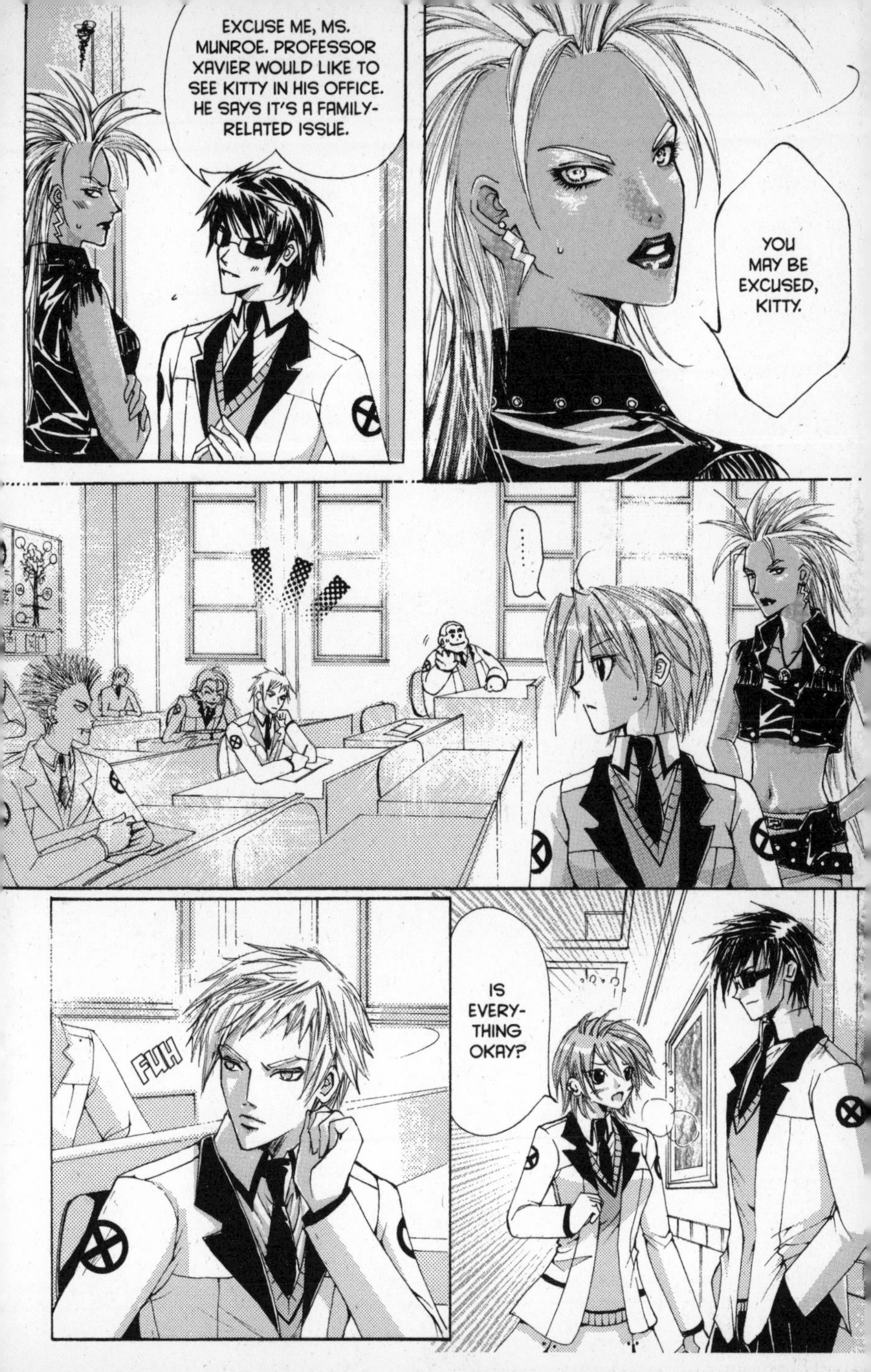
EXCUSE ME, MS. MUNROE. PROFESSOR XAVIER WOULD LIKE TO SEE KITTY IN HIS OFFICE. HE SAYS IT'S A FAMILY-RELATED ISSUE.
YOU MAY BE EXCUSED, KITTY.
......
FUH
IS EVERY-THING OKAY?

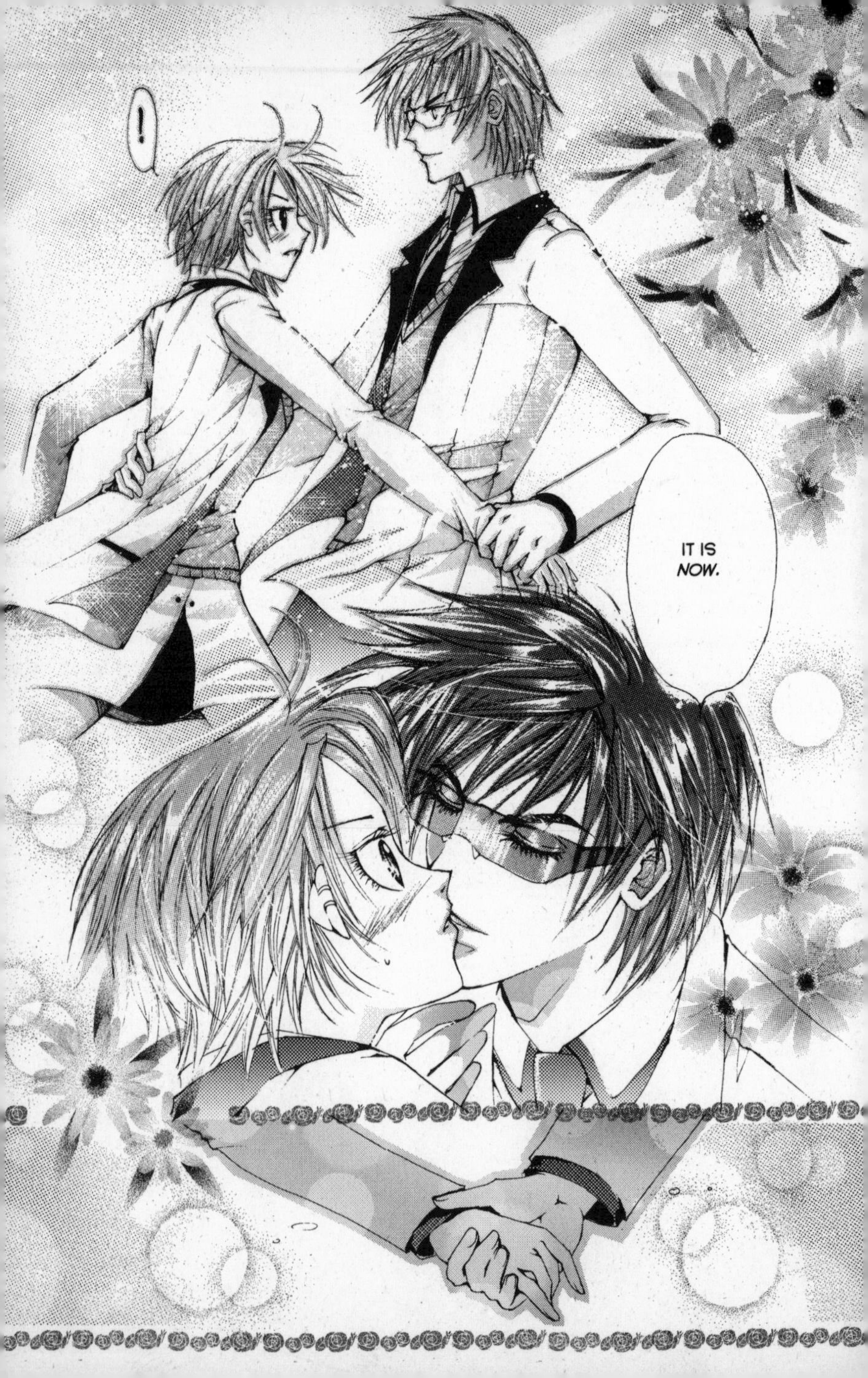
!
IT IS NOW.

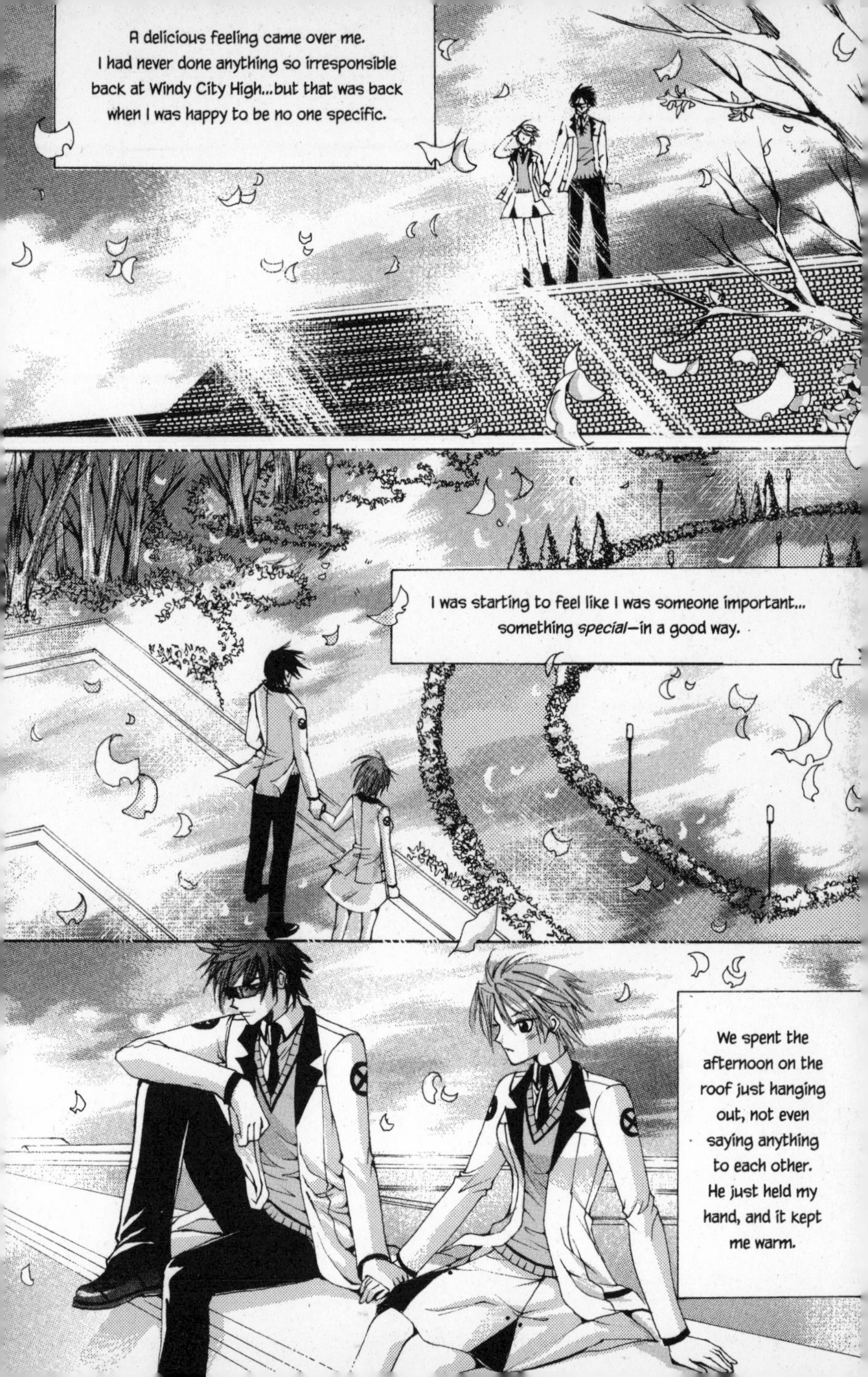
A delicious feeling came over me. I had never done anything so irresponsible back at Windy City High...but that was back when I was happy to be no one specific.
I was starting to feel like I was someone important... something *special*—in a good way.
We spent the afternoon on the roof just hanging out, not even saying anything to each other. He just held my hand, and it kept me warm.

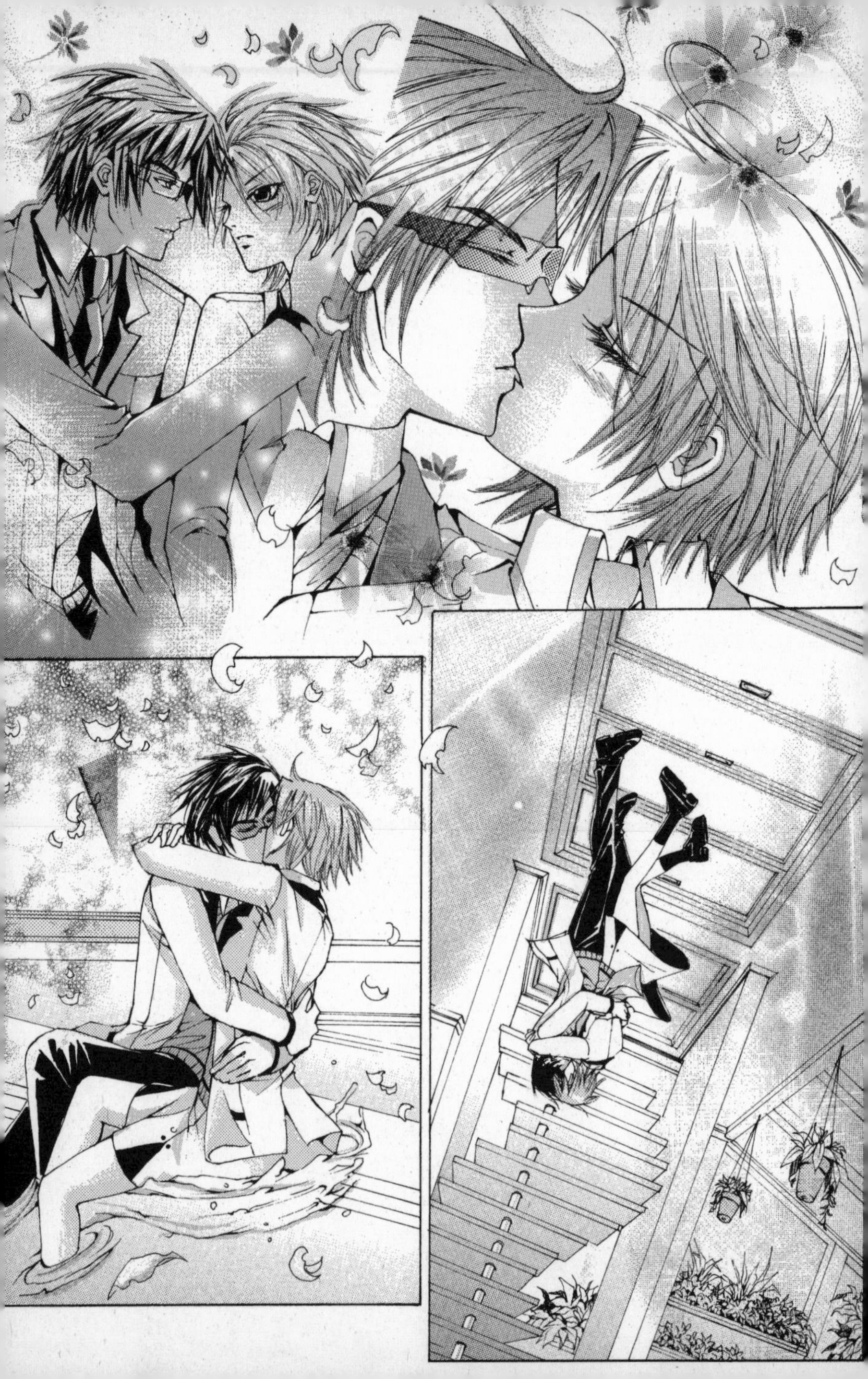

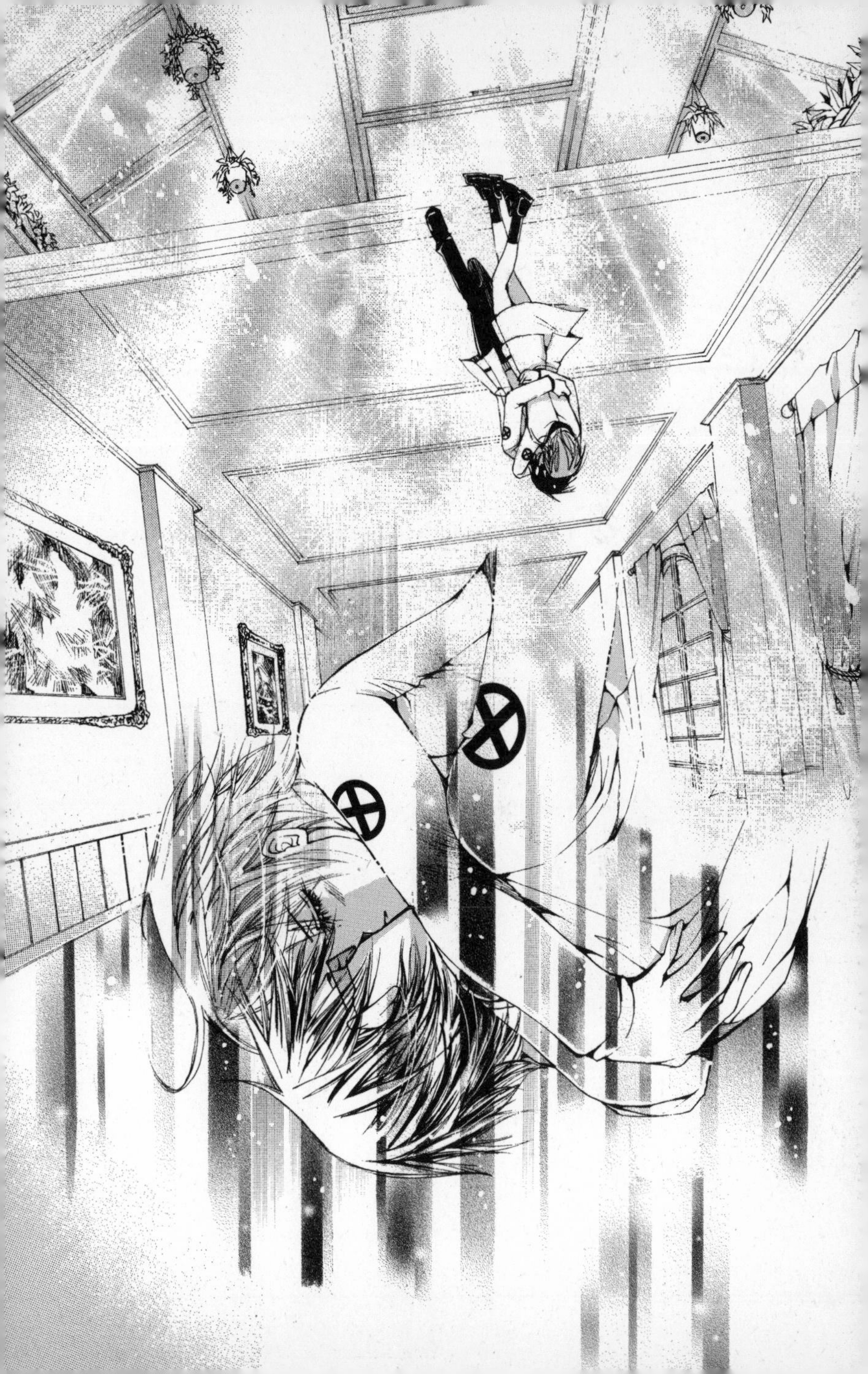

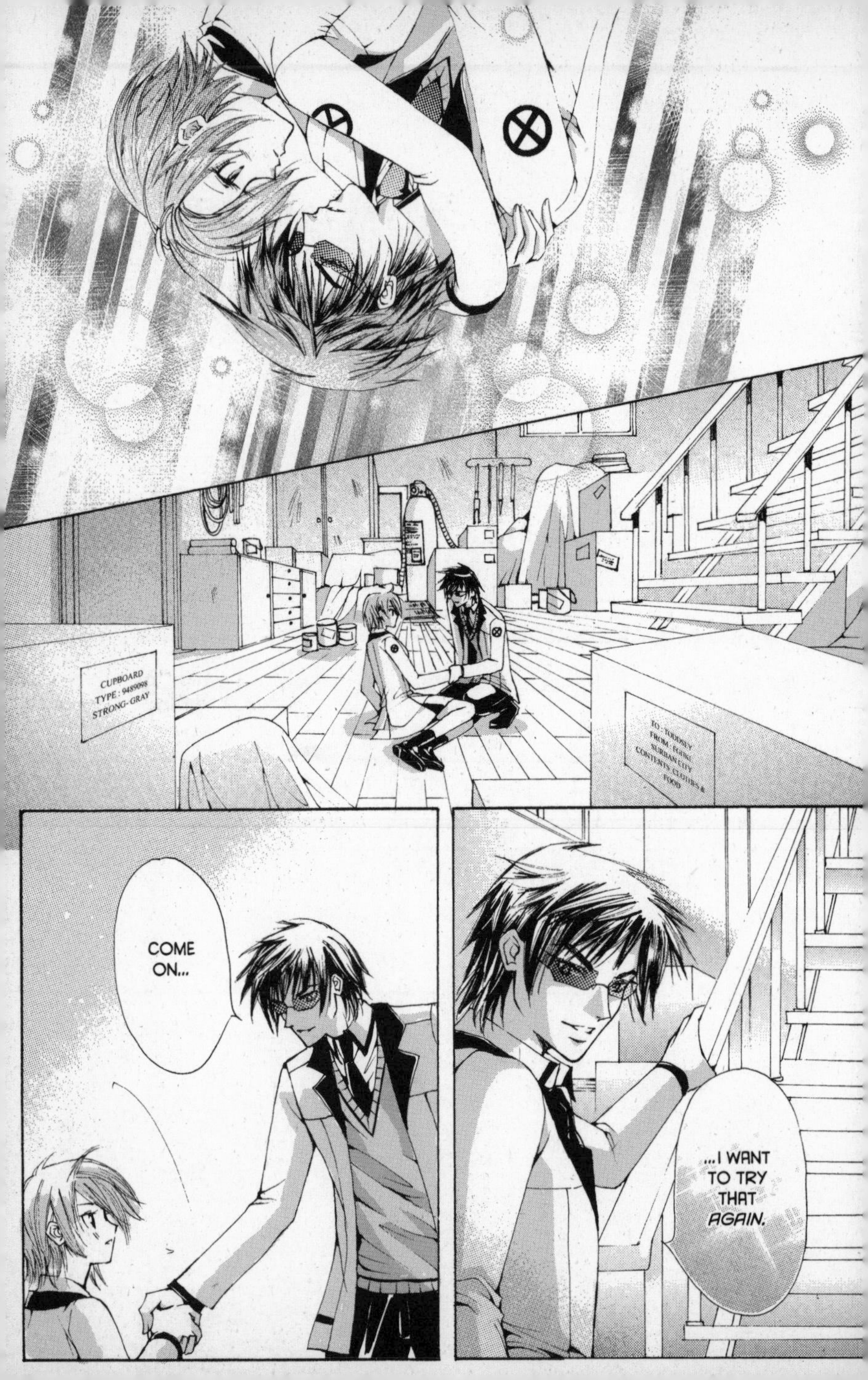
CUPBOARD
TYPE : 9489098
STRONG-GRAY
TO : TODDSEY
SURBAN CITY
CONTENTS : CLOTHES & FOOD
COME ON...
...I WANT TO TRY THAT *AGAIN.*

Chapter Three

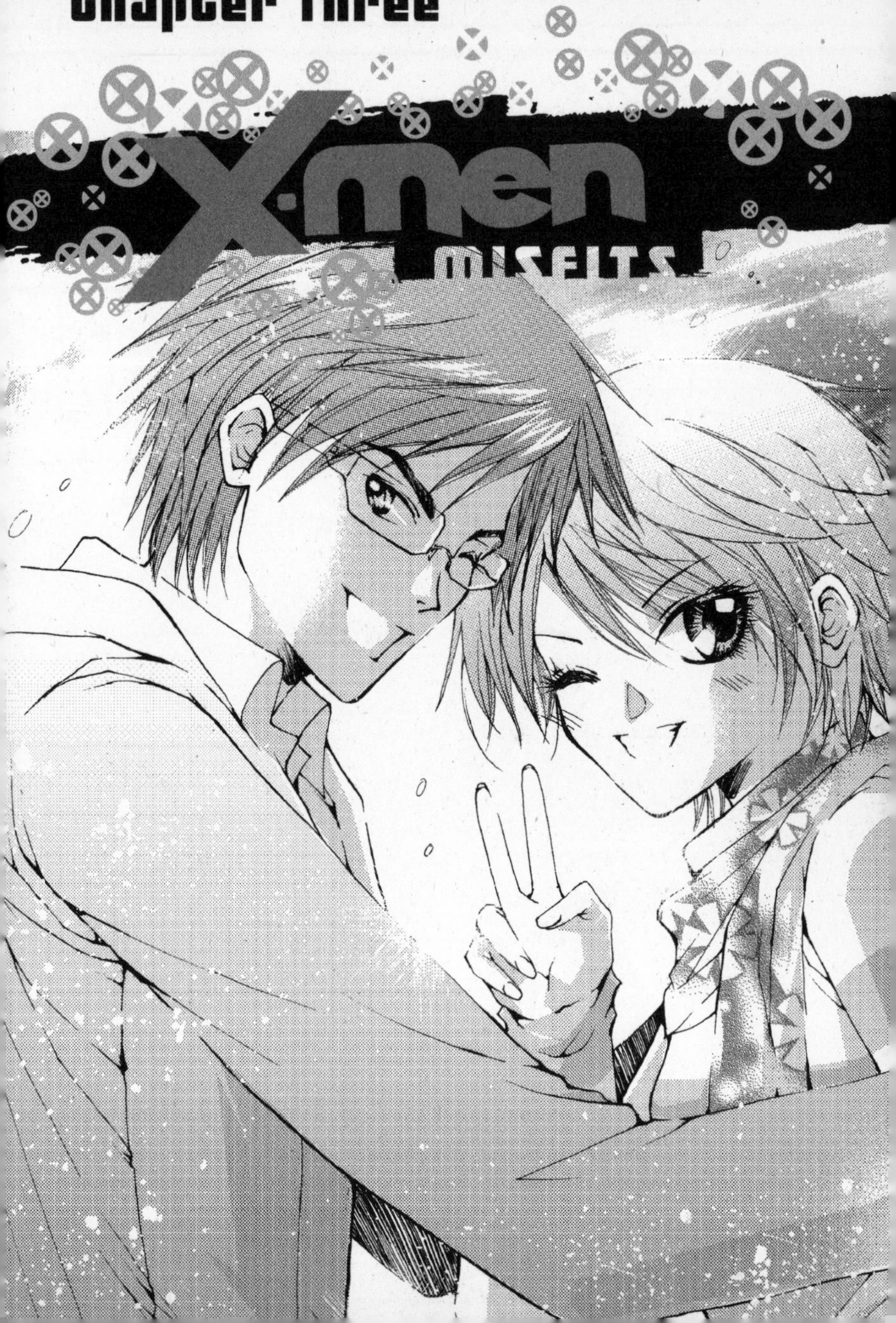
X-men
MISFITS

XAVIER'S SCHOOL
FOR GIFTED YOUNGSTERS

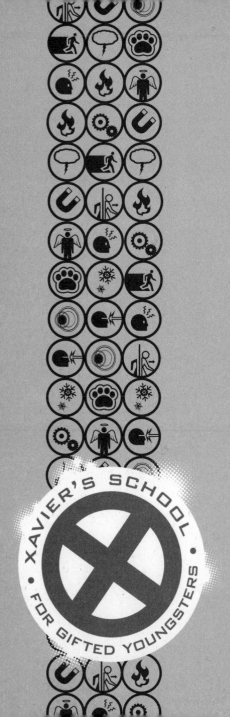

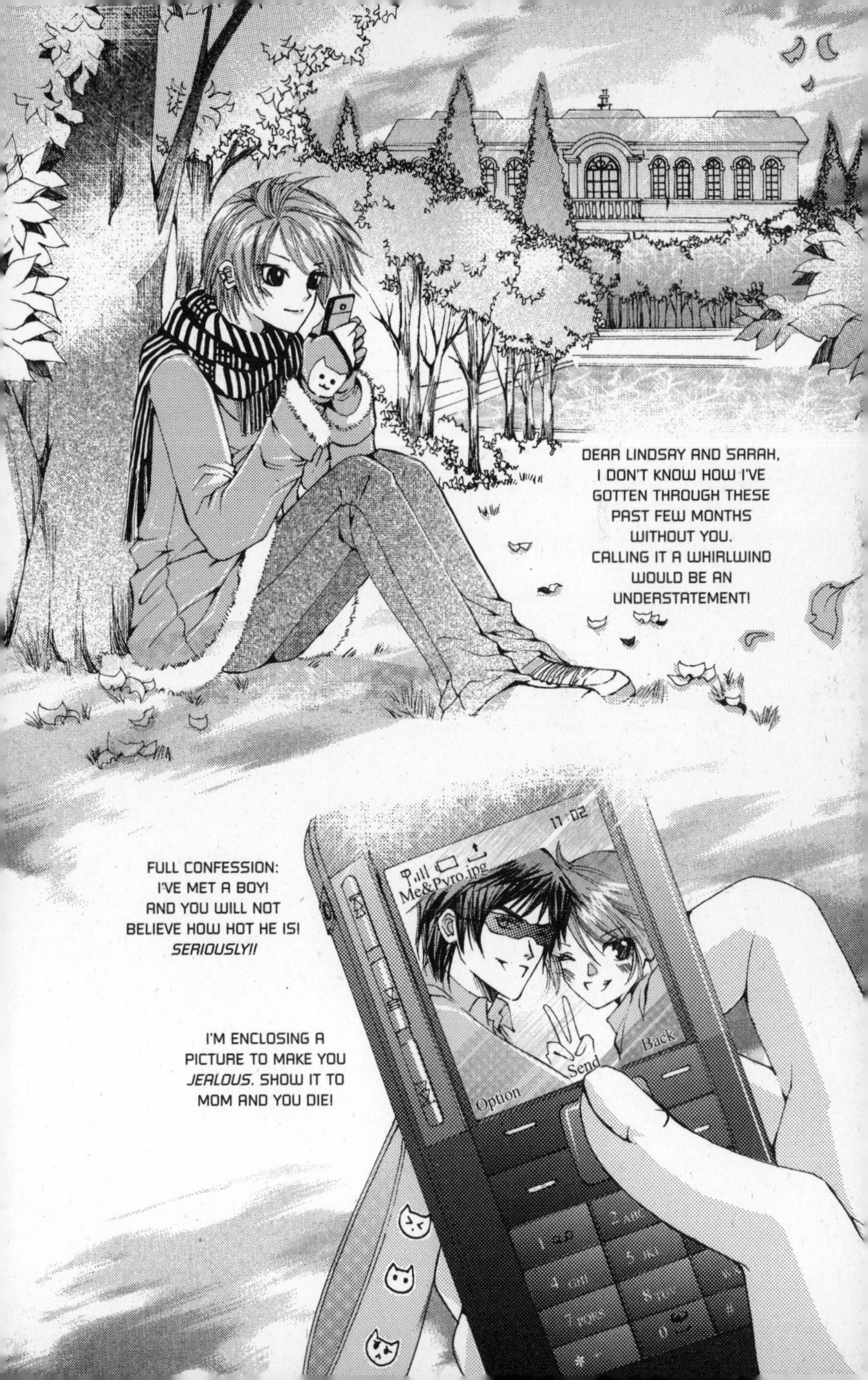
DEAR LINDSAY AND SARAH, I DON'T KNOW HOW I'VE GOTTEN THROUGH THESE PAST FEW MONTHS WITHOUT YOU. CALLING IT A WHIRLWIND WOULD BE AN UNDERSTATEMENT!
FULL CONFESSION: I'VE MET A BOY! AND YOU WILL NOT BELIEVE HOW HOT HE IS! *SERIOUSLY!!*
11:02
Me&Pyro.jpg
Back
Send
Option
I'M ENCLOSING A PICTURE TO MAKE YOU *JEALOUS.* SHOW IT TO MOM AND YOU DIE!

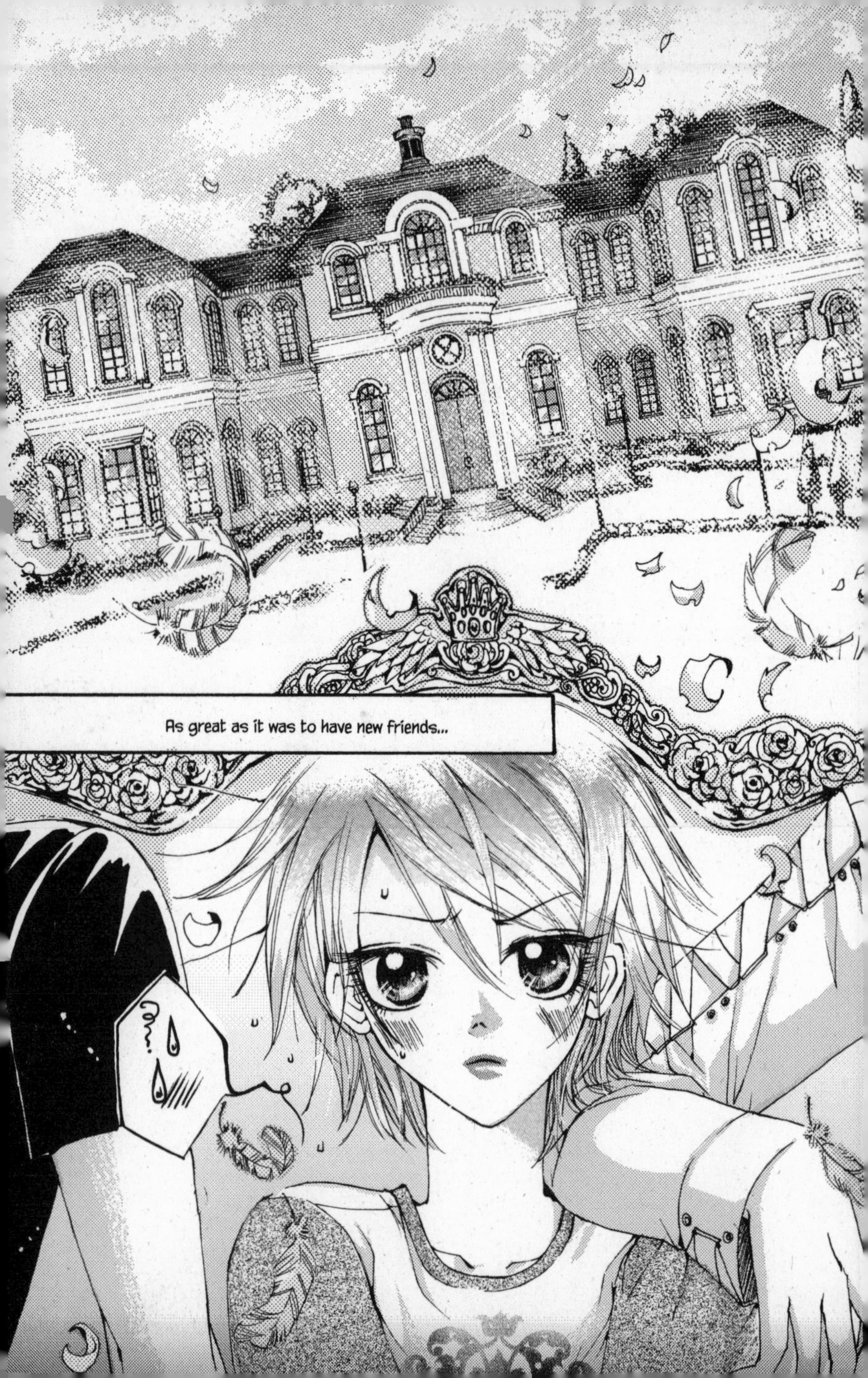
As great as it was to have new friends...

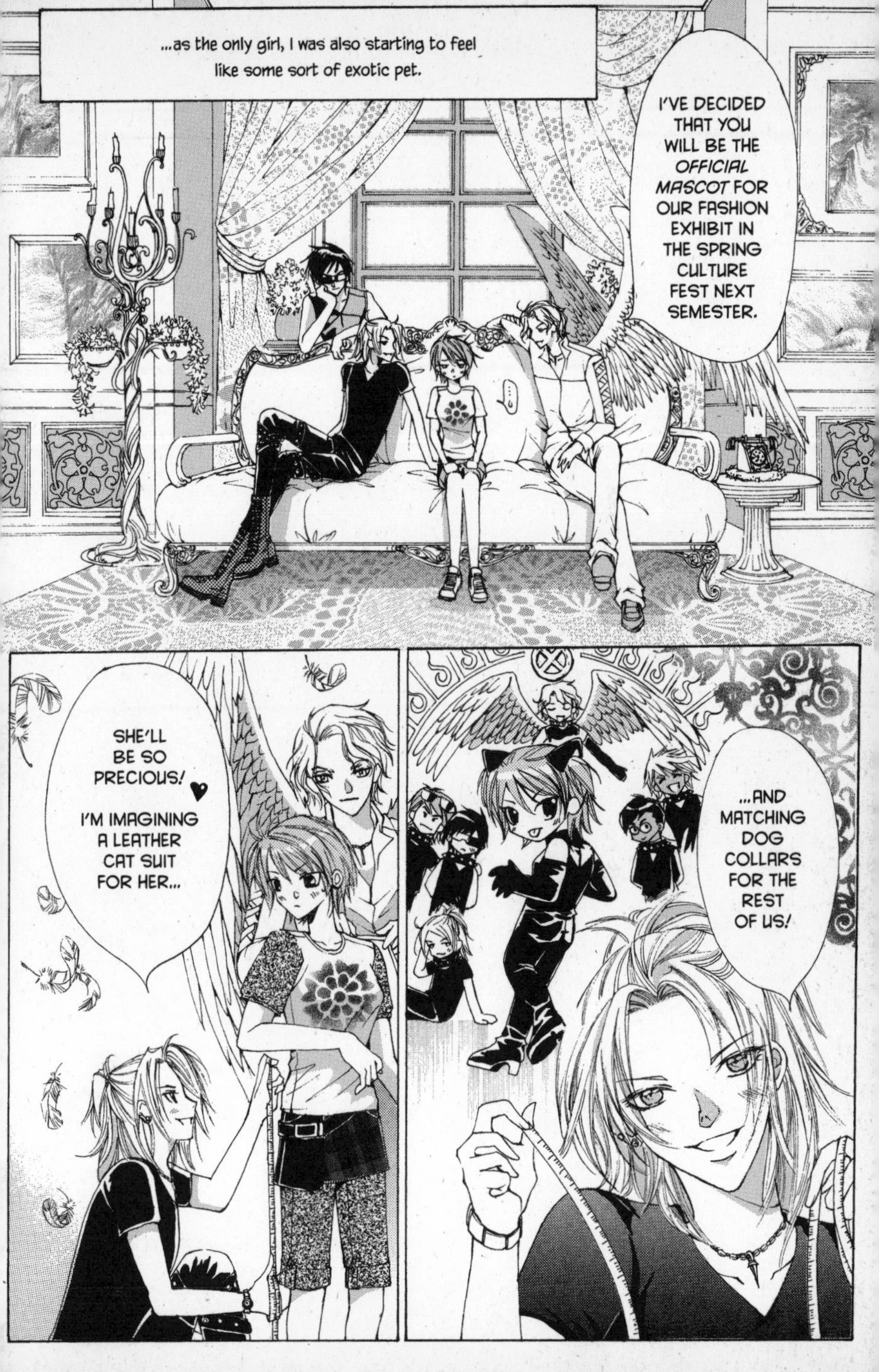
...as the only girl, I was also starting to feel like some sort of exotic pet.
I'VE DECIDED THAT YOU WILL BE THE *OFFICIAL MASCOT* FOR OUR FASHION EXHIBIT IN THE SPRING CULTURE FEST NEXT SEMESTER.
SHE'LL BE SO PRECIOUS! ♥ I'M IMAGINING A LEATHER CAT SUIT FOR HER...
...AND MATCHING DOG COLLARS FOR THE REST OF US!

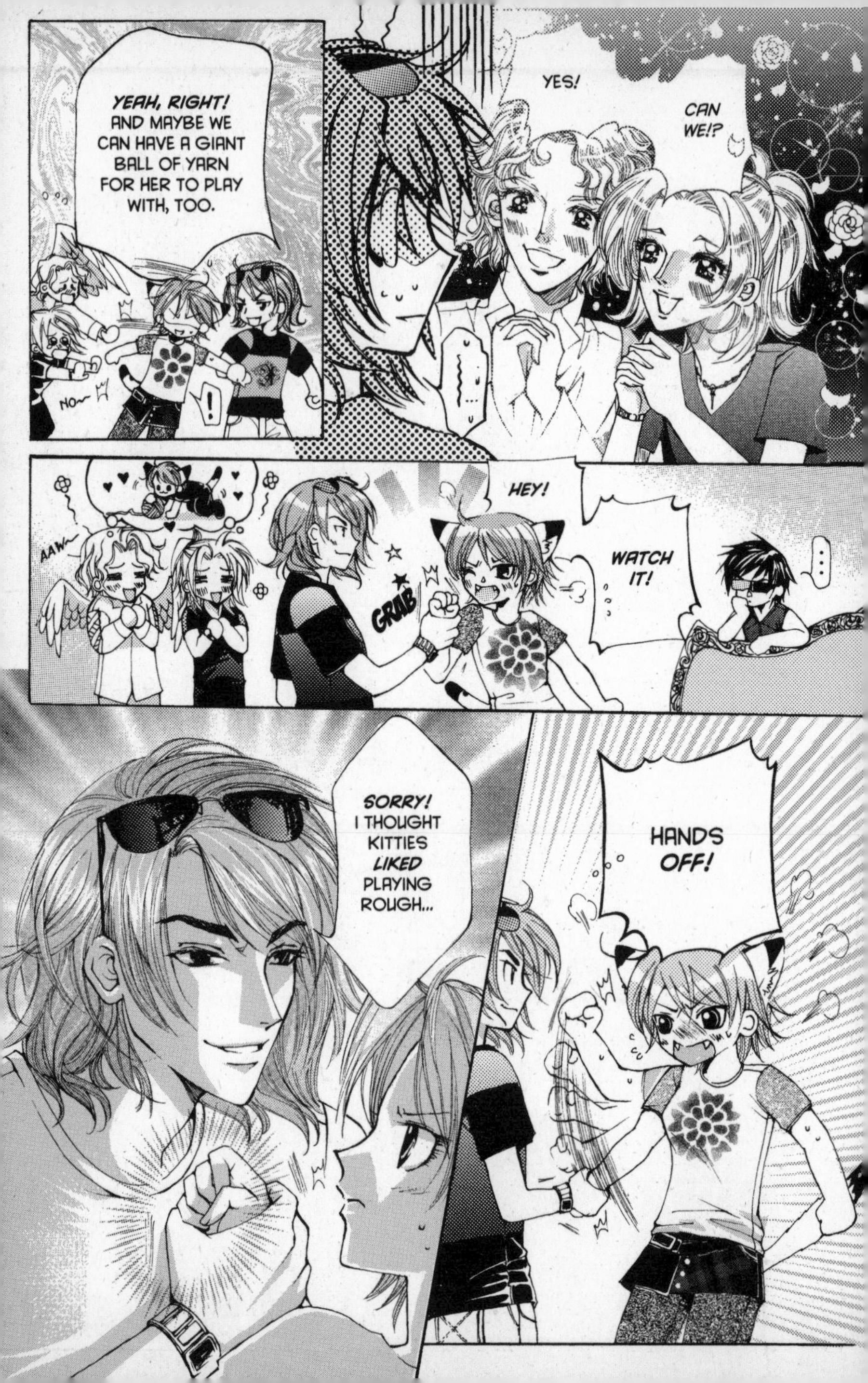
YEAH, RIGHT! AND MAYBE WE CAN HAVE A GIANT BALL OF YARN FOR HER TO PLAY WITH, TOO.
NO~
!
YES!
CAN WE!?
......
AAW~
HEY!
GRAB
WATCH IT!
...
SORRY! I THOUGHT KITTIES LIKED PLAYING ROUGH...
HANDS OFF!

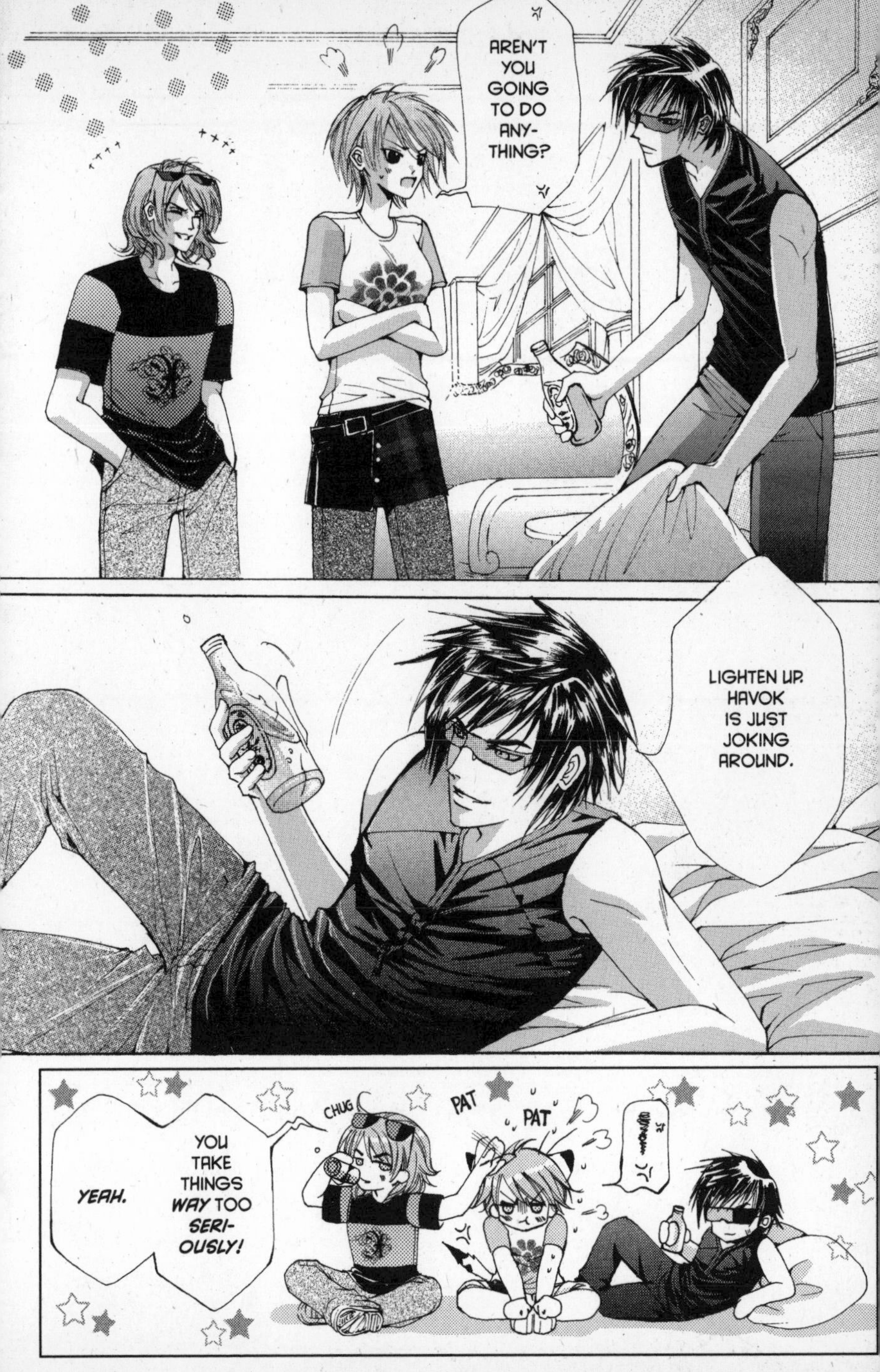
AREN'T YOU GOING TO DO ANY-THING?
LIGHTEN UP. HAVOK IS JUST JOKING AROUND.
YEAH.
CHUG
YOU TAKE THINGS *WAY* TOO SERI-OUSLY!
PAT
PAT

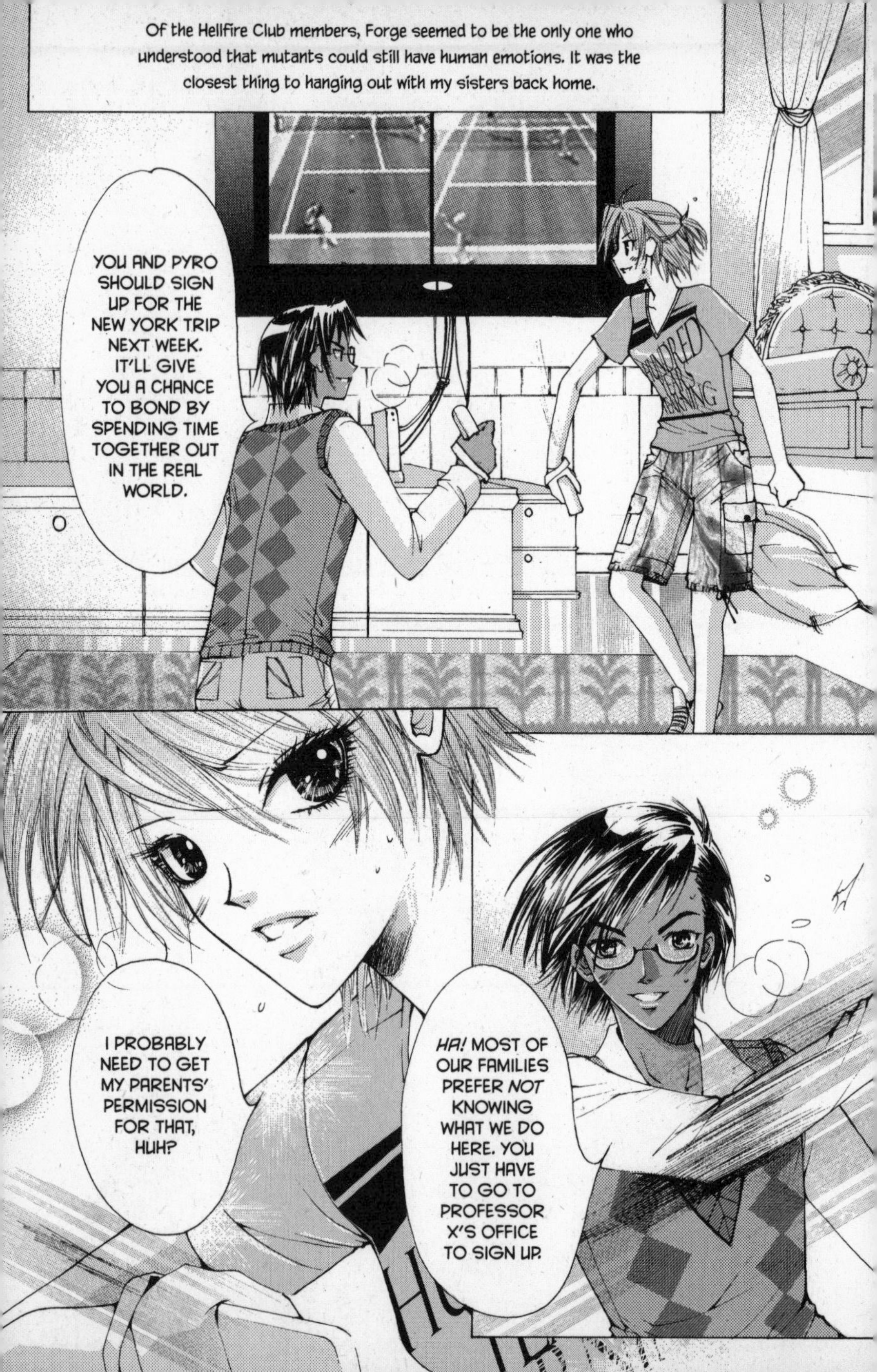
Of the Hellfire Club members, Forge seemed to be the only one who understood that mutants could still have human emotions. It was the closest thing to hanging out with my sisters back home.
YOU AND PYRO SHOULD SIGN UP FOR THE NEW YORK TRIP NEXT WEEK. IT'LL GIVE YOU A CHANCE TO BOND BY SPENDING TIME TOGETHER OUT IN THE REAL WORLD.
I PROBABLY NEED TO GET MY PARENTS' PERMISSION FOR THAT, HUH?
HA! MOST OF OUR FAMILIES PREFER *NOT* KNOWING WHAT WE DO HERE. YOU JUST HAVE TO GO TO PROFESSOR X'S OFFICE TO SIGN UP.

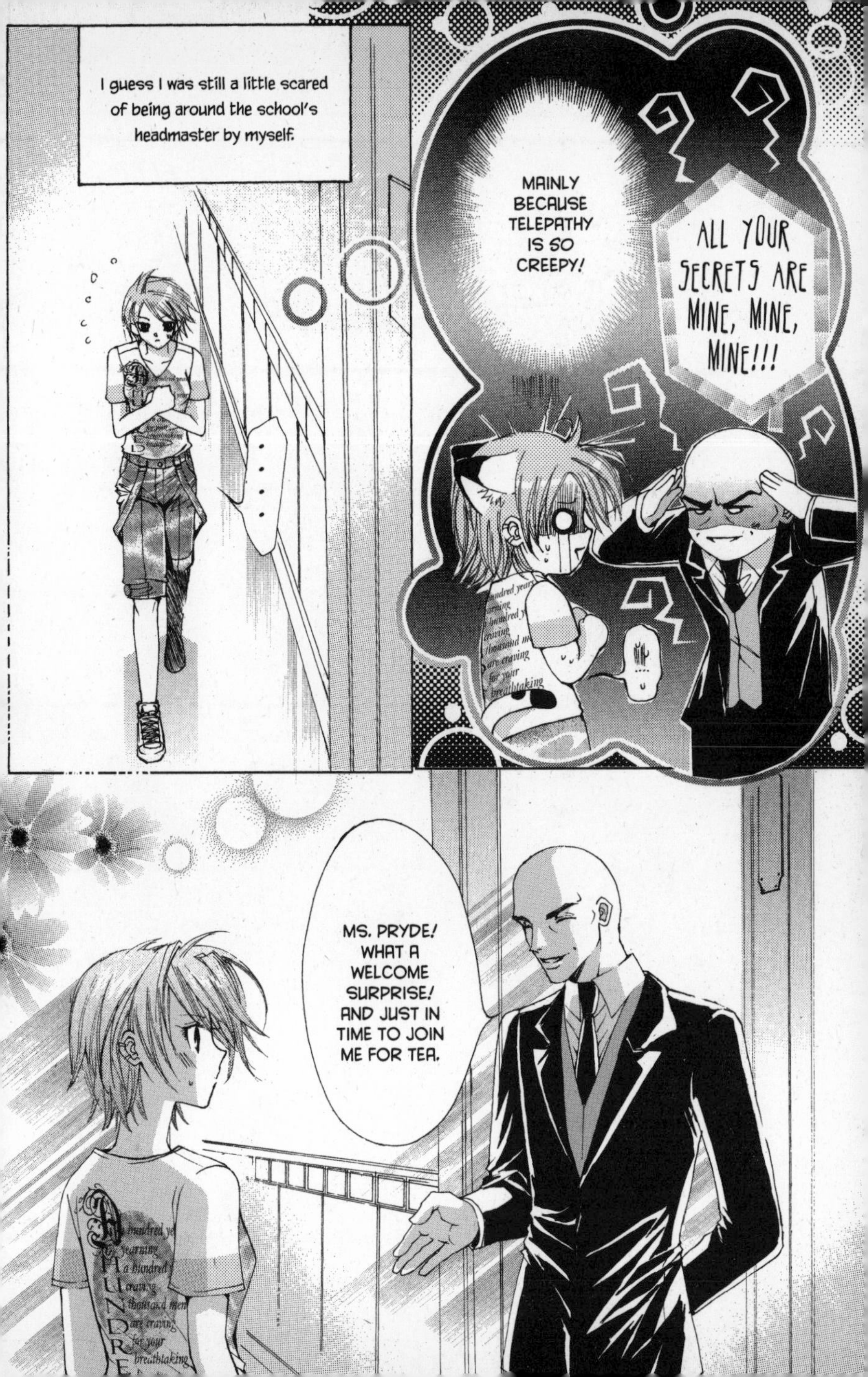
I guess I was still a little scared of being around the school's headmaster by myself.
MAINLY BECAUSE TELEPATHY IS SO CREEPY!
ALL YOUR SECRETS ARE MINE, MINE, MINE!!!
MS. PRYDE! WHAT A WELCOME SURPRISE! AND JUST IN TIME TO JOIN ME FOR TEA.

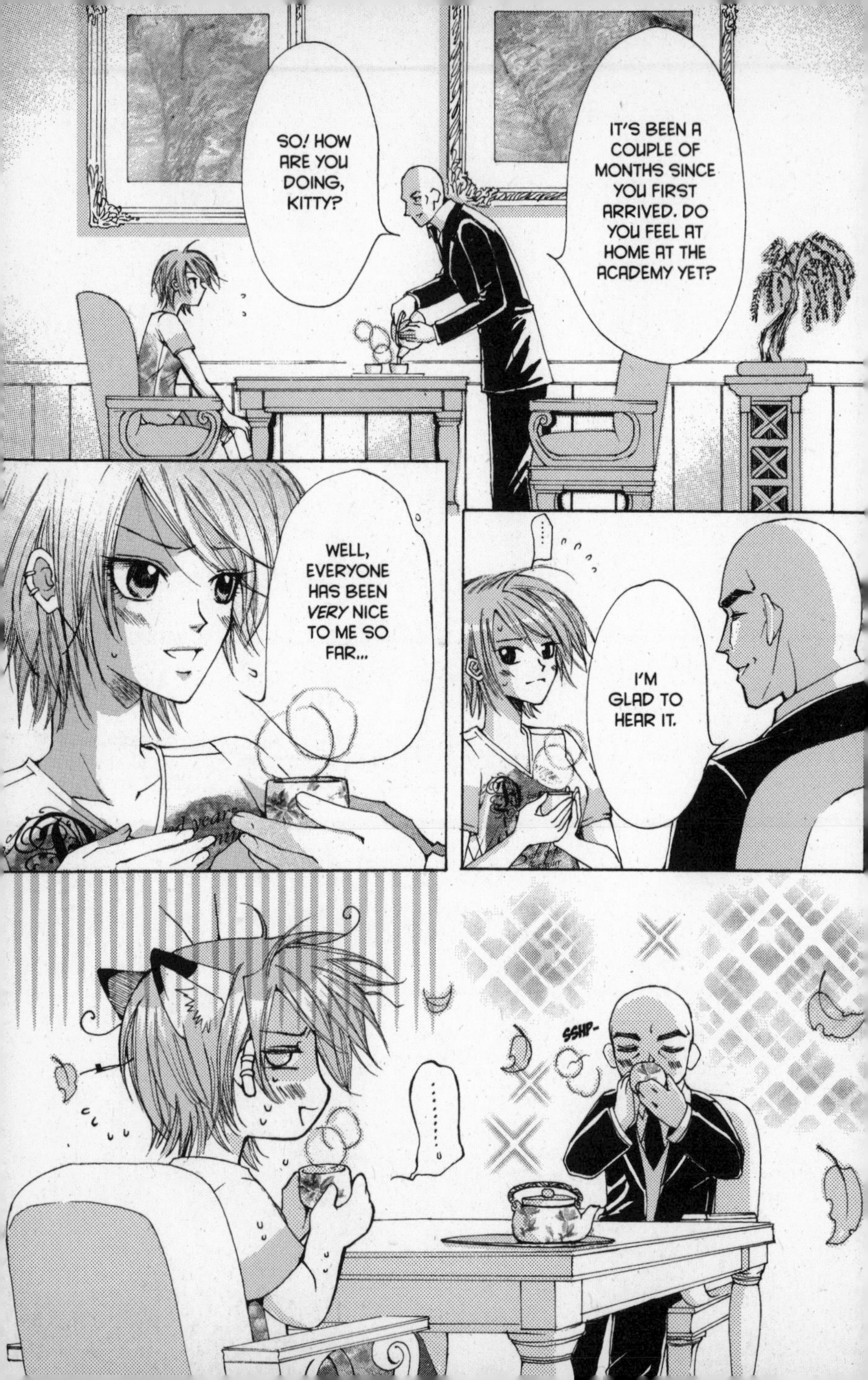
SO! HOW ARE YOU DOING, KITTY?
IT'S BEEN A COUPLE OF MONTHS SINCE YOU FIRST ARRIVED. DO YOU FEEL AT HOME AT THE ACADEMY YET?
WELL, EVERYONE HAS BEEN *VERY* NICE TO ME SO FAR...
...
I'M GLAD TO HEAR IT.
...
SSHP-

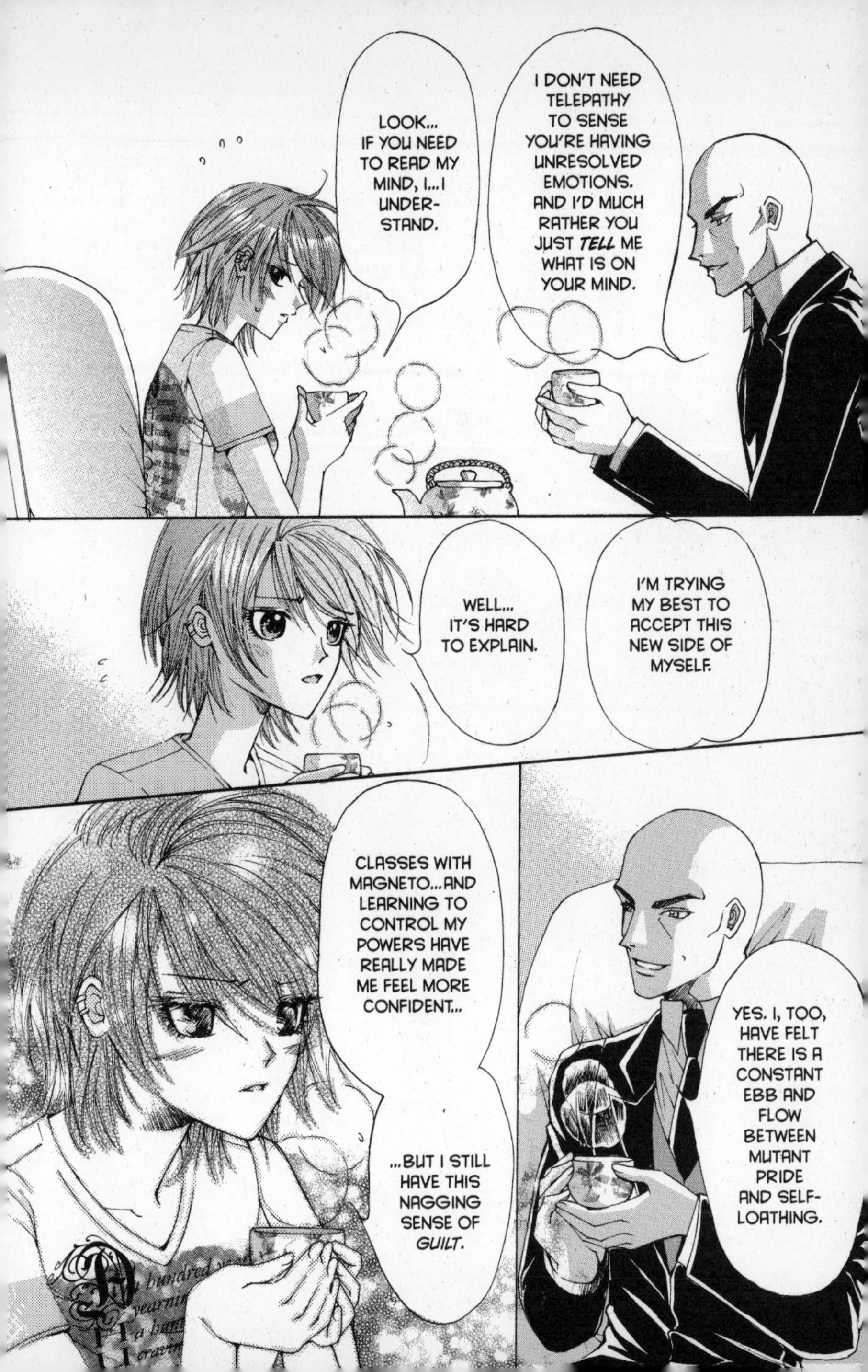
LOOK... IF YOU NEED TO READ MY MIND, I...I UNDER-STAND.
I DON'T NEED TELEPATHY TO SENSE YOU'RE HAVING UNRESOLVED EMOTIONS. AND I'D MUCH RATHER YOU JUST *TELL* ME WHAT IS ON YOUR MIND.
WELL... IT'S HARD TO EXPLAIN.
I'M TRYING MY BEST TO ACCEPT THIS NEW SIDE OF MYSELF.
CLASSES WITH MAGNETO...AND LEARNING TO CONTROL MY POWERS HAVE REALLY MADE ME FEEL MORE CONFIDENT...
...BUT I STILL HAVE THIS NAGGING SENSE OF *GUILT*.
YES. I, TOO, HAVE FELT THERE IS A CONSTANT EBB AND FLOW BETWEEN MUTANT PRIDE AND SELF-LOATHING.

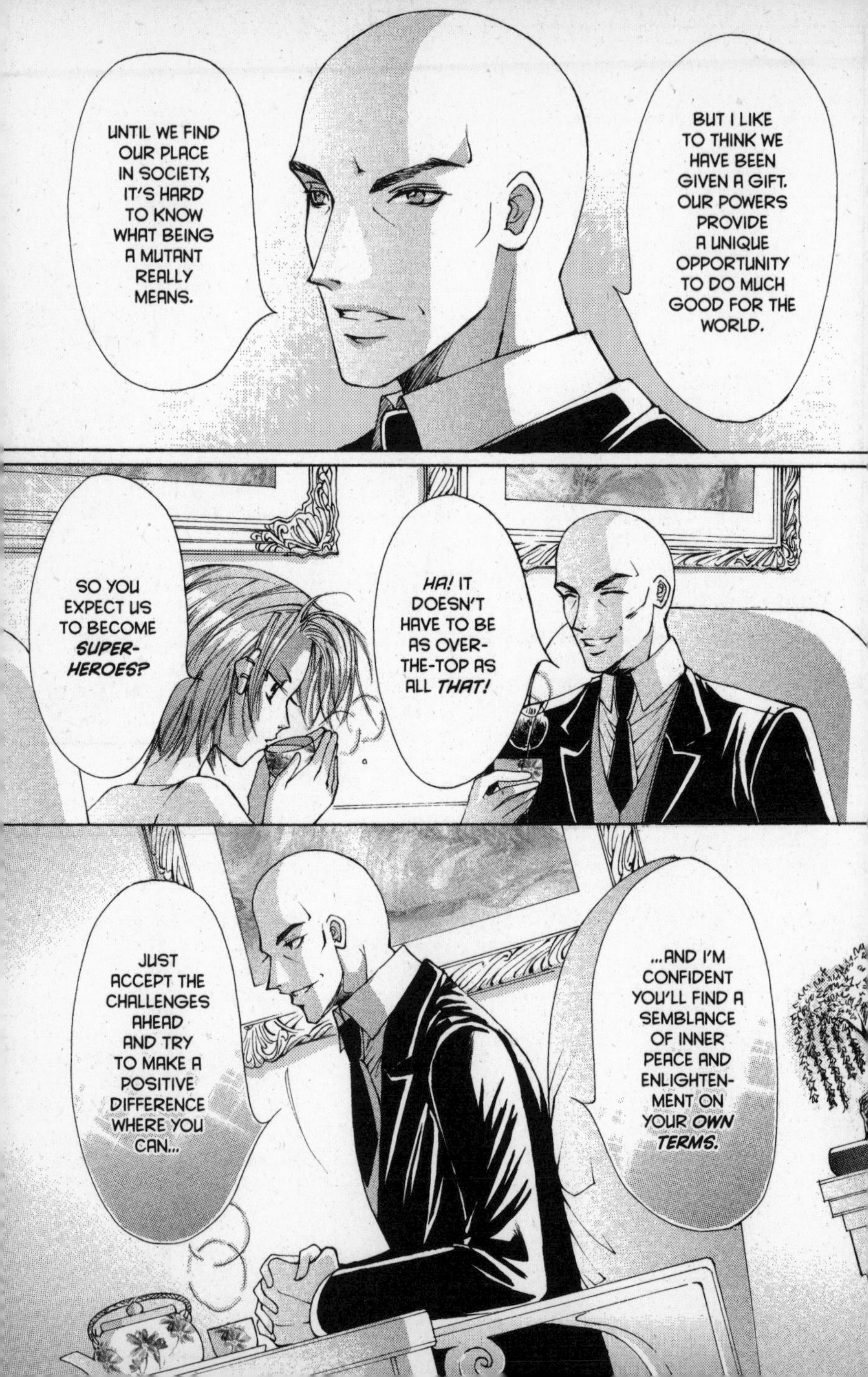
UNTIL WE FIND OUR PLACE IN SOCIETY, IT'S HARD TO KNOW WHAT BEING A MUTANT REALLY MEANS.
BUT I LIKE TO THINK WE HAVE BEEN GIVEN A GIFT. OUR POWERS PROVIDE A UNIQUE OPPORTUNITY TO DO MUCH GOOD FOR THE WORLD.
SO YOU EXPECT US TO BECOME *SUPER-HEROES?*
HA! IT DOESN'T HAVE TO BE AS OVER-THE-TOP AS ALL *THAT!*
JUST ACCEPT THE CHALLENGES AHEAD AND TRY TO MAKE A POSITIVE DIFFERENCE WHERE YOU CAN...
...AND I'M CONFIDENT YOU'LL FIND A SEMBLANCE OF INNER PEACE AND ENLIGHTEN-MENT ON YOUR *OWN TERMS.*

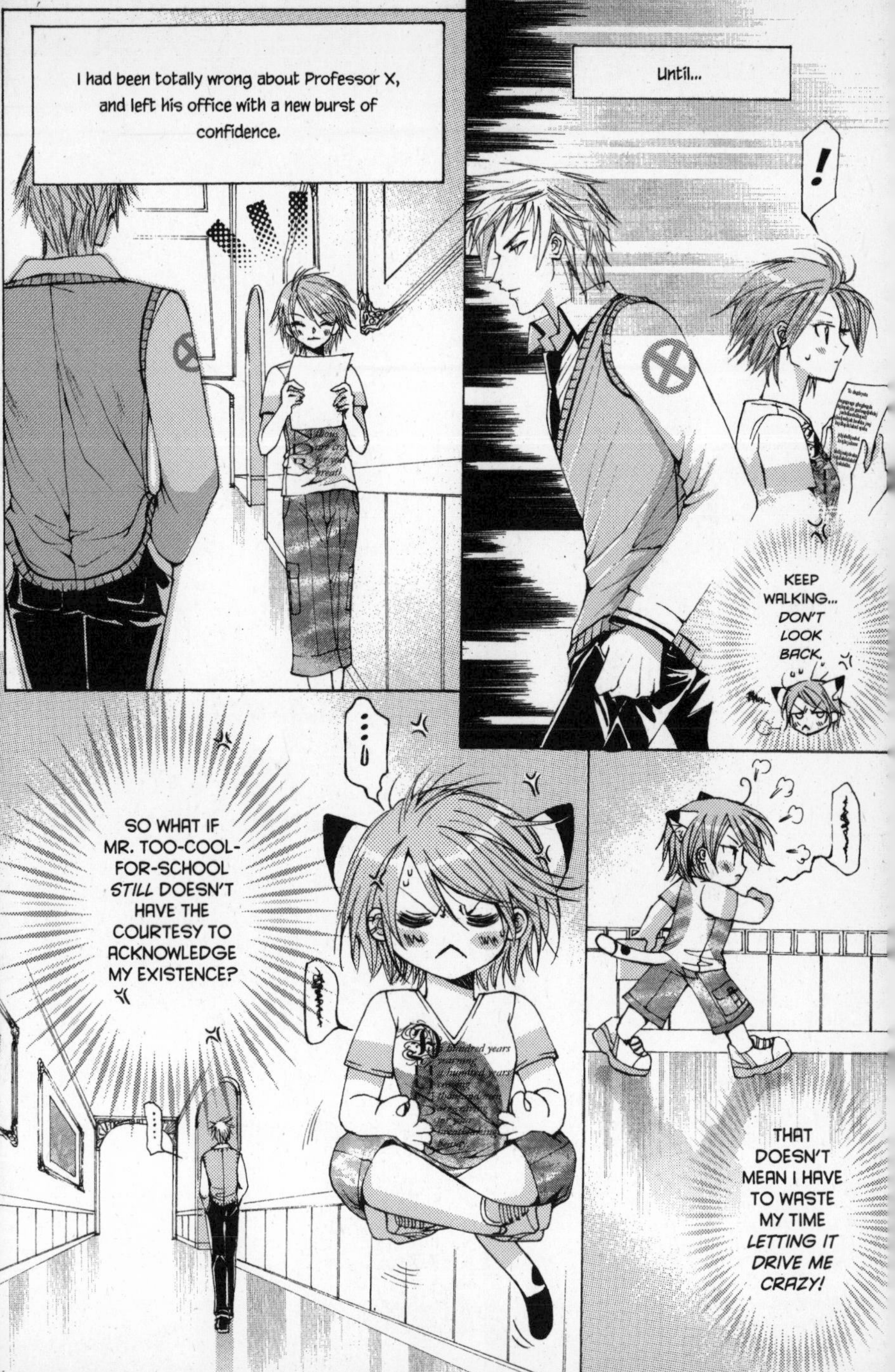
I had been totally wrong about Professor X, and left his office with a new burst of confidence.
Until...
!
KEEP WALKING... DON'T LOOK BACK.
SO WHAT IF MR. TOO-COOL-FOR-SCHOOL STILL DOESN'T HAVE THE COURTESY TO ACKNOWLEDGE MY EXISTENCE?
...!
.....
THAT DOESN'T MEAN I HAVE TO WASTE MY TIME LETTING IT DRIVE ME CRAZY!

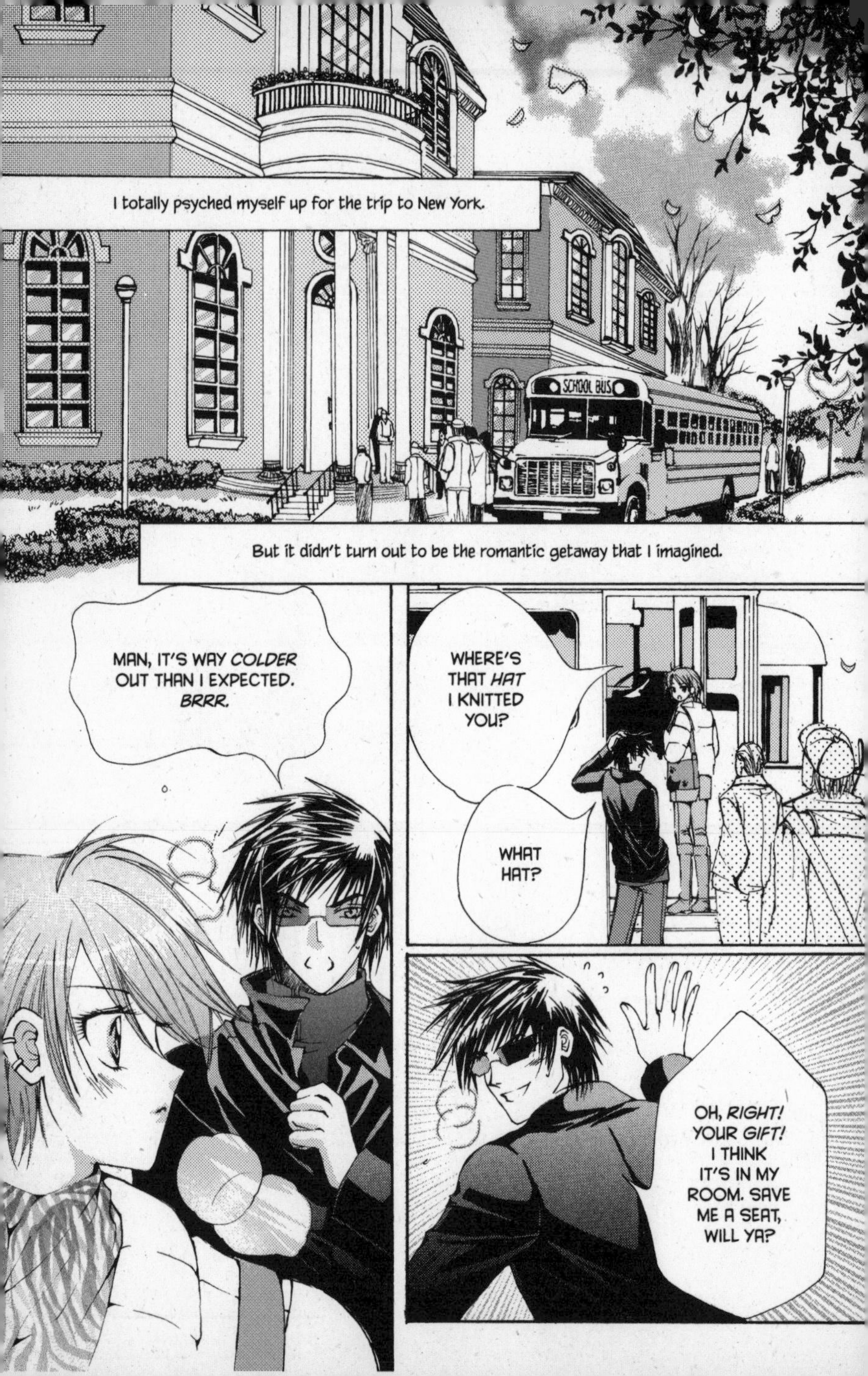
I totally psyched myself up for the trip to New York.
But it didn't turn out to be the romantic getaway that I imagined.
MAN, IT'S WAY COLDER OUT THAN I EXPECTED. BRRR.
WHERE'S THAT HAT I KNITTED YOU?
WHAT HAT?
OH, RIGHT! YOUR GIFT! I THINK IT'S IN MY ROOM. SAVE ME A SEAT, WILL YA?

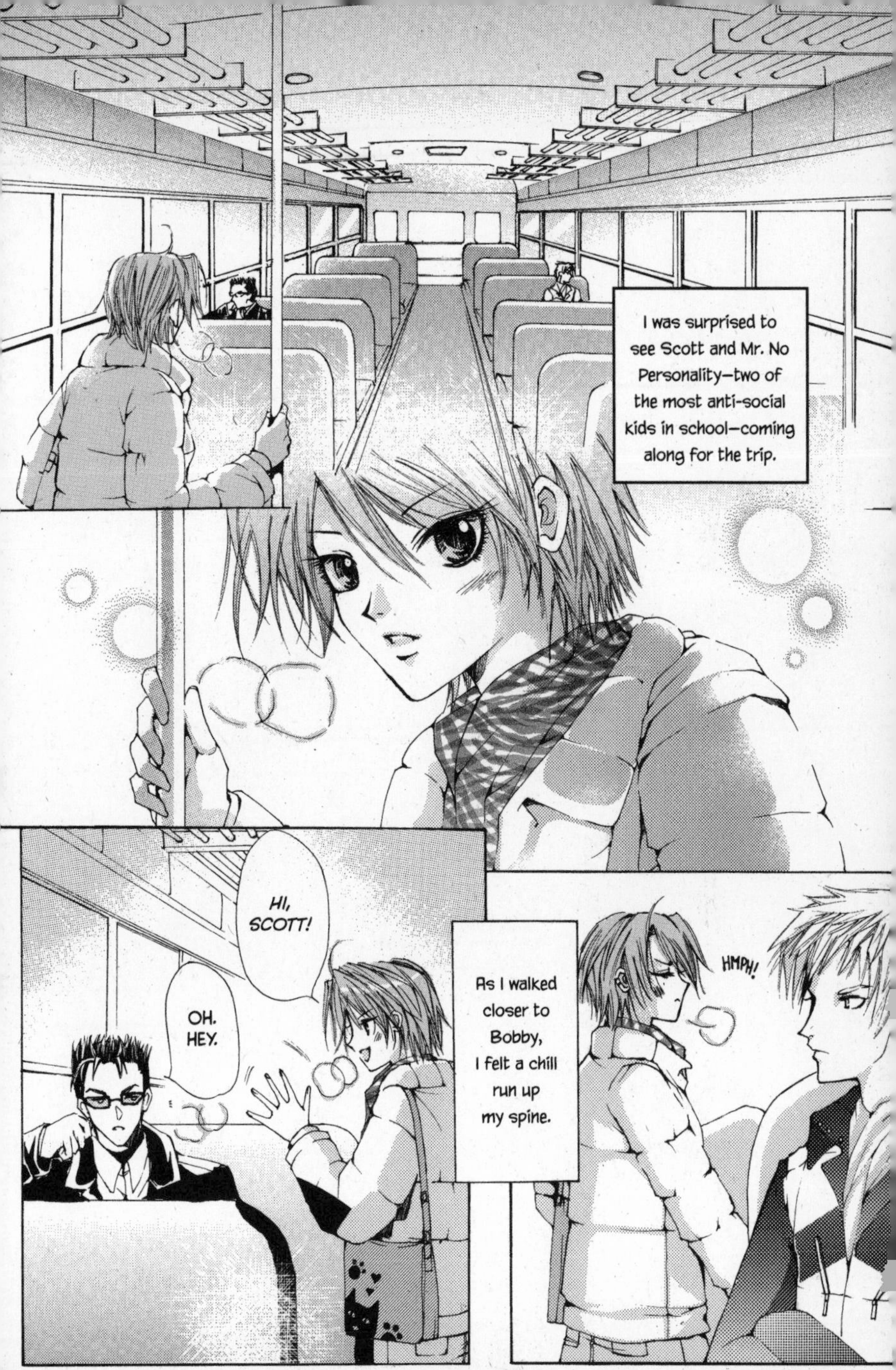
I was surprised to see Scott and Mr. No Personality—two of the most anti-social kids in school—coming along for the trip.
HI, SCOTT!
OH. HEY.
As I walked closer to Bobby, I felt a chill run up my spine.
HMPH!

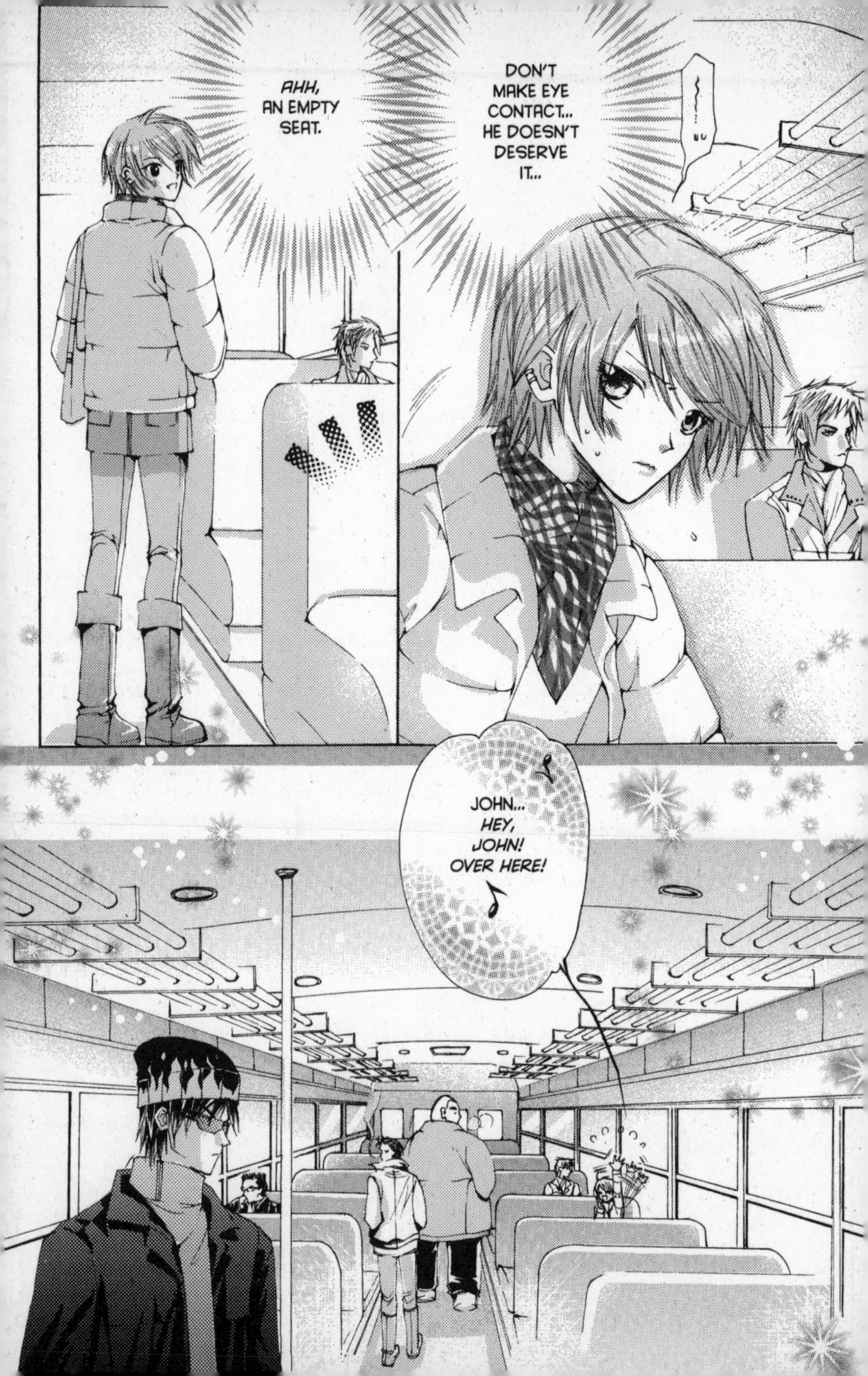
AHH, AN EMPTY SEAT.
DON'T MAKE EYE CONTACT... HE DOESN'T DESERVE IT...
JOHN... HEY, JOHN! OVER HERE!

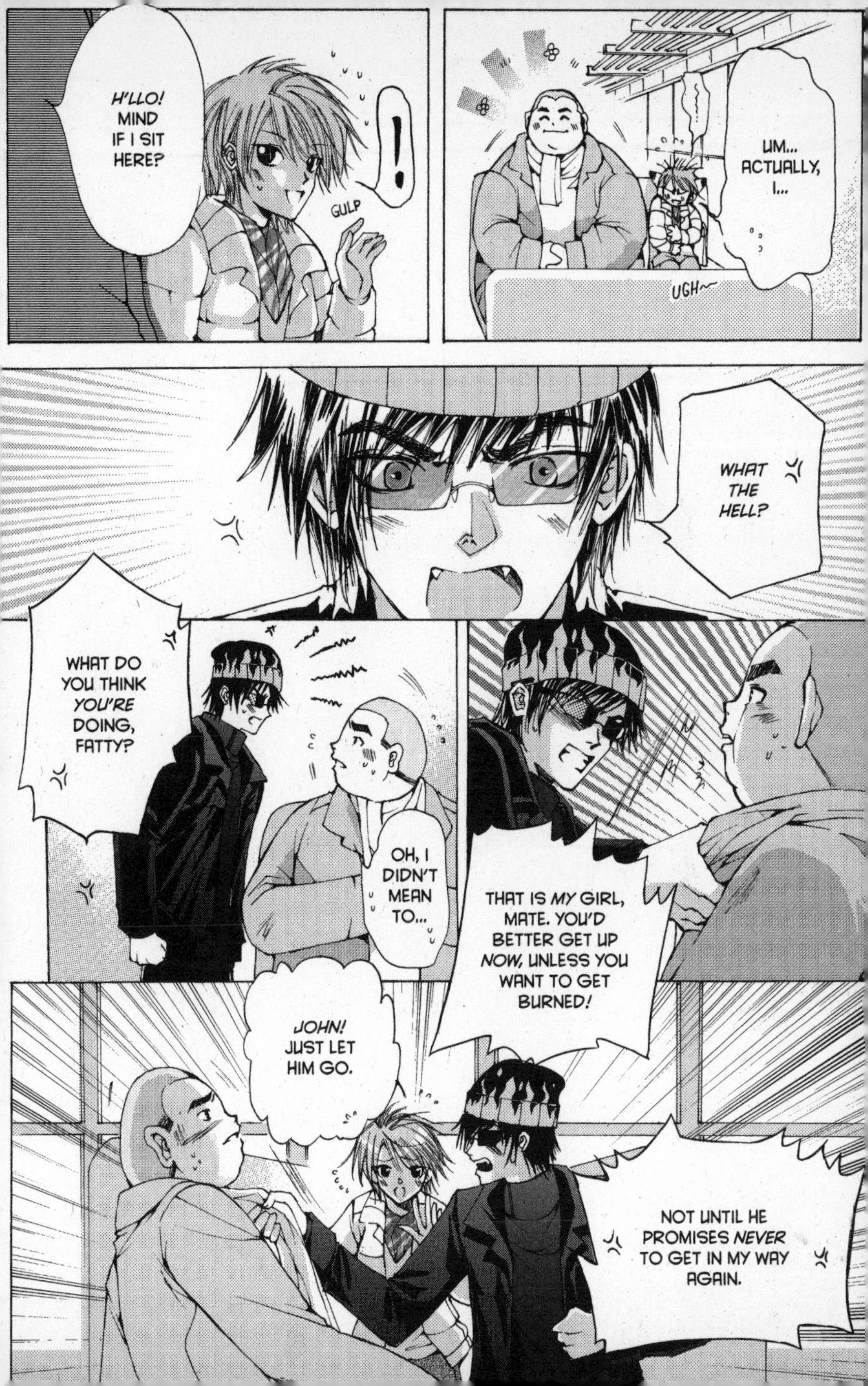
H'LLO! MIND IF I SIT HERE?
!
GULP
UM... ACTUALLY, I...
UGH~
WHAT THE HELL?
WHAT DO YOU THINK YOU'RE DOING, FATTY?
OH, I DIDN'T MEAN TO...
THAT IS MY GIRL, MATE. YOU'D BETTER GET UP NOW, UNLESS YOU WANT TO GET BURNED!
JOHN! JUST LET HIM GO.
NOT UNTIL HE PROMISES NEVER TO GET IN MY WAY AGAIN.

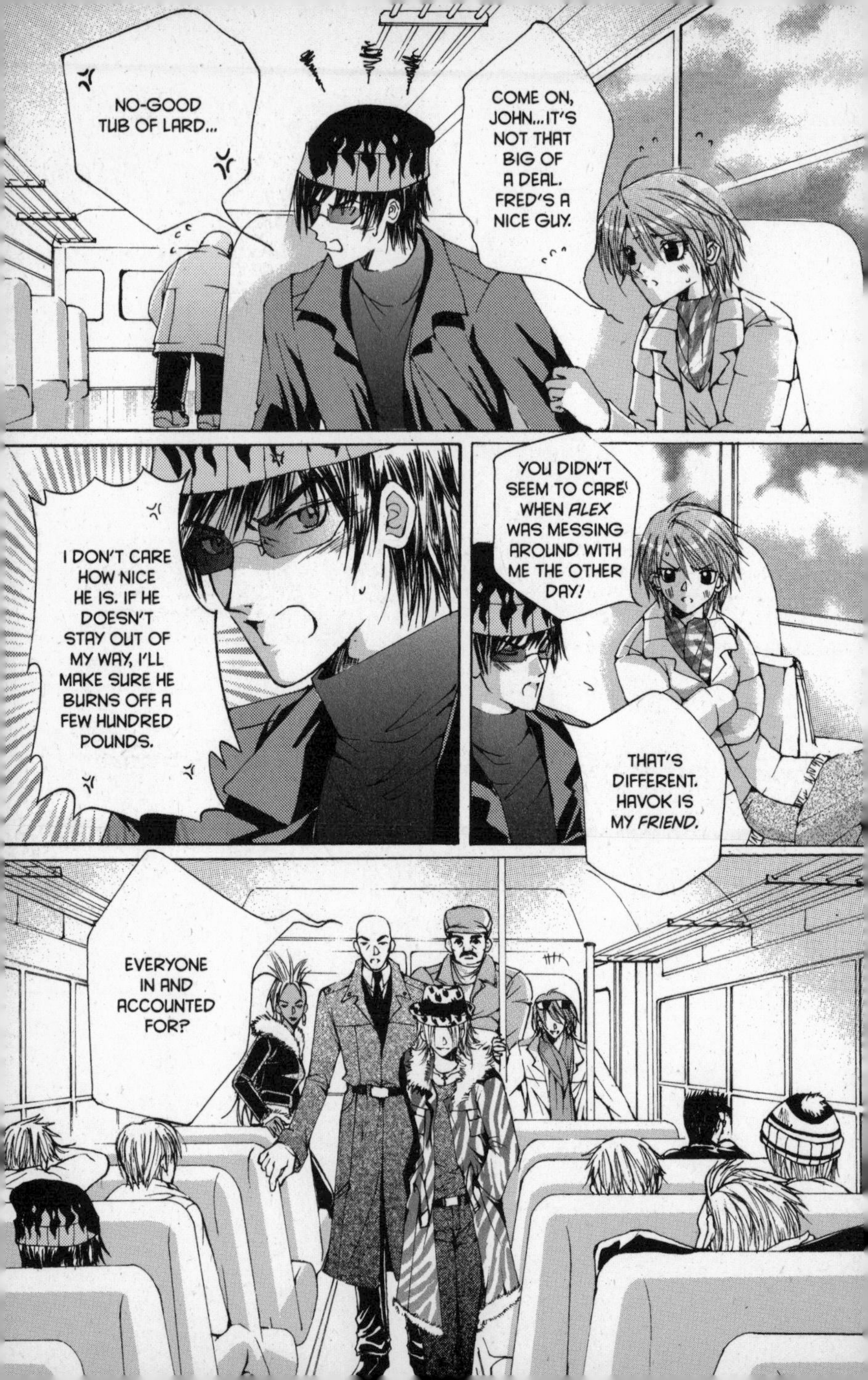
NO-GOOD TUB OF LARD...
COME ON, JOHN...IT'S NOT THAT BIG OF A DEAL. FRED'S A NICE GUY.
I DON'T CARE HOW NICE HE IS. IF HE DOESN'T STAY OUT OF MY WAY, I'LL MAKE SURE HE BURNS OFF A FEW HUNDRED POUNDS.
YOU DIDN'T SEEM TO CARE WHEN *ALEX* WAS MESSING AROUND WITH ME THE OTHER DAY!
THAT'S DIFFERENT. HAVOK IS MY *FRIEND*.
EVERYONE IN AND ACCOUNTED FOR?

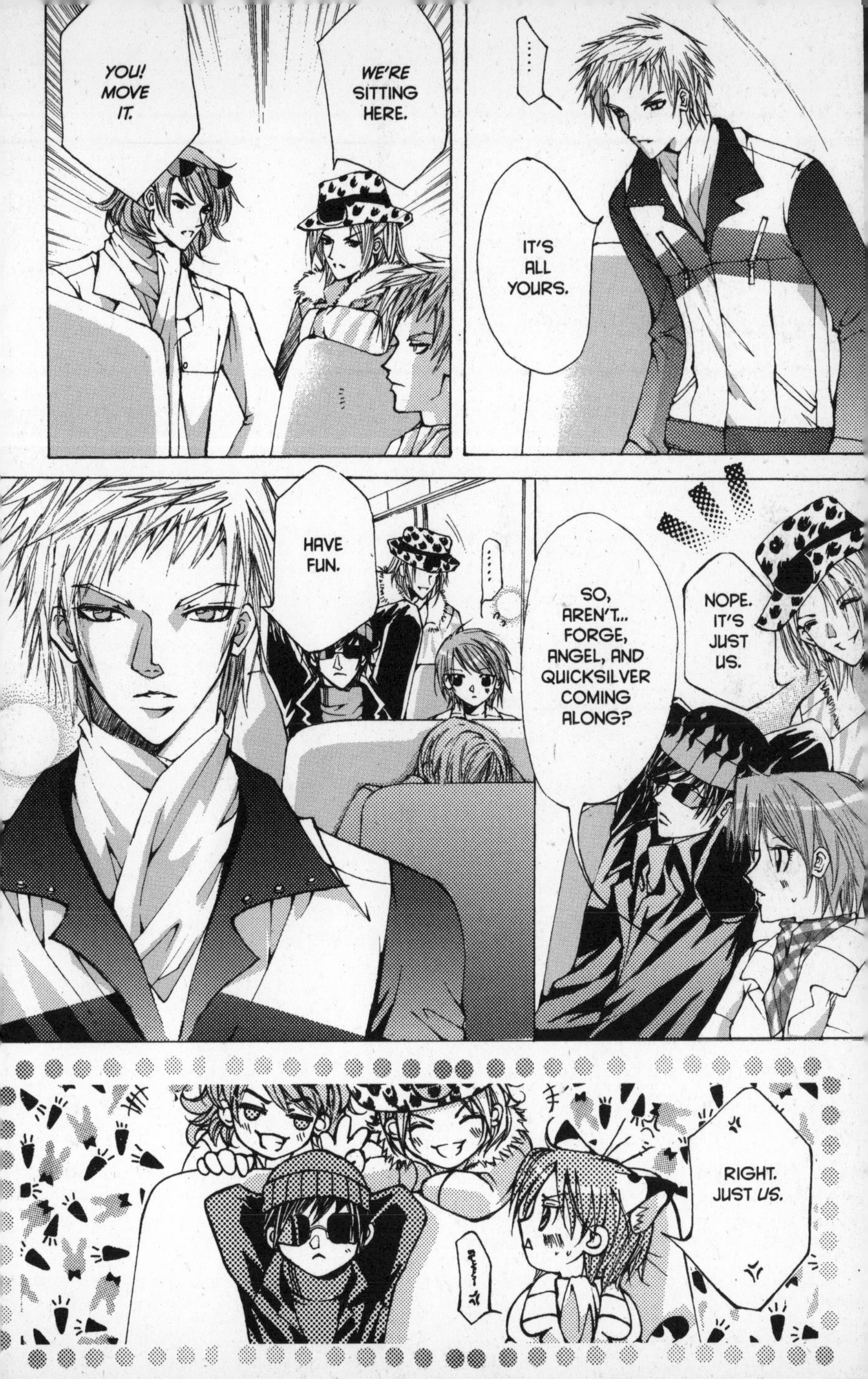
YOU! MOVE IT.
WE'RE SITTING HERE.
......
IT'S ALL YOURS.
HAVE FUN.
......
SO, AREN'T... FORGE, ANGEL, AND QUICKSILVER COMING ALONG?
NOPE. IT'S JUST US.
RIGHT. JUST US.

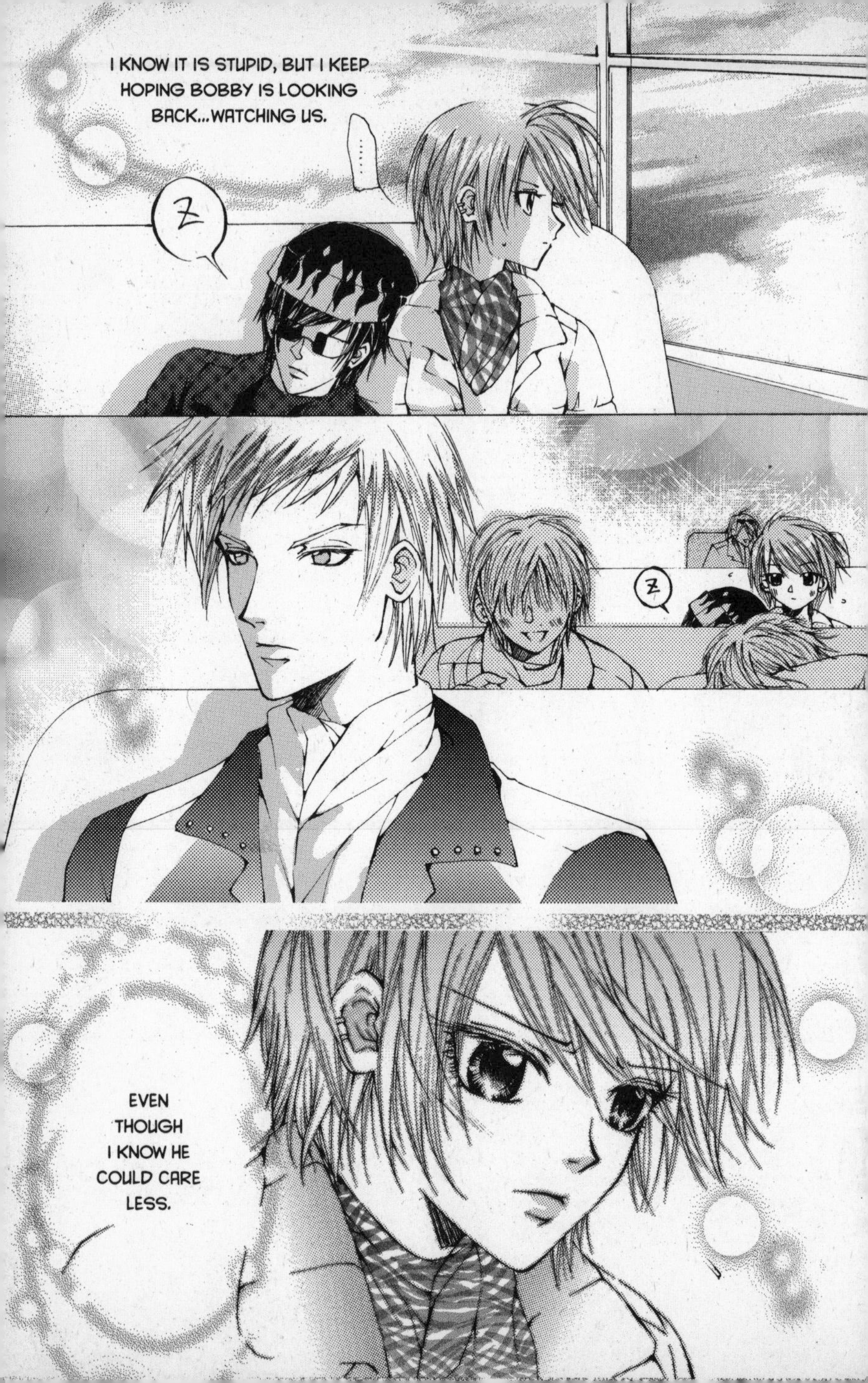
I KNOW IT IS STUPID, BUT I KEEP HOPING BOBBY IS LOOKING BACK...WATCHING US.
......
Z
Z
EVEN THOUGH I KNOW HE COULD CARE LESS.

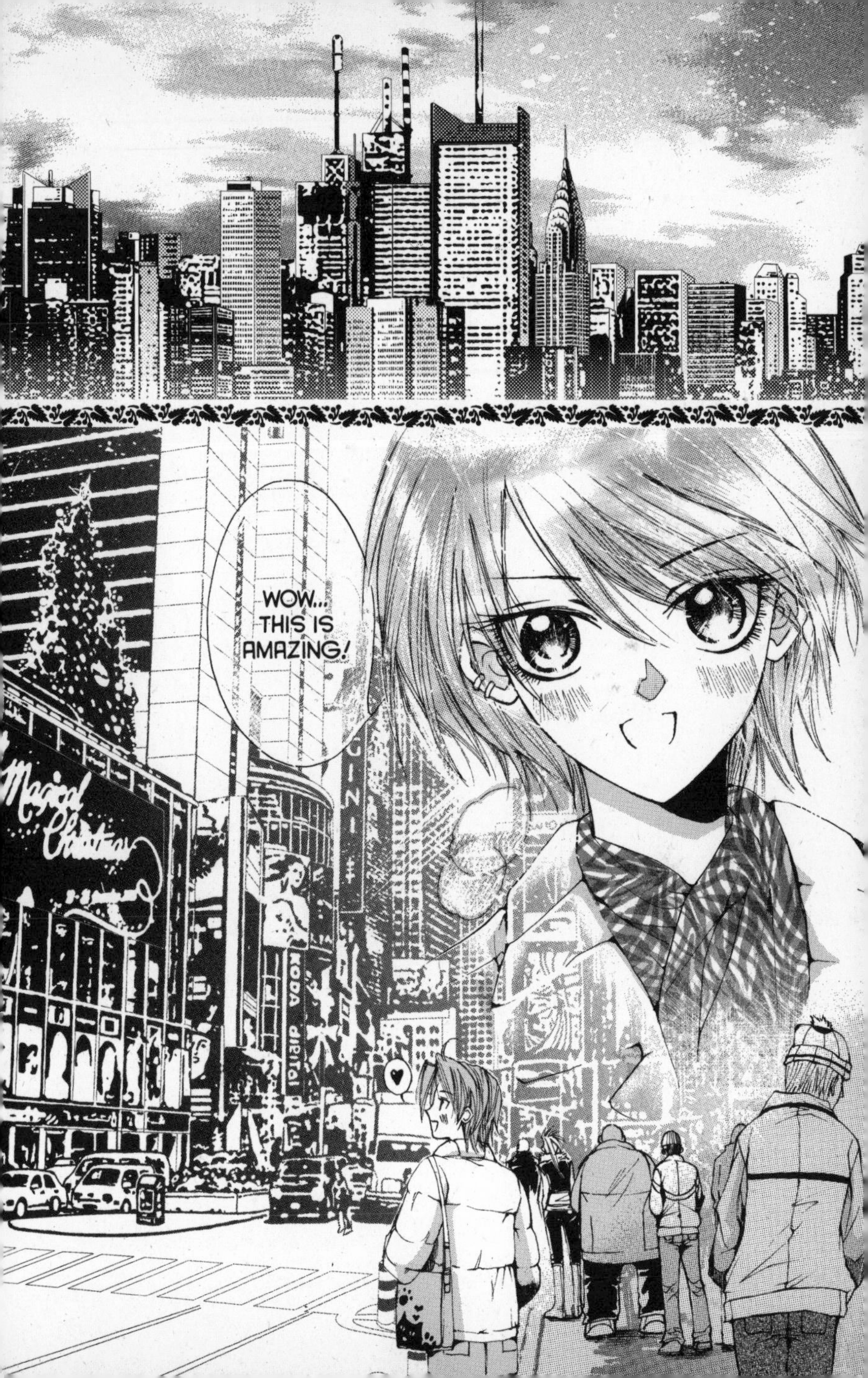
WOW... THIS IS AMAZING!

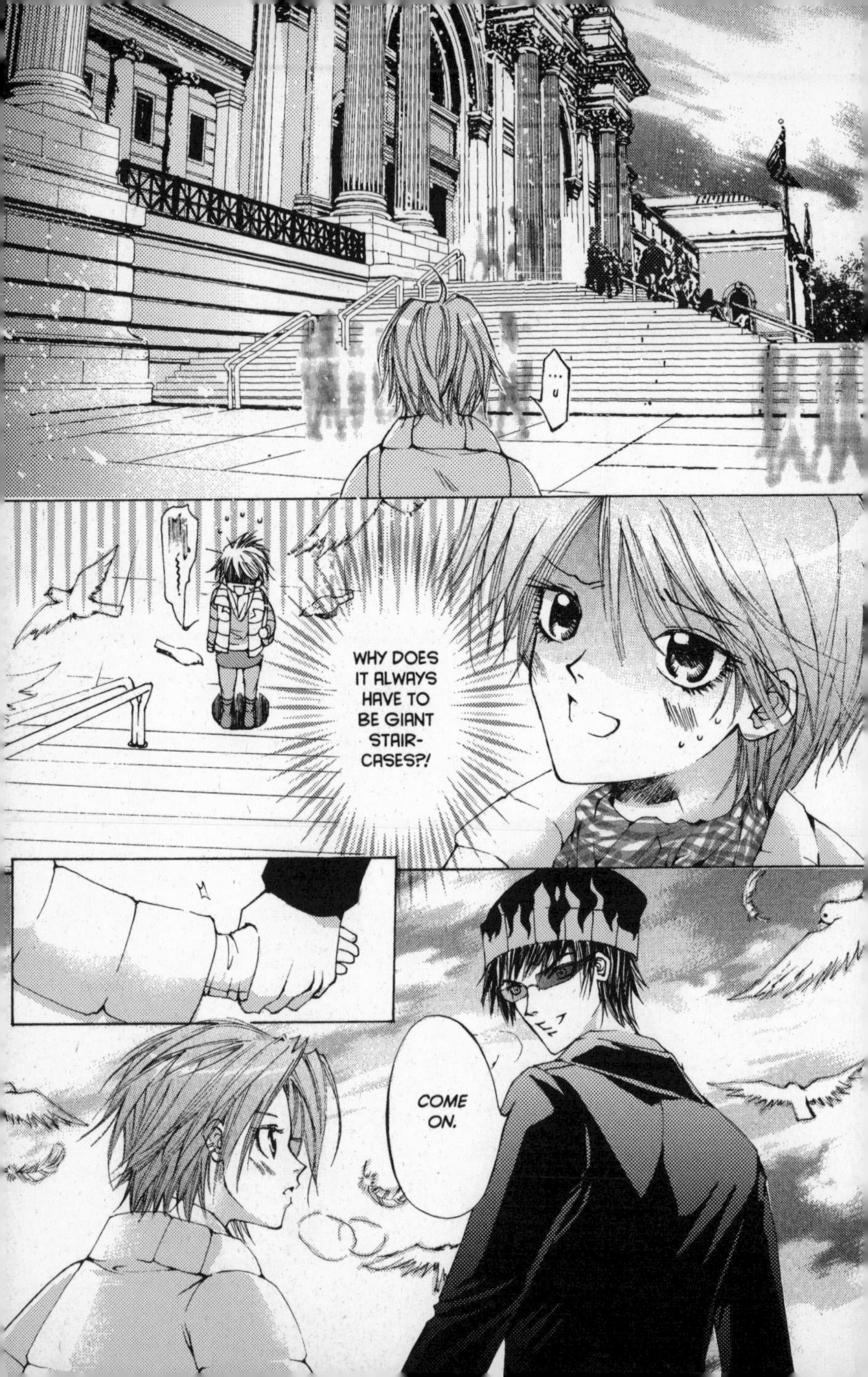
WHY DOES IT ALWAYS HAVE TO BE GIANT STAIR-CASES?!
COME ON.

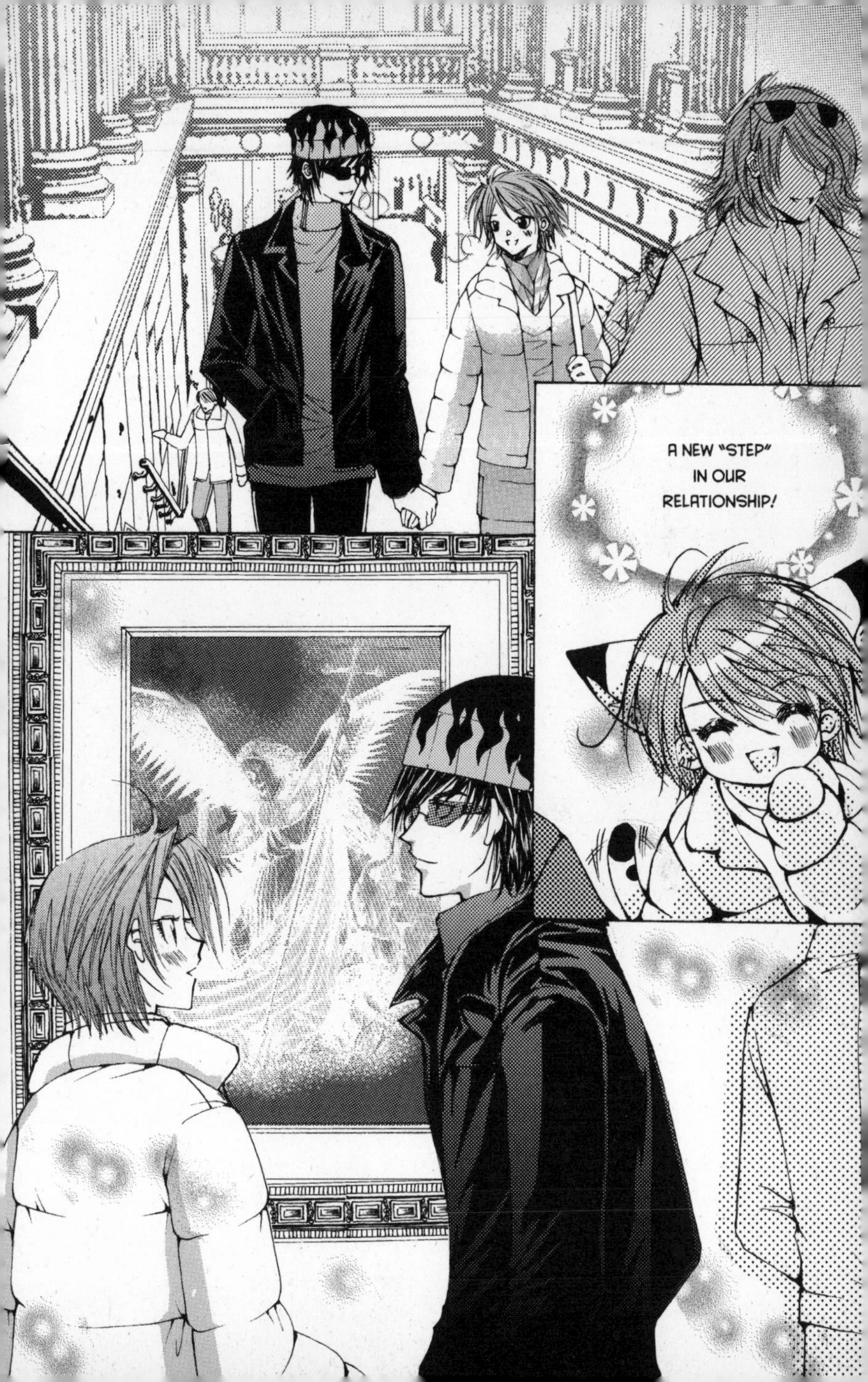
A NEW "STEP" IN OUR RELATIONSHIP!

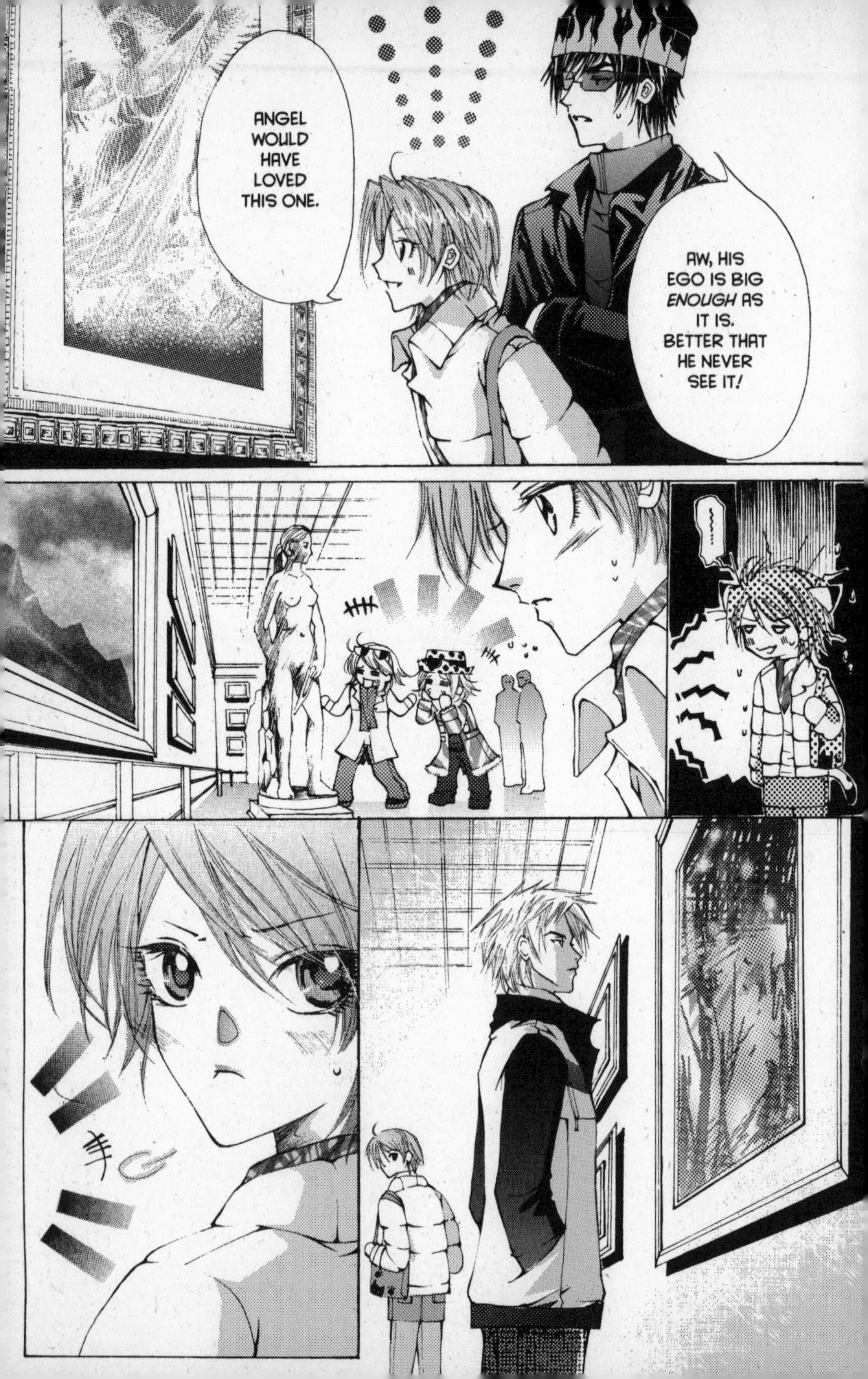
ANGEL WOULD HAVE LOVED THIS ONE.
AW, HIS EGO IS BIG *ENOUGH* AS IT IS. BETTER THAT HE NEVER SEE IT!

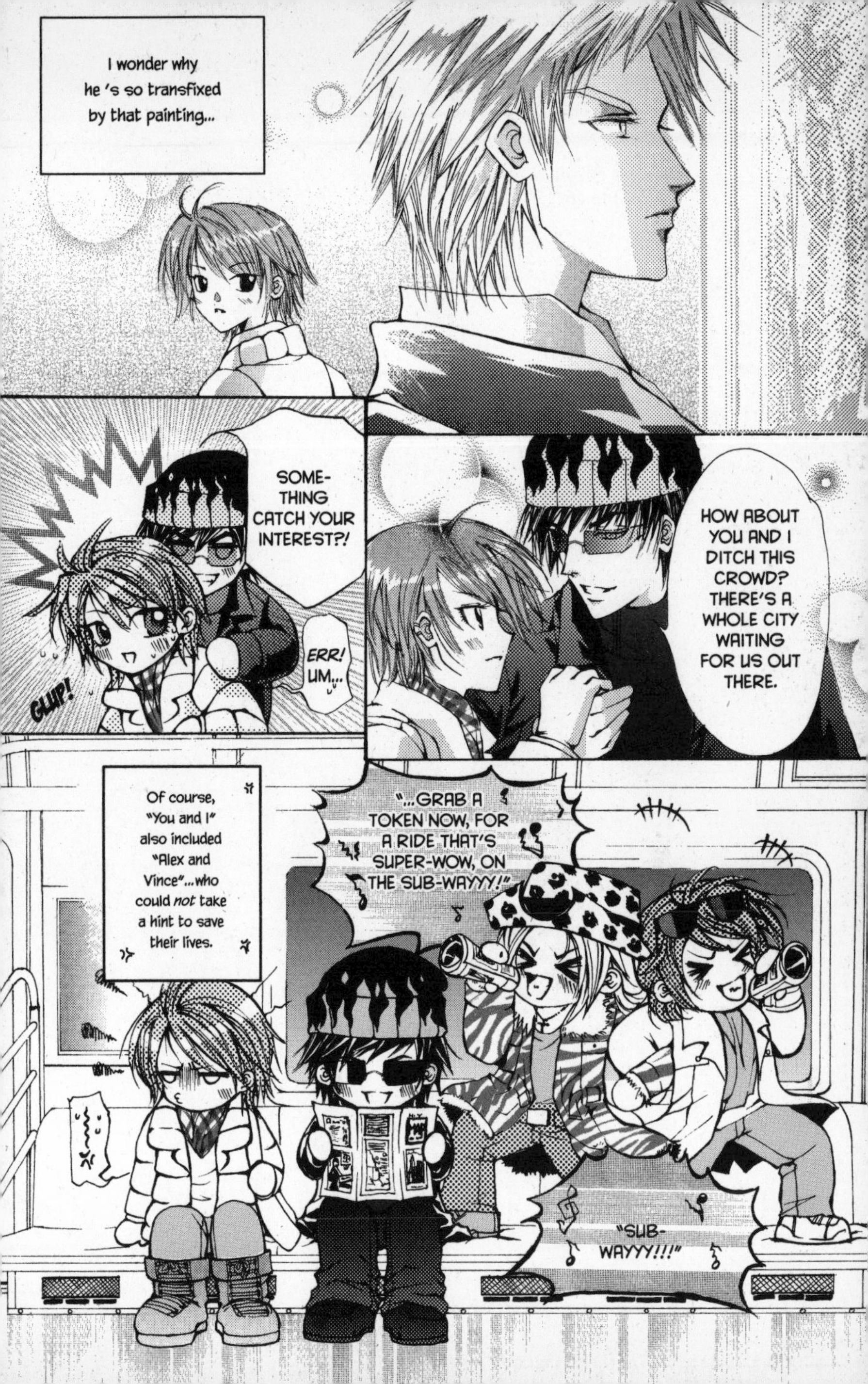
I wonder why he's so transfixed by that painting...
SOME-THING CATCH YOUR INTEREST?!
ERR! UM...
GLUP!
HOW ABOUT YOU AND I DITCH THIS CROWD? THERE'S A WHOLE CITY WAITING FOR US OUT THERE.
Of course, "You and I" also included "Alex and Vince"...who could *not* take a hint to save their lives.
"...GRAB A TOKEN NOW, FOR A RIDE THAT'S SUPER-WOW, ON THE SUB-WAYYY!"
"SUB-WAYYY!!!"

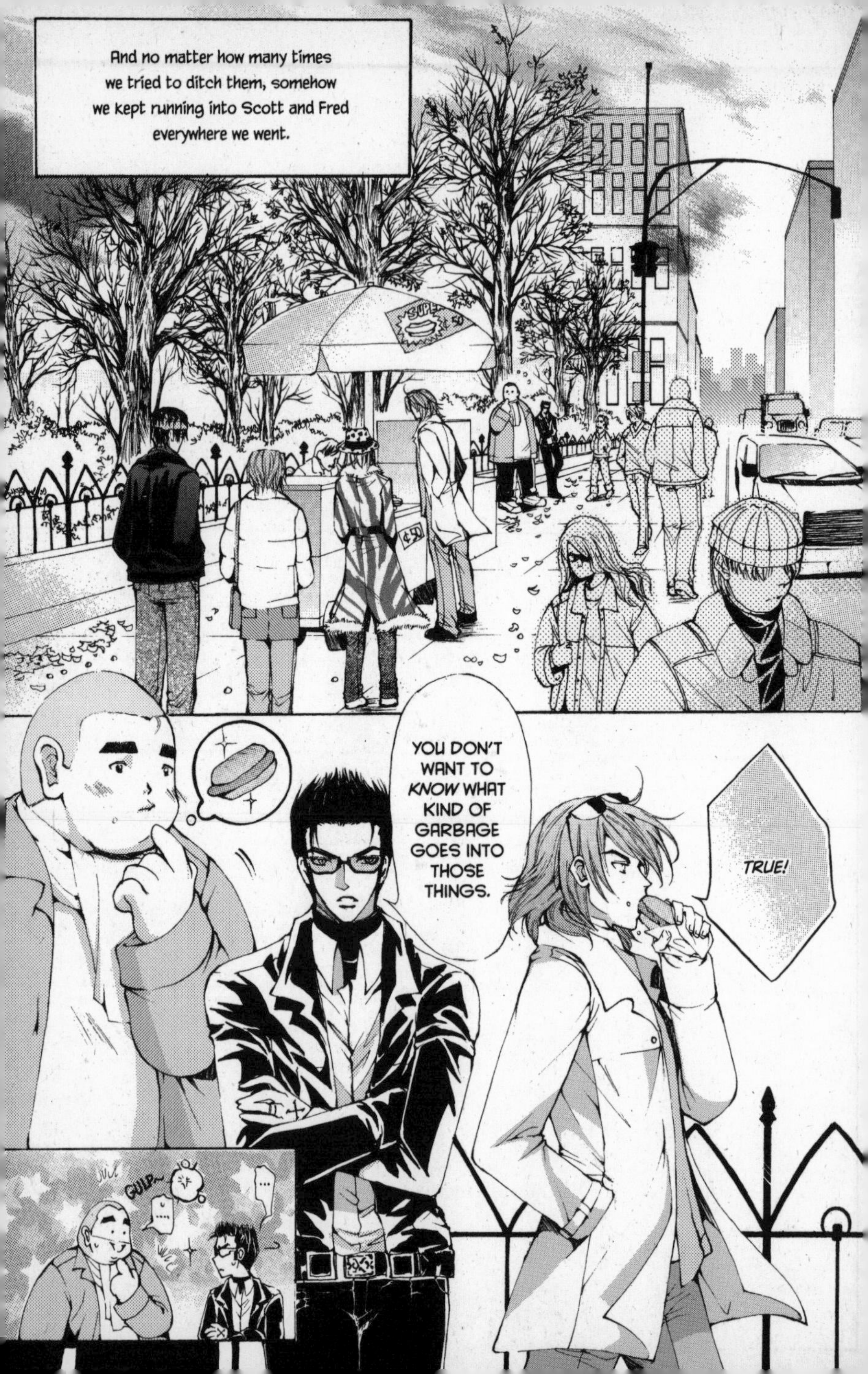
And no matter how many times we tried to ditch them, somehow we kept running into Scott and Fred everywhere we went.
YOU DON'T WANT TO *KNOW* WHAT KIND OF GARBAGE GOES INTO THOSE THINGS.
TRUE!
GULP~
...
....

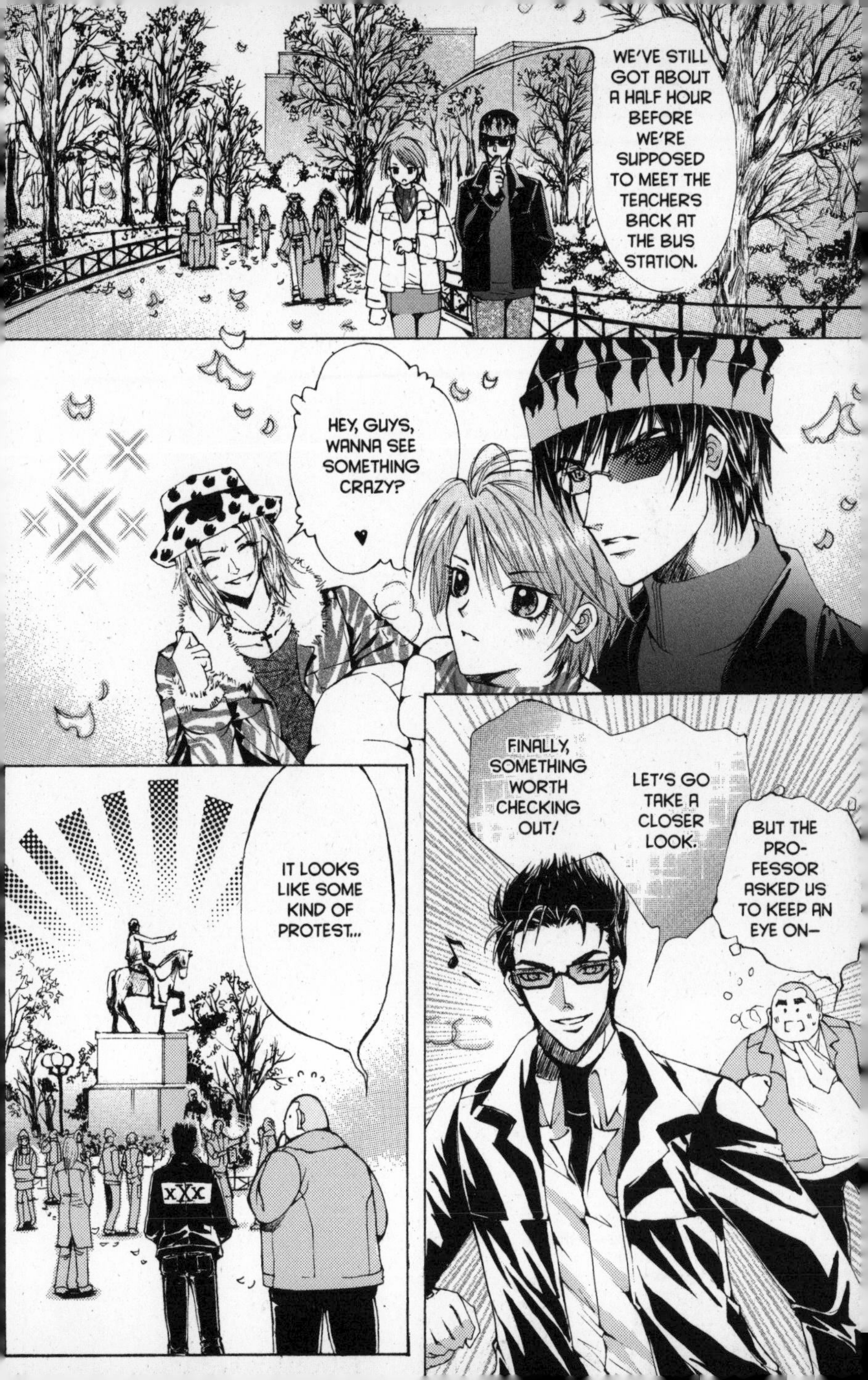

WE'VE STILL GOT ABOUT A HALF HOUR BEFORE WE'RE SUPPOSED TO MEET THE TEACHERS BACK AT THE BUS STATION.
HEY, GUYS, WANNA SEE SOMETHING CRAZY?
IT LOOKS LIKE SOME KIND OF PROTEST...
FINALLY, SOMETHING WORTH CHECKING OUT!
LET'S GO TAKE A CLOSER LOOK.
BUT THE PRO-FESSOR ASKED US TO KEEP AN EYE ON–

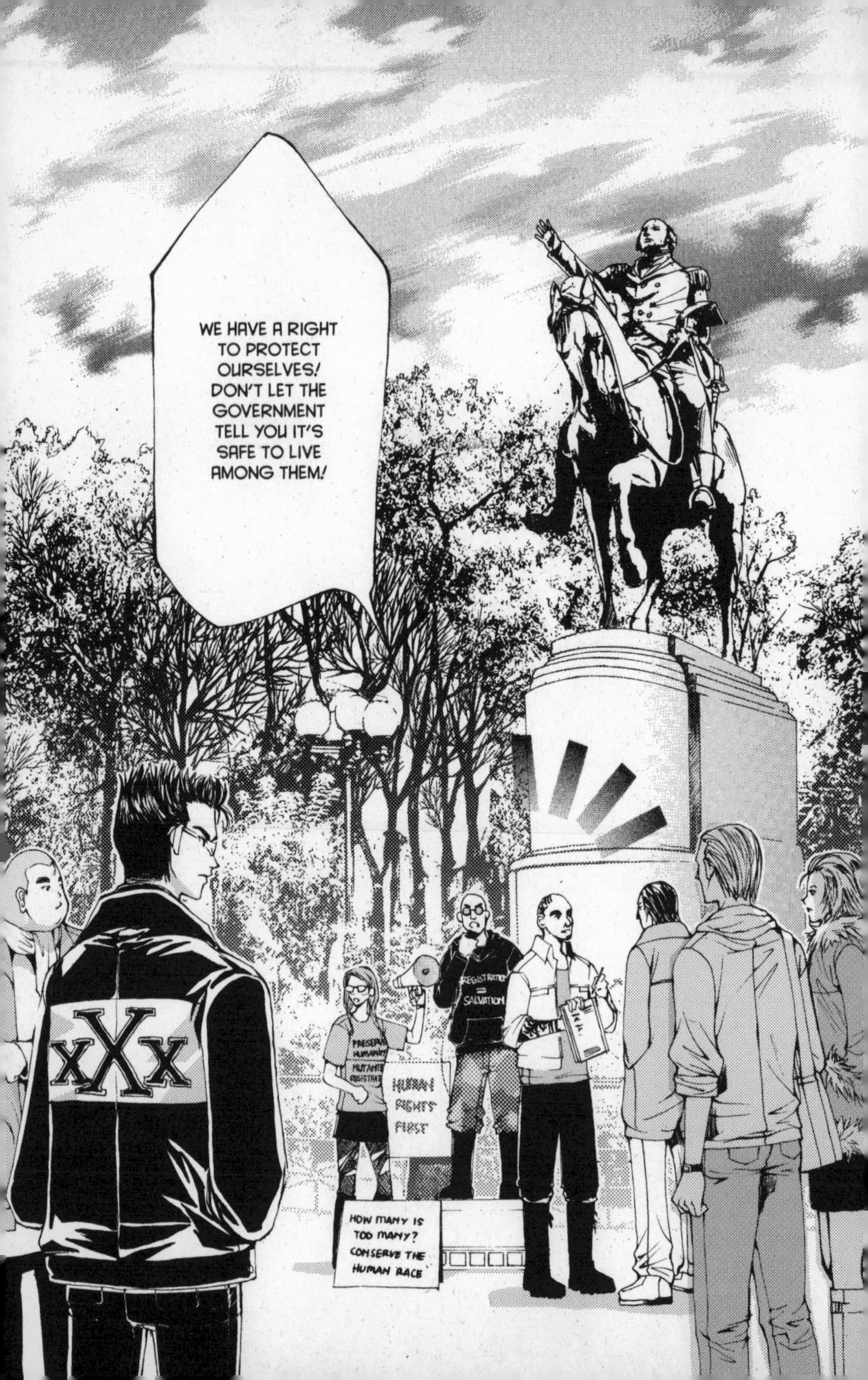
WE HAVE A RIGHT TO PROTECT OURSELVES! DON'T LET THE GOVERNMENT TELL YOU IT'S SAFE TO LIVE AMONG THEM!
xXx
HUMAN RIGHTS FIRST
HOW MANY IS TOO MANY? CONSERVE THE HUMAN RACE

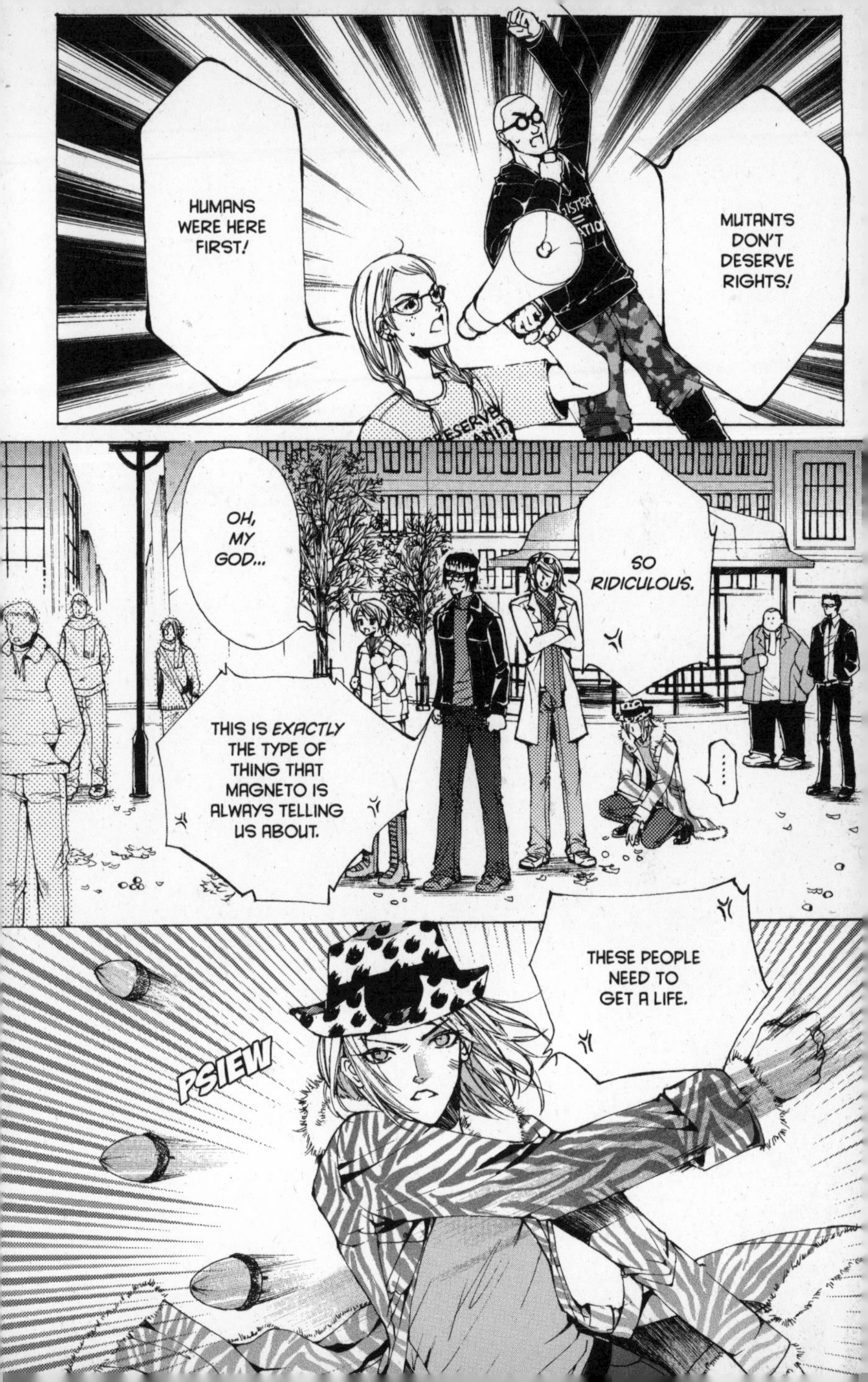
HUMANS WERE HERE FIRST!
MUTANTS DON'T DESERVE RIGHTS!
OH, MY GOD...
SO RIDICULOUS.
THIS IS *EXACTLY* THE TYPE OF THING THAT MAGNETO IS ALWAYS TELLING US ABOUT.
......
THESE PEOPLE NEED TO GET A LIFE.
PSIEW

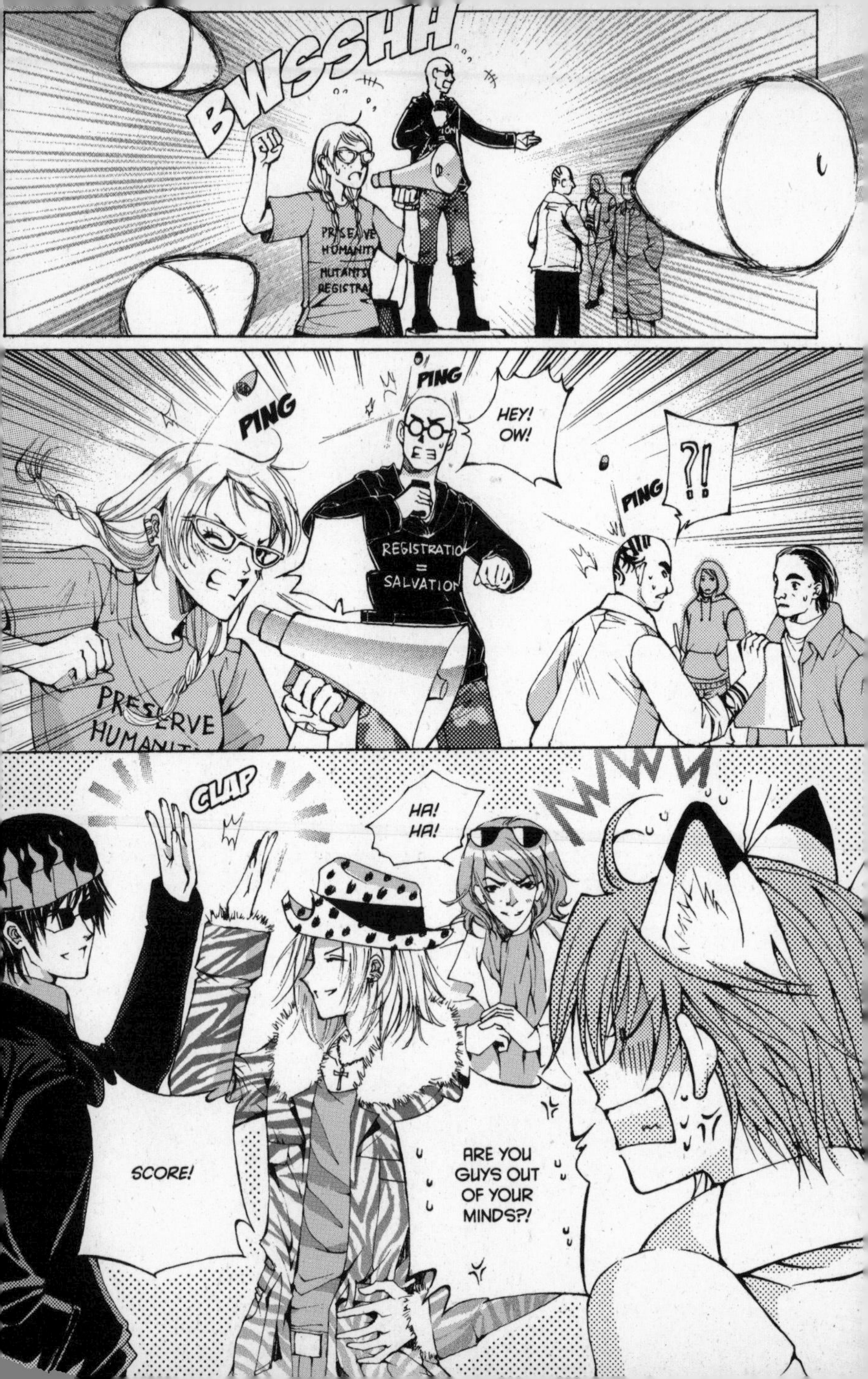
BWSSHH
PING
PING
HEY! OW!
PING
?!
CLAP
HA! HA!
SCORE!
ARE YOU GUYS OUT OF YOUR MINDS?!

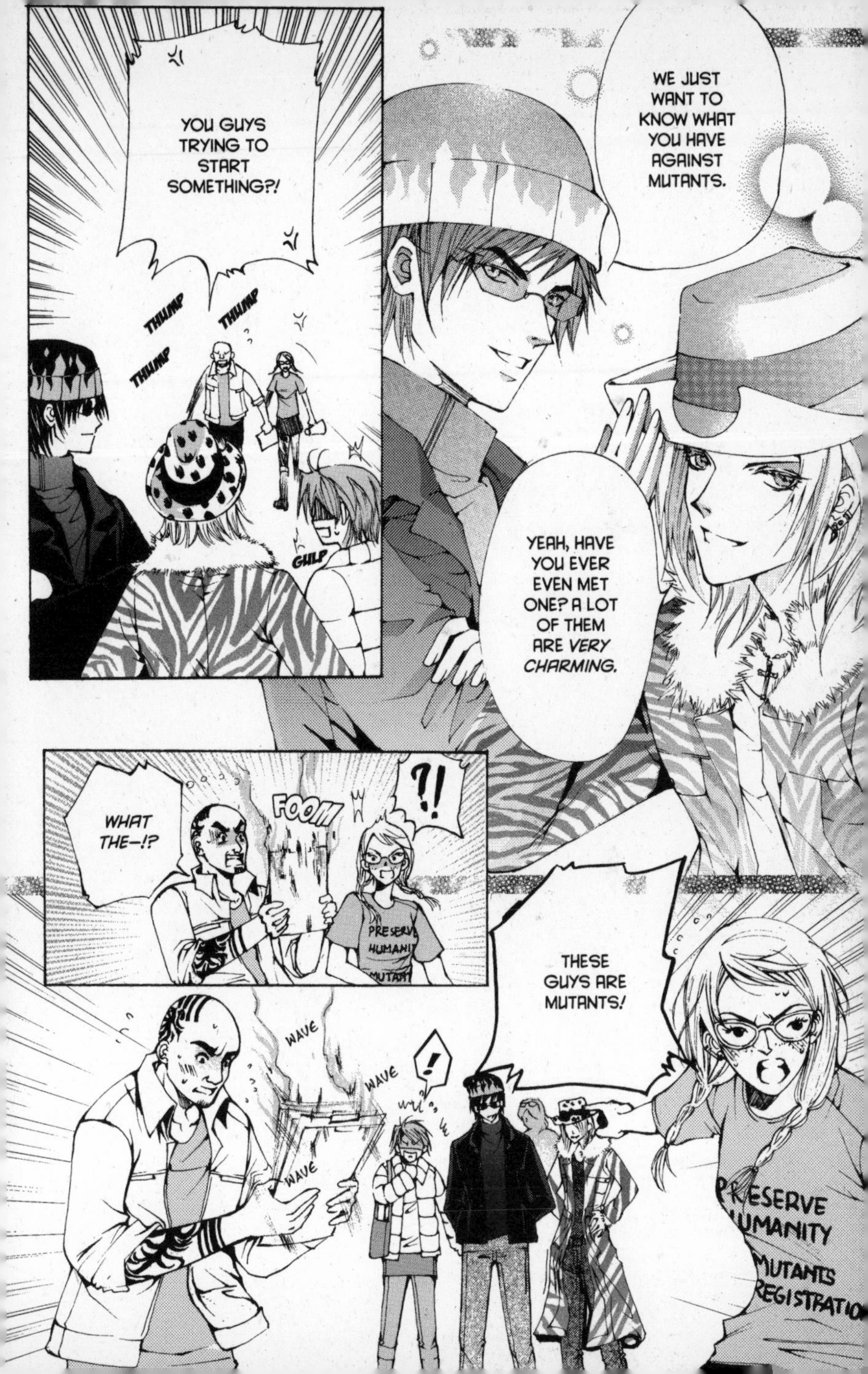
YOU GUYS TRYING TO START SOMETHING?!
THUMP
THUMP
THUMP
GULP
WE JUST WANT TO KNOW WHAT YOU HAVE AGAINST MUTANTS.
YEAH, HAVE YOU EVER EVEN MET ONE? A LOT OF THEM ARE *VERY CHARMING.*
WHAT THE-!?
FOOM
?!
PRESERVE HUMANI
MUTANT
THESE GUYS ARE MUTANTS!
WAVE
WAVE
WAVE
!
PRESERVE HUMANITY
MUTANTS REGISTRATIO

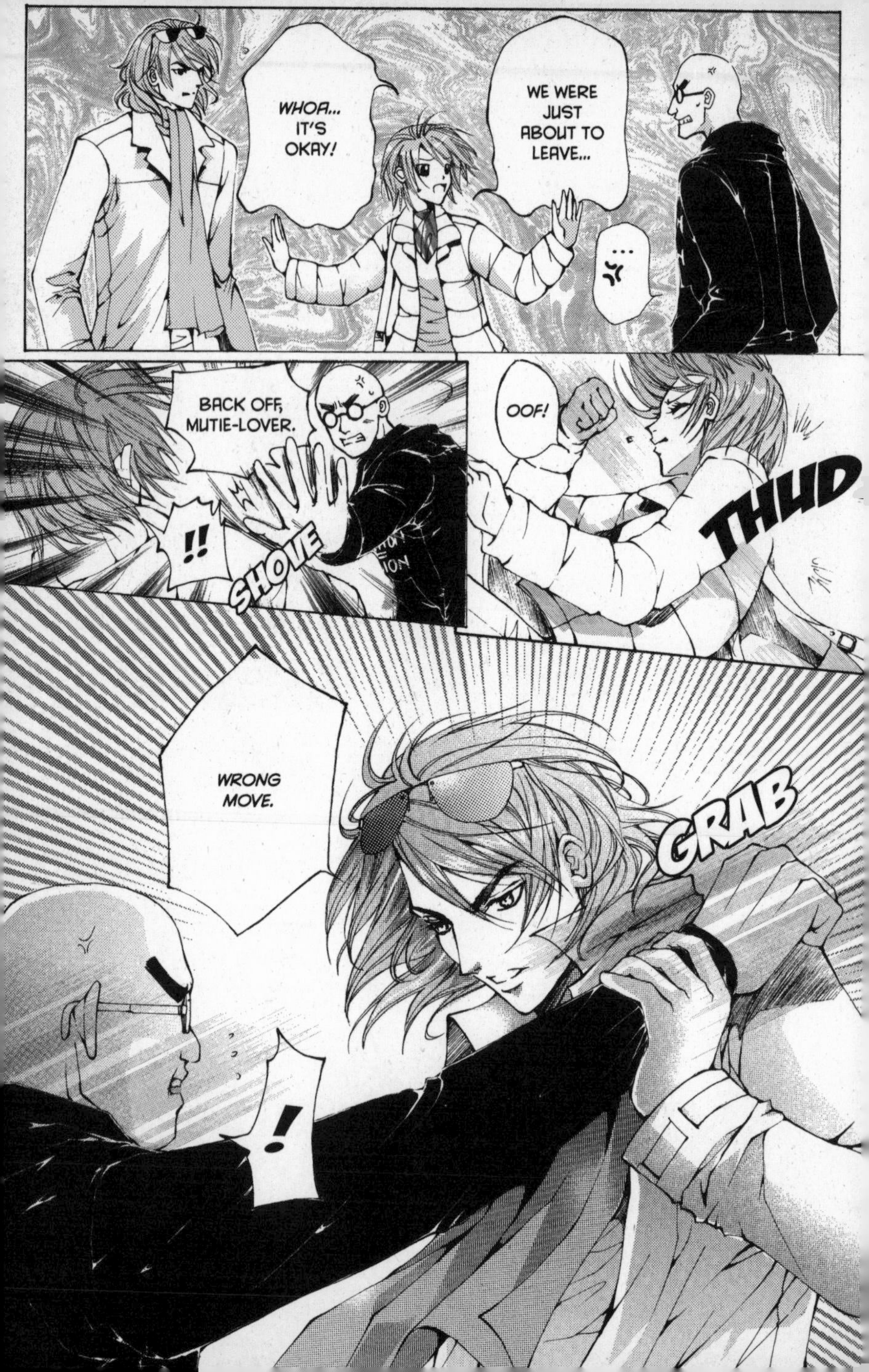
WHOA... IT'S OKAY!
WE WERE JUST ABOUT TO LEAVE...
...
BACK OFF, MUTIE-LOVER.
!!
SHOVE
OOF!
THUD
WRONG MOVE.
GRAB
!

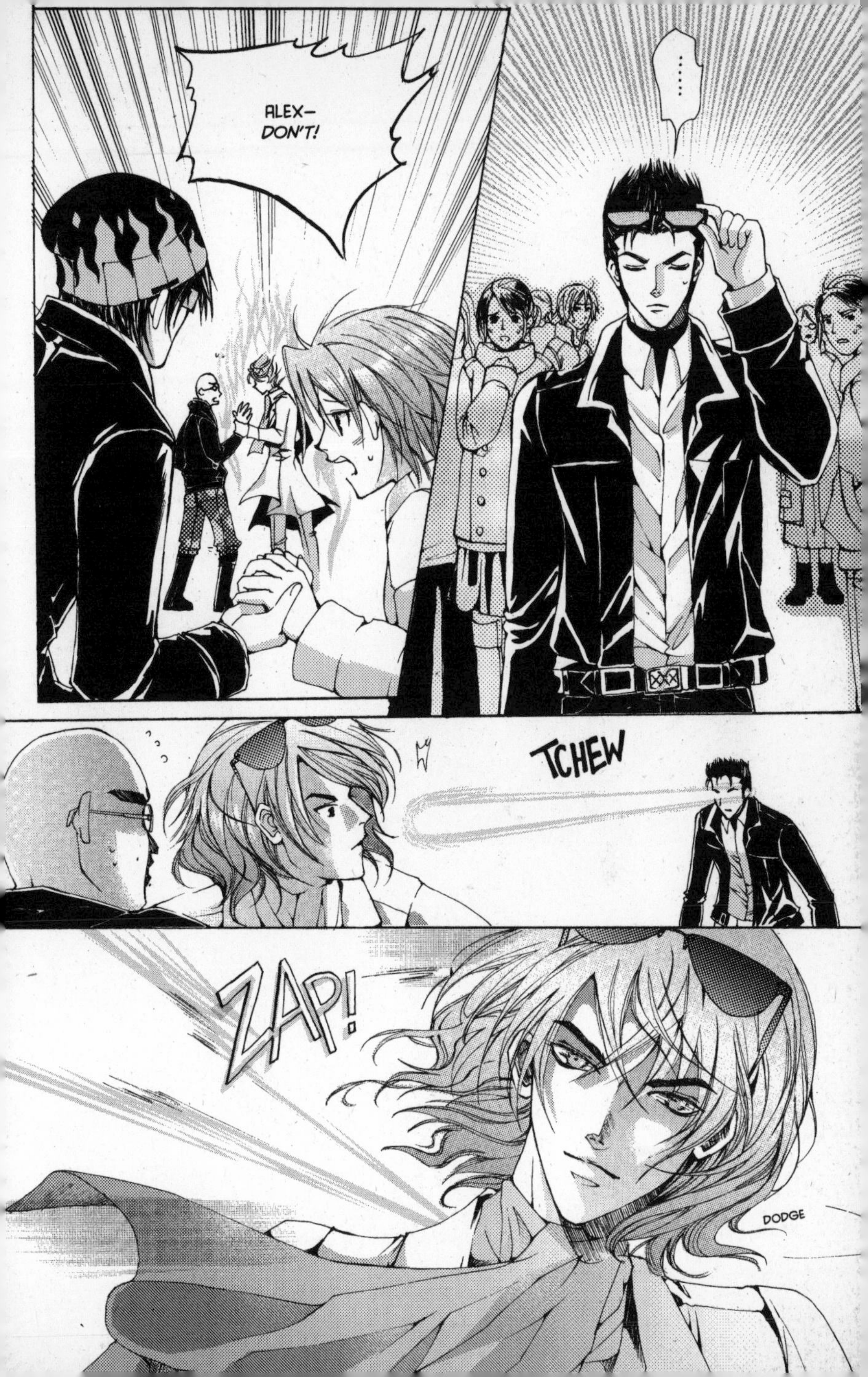
ALEX—
DON'T!
......
TCHEW
ZAP!
DODGE

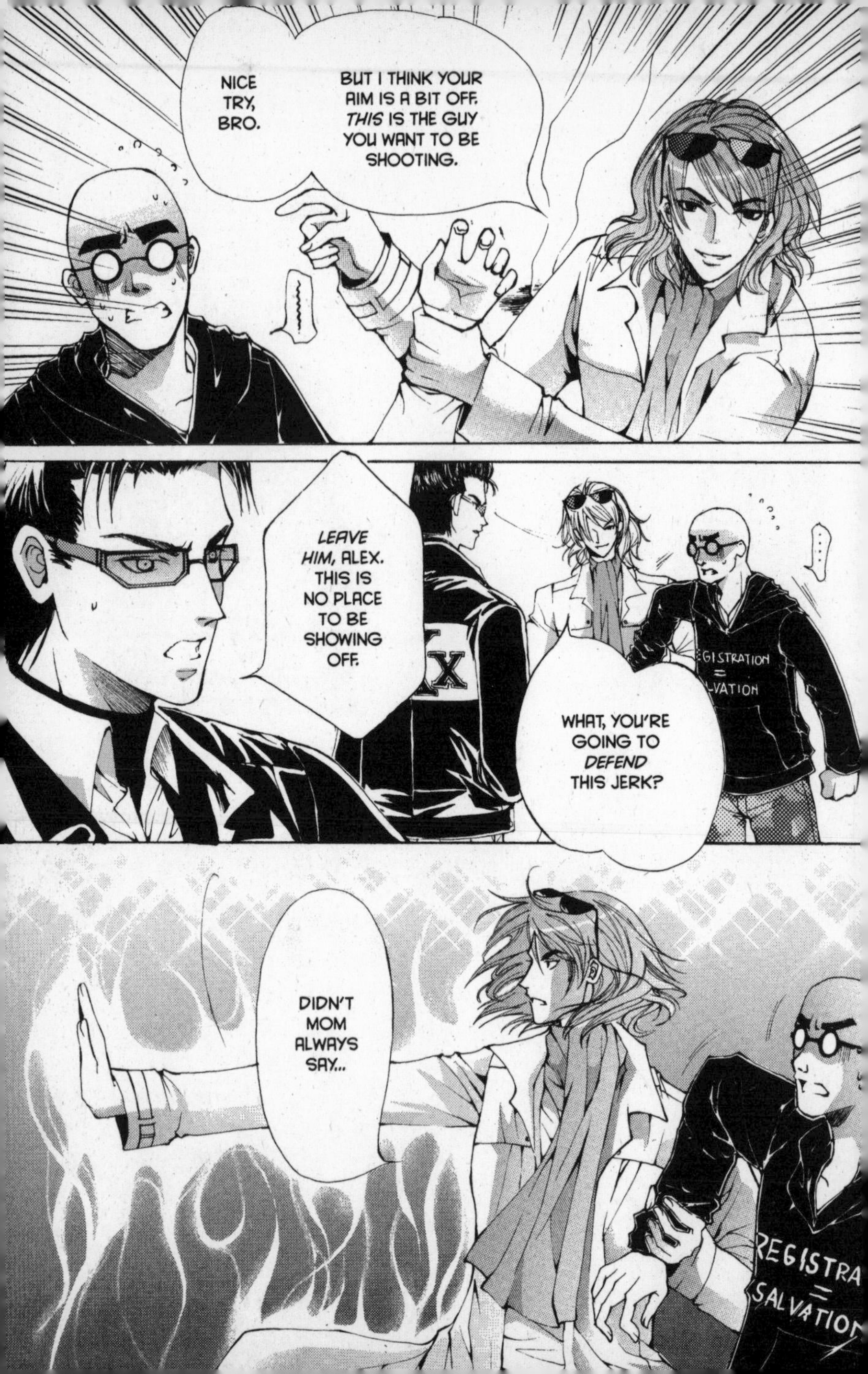
NICE TRY, BRO.
BUT I THINK YOUR AIM IS A BIT OFF. *THIS* IS THE GUY YOU WANT TO BE SHOOTING.
LEAVE HIM, ALEX. THIS IS NO PLACE TO BE SHOWING OFF.
WHAT, YOU'RE GOING TO *DEFEND* THIS JERK?
DIDN'T MOM ALWAYS SAY...

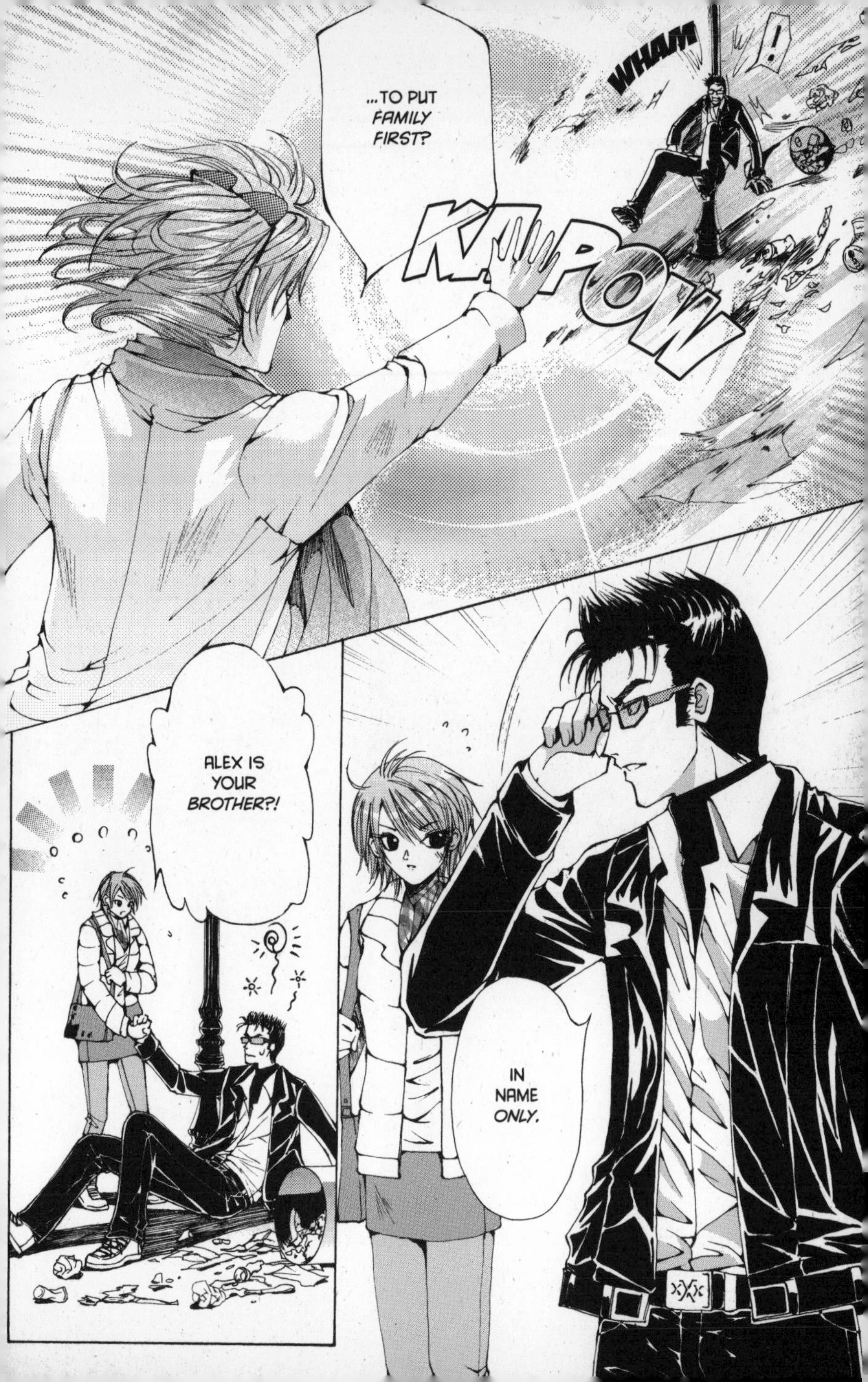
...TO PUT FAMILY FIRST?
KAPOW
WHAM
!
ALEX IS YOUR BROTHER?!
IN NAME ONLY.

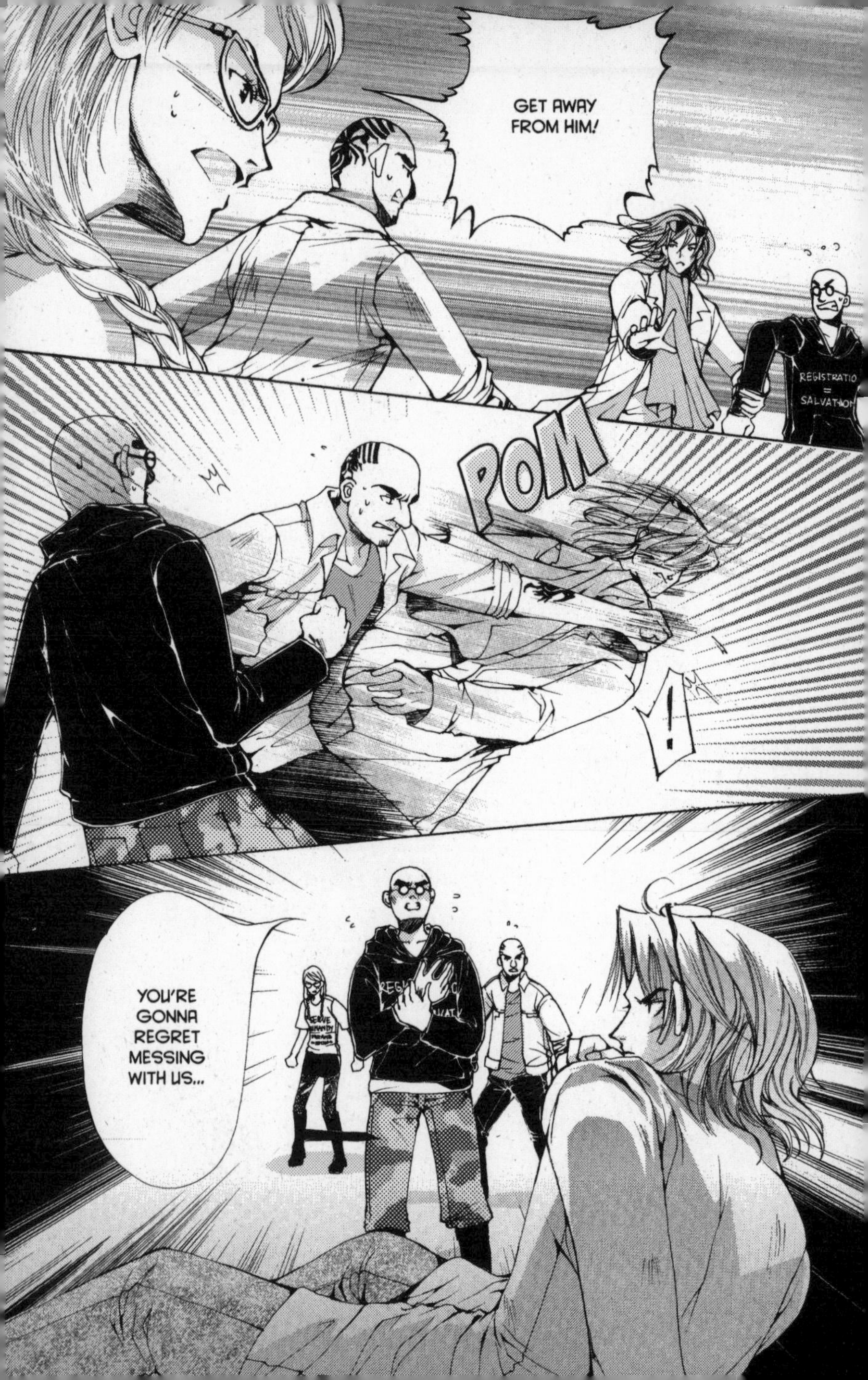
GET AWAY FROM HIM!
REGISTRATIO = SALVATION
POM
!
YOU'RE GONNA REGRET MESSING WITH US...

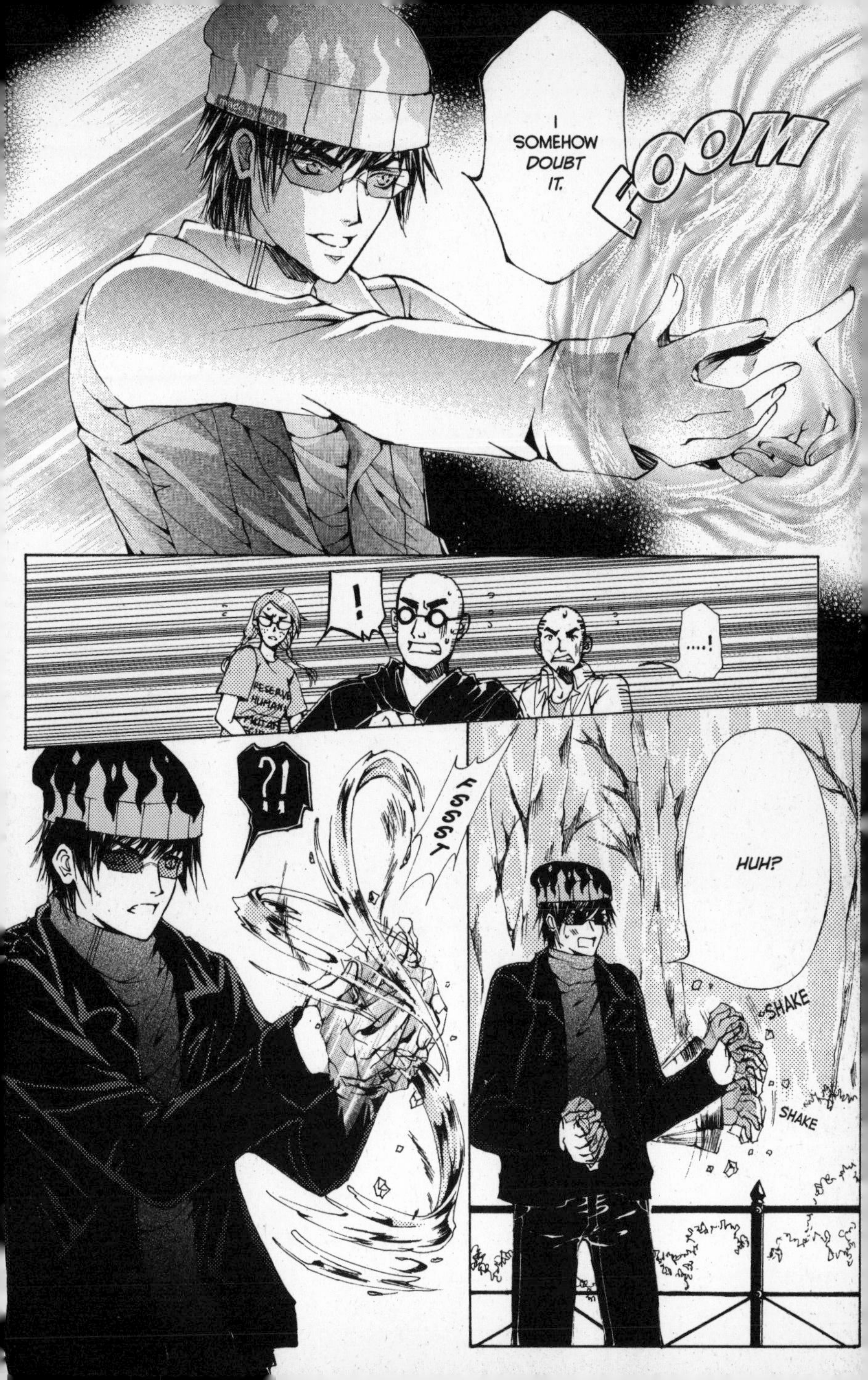
I SOMEHOW DOUBT IT.
FOOM
!
....!
?!
FOOOOT
HUH?
SHAKE
SHAKE

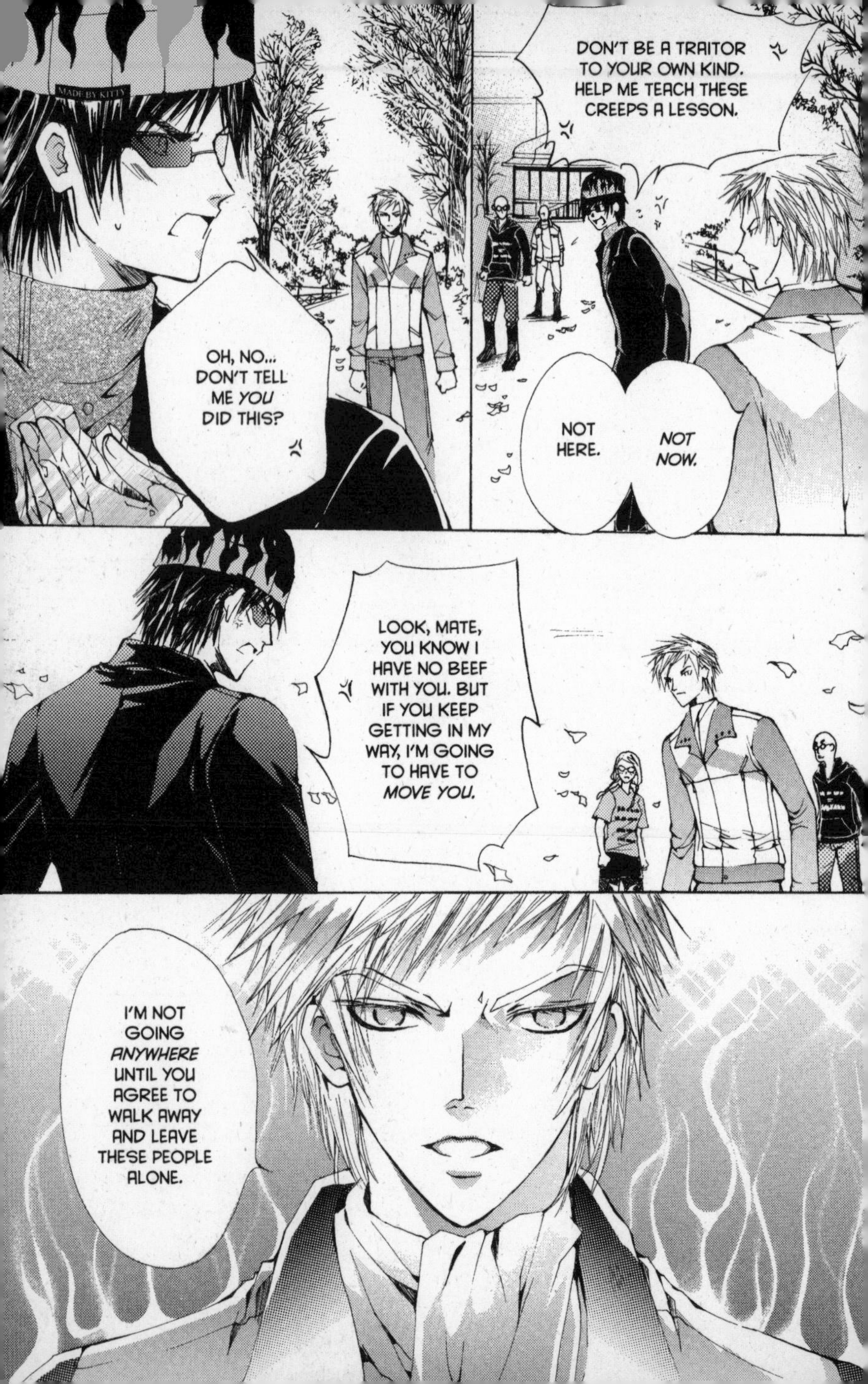
MADE BY KITTY
OH, NO... DON'T TELL ME *YOU* DID THIS?
DON'T BE A TRAITOR TO YOUR OWN KIND. HELP ME TEACH THESE CREEPS A LESSON.
NOT HERE.
NOT NOW.
LOOK, MATE, YOU KNOW I HAVE NO BEEF WITH YOU. BUT IF YOU KEEP GETTING IN MY WAY, I'M GOING TO HAVE TO *MOVE YOU.*
I'M NOT GOING *ANYWHERE* UNTIL YOU AGREE TO WALK AWAY AND LEAVE THESE PEOPLE ALONE.

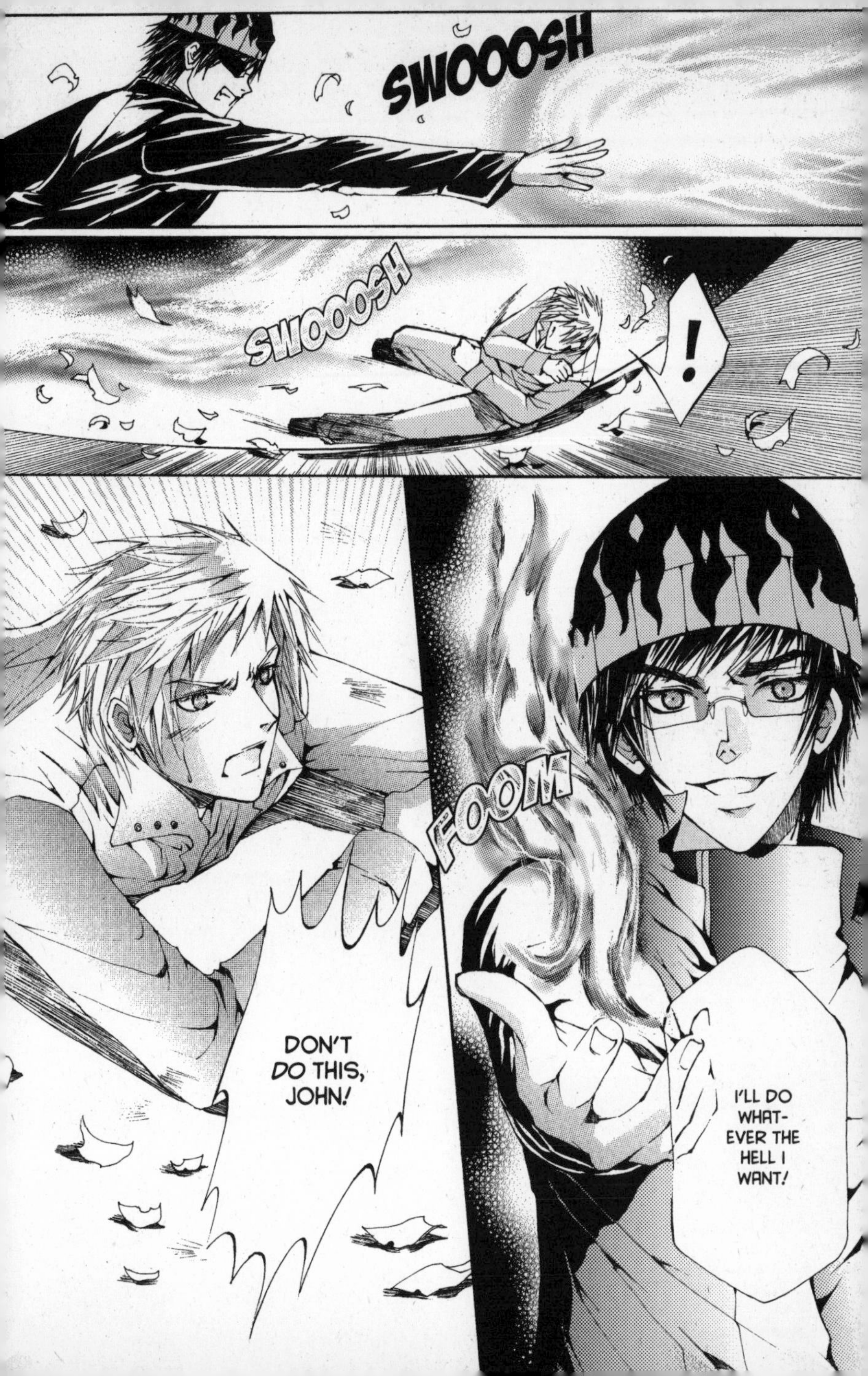
SWOOOSH
SWOOOSH
!
DON'T DO THIS, JOHN!
FOOM
I'LL DO WHAT-EVER THE HELL I WANT!

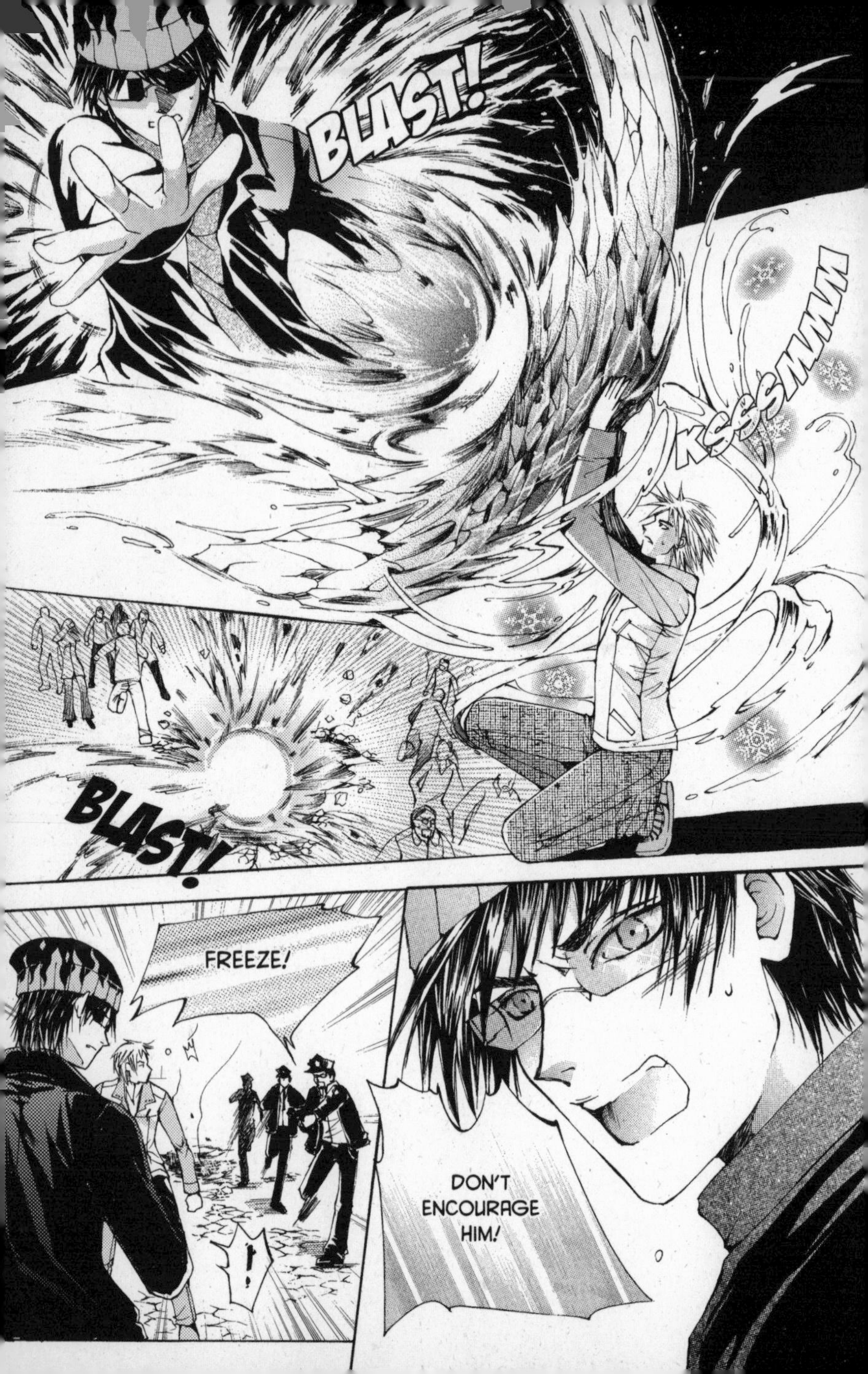
BLAST!
KSSSMMM
BLAST!
FREEZE!
!
!
DON'T ENCOURAGE HIM!

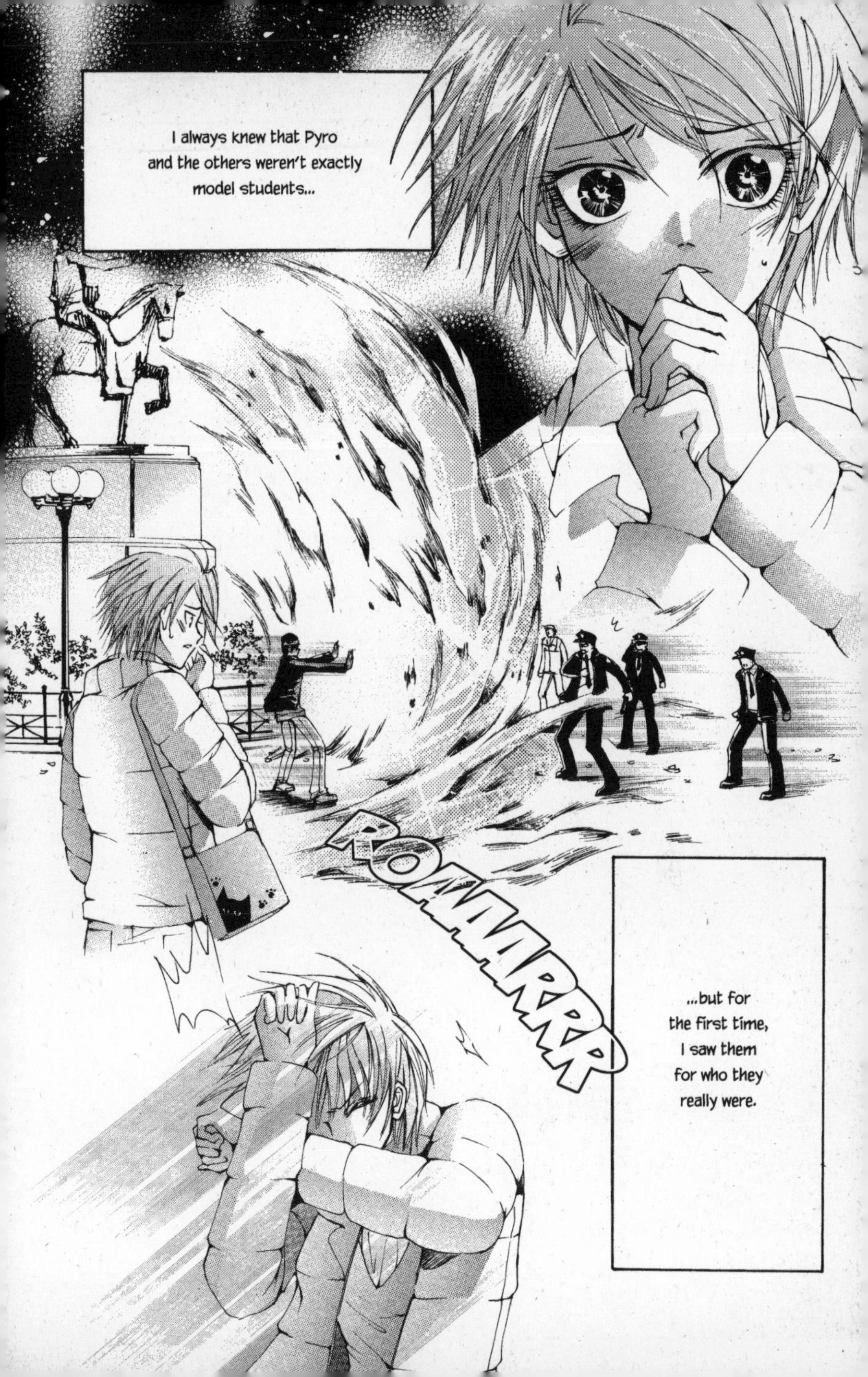
I always knew that Pyro and the others weren't exactly model students...
ROWWRRR
...but for the first time, I saw them for who they really were.

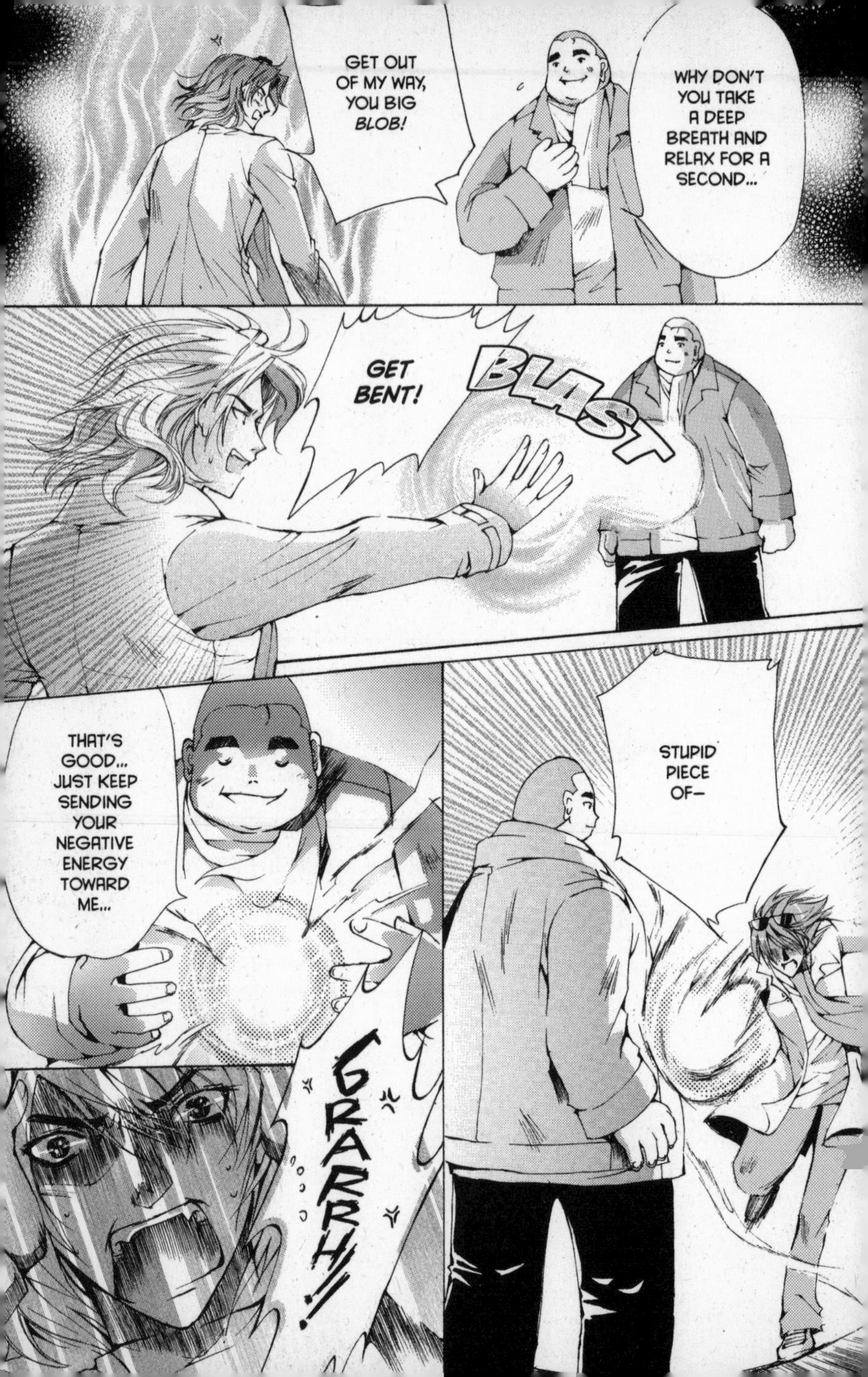
GET OUT OF MY WAY, YOU BIG *BLOB!*
WHY DON'T YOU TAKE A DEEP BREATH AND RELAX FOR A SECOND...
GET BENT!
BLAST
THAT'S GOOD... JUST KEEP SENDING YOUR NEGATIVE ENERGY TOWARD ME...
GRARRH!!
STUPID PIECE OF–

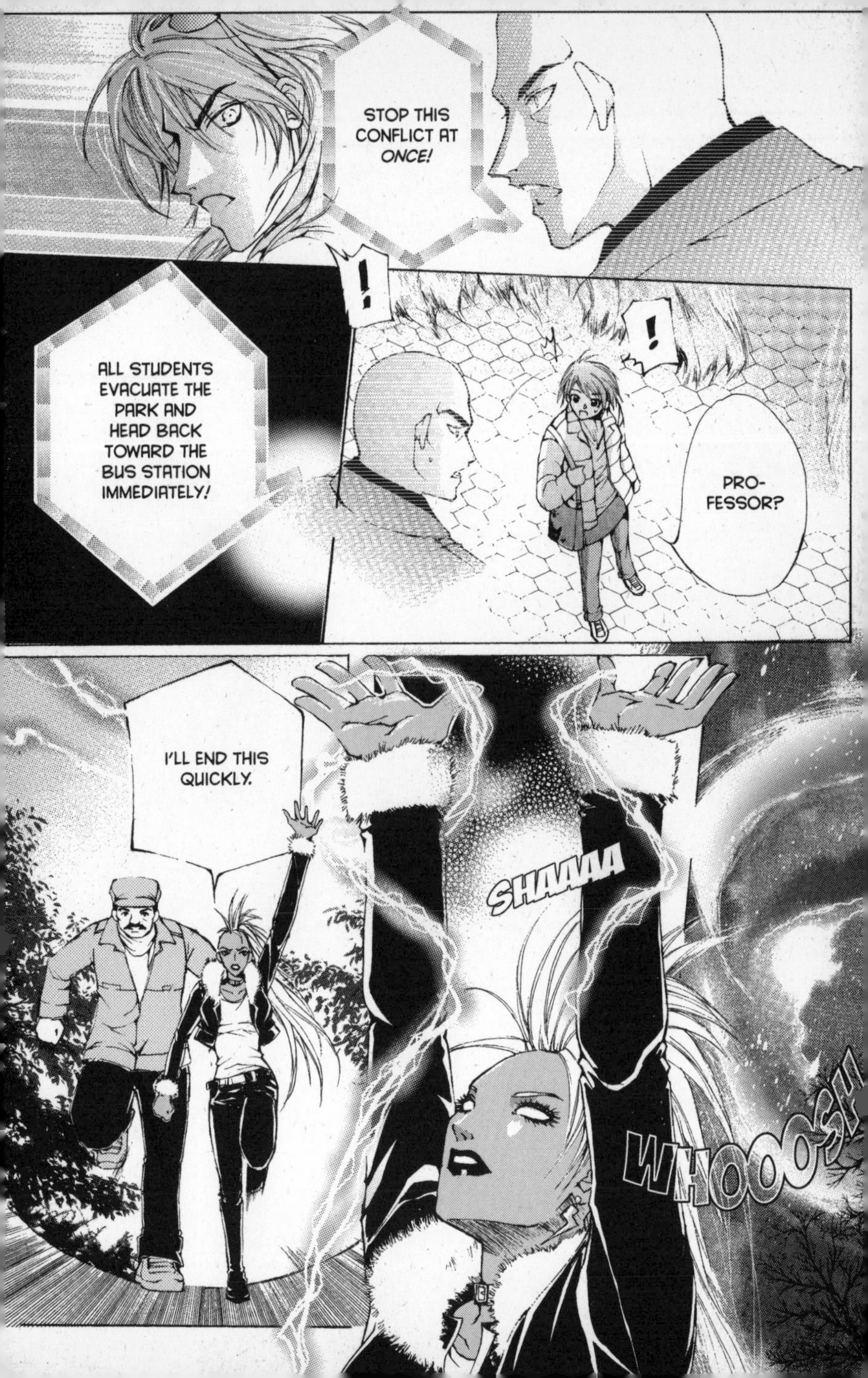
STOP THIS CONFLICT AT ONCE!
ALL STUDENTS EVACUATE THE PARK AND HEAD BACK TOWARD THE BUS STATION IMMEDIATELY!
!
!
PRO-FESSOR?
I'LL END THIS QUICKLY.
SHAAAA
WHOOOSH

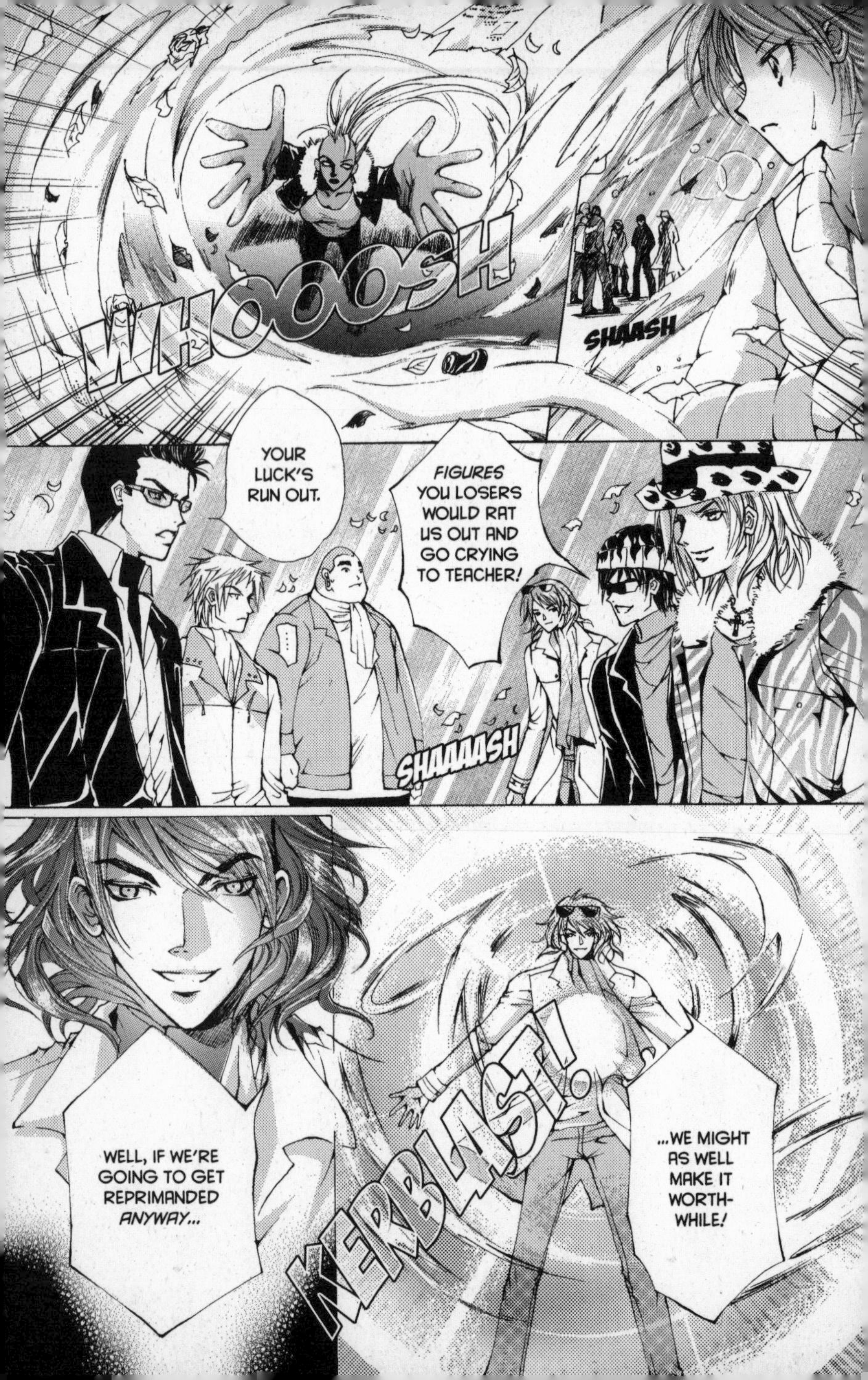
WHOOOOSH
SHAASH
YOUR LUCK'S RUN OUT.
FIGURES YOU LOSERS WOULD RAT US OUT AND GO CRYING TO TEACHER!
SHAAAASH
WELL, IF WE'RE GOING TO GET REPRIMANDED *ANYWAY*...
KERBLAST!
...WE MIGHT AS WELL MAKE IT WORTH-WHILE!

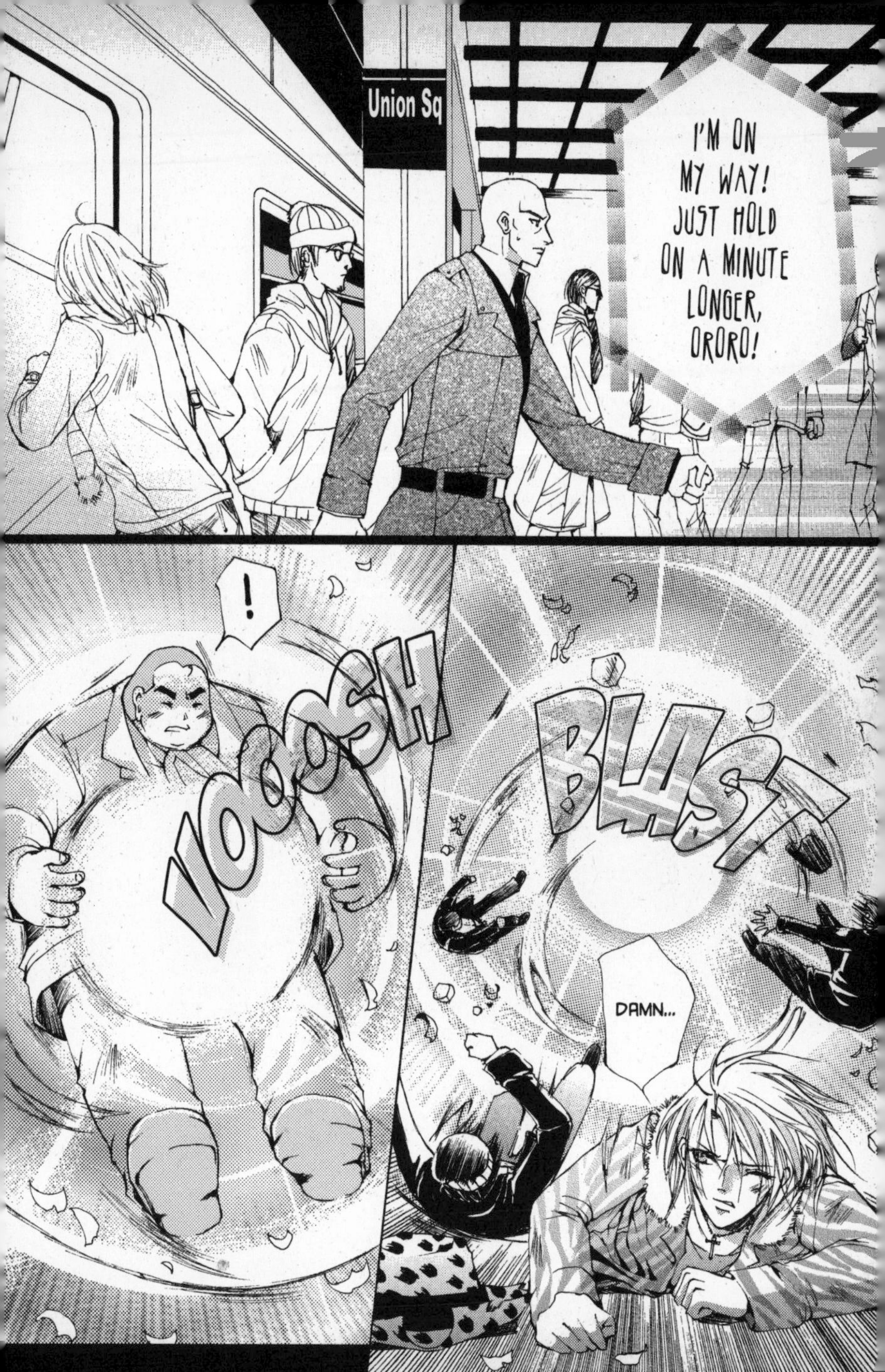
Union Sq
I'M ON MY WAY! JUST HOLD ON A MINUTE LONGER, ORORO!
!
VOOOOSH
BLAST
DAMN...

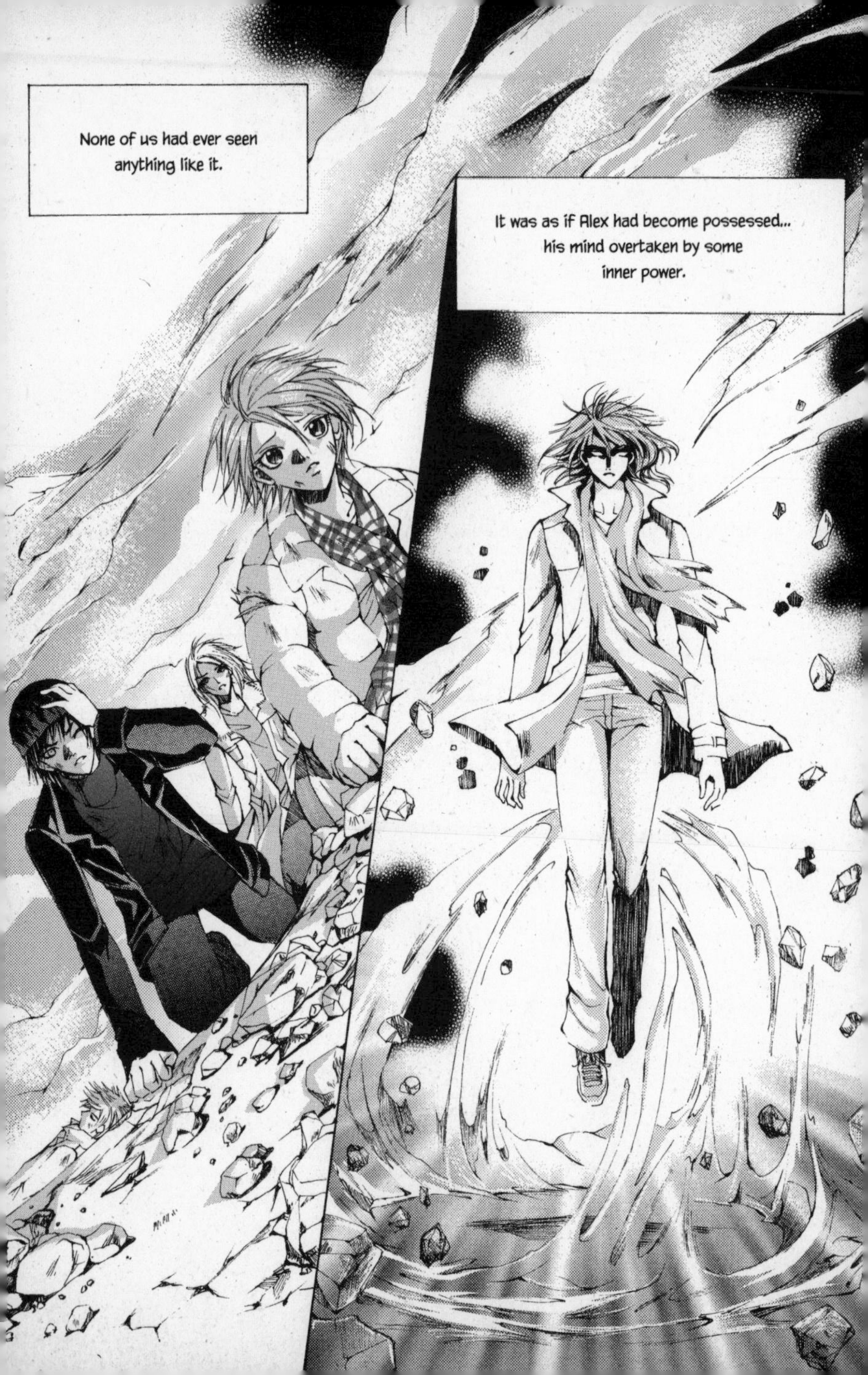
None of us had ever seen anything like it.
It was as if Alex had become possessed... his mind overtaken by some inner power.

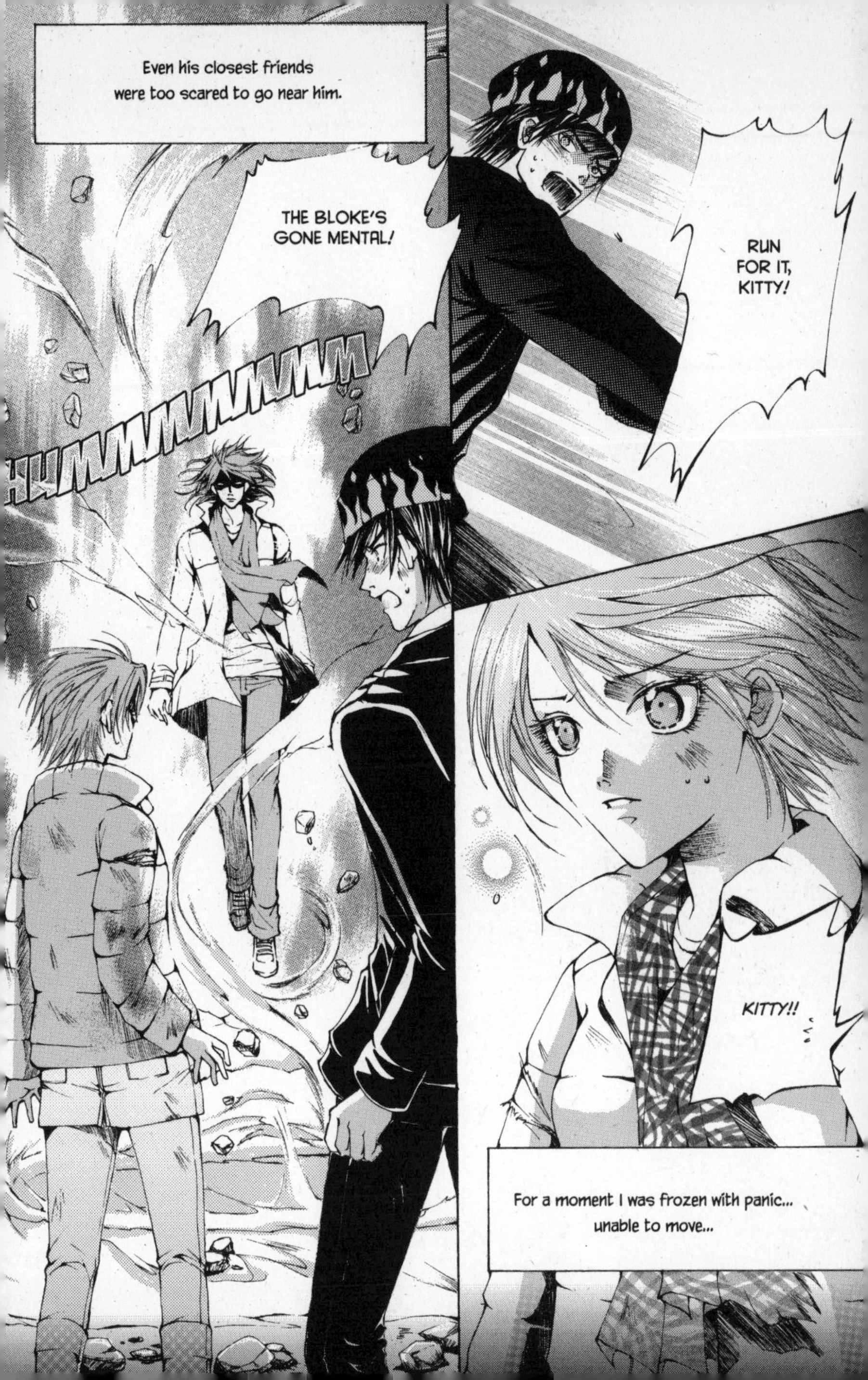
Even his closest friends
were too scared to go near him.
THE BLOKE'S GONE MENTAL!
HUMMMMMMMMM
RUN FOR IT, KITTY!
KITTY!!
For a moment I was frozen with panic...
unable to move...

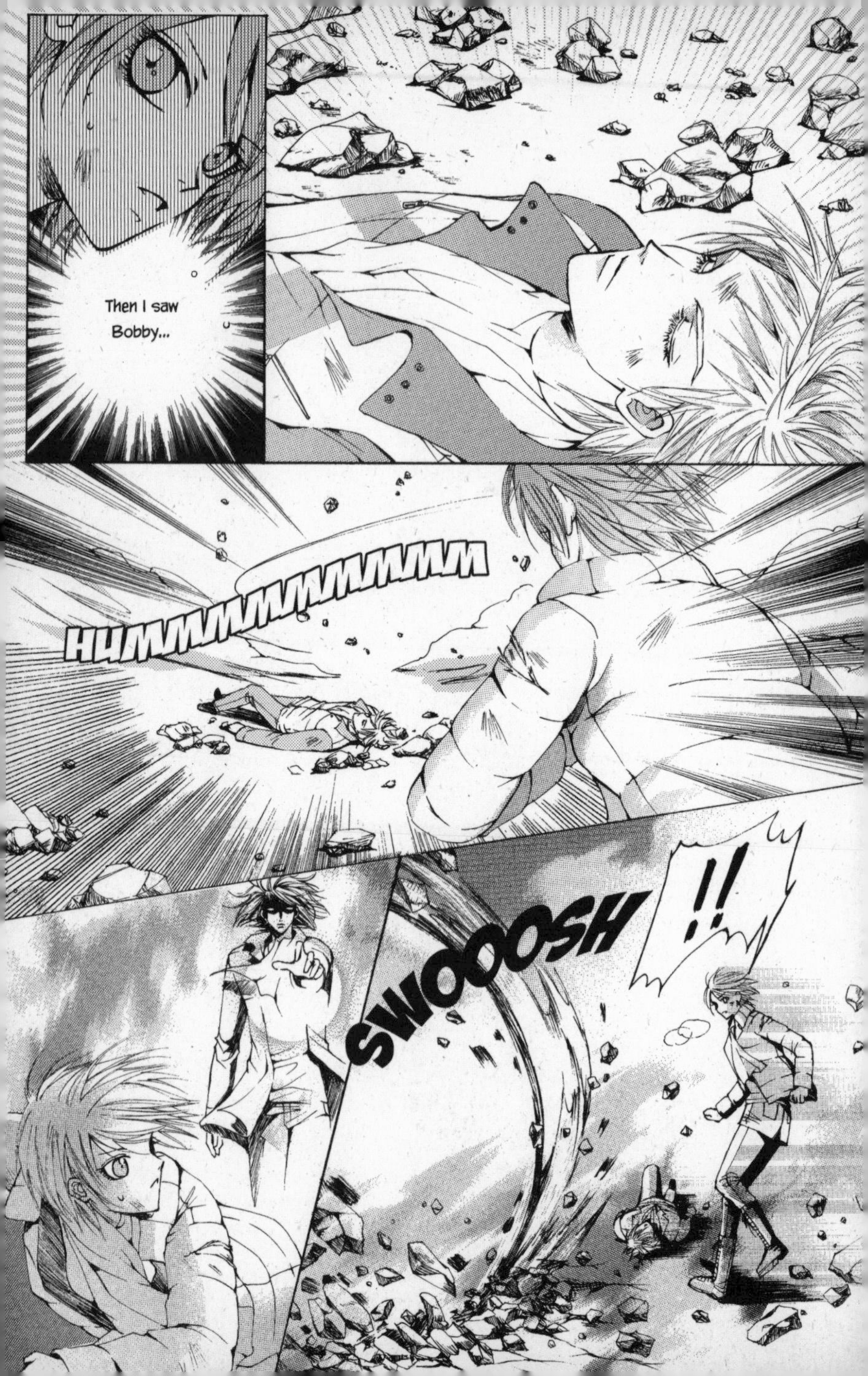
Then I saw Bobby...
HUMMMMMMMMMMMM
SWOOOSH
!!

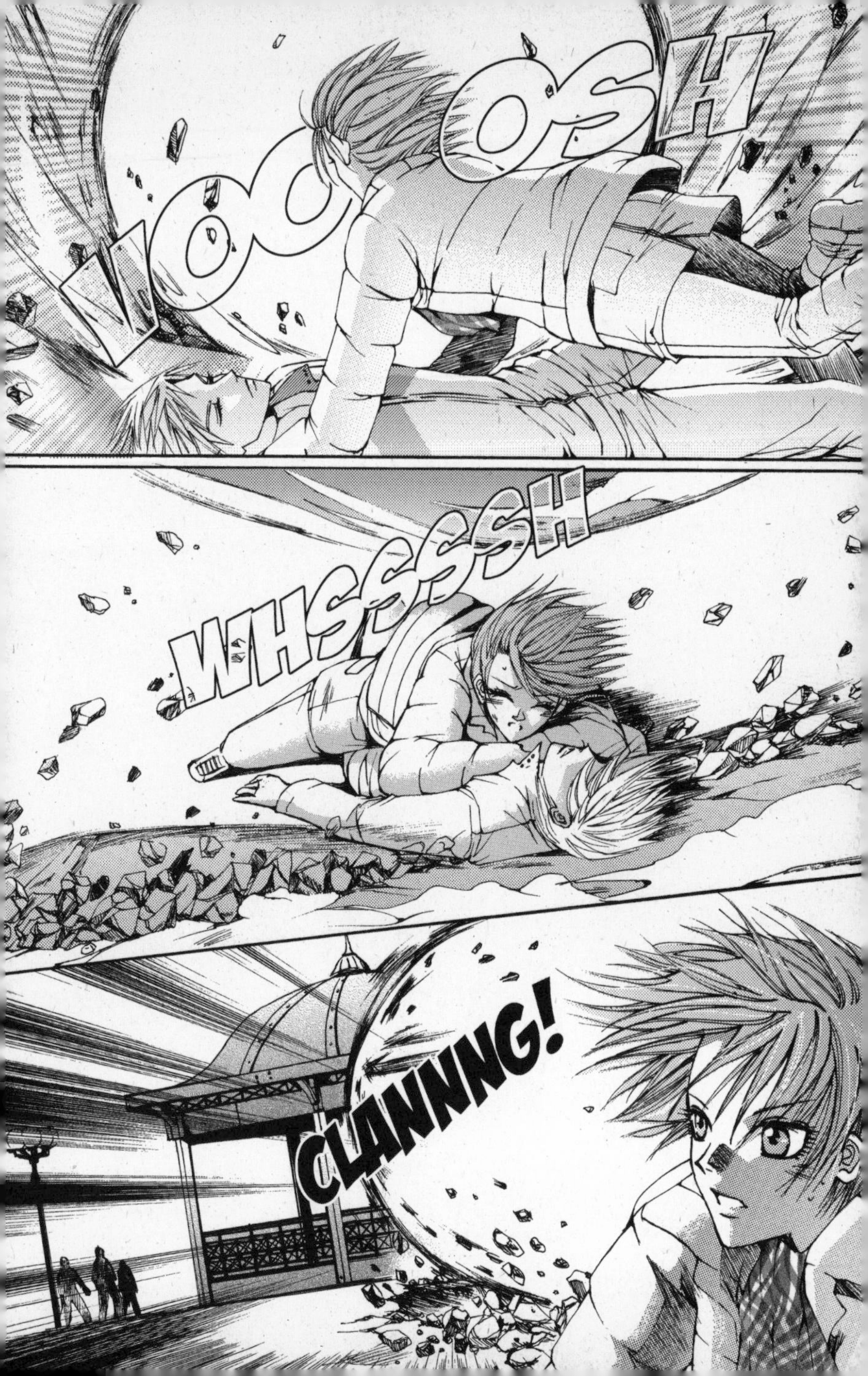
VOOOOSH
WHSSSSH
CLANNNG!

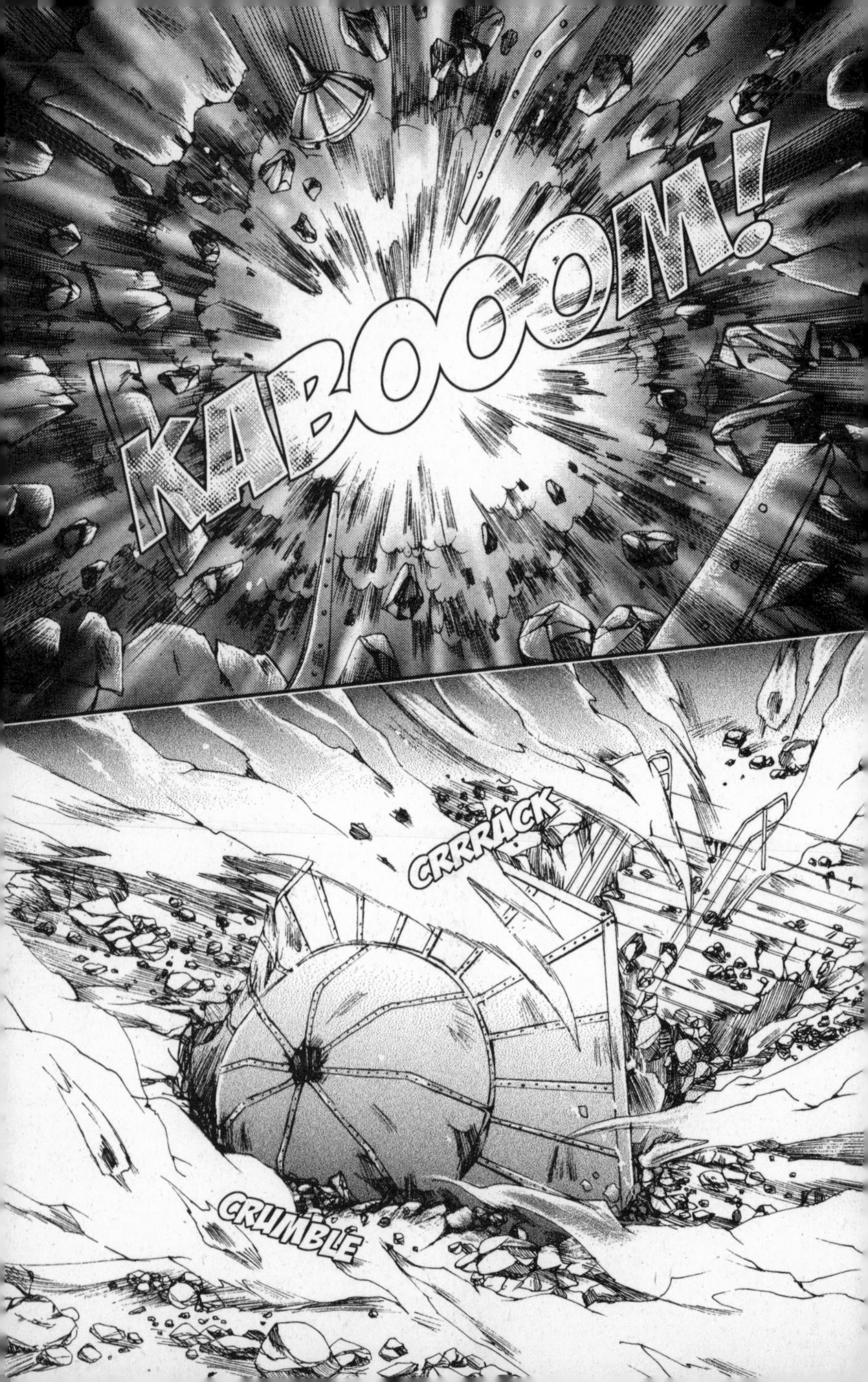
KABOOOM!
CRRRACK
CRUMBLE

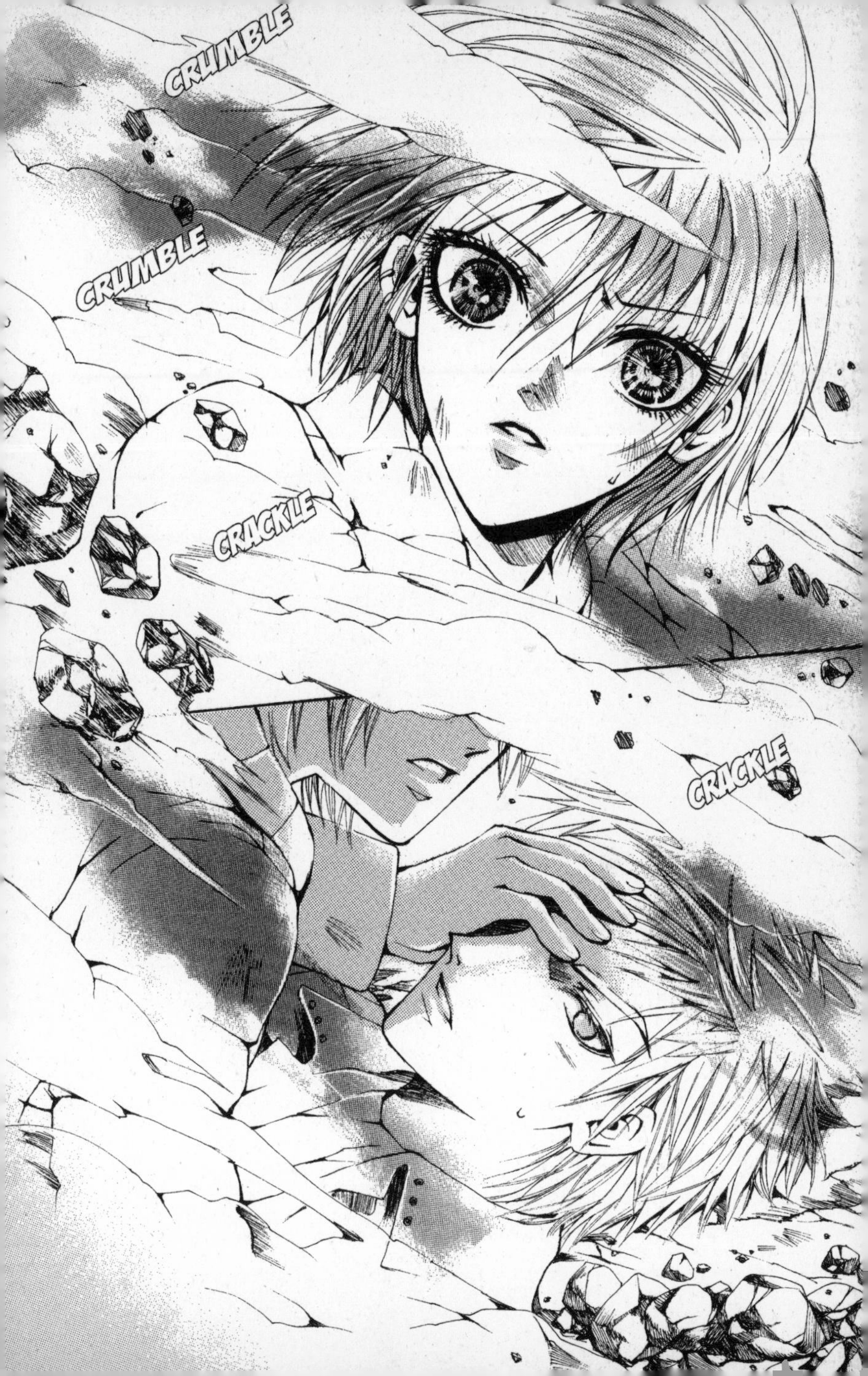
CRUMBLE
CRUMBLE
CRACKLE
CRACKLE

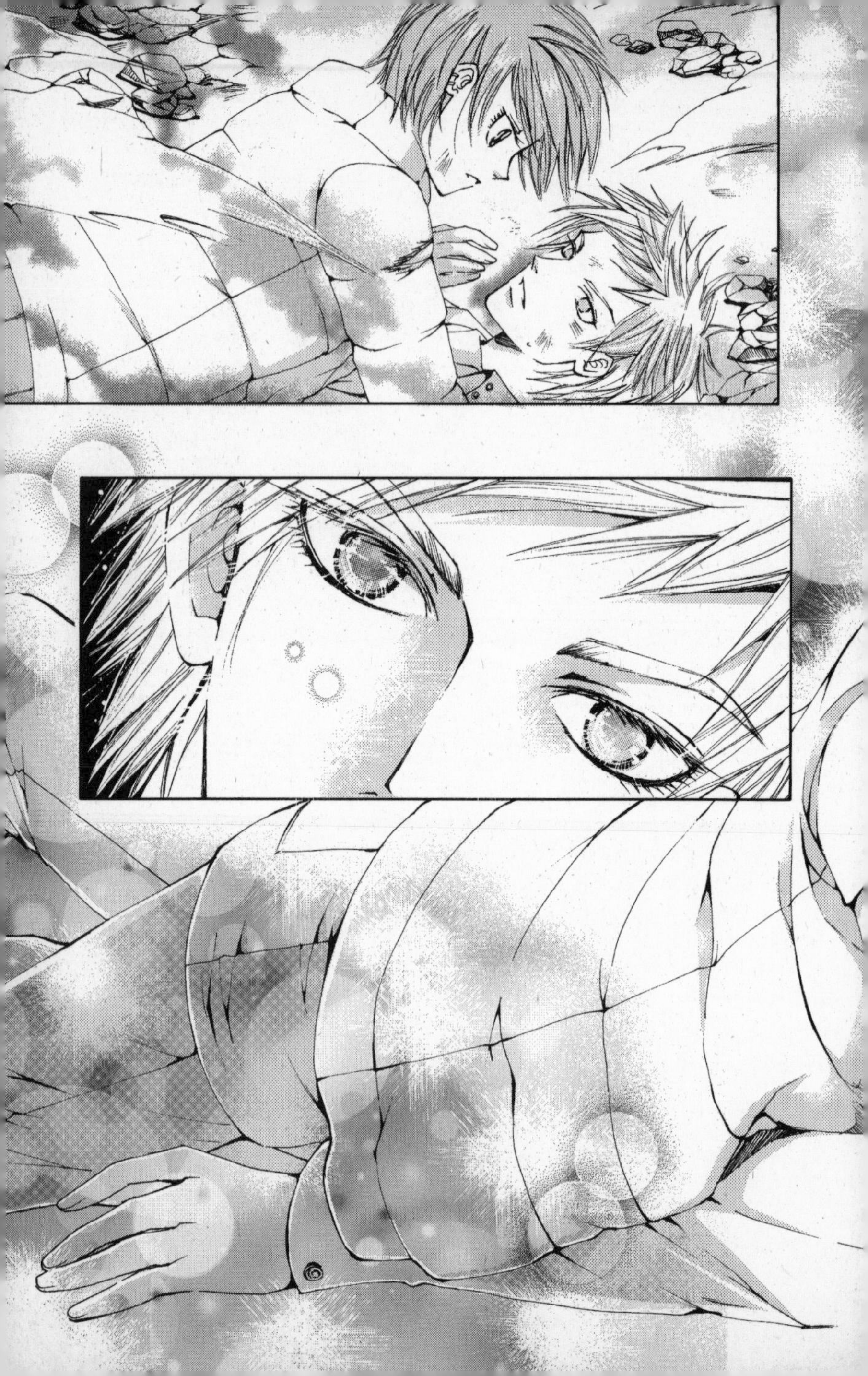

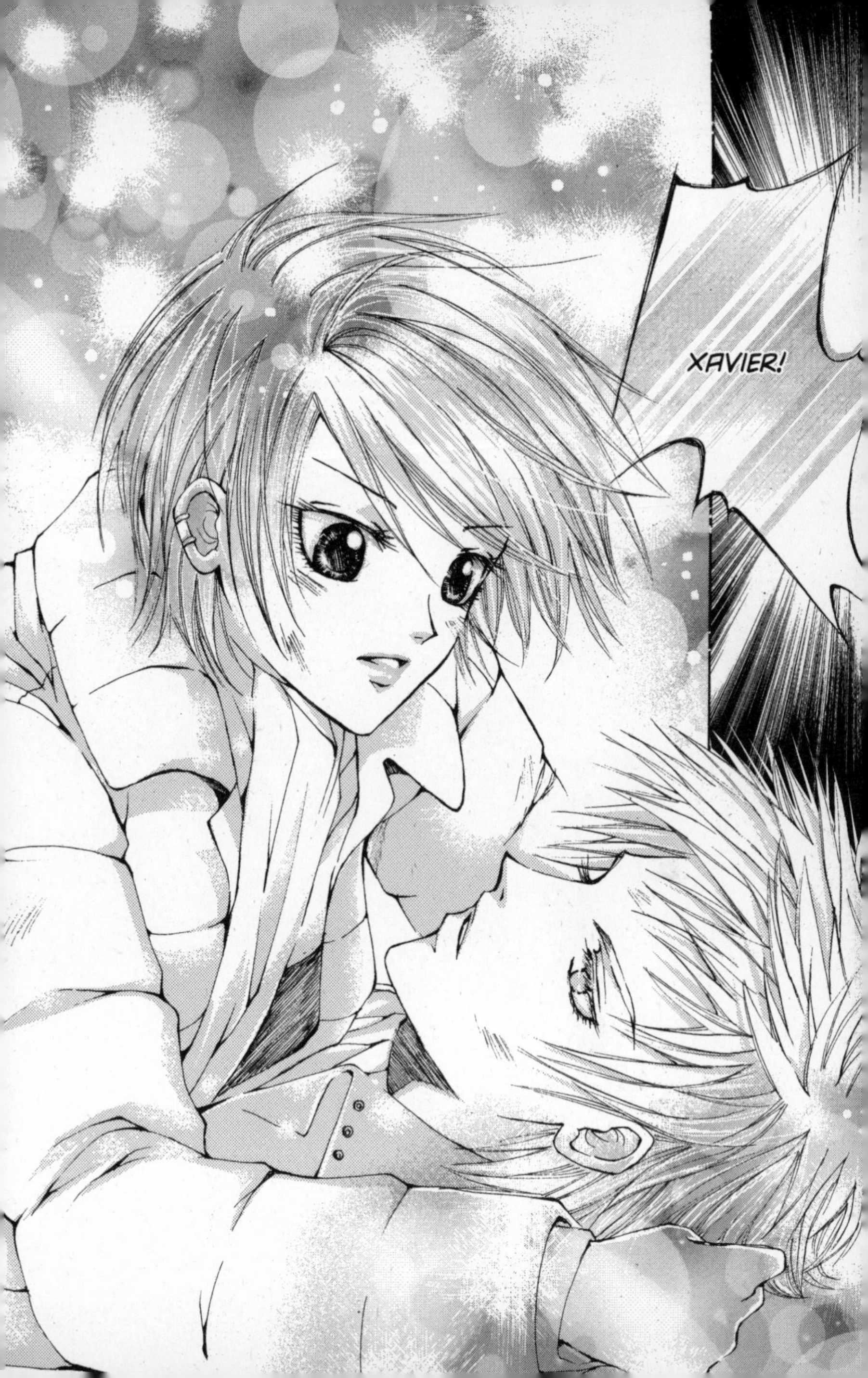
XAVIER!

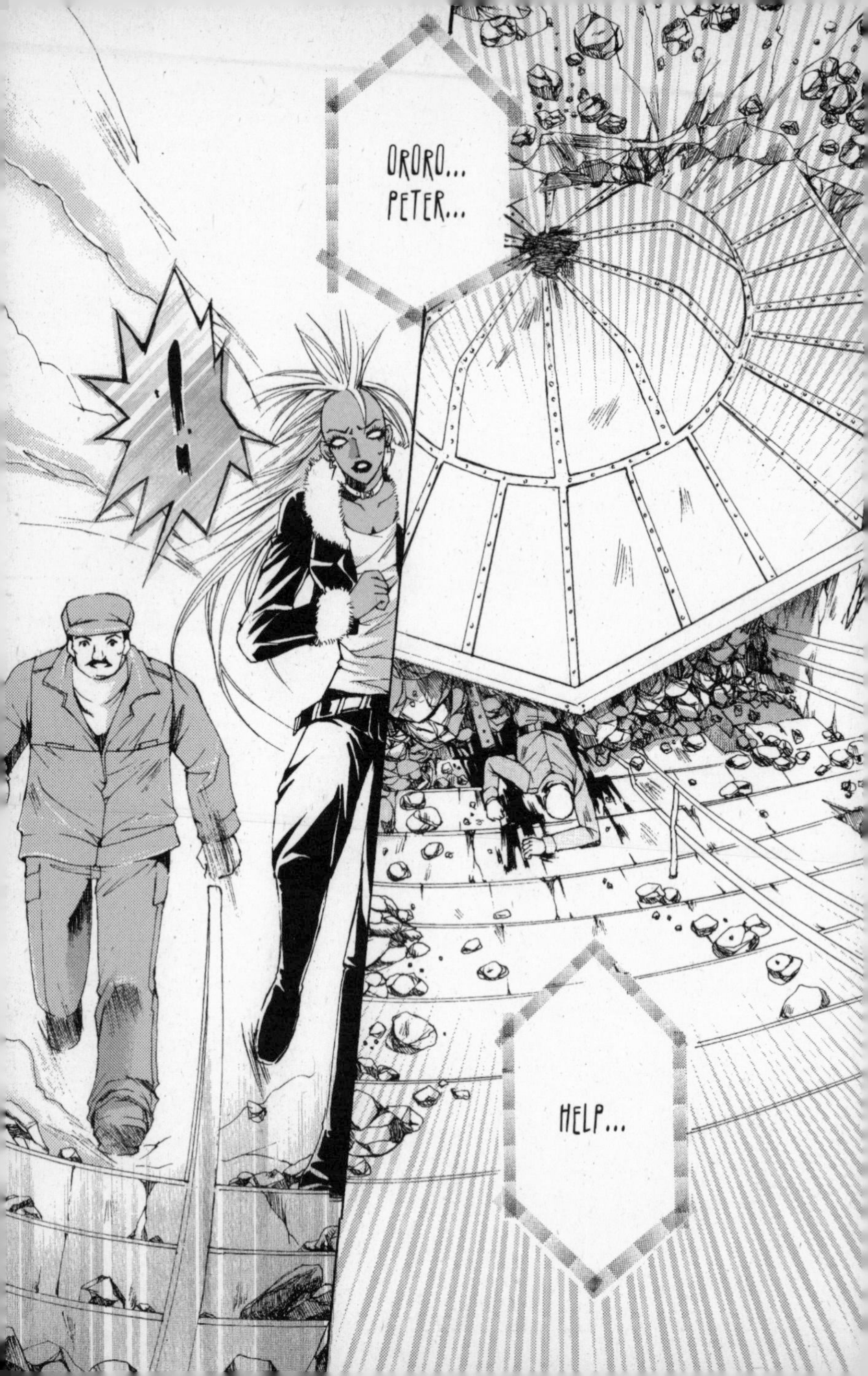
!
ORORO...
PETER...
HELP...

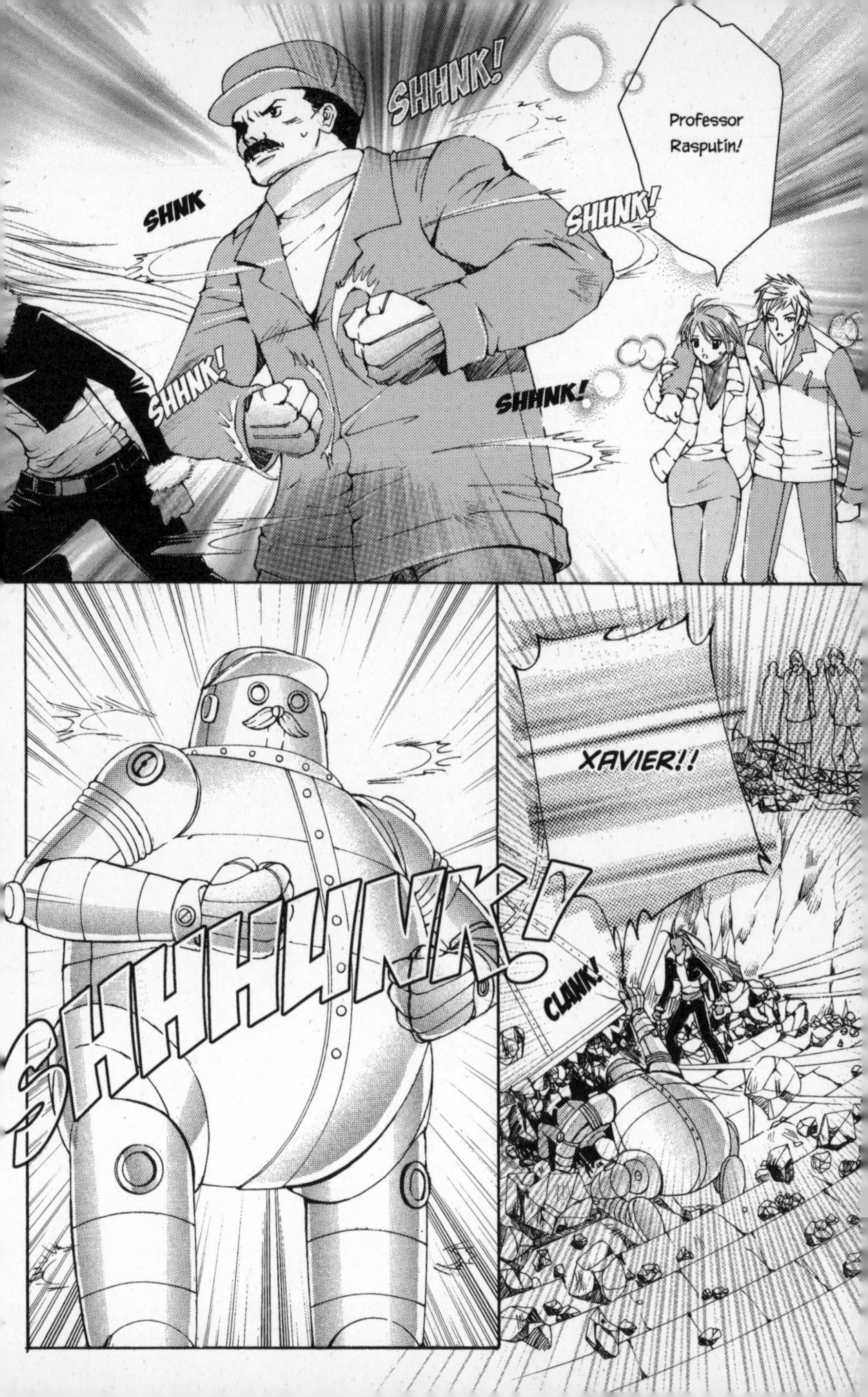
SHHNK!
Professor Rasputin!
SHNK
SHHNK!
SHHNK!
SHHNK!
SHHHHNK!
XAVIER!!
CLANK!

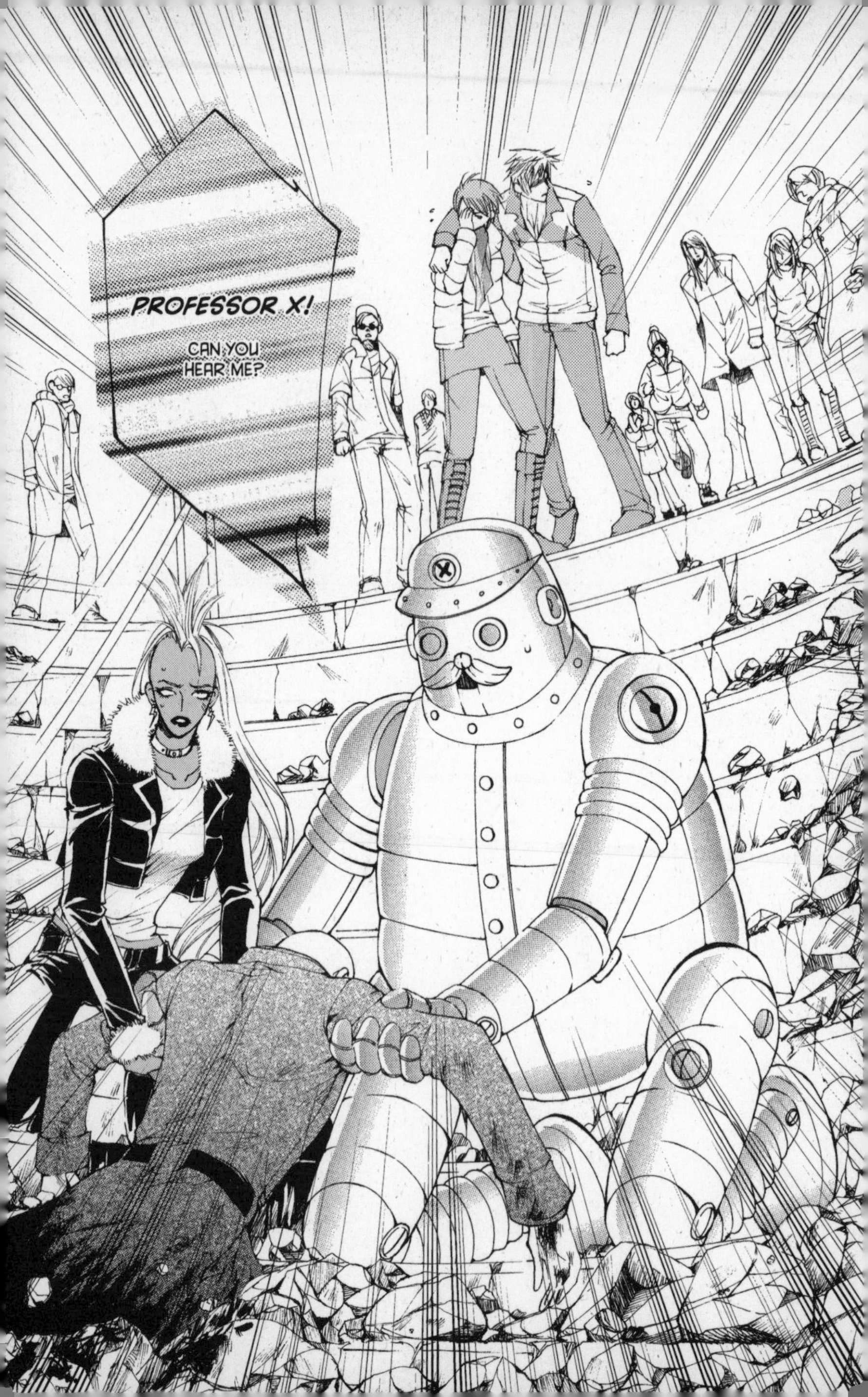
PROFESSOR X!
CAN YOU HEAR ME?

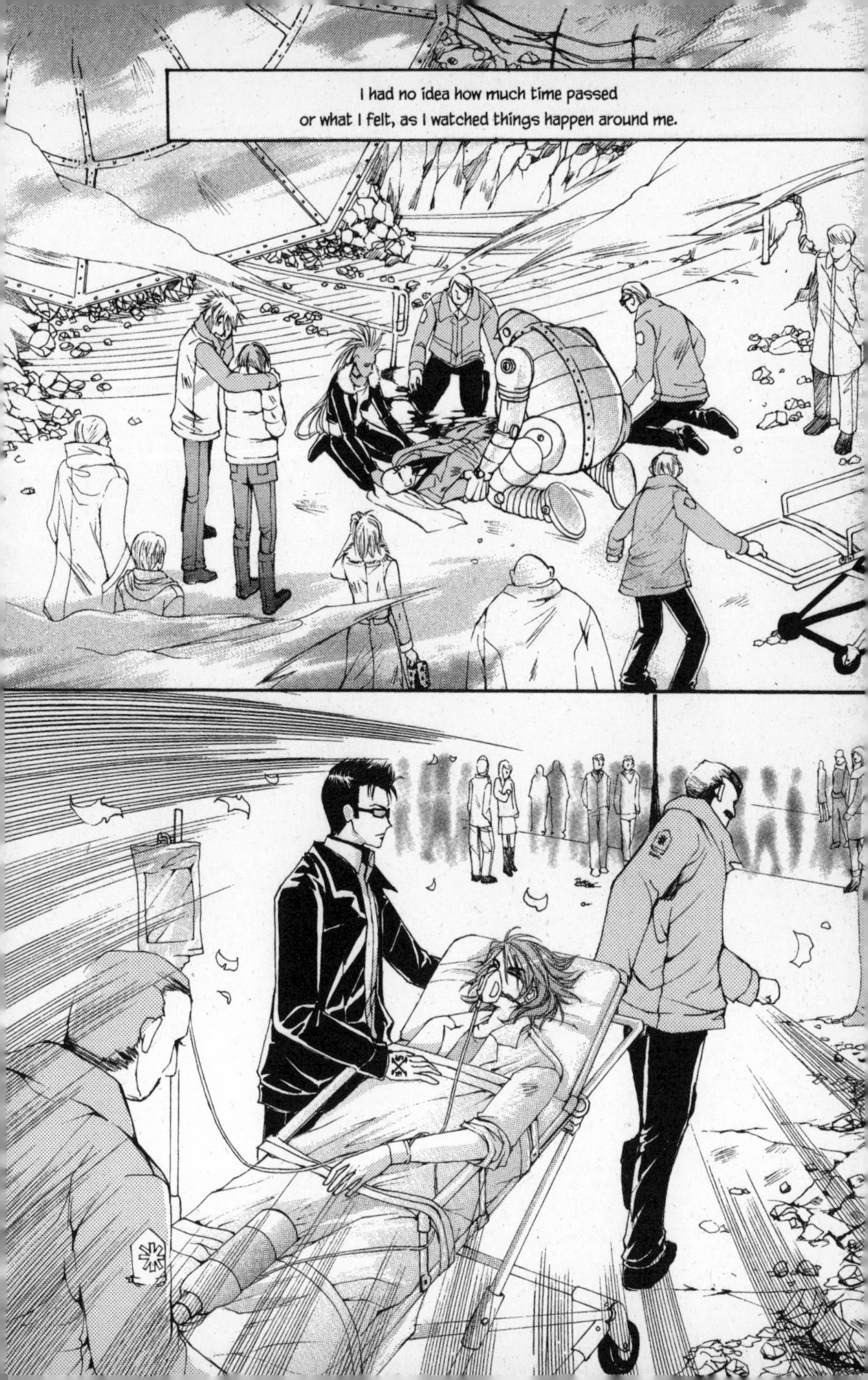
I had no idea how much time passed
or what I felt, as I watched things happen around me.

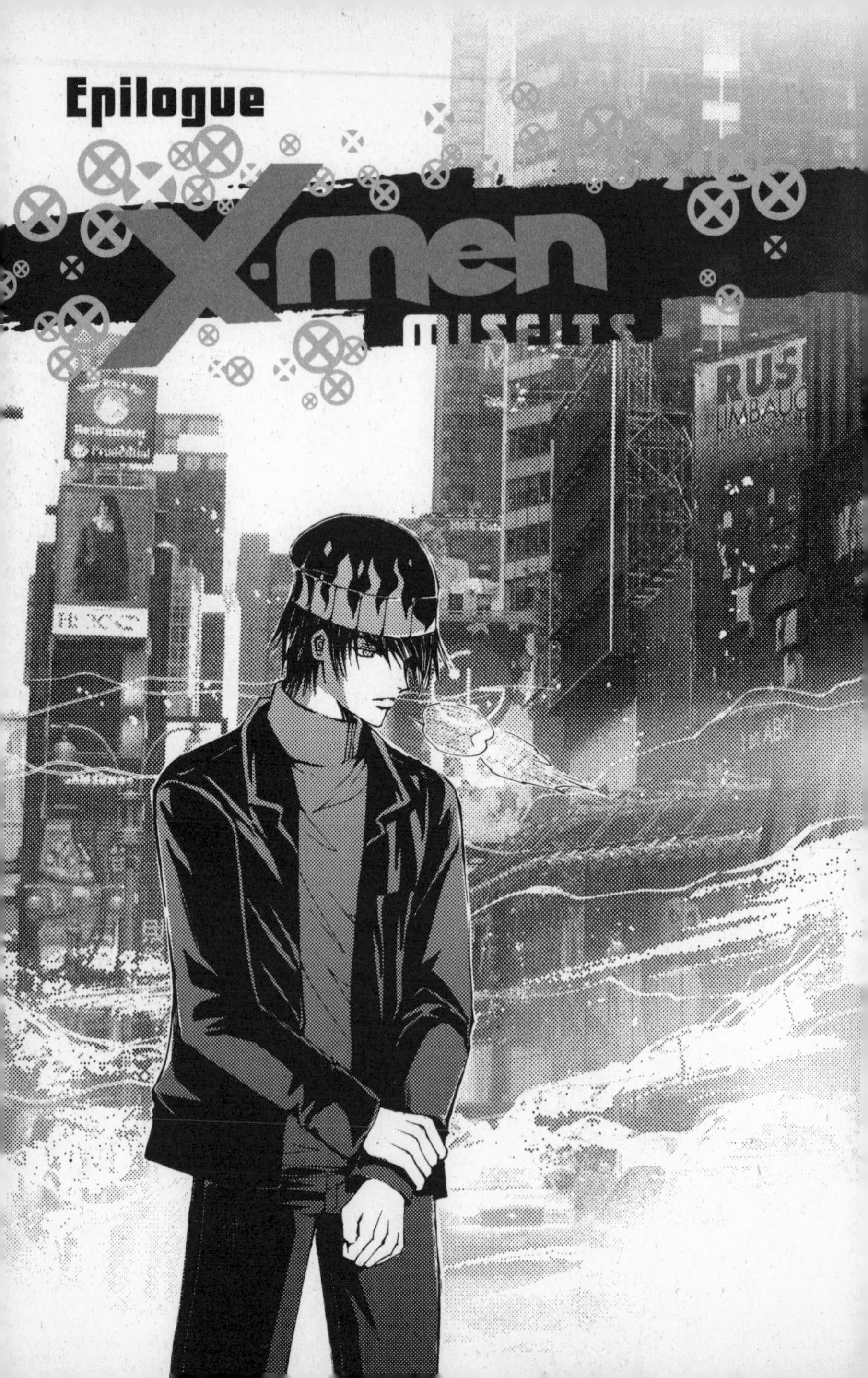
Epilogue
X-men
Misfits

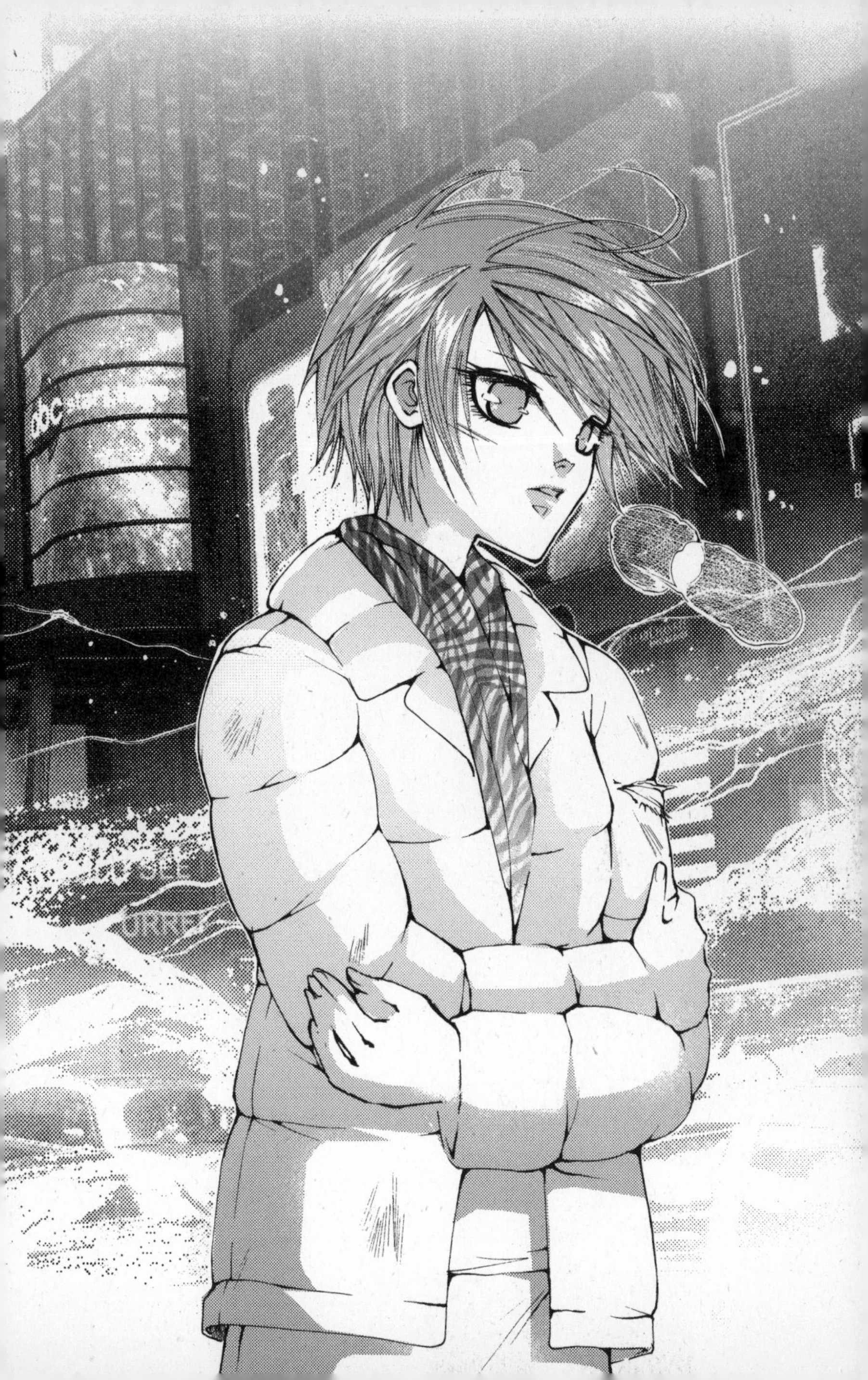
abc

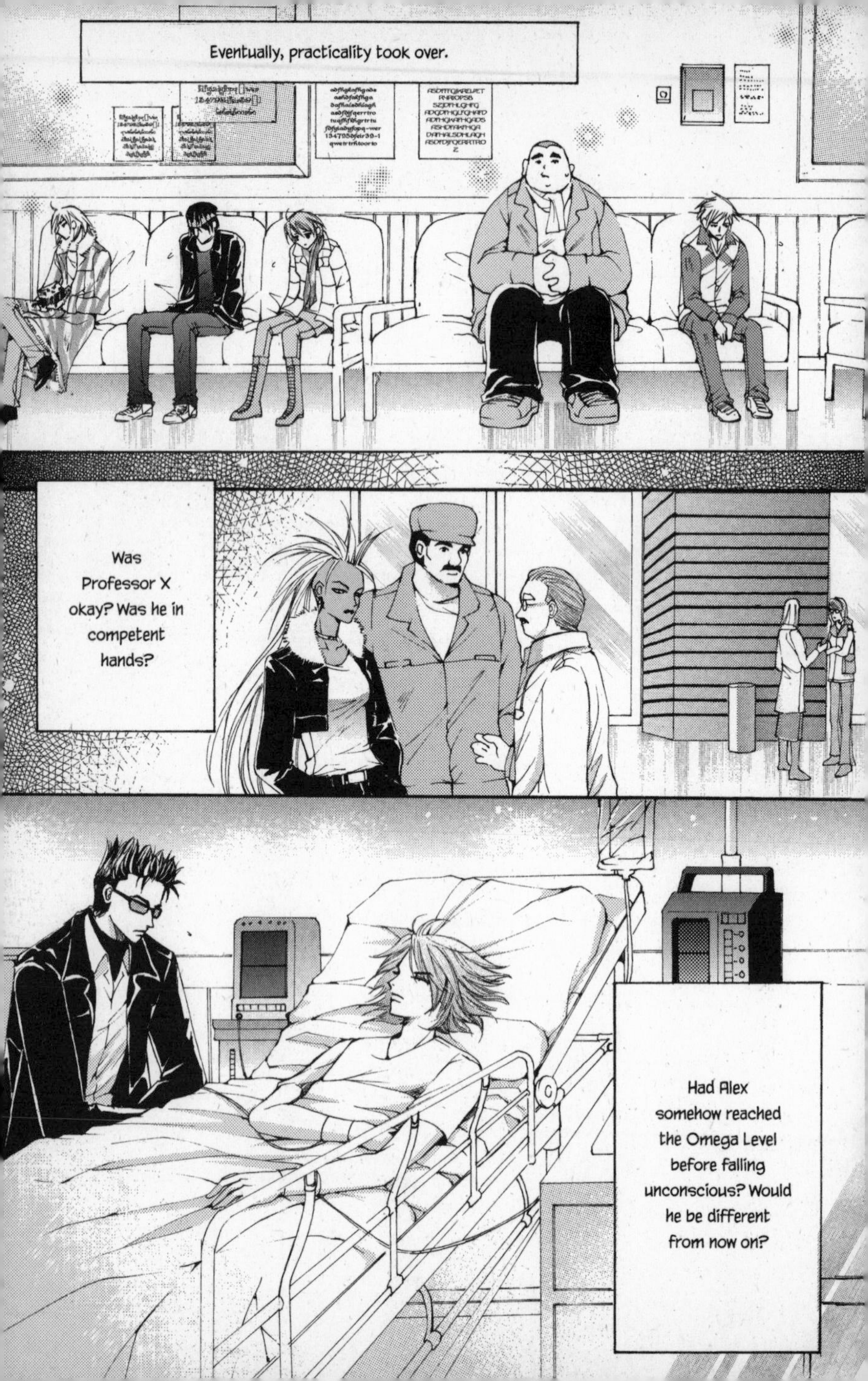
Eventually, practicality took over.
Was Professor X okay? Was he in competent hands?
Had Alex somehow reached the Omega Level before falling unconscious? Would he be different from now on?

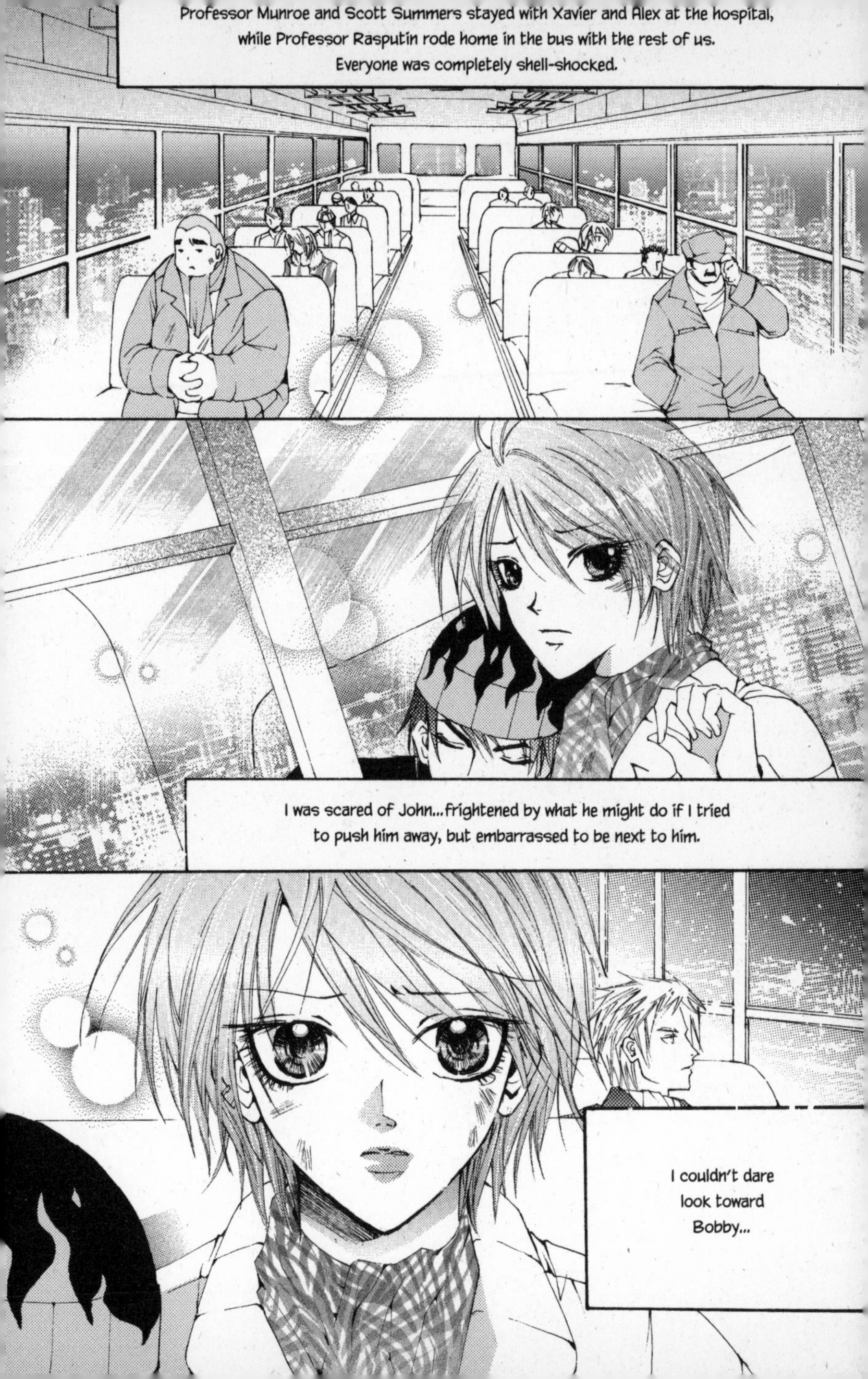
Professor Munroe and Scott Summers stayed with Xavier and Alex at the hospital, while Professor Rasputin rode home in the bus with the rest of us. Everyone was completely shell-shocked.
I was scared of John...frightened by what he might do if I tried to push him away, but embarrassed to be next to him.
I couldn't dare look toward Bobby...

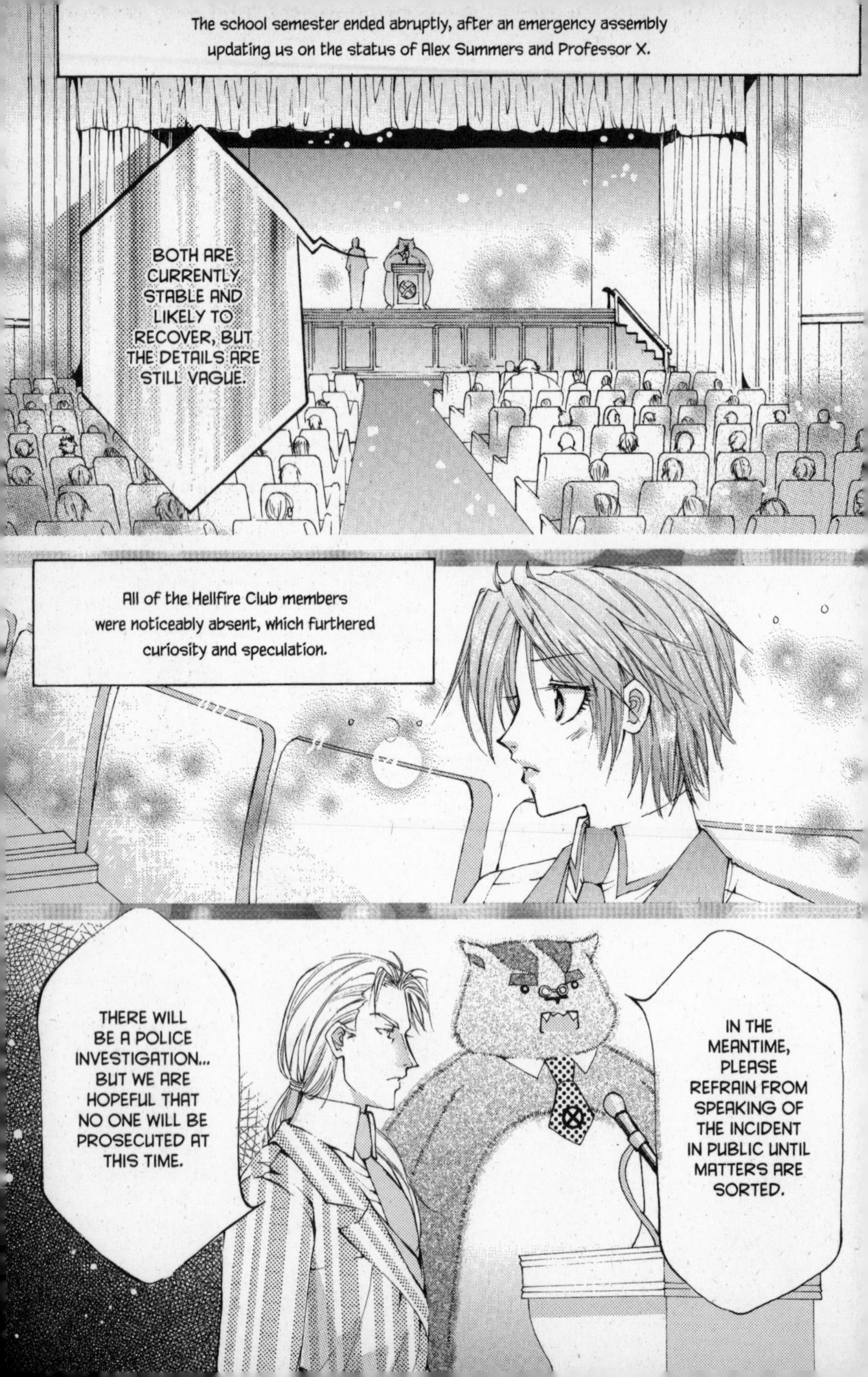
The school semester ended abruptly, after an emergency assembly updating us on the status of Alex Summers and Professor X.
BOTH ARE CURRENTLY STABLE AND LIKELY TO RECOVER, BUT THE DETAILS ARE STILL VAGUE.
All of the Hellfire Club members were noticeably absent, which furthered curiosity and speculation.
THERE WILL BE A POLICE INVESTIGATION... BUT WE ARE HOPEFUL THAT NO ONE WILL BE PROSECUTED AT THIS TIME.
IN THE MEANTIME, PLEASE REFRAIN FROM SPEAKING OF THE INCIDENT IN PUBLIC UNTIL MATTERS ARE SORTED.

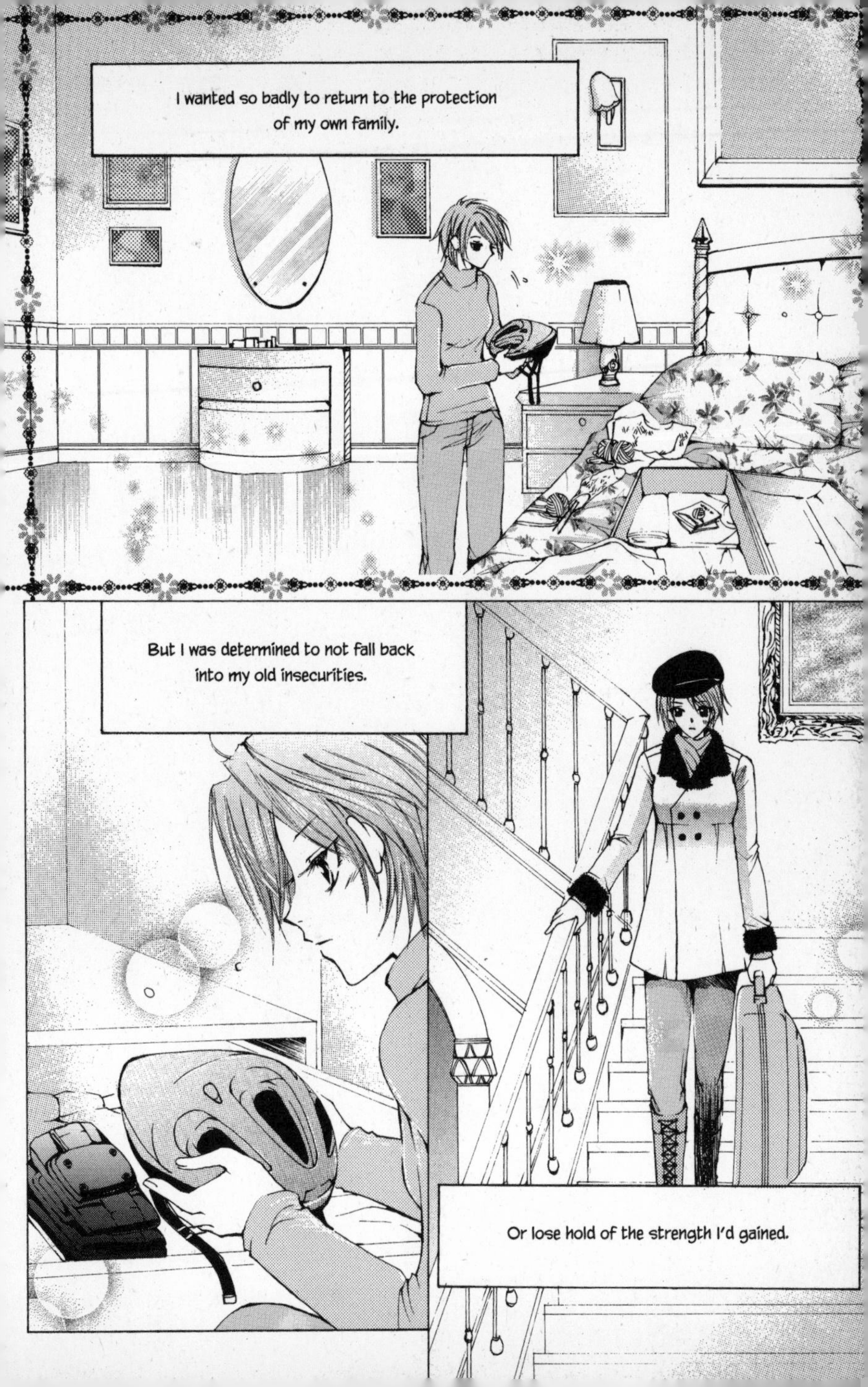
I wanted so badly to return to the protection of my own family.
But I was determined to not fall back into my old insecurities.
Or lose hold of the strength I'd gained.

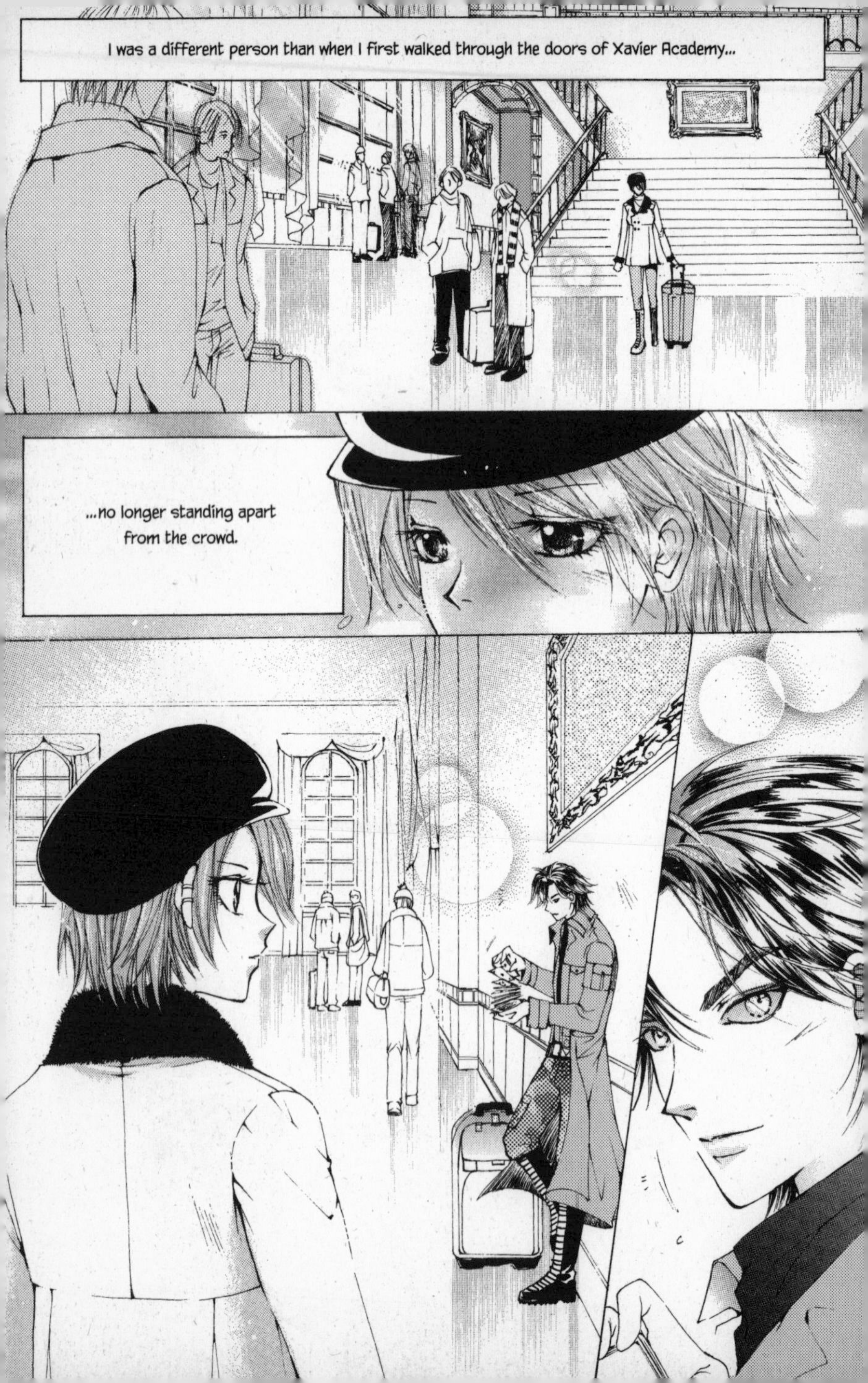
I was a different person than when I first walked through the doors of Xavier Academy...
...no longer standing apart from the crowd.

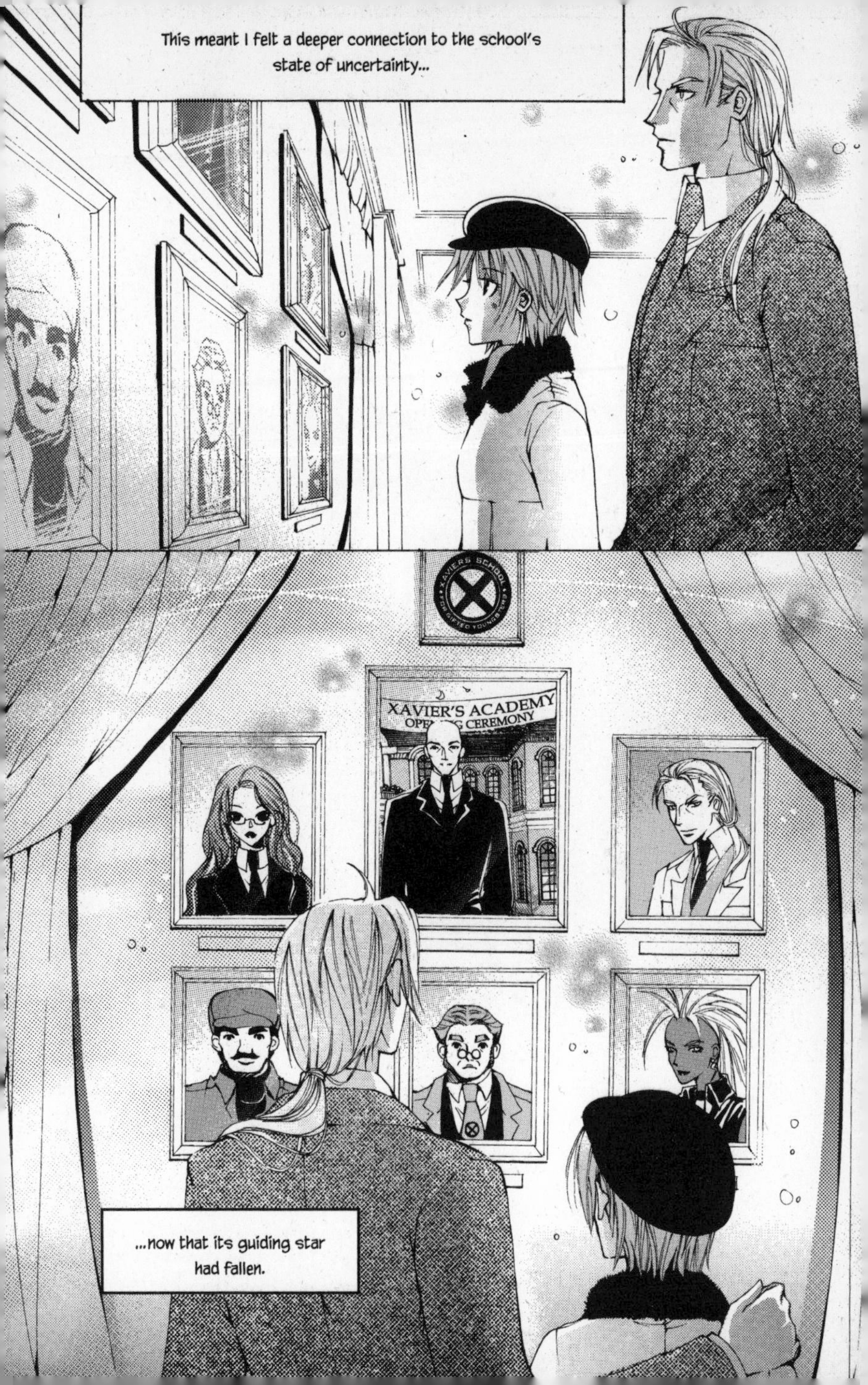
This meant I felt a deeper connection to the school's state of uncertainty...
XAVIER'S ACADEMY
...now that its guiding star had fallen.

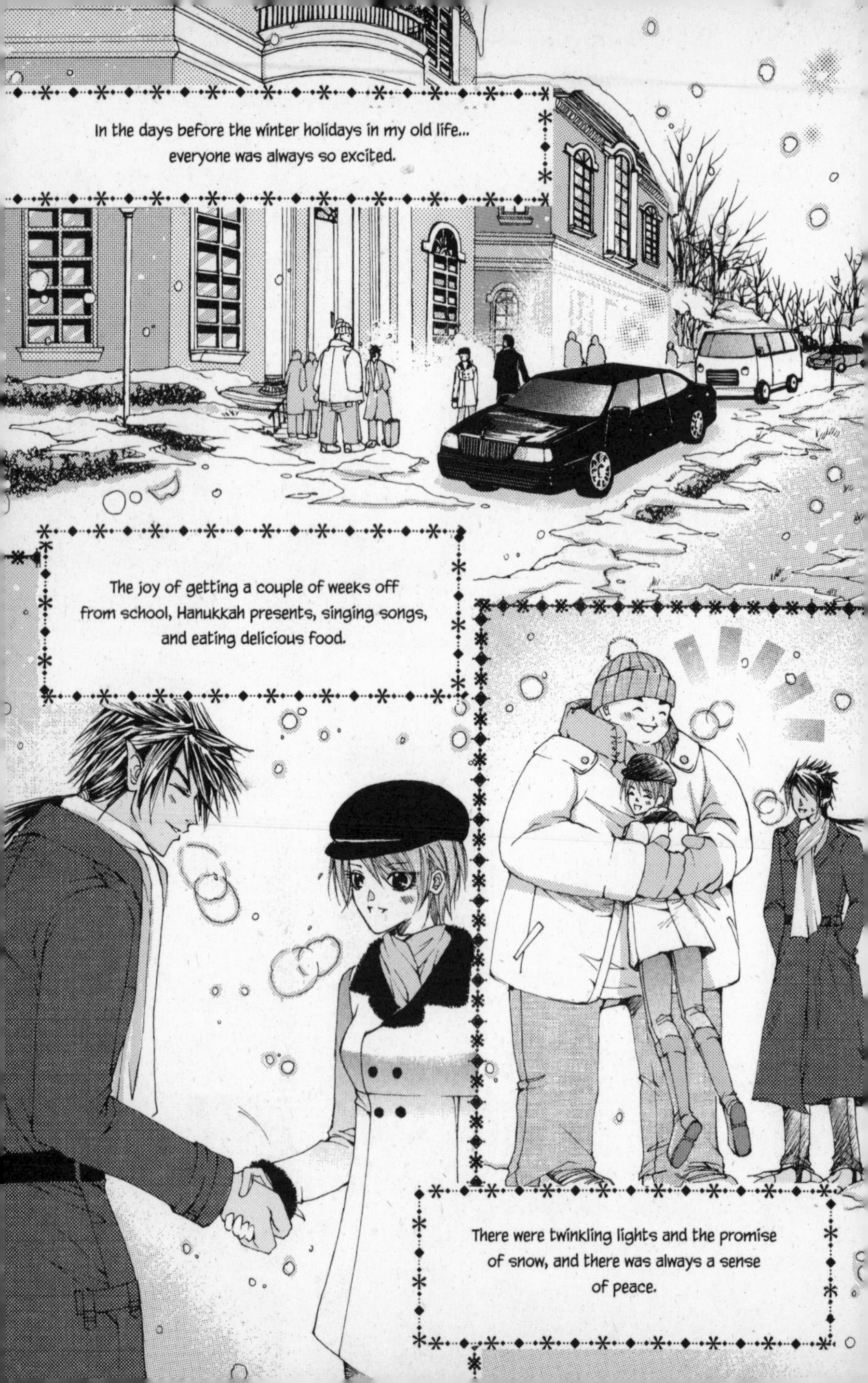
In the days before the winter holidays in my old life... everyone was always so excited.
The joy of getting a couple of weeks off from school, Hanukkah presents, singing songs, and eating delicious food.
There were twinkling lights and the promise of snow, and there was always a sense of peace.

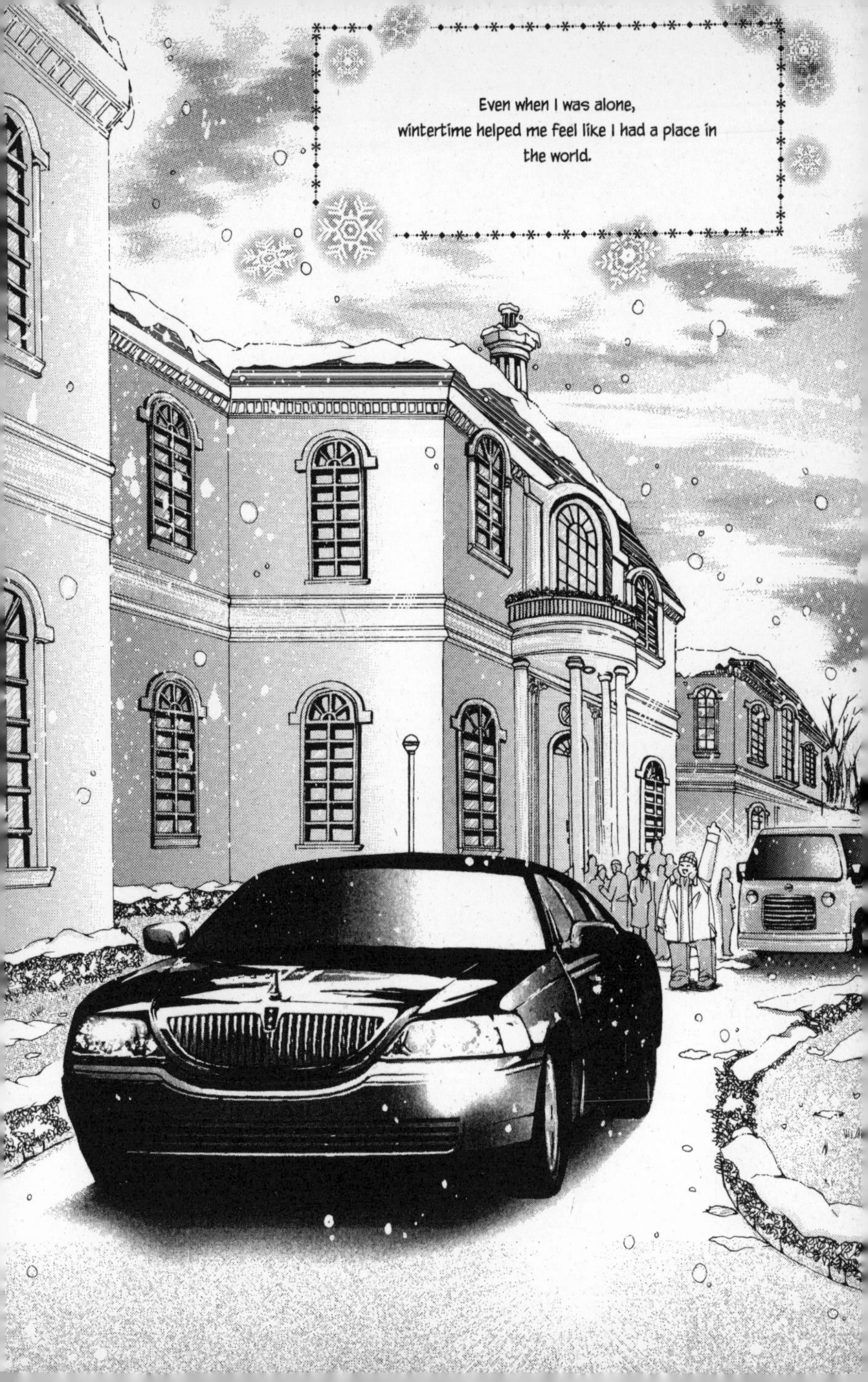
Even when I was alone, wintertime helped me feel like I had a place in the world.

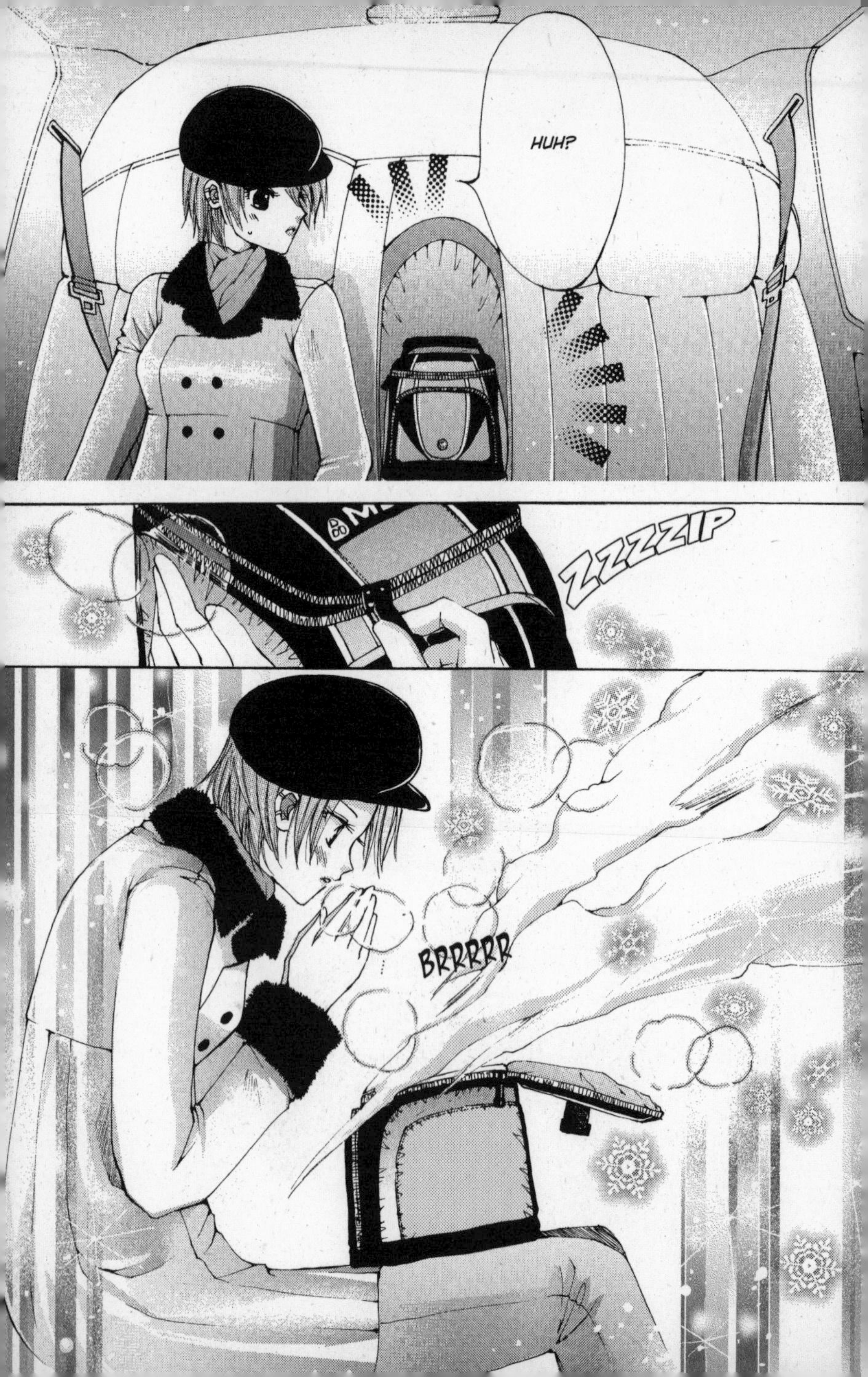
HUH?
ZZZZIP
BRRRRR

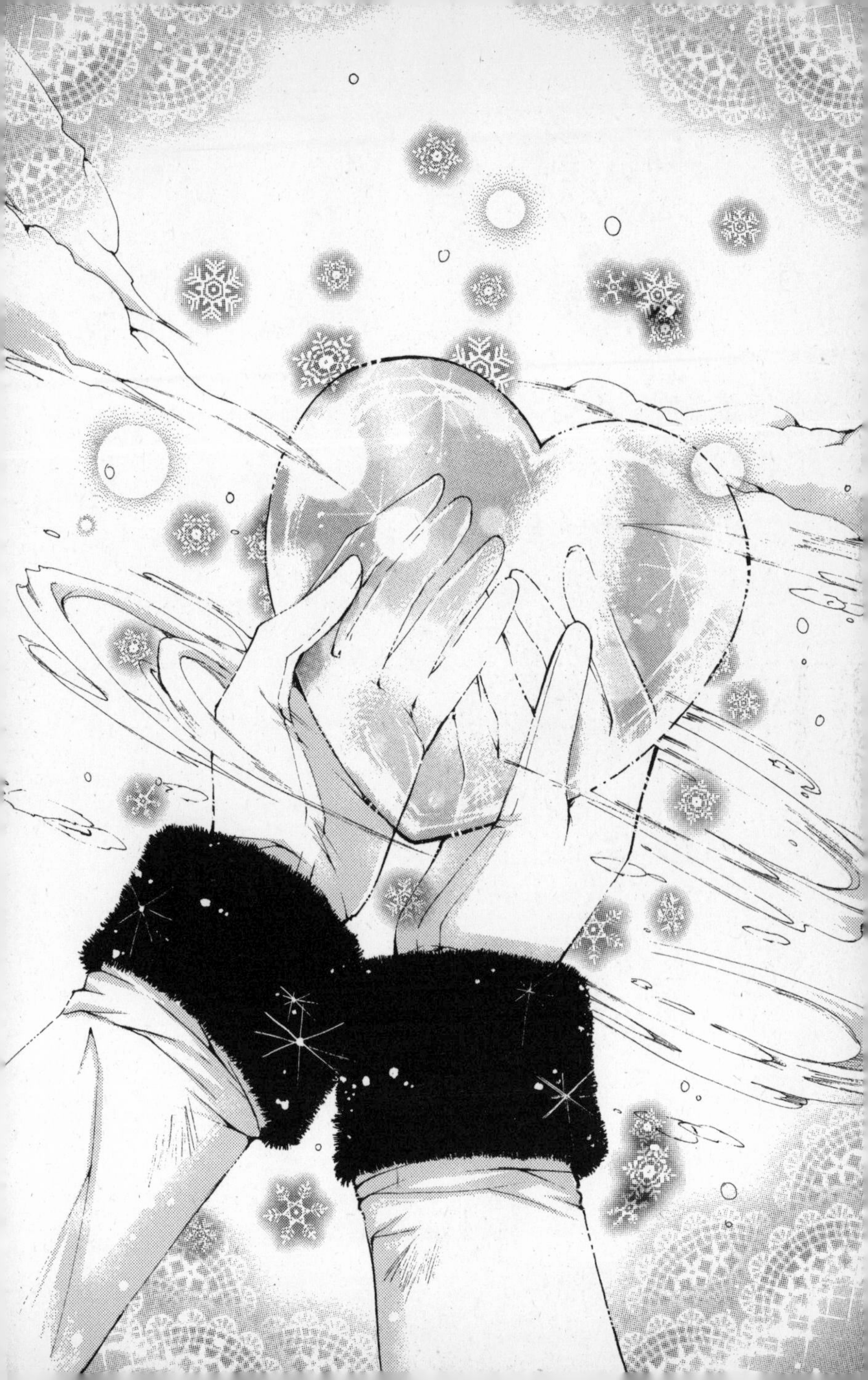

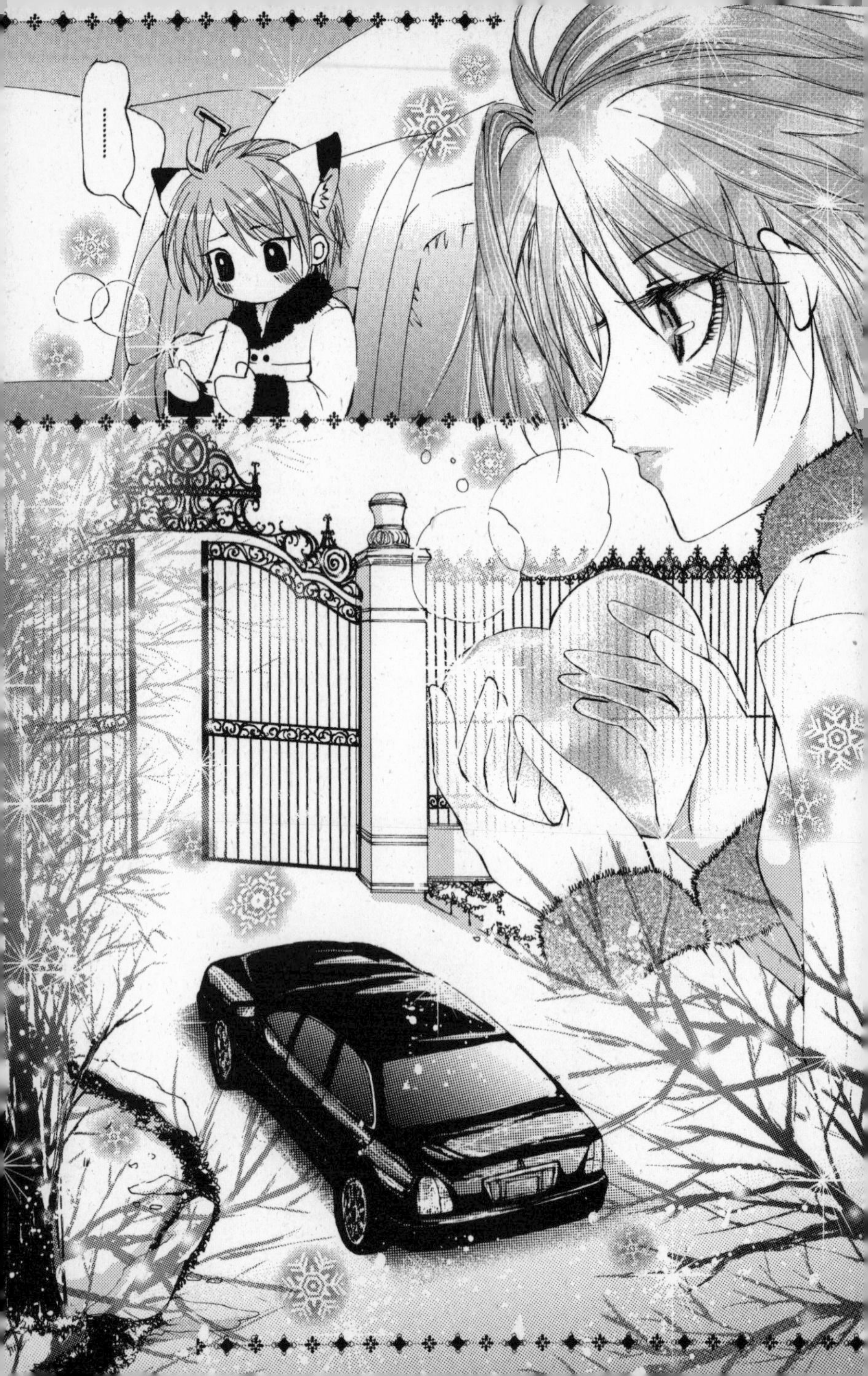
……

Preview of volume 2

It's not easy starting a new school year…especially when you're a student at Xavier's School! And Kitty Pryde is starting the semester with classic first-day jitters. Will the place be the same without Professor X? She's been thinking about Iceman all summer—but has he been thinking about her? And she's so not looking forward to running into her hotheaded ex, Pyro, and his buddies in the Hellfire Club.

But this year, boys will be the *least* of Kitty's troubles, because Kitty's no longer the only girl at Professor X's academy! Between sharing the boys of Xavier's School with the new girls, and an action-packed school tournament—with an obstacle course, a fashion show, and a cooking showdown—it's going to be one crazy semester!

XAVIER'S SCHOOL · FOR GIFTED YOUNGSTERS

About the Artist

Just a couple of silly poses
Hello!!
ANZU

Visit me on the web
ANZU-art.com

Anzu-manga.deviantart.com

http://Thirst.thewebcomic.com

I'll see u there!

Special thanks
—To MY LORD, Jesus Christ.
—To my assistants Yuu-An, UV, Liwa, and Nico, for helping me this whole time, through the hard times and tears…I love you all!
—To my editor, Tricia: I'm sorry for always making you wait for the pages! I'll work harder on the next book.
—To Dave and Raina. It was so nice to meet you two. (Looks like I've become one of your fans!) I liked your story soooo much, and I'm having a good time reading your comics ☺. And I'm so excited to read book two!
—To Marilyn Allen—thank you so much for always helping me.
—To the rest of the Del Rey team and Marvel Comics. Thank you so much for giving me this opportunity!
—To, at last, my readers. Thank you so much for spending your time reading my work. I'll keep working hard for you!

I'll see you in Book 2!

The last day in the studio

6:00 AM
HA HA HA!
5 PAGES LEFT! OK, GIRLS, LET'S END THIS PERFECTLY!
SNAP
YEAH!
YEE-HA!
HOORAY!
HEY, I'M A GUY!
THE ONLY GUY HERE
CLAP CLAP
4:00 AM The Next Day
DIZZY
DIZZY
HUH? WHAT AM I TRYING TO DRAW?
ONE MORE PAGE LEFT... LET'S END THIS...
HOORAY!
THE LAST SURVIVOR
I CAN'T SEE CLEARLY!

Finally, we got to the end of the book! I can't wait to start on Book 2!

About the Writers

We'd like to thank Anzu and Dave, our editor, Tricia, and everyone at Del Rey and Marvel!

Dave would also like to thank his sister, Michele, who as a kid read countless X-Men comics (plus the spin-offs) and would talk endlessly about her favorite characters, explaining with great enthusiasm which ones were the *hottest*!

Raina Telgemeier is the adaptor and illustrator of the *Baby-sitters Club* graphic novel series (Scholastic/Graphix), which were selected by YALSA for their Great Graphic Novels for Teens list in 2006, as well as *Booklist's* Top 10 Graphic Novels for Youth list. She's drawn stories for several anthologies including *Flight* Volume 4, *Awesome,* and *Bizarro World.* Her graphic memoir, *SMILE,* will be published by Scholastic/Graphix in 2010. Raina's comics have been nominated for the Ignatz, Cybil, and Eisner awards. Visit her online at goraina.com.

Dave Roman draws the webcomic series *Astronaut Elementary,* and has written several graphic novels including *Agnes Quill: An Anthology of Mystery* (SLG Publishing), *Jax Epoch and the Quicken Forbidden* (AiT/PlanetLar), and *The Adventures of Tymm: Alien Circus* (Platinum Studios). He's had stories appear in the *Flight* series (Villard), and is one of the co-founders of the video game art site lifemetercomics.com. Visit him online at yaytime.com.

PHOENIX WRIGHT ACE ATTORNEY: OFFICIAL CASEBOOK

BASED ON THE HIT VIDEO GAME FROM CAPCOM!

VOLUME ONE: THE PHOENIX WRIGHT FILES
VOLUME TWO: THE MILES EDGEWORTH FILES

OFFICIAL CASEBOOK VOL.1
The Phoenix Wright Files
Ace Attorney
Phoenix Wright
BASED ON THE HIT
VIDEO GAME FROM CAPCOM!

OFFICIAL CASEBOOK VOL.2
The Miles Edgeworth Files
Ace Attorney
Phoenix Wright
BASED ON THE HIT
VIDEO GAME FROM CAPCOM!

Available anywhere books or comics are sold!

VISIT WWW.DELREYMANGA.COM TO:

- Read sample pages
- View release date calendars for upcoming volumes
- Sign up for Del Rey's free manga e-newsletter
- Find out the latest about new Del Rey Manga series

RATING T AGES 13+

DEL REY MANGA

www.delreymanga.com

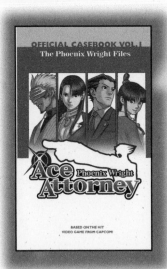

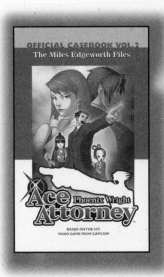

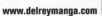